Adobe

After Effects CS5
Visual Effects and Compositing
STUDIO TECHNIQUES

Mark Christiansen

Adobe

Adobe® After Effects® CS5 Visual Effects and Compositing Studio Techniques

Mark Christiansen

This Adobe Press book is published by Peachpit.
For information on Adobe Press books, contact:

Peachpit
1249 Eighth Street
Berkeley, CA 94710
(510) 524-2178
Fax: (510) 524-2221

To report errors, please send a note to errata@peachpit.com

Peachpit is a division of Pearson Education
Copyright © 2011 Mark Christiansen
For the latest on Adobe Press books, go to www.adobepress.com

Senior Editor: Karyn Johnson
Development and Copy Editor: Peggy Nauts
Production Editor: Cory Borman
Technical Editor: Todd Kopriva
Proofreader: Kelly Kordes Anton
Composition: Kim Scott, Bumpy Design
Indexer: Jack Lewis
Cover design: Peachpit Press/Charlene Will
Cover illustration: Regina Cleveland

ISBN 13: 978-0-321-71962-1
ISBN 10:   0-321-71962-X

9 8 7 6 5 4 3 2 1

Printed and bound in the United States of America

Contents

Scripting appendix by Jeff Almasol and
After Effects JavaScript Guide by Dan Ebberts
available on the accompanying DVD-ROM

About the Author

Mark Christiansen is a San Francisco–based visual effects supervisor and creative director. Some of his Hollywood feature and independent film credits include *Avatar*, *All About Evil*, *The Day After Tomorrow* and *Pirates of the Caribbean 3: At World's End*. As a director, producer, designer, and compositor/animator, he has worked on a diverse slate of commercial, music video, live event, and television documentary projects for clients as diverse as Sony, Interscope, HBO, and many of the world's best-known Silicon Valley companies.

Mark has used After Effects since version 2.0 and has worked directly with the After Effects development and marketing teams over the years. He has written four previous editions of this book as well as *After Effects 5.5 Magic* (with Nathan Moody), and has contributed to other published efforts including the Adobe After Effects Classroom in a Book.

Mark is a founder of Pro Video Coalition (providecoalition.com). He has created video training for Digieffects, lynda.com, and others; has taught courses at fxphd.com and Academy of Art University; and has been a guest host of popular podcasts such as "The VFX Show." You can find him at christiansen.com.

About the Contributors

Jeff Almasol (Appendix: Scripting) is a senior quality engineer on the Adobe After Effects team by day and crafter of After Effects scripts at his redefinery.com site by night. His site provides numerous free scripts, reference material, and links to other scripting resources. Prior to Adobe, Jeff worked at Elastic Reality Inc. and Avid Technology on Elastic Reality, Marquee, AvidProNet, and other products; and at Profound Effects on Useful Things and Useful Assistants. You might find him talking in the third person on Twitter (redefinery) and other sites.

Dan Ebberts (Chapter 10: Expressions and After Effects Javascript Guide) is a freelance After Effects script author and animation consultant. His scripting services have been commissioned for a wide range of projects, including workflow automation and complex animation rigging. He is a frequent contributor to the various After Effects forums and has a special interest in expressions and complex algorithms. Dan is an electrical engineer by training, with a BSEE degree from the University of California, but has spent most of his career writing software. He can be reached through his web site at http://motionscript.com.

Stu Maschwitz (Foreword) is a writer and director, and the creator of the Magic Bullet Suite from Red Giant Software. Maschwitz spent four years as a visual effects artist at George Lucas's Industrial Light & Magic (ILM), working on such films as *Twister* and *Men in Black*. He cofounded and was CTO of The Orphanage, a San Francisco-based visual effects and film production company. Maschwitz has directed numerous commercials and supervised effects work on films including *Sin City* and *The Spirit*. Maschwitz is a guerilla filmmaker at heart and combined this spirit and his effects knowledge into a book: *The DV Rebel's Guide: An All-Digital Approach to Making Killer Action Movies on the Cheap* (Peachpit Press).

To the muse, in all of her guises.

Acknowledgments

When I started the first edition of this book, I may have guessed there was a chance it would be a success and find its way into multiple editions, but I certainly wasn't focused on that. Some fundamental things about the book, like its basic structure, have not changed, but other aspects have been radically revamped for this one.

That parallels the development of After Effects itself. I can still vividly remember the excitement of getting started creating shots in After Effects before I even had heard the term "compositor," and fooling a renowned visual effects veteran—a veteran, who shall remain nameless, who had no idea the tools existed on the desktop to do this kind of stuff. After Effects is compelling enough on its own to make it worth becoming an expert.

Thank you in particular to Adobe for loaning the time and energy of Todd Kopriva to work on this edition. Todd doesn't let you get away with anything and, as Michael Coleman said to me, he represents the "gold standard" for technical editorial work. I can't imagine a better person for that role on this edition of the book.

It can be difficult to properly acknowledge the deceased. When the last version of this book came out, The Orphanage, the facility where my After Effects chops found a setting in which we could push compositing in this software to the maximum, was still very much alive. I remain grateful to filmmaker Stu Maschwitz, who cofounded and was CTO of The Orphanage, for helping to guide the first edition to truly reflect best practices in VFX and help set a standard for this book.

Maintaining that standard has been possible only with the collaboration of others. In the last edition, I brought in the best guy I knew to explain expressions, Dan Ebberts, and a counterpart on the scripting side, Jeff Almasol, to contribute chapters on their respective specialties, and those remain in this edition.

But there have been other, perhaps less likely contributors to the book and disc you have before you. It was a challenge from a reader, a filmmaker in Switzerland named Sergio Villalpando, that caused me to completely redo a chapter that I had considered the heart of the book (Chapter 6: Color Keying). He encountered difficulty putting the techniques described into practice, and the way in which he articulated his frustration was clear and concise enough to motivate me to approach it as if starting over, basing the new version much more closely on a step-by-step example.

My students at Academy of Art made me realize that—although it's great to impress everyone with a mind-blowingly clever technique—clear, patient elucidation of fundamentals is far more valuable. The personal experience of using the previous edition of the book to teach this material led to many changes in this edition, including the addition of a simple example comp in the very first chapter. Students have a better understanding of this process before even beginning it these days, and even though this is not a beginner book, the patient novice may now find an easier way in, thanks to my classroom experience.

Collaboration is key to this work. In gathering new material for this edition I had a few collaborators who were willing to shoot material, either with me on a day out (thanks Tyler McPherron) or remotely (gratitude to Chris Meyer—yes, that Chris Meyer—and to Eric Escobar). Brendan Bolles provided a wonderful description of the difference between low and high dynamic range imaging, which remains lucid and lively enough that I've left a lot of it intact in Chapter 11.

More and other contributors have been essential to past, current, and future book editions including Kontent, Pixel Corps, Artbeats, fxphd, Case Films, Creative COW, Kenwood Group, Inhance, Sony, ABC, Red Bull USA, and individuals such as Pete O'Connell, Benjamin Morgan, Matt Ward, Ross Webb, Luis Bustamente, Micah Parker, Jorge L. Peschiera, Shuets Udono, Eric E. Yang, and Kevin Miller.

This book's cover was designed by Regina Cleveland with the guidance of Charlene Will. Thanks to both of you for taking a bunch of ideas I put out there, from the ridiculous to the even more ridiculous, and coming up with a design that feels fresh and lively without causing any corporate powers-that-be to collapse.

It's the people at Adobe who've made After Effects what it is, in particular Dave Simons and Dan Wilk, as well as Michael Natkin, Chris Prosser, John Nelson, Ellen Wixted, and Michael Coleman plus the many—but not as many as you might think—other members of the development team.

Thanks to the companies whose tools are included on the book's DVD: Jack Binks at The Foundry, Peder Norrby, who *is* Trapcode, Russ Andersson of Andersson Technologies, Sean Safreed of Red Giant Software, Andrew Millin of ObviousFX LLC, Marco Paolini of SilhouetteFX, Pierre Jasmin and Pete Litwinowicz of RevisionFX, Robert Sharp and the whole crew at Digieffects, and Philipp Spoth of Frischluft. Why bother discussing tools that aren't worth using, when there are great ones like these?

This is the best edition yet of this book thanks to the efforts and commitment of the many good people at Peachpit, all of whose best qualities are embodied in one Karyn Johnson. Without you, the pieces would not have come together in the way they did, the book would not be written the same, and the entire process would have been a whole lot less fun. Your humor, patience, commitment, and professionalism make this process of publishing a book relevant and vital, and you are truly able to bring out the best in others.

Finally, thank you to you, the people who read, teach, and respond to the material in this book. Your comments and questions are welcome at aestudiotechniques@gmail.com.

Foreword to This Edition

Face it, Bart, Sideshow Bob has changed.
No, he hasn't. He's more the same than ever!
> —Lisa and Bart Simpson in "Brother from
> Another Series," The Simpsons, Season 8

The first edition of this book was published in 2005 and I wrote the foreword for the third edition in 2008. I just read it, with an eye to updating it. I didn't change a word.

Everything I wrote then is even more true today. I'm seeing it every time I turn on my television—people are losing their preoccupation with realism and just telling stories. Certainly in many cases this is due to drastically reduced budgets. Nothing inspires creativity like limited resources. But if you can make your point as effectively with a stylized-but-beautiful animation, suddenly spending months of work to "do it photo-real" seems like more than just squandered resources; it seems to miss the point altogether.

Now we're shooting sumptuous moving images on inexpensive DSLR cameras. Laptop computers are every bit as powerful as tower workstations from two years ago. Our phones have HD video cameras and our favorite visual effects application comes bundled with a competent roto artist in the box. We're expected to make even more for even less.

The combination of Adobe After Effects CS5 and this book remains your best asset in that battle. What I wrote in 2008's foreword was controversial and challenging at the time, but today it just feels like common sense. When the season finale of a hit TV show is shot using a camera that you can buy at the corner camera store—when a professional cinematographer is willing to suffer through compression artifacts and other technical shortcomings of that camera because the images he makes with it create an emotional experience he can't achieve any other way— you're in the middle of a sea change. It's not the 100-artist facilities or the shops with investments in "big iron" that are going to come out on top. The victory will go to the artists who generate an emotional reaction by any means necessary. The filmmaker with an entire studio in her backpack. The visual effects artist who has an entire show's worth of shots slap-comped while the editor is still loading footage. The graphic designer who ignores the stale collection of stock footage and shoots his own cloud time-lapse using a $.99 iPhone app.

Two years ago it was fun to think about bringing the sex to your work. Today it's necessary for survival. Use what you learn in this book to make beautiful things that challenge and excite people. The tools have gotten better. It's up to you to translate that into a better audience experience.

Stu Maschwitz
San Francisco, August 2010

Foreword

I can't see the point in the theatre. All that
sex and violence. I get enough of that at home.
Apart from the sex, of course.
> —Tony Robinson as Baldrick, *Blackadder*

Who Brings the Sex?

"Make it look real." That would seem to be the mandate of the visual effects artist. Spielberg called and he wants the world to believe, if only for 90 minutes, that dinosaurs are alive and breathing on an island off the coast of South America. Your job: Make them look real. Right?

Wrong.

I am about to tell you, the visual effects artist, the most important thing you'll ever learn in this business: Making those Velociraptors (or vampires or alien robots or bursting dams) "look real" is absolutely *not* what you should be concerned with when creating a visual effects shot.

Movies are not reality. The reason we love them is that they present us with a heightened, idealized version of reality. Familiar ideas—say, a couple having an argument—but turned up to eleven: The argument takes place on the observation deck of the Empire State building, both he and she are perfectly backlit by the sun (even though they're facing each other), which is at the exact same just-about-to-set golden-hour position for the entire 10-minute conversation. The couple are really, really charming and impossibly good-looking—in fact, one of them is Meg Ryan. Before the surgery. Oh, and music is playing.

What's real about that? Nothing at all—and we love it.

Do you think director Alejandro Amenábar took Javier Aguirresarobe, cinematographer on *The Others*, aside and said, "Whatever you do, be sure to make Nicole Kidman look *real?*" Heck no. Directors say this kind of stuff to their DPs: "Make her look like a statue." "Make him look bullet-proof." "Make her look like she's sculpted out of ice."

Did It Feel Just Like It Should?

Let's roll back to *Jurassic Park*. Remember how terrific the T-rex looked when she stepped out of the paddock? Man, she looked good.

She looked *good*.

The realism of that moment certainly did come in part from the hard work of Industrial Light and Magic's fledgling computer graphics department, who developed groundbreaking technologies to bring that T-rex to life. But mostly, that T-rex *felt real* because she *looked good*. She was wet. It was dark. She had a big old Dean Cundey blue rim light on her coming from nowhere. In truth, you could barely see her.

But you sure could hear her. Do you think a T-rex approaching on muddy earth would really sound like the first notes of a new THX trailer? Do you think Spielberg ever sat with sound designer Gary Rydstrom and said, "Let's go out of our way to make sure the footstep sounds are authentic?" No, he said, "Make that mofo sound like the *Titanic* just rear-ended the Hollywood Bowl" (may or may not be a direct quote).

It's the sound designer's job to create a soundscape for a movie that's emotionally true. They make things feel right even if they skip over the facts in the process. Move a gun half an inch and it sounds like a shotgun being cocked. Get hung up on? Instant dial tone. Modern computer displaying something on the screen? Of course there should be the sound of an IBM dot-matrix printer from 1978.

Sound designers don't bring facts. They bring the sex. So do cinematographers, makeup artists, wardrobe stylists, composers, set designers, casting directors, and even the practical effects department.

And yet somehow, we in the visual effects industry are often forbidden from bringing the sex. Our clients pigeonhole us into the role of the prop maker: Build me a T-rex, and it better look real. But when it comes time to put that T-rex on screen, we are also the cinematographer (with our CG lights), the makeup artist (with our "wet look" shader), and the practical effects crew (with our rain). And although he may forget to speak with us in the same flowery terms that he used with Dean on set, Steven wants us to make sure that T-rex looks like a T-rex should in a movie. Not just good—*impossibly* good. Unrealistically blue-rim-light-outa-nowhere good. Sexy good.

Have you ever argued with a client over aspects of an effects shot that were immutable facts? For example, you may have a client who inexplicably requested a little less motion blur on a shot, or who told you "just a little slower" for an object after you calculated its exact rate of fall? Do you ever get frustrated with clients who try to art-direct reality in this way?

Well, stop it.

Your client is a director, and it's their *job* to art-direct reality. It's not their job to know (or suggest) the various ways that it may or may not be possible to selectively reduce motion blur, but it is their job to feel it in their gut that somehow this particular moment should feel "crisper" than normal film reality. And you know what else? It's your job to predict that they might want this and even propose it. In fact, you'd better have this conversation early, so you can shoot the plate with a 45-degree shutter, that both the actors and the T-rex might have a quarter the normal motion blur.

Was It Good for You?

The sad reality is that we, the visual effects industry, pigeonhole *ourselves* by being overly preoccupied with reality. We have no one to blame but ourselves. No one else on the film set does this. If you keep coming back to your client with defenses such as "That's how it would really look" or "That's how fast it would really fall," then not only are you going to get in some arguments that you will lose, but you're actually setting back our entire industry by perpetuating the image of visual effects artists as blind to the importance of the sex. On the set, after take one of the spent brass shell falling to the ground, the DP would turn to the director and say, "That felt a bit fast. Want me to do one at 48 frames?" And the director would say yes, and they'd shoot it, and then months later the editor would choose take three, which they shot at 72 frames per second "just in case." That's the filmmaking process, and when you take on the task of creating that same shot in CG, you need to represent, emulate, and embody that entire process. You're the DP, both lighting the shot and determining that it might look better overcranked. You're the editor, confirming that choice in the context of the cut. And until you show it to your client, you're the director, making sure this moment *feels* right in all of its glorious unreality.

The problem is that the damage is already done. The client has worked with enough effects people who have willingly resigned themselves to not bringing the sex that they now view all of us as geeks with computers rather than fellow filmmakers. So when you attempt to break our self-imposed mold and bring the sex to your client, you will face an uphill battle. But here's some advice to ease the process: Do it without asking. I once had a client who would pick apart every little detail of a matte painting, laying down accusations of "This doesn't look real!"—until we color corrected the shot cool, steely blue with warm highlights. Then all the talk of realism went away, and the shot got oohs and ahs.

Your client reacts to your work *emotionally*, but they critique *technically*. When they see your shot, they react with their gut. It's great, it's getting better, but there's still something not right. What they *should* do is stop there and let you figure out what's not right, but instead, they somehow feel the need to analyze their gut reaction and turn it into action items: "That highlight is too hot" or "The shadows under that left foot look too dark." In fact it would be better if they focused on vocalizing their gut reactions: "The shot feels a bit lifeless," or "The animation feels too heavy somehow." Leave the technical details to the pros.

You may think that those are the worst kind of comments, but they are the best. I've seen crews whine on about "vague" client comments like "give the shot more oomf." But trust me, this is exactly the comment you want.

Because clients are like customers at a restaurant, and you are the chef. The client probably wants to believe that "more oomf" translates into something really sophisticated, like volumetric renderings or level-set fluid dynamics, in the same way that a patron at a restaurant would hope that a critique like "this dish needs more flavor" would send the chef into a tailspin of exotic ingredients and techniques. Your client would never admit (or suggest on their own) that "oomf" is usually some combination of "cheap tricks" such as camera shake, a lens flare or two, and possibly some God rays—just like the diner would rather not know that their request for "more flavor" will probably be addressed with butter, salt, and possibly MSG.

The MSG analogy is the best: Deep down, you want to go to a Chinese restaurant that uses a little MSG but doesn't admit it. You want the cheap tricks because they work, but you'd rather not think about it. Your client wants you to use camera shake and lens flares, but *without telling them.* They'd never admit that those cheap tricks "make" a shot, so let them off the hook and do those things without being asked. They'll silently thank you for it. Bringing the sex is all about cheap tricks.

Lights On or Off?

There are some visual effects supervisors who pride themselves on being sticklers for detail. This is like being an architect whose specialty is nails. I have bad news for the "Pixel F*ckers," as this type are known: Every shot will always have something wrong with it. There will forever be something more you could add, some shortcoming that could be addressed. What makes a visual effects supervisor good at their job is knowing which of the infinitely possible tweaks are important. Anyone can nitpick. A good supe focuses the crew's efforts on the parts of the shot that impact the audience most. And this is always the sex. Audiences don't care about matte lines or mismatched black levels, soft elements or variations in grain. If they did, they wouldn't have been able to enjoy *Blade Runner* or *Back to the Future* or that one *Star Wars* movie—what was it called? Oh yeah: *Star Wars.* Audiences only care about the sex.

On a recent film I was struggling with a shot that was just kind of sitting there. It had been shot as a pick-up, and it needed some help fitting into the sequence that had been shot months earlier. I added a layer of smoke to technically match the surrounding shots. Still, the shot died on the screen. Finally, I asked my compositor to softly darken down the right half of the shot by a full stop, placing half the plate along with our CG element in a subtle shadow. Boom, the shot sang.

What I did was, strictly speaking, the job of the cinematographer, or perhaps the colorist. The colorist, the person who designs the color grading for a film, is the ultimate bringer of the sex. And color correction is the ultimate cheap trick. There's nothing fancy about what a Da Vinci 2K or an Autodesk Lustre does with color. But what a good colorist does with those basic controls is bring heaping, dripping loads of sex to the party. The problem is (and I mean *the* problem—the single biggest problem facing our industry today), the colorist gets their hands on a visual effects shot only *after it has already been approved*. In other words, the film industry is currently shooting itself in the foot (we, the visual effects artists, being that foot) by insisting that our work be approved in a sexless environment. This is about the stupidest thing ever, and until the industry works this out, you need to fight back by taking on some of the role of the colorist as you finalize your shots, just like we did when we made those matte paintings darker and bluer with warm highlights.

Filmmaking is a battleground between those who bring the sex and those who don't. The non-sex-bringing engineers at Panavision struggle to keep their lenses from flaring, while ever-sexy cinematographers fight over a limited stock of 30-year-old anamorphic lenses because they love the flares. I've seen DPs extol the unflinching sharpness of a priceless Panavision lens right before adding a smear of nose grease (yes, the stuff on your nose) to the rear element to soften up the image to taste. Right now this battle is being waged on every film in production between the visual effects department and the colorists of the world. I've heard effects artists lament that after all their hard work making something look real, a colorist then comes along and "wonks out the color." In truth, all that colorist did was bring the sex that the visual effects should have been starting to provide on their own. If what the colorist did to your shot surprised you, then you weren't thinking enough about what makes a movie a movie.

In Your Hands

You're holding a book on visual effects compositing in Adobe After Effects. There are those who question the validity of such a thing. Some perpetuate a stigma that After Effects is for low-end TV work and graphics only. To do "real" effects work, you should use a program such as Nuke or Shake. Those techy, powerful applications are good for getting shots to look technically correct, but they do not do much to help you sex them up. After Effects may not be on par with Nuke and Shake in the tech department, but it beats them handily in providing a creative environment to experiment, create, and reinvent a shot. In that way it's much more akin to the highly respected Autodesk Flame and Inferno systems—it gives you a broad set of tools to *design* a shot, and has enough horsepower for you to finish it, too. It's the best tool to master if you want to focus on the creative aspects of visual effects compositing. That's why this book is unique. Mark's given you the good stuff here, both the nitty-gritty details as well as the aerial view of extracting professional results from an application that's as maligned as it is loved. No other book combines real production experience with a deep understanding of the fundamentals, aimed at the most popular compositing package on the planet.

Bring It

One of the great matte painters of our day once told me that he spent only the first few years of his career struggling to make his work look *real*, but that he'll spend the rest of his life learning new ways of making his work look *good*. It's taken me years of effects supervising, commercial directing, photography, wandering the halls of museums, and waking up with hangovers after too much really good wine to fully comprehend the importance of those words. I can tell you that it was only after this particular matte painter made this conscious choice to focus on making things look *good*, instead of simply real, that he skyrocketed from a new hire at ILM to one of their top talents. Personally, it's only after I learned to bring the sex that I graduated from visual effects supervising to become a professional director.

So who brings the sex? The answer is simple: The people who care about it. Those who understand the glorious unreality of film and their place in the process of creating it. Be the effects artist who breaks the mold and thinks about the story more than the bit depth. Help turn the tide of self-inflicted prejudice that keeps us relegated to creating boring reality instead of glorious cinema. Secretly slip your client a cocktail of dirty tricks and fry it in more butter than they'd ever use at home.

Bring the sex.

Stu Maschwitz
San Francisco, October 2008

I

Introduction

If you aren't fired with enthusiasm, you will be fired—with enthusiasm.

—Vince Lombardi

Why This Book?

This book is about creating visual effects—the art and science of assembling disparate elements so that they appear to have been taken with a single camera, of making an ordinary shot extraordinary without making it unbelievable. The subject matter goes deep into core visual effects topics—color correction, keying, tracking, and roto among them—that are only touched on by other After Effects books, while leaving tools more dedicated to motion graphics (Text, Shape layers, many effects, and even a few specialized tools such as Motion Sketch) more or less alone.

I do not shy away from strong opinions, even when they deviate from the official line. My opinions and techniques have been refined through actual work in production at a few of the finest visual effects facilities in the world, and they're valid not only for "high-end" productions but for any composited shot. Where applicable, the reasoning behind using one technique over another is provided. I aim to make you not a better button-pusher but a more effective artist and technician.

The visual effects industry is historically protective of trade secrets, often reflexively treating all production information as proprietary. Work on a major project, however, and you will soon discover that even the most complex shot is made up largely of repeatable techniques and practices; the art is in how these are applied, combined, and customized, and what is added (or taken away).

Each shot is unique, and yet each relies on techniques that are tried and true. This book offers you as much of the latter as possible so that you can focus on the former. There's not much here in the way of step-by-step instructions; it's more important that you grasp how things work so that you can repurpose the technique for your individual shot.

This is emphatically not a book for beginners. Although the first section is designed to make sure you are making optimal use of the software, it's not an effective primer on After Effects in particular or digital video in general. If you're new to After Effects, first spend some time with its excellent documentation or check out one of the many books available to help beginners learn to use After Effects.

On the other hand, I have noticed recently that even beginners often understand more than they used to about the compositing process in general and about Adobe software in particular. In both cases it is the rise of Photoshop as the worldwide standard tool for image editing that has provided amateurs and students alike a leg up. Photoshop users have an advantage when working with After Effects as it, more than other compositing applications, employs a user interface whose specific tools and shortcuts as well as overall design mirror that of Photoshop. If you've hardly touched After Effects but feel confident working with digital images and video, try diving into the redesigned Chapter 1 of this book and let me know how it goes.

Organization of This Book, and What's New

Like its predecessors, *Adobe After Effects CS5 Visual Effects and Compositing Studio Techniques* is organized into three sections. Although each chapter has been refined and updated, the broad organization of the book remains as follows.

▶ Section I, "Working Foundations," is predominantly about the After Effects UI itself. I don't drag you through each menu and button; instead I attempt to offer some advice to novices and pros alike to improve your state of flow with the software. This means that we focus on workflows, shortcuts, and principles of how things work in After Effects when compositing.

I encourage you not to assume that you're too advanced to at least skim this section; it's virtually guaranteed that there's information in there you don't already know. In this edition I've also attempted to make the first chapter friendlier to new users.

▶ Section II, "Effects Compositing Essentials," focuses on the core techniques at the heart of effects compositing. Color matching, keying, rotoscoping, and motion tracking are the topics that are essential throughout the rest of the book and in your compositing experience generally. There is also a chapter that handles the camera and 3D, one on expressions, and one about working in 32-bpc linear color as well as handling film and high dynamic range images.

▶ This section is the true heart of the book. In this edition I've added new and expanded examples to elucidate high-level principles. Chapter 6, on keying (which I long considered one of the strongest), received a thorough rewrite, as did Chapter 7, which focuses on rotoscoping. Chapter 11, on working beyond the standard 8 bits per channel, 2.2 gamma pipeline, has also been heavily edited for greater clarity.

▶ Section III, "Creative Explorations," demonstrates actual shots you are likely to re-create, offering best practices for techniques every effects artist needs to know. Some of these examples are timeless, but where applicable I have refined what was there, either because of new insights in my own craft or because I thought of more and newer techniques to share.

In all cases, the focus is on explaining how things work so that you can put these techniques to use on your own shot, instead of taking a simple "paint by numbers" approach to prefabricated shots.

The biggest change in After Effects CS5 is that the software now makes use of 64-bit memory addressing. This does not change a whole lot about how you work with the software, though, other than making it far less likely you will encounter out-of-memory errors as you work and far more likely that you can make better use of a multiprocessor system with an up-to-date graphics card.

The addition of Roto Brush certainly changed the landscape of Chapter 7, on rotoscoping, although it has not obviated the need for tried-and-true techniques to refine a matte.

Artistry

When I was working on the first edition of this book I used to ride my bicycle home up the hill out of the Presidio, where The Orphanage was located, and think about what people really needed to know in order to move their work to the level of a visual effects pro. Here's what I came up with:

▶ **Get reference.** You can't re-create what you can't clearly see. Too many artists skip this step.

▶ **Simplify.** To paraphrase Einstein, a good solution is as simple as possible, but no simpler.

▶ **Break it down.** If even the most complicated shot consists of small, comprehensible steps—perhaps thousands of them—any visual problem can be solved by patiently being reduced to the point where it's simply a question of performing the steps in the correct order. Easier said than done in many cases, certainly, but there's still a huge difference between difficult and impossible.

▶ **Don't expect a perfect result on the first try.** My former colleague Paul Topolos (now in the art department at Pixar) used to say that "recognizing flaws in your work doesn't mean you're a bad artist. It only means you have taste."

This is how it's done at the best studios, and even if you're not currently working at one of them, this is how you should do it, too.

Compositing in After Effects

Some users may be coming to this book unfamiliar with After Effects but experienced in other compositing software. Here's a brief overview of how the After Effects workflow is unique from every other compositing application out there. Each application is somewhat different, and yet the main competitors to After Effects—Nuke, Shake, Flame, Fusion, and Toxic, to name a few—are probably more similar to one another than any of them is to After Effects, which is in many ways a lot more like Photoshop.

Here are some of the features that can make After Effects easier for the beginner to use but can constrain others:

▶ Render order is established in the Timeline and via nested compositions: layers, not nodes. After Effects has Flowchart view, but you don't create your composition there the way you would with a tree/node interface.

▶ Transforms, effects, and masks are embedded in every layer and render in a fixed order.

▶ After Effects has a persistent concept of an alpha channel in addition to the three color channels. The alpha is always treated as if it is straight (not premultiplied) once an image has been imported and interpreted.

▶ An After Effects project is not a script, although version CS4 introduced a text version of the After Effects Project (.aep) file, the XML-formatted .aepx file. Most of its contents are inscrutable other than source file paths. Actions are not recordable and there is no direct equivalent to Shake macros.

▶ Temporal and spatial settings tend to be absolute in After Effects because it is composition- and timeline-based. This is a boon to projects that involve complex timing and animation, but it can snare users who aren't used to it and suddenly find pre-comps that end prematurely or are cropped. Best practices to avoid this are detailed in Chapter 4.

Of these differences, some are arbitrary, most are a mixed bag of advantages and drawbacks, and a couple are constantly used by the competition as a metaphorical stick with which to beat After Effects. The two that come up the most are the handling of precomposing and the lack of macros.

This book attempts to shed light on these and other areas of After Effects that are not explicitly dealt with in its user interface or documentation. After Effects itself spares you details that as a casual user you might never need to know about but that as a professional user you should understand thoroughly. This book is here to help.

What's on the DVD

Jeff Almasol's scripting chapter is in an appendix, found on the disc as a PDF. It is the most accessible resource available on this complicated and much-feared topic, walking you through three scripts, each of which builds upon the complexity of the previous. Scripting provides the ability to create incredibly useful extensions to After Effects to eliminate tedious tasks. Several of these are included in the scripts folder on the disc as exclusives to this book.

In order to focus on more advanced and applied topics in the print edition, Dan Ebberts kicked JavaScript fundamentals to a special JavaScript addendum, also included as a PDF. This is in many ways the "missing manual" for the After Effects implementation of JavaScript, omitting all of the useless web-only scripting commands found in the best available books, but extending beyond the material in After Effects help.

If you want to find out more about some of the plug-ins and software mentioned in this book, look no further than its DVD-ROM. For example, the disc includes demos of

- SynthEyes from Andersson Technologies
- Camera Tracker and Kronos from the Foundry
- Red Giant Software's Magic Bullet Looks, Knoll Light Factory Pro, Key Correct Pro, Magic Bullet Colorista 2, Trapcode Lux, Trapcode Horizon, Trapcode Form, Trapcode Particular 2, Warp, and more
- ReelSmart Motion Blur and PV Feather from RE: Vision Effects
- Lenscare from Frischluft

You'll also find HD footage with which you can experiment and practice your techniques. There are dozens of example files to help you deconstruct the techniques described.

Finally, there are also a few useful and free third-party scripts mentioned throughout the book; for more of these, see the script links PDF in the scripts folder on the disc.

NOTES

To install the lesson files, footage, and software demos included on the DVD, simply copy each chapter folder in its entirety to your hard drive. Note that all .aep files are located in the subfolder of each chapter folder on the disc.

If you have comments or questions you'd like to share with the author, please email them to AEStudioTechniques@gmail.com.

The Bottom Line

Just like the debates about which operating system is best, debates about which compositing software is tops are largely meaningless—especially when you consider that the majority of first-rate, big-budget movie effects extravaganzas are created with a variety of software applications on a few different platforms. Rarely is it possible to say what software was used to composite a given shot just by looking at it, because it's about the artist, not the tools.

The goal is to understand the logic of the software so that you can use it to think through your artistic and technical goals. This book will help you do that.

SECTION I

Working Foundations

1

Composite in After Effects

All science touches on art; all art has its scientific side.
The worst scientist is he who is not an artist; the worst
artist is he who is no scientist.

—Armand Trousseau

Composite in After Effects

This book is about creating visual effects using Adobe After Effects, the world's most ubiquitous compositing application. It helps you create believable, fantastic moving images using elements from disparate sources, and do so with the least possible effort. This first section offers a jump-start (if you're relatively new) or a refresher (if you're already an After Effects artist) on the After Effects workflow.

Effective visual effects compositing uses your best skills as both artist and engineer. As an artist, you make creative and aesthetic decisions that are uniquely your own, but if you are not also able to understand how to implement those decisions effectively, your artistry will suffer. If I had to say what most often separates a great result from mediocrity, the answer is iteration—multiple passes—and solid technical skills enable these to happen most quickly and effectively, so your creative abilities can take over.

This chapter and the rest of Section I focus on how to get things done in After Effects as effortlessly as possible. It is assumed that you already know your way around the basics of After Effects and are ready to learn to fly.

A over B

After Effects is full of so many panels, effects, and controls, not to mention custom tools and powerful modifiers such as scripts and expressions, that it's easy to feel overwhelmed. Let's take a look at a simple yet real-world composite to help reveal the true essentials of the application.

NOTES

If this book opens at too advanced a level for you, see the Introduction for more resources to help you get up to speed with the basic operations of After Effects.

You may have heard the expression, "If you can imagine it, you can create it in After Effects." I first heard it working alongside Trish Meyer in the era of After Effects 3.0, and I'm sure you can appreciate that it has only become more true with time. So the following example is by no means comprehensive, nor is adding an element to a scene in this manner even necessarily what you'll be doing in After Effects. But the basic principle is that After Effects lets you go beyond what you can otherwise do editing footage by actually changing what appears in the scene itself.

Let's suppose that your independent film just got a great opportunity from a commercial sponsor to add its product into a scene. The challenge is that the scene has already been shot, and so you must "fix it in post"—a process that has become so common it's now an on-set joke. It's also the reality of how all of the top-grossing movies of our time have been made, not to mention virtually every commercial and many television, Internet, industrial, and student projects.

Figure 1.1 on the next page shows the elements we have to work with: a background *plate* image sequence and the foreground element to be added. Your author was in fact paid to create the 3D model as a viral product endorsement a few years back.

Workspace Setup

To get to this starting point, try this: Navigate (in the Windows Explorer or Mac Finder) to the source elements you moved from this chapter's folder on the book's disc to your local drive. Find the 01_a_over_b example project. Arrange your windows so that you can see both that Explorer/Finder window and the After Effects Project panel, then drag both source items—jf_table and RBcan_jf_table.tif—into that panel. (You can actually drag them anywhere onto the After Effects user interface (UI), and they should end up there.) If this presents any difficulty, you can instead choose File > Import > Multiple Files (**Ctrl+Alt+I/Cmd+Opt+I**), choose the single TIFF image, and then go into the jf_table folder to select any of those TIFF images with TIFF Sequence checked at the bottom of

The term "plate" stretches back to the earliest days of optical compositing (and even further to still photography) and refers to the glass plate that held the source footage. It now generally means the background onto which foreground elements are composited, although the foreground can also be the plate, and there are other kinds of plates such as effects plates.

Figure 1.1 This comp begins as simple as can be, with element A (the can image with alpha channel, where source is displayed in the footage channel) laid over element B (the background clip).

the Import Multiple Files dialog—but see how much more complicated that is?

Make a folder by clicking on the New Folder icon along the bottom of the Project panel, typing **Source** or **src** in the live text field to label it. Drag those elements into that folder. If you've done it right, your project panel should look something like the one you see in **Figure 1.1**.

How After Effects looks at program startup depends on its most recent usage, if any. You probably see a menu labeled Workspace; if not, reveal the Tools panel (**Ctrl+1/Cmd+1**) or just use Window > Workspace instead (most everything in the application exists in more than one place, allowing you to pick your favorite approach and find the controls more easily). Choose the Standard workspace and then, further down the same menu, pick Reset "Standard"—you are now back to the factory defaults.

Does the user interface seem complicated? You can make it even more so—go to Window > Workspace (or the

Workspace menu in the toolbar) and choose All Panels. You're likely to see a bunch of tabs crammed up and down the right side of the screen. Now breathe a sigh of relief, since I can tell you that there are a few in there I no longer even use—Wiggler and Smoother being two that have been effectively rendered obsolete by expressions (Chapter 10). In any case, I would never recommend leaving so many controls open at once. To swing radically in the opposite direction, try the Minimal workspace (and if necessary, Reset "Minimal"). This is closer to my own optimum, but then, I don't generally object when labeled a minimalist.

The Standard workspace is also a fine place to start. In Standard, click on the Audio tab and close it—unless you're timing animations to sound or mastering an entire movie in After Effects you won't need that panel.

Now try tearing off the Info panel—hold down **Ctrl** (**Cmd**) as you drag it by its tab away from its current position. You can do this with any panel: It is now undocked. I often work with Info this way, letting it float above my Composition viewer panel so that the pixel and position values are directly adjacent. This may be too much hot-rodding for you right away, so now try dragging it over a few of the other panels without letting go. You'll see violet-colored hit areas—six of them—on each panel, and at the four edges of the screen, teal-colored gutters.

If you actually drop the Info panel into any of these areas you may notice a pretty major flaw in all of this freedom— poorly placed, the Info panel can generate a lot of extra wasted space. You can drag it elsewhere or **Ctrl** (**Cmd**) drag and drop it to tear it off again. You can combine it with the Preview panel to save space: Drag the Info panel over the Preview panel or vice versa using the tab at the upper left.

Now try Window > Effects & Presets, or even better, use the shortcut **Ctrl+5** (**Cmd+5**). The Window menu contains all of the panels, and each can be toggled here. The need for the Effects & Presets panel is only occasional, so why take up space with it when you could instead have a bigger Composition panel (or a couple of viewers side-by-side as shown in Figure 1.1)?

Figure 1.2 Highlight an item in the Project panel and useful information appears adjacent to that item's thumbnail at the top.

Set Up the Composition

This is all a little abstract without working on the actual elements. I have done whole After Effects animations that have no source elements at all, but these are typically type animations with solid, shape, and particle-based effects created right in the application—in other words, they are more motion graphics than visual effects, which are almost always based on source footage—on the effects plate.

Let's have a look. Select jf_table in the Project panel and take a look at the info at the top of the panel (**Figure 1.2**). Listed are its pixel dimensions (1280 x 720), pixel aspect ratio (1 or square), duration (in frames or time, depending on your project settings—more on all of these later), frame rate, and color depth. If the frame rate isn't 24 fps (**Figure 1.1** shows the After Effects default of 30 fps), click the Interpret Footage icon along the bottom of the panel and change it by typing 24 and clicking OK.

Now select the other layer, RBcan_jf_table.tif. It differs from the first in a couple of significant ways. As a still image, it has no duration or frame rate, although because it was rendered specifically for this scene it does have matching pixel dimensions and aspect. Most significantly for our purposes, its pixel depth is Millions of Colors+— (that is After Effects-speak for 8-bit RGBA, a 32-bit-per-pixel image with four 8-bit channels instead of three). This image includes an alpha channel to store transparency data, which is covered in depth in Chapter 3.

To get to work, place your elements in a composition, or comp. Start with whichever layer contains the plate—in this case, jf_table—by dragging it to the New Composition icon. With no extra effort you automatically set a comp whose size, aspect, duration, and frame rate match those of the source.

Now add the Red Bull can. There are a few ways to do this. You can simply drag it into the Timeline panel to where you see a black line above the existing layer and drop it. Instead, you can drag it to the Composition icon in the Project panel, or, easiest of all, you can select the image and use **Ctrl+/** (**Cmd+/**).

Just like in Photoshop, simply positioning one layer above another in the stack—in this case, the Timeline panel (instead of a Layer panel) creates a composite image. The operation is seamless only because the can was generated with an alpha channel, but this isn't the only way to combine layers in After Effects—not by a long shot. Chapter 3 introduces the full variety of options beyond this no-brainer, and even illustrates how this simplest of composites actually works.

Preview and Refine

Now is a good time to preview the composition and see how it looks. Here you can make use of the Preview panel, at least until you learn the one essential shortcut from it—0 (zero) on the numeric keypad (which is on the side or, on a laptop, embedded with the function key shortcuts) stands in for the RAM Preview icon . Beginners often mistakenly hit the spacebar to play compositions in After Effects. With faster and faster systems, this increasingly works, but only a RAM preview buffers the composition into memory and locks its playback to the correct frame rate, and only it includes audio playback.

Once the shot is looping, you can use the spacebar to stop it at any point, and then, with your cursor over the Composition panel, click the key at the upper left of your keyboard, just below Esc—it's usually called the tilde (~) key even though it's actually the backward accent (`) key. We'll call it the tilde—that's easier to say and remember. It brings the panel up full screen for easier examination.

The shot needs work. What do you see? If you said

- **color matching**—that is covered in Chapter 5
- **motion tracking**, so that it matches the slight camera move in the source shot—Chapter 8
- **adding a cast shadow**—this has a few components, which are addressed in Chapters 3, 7, and 12
- **foreground smoke**—fully addressed in Chapter 13
- **grain matching**—Chapter 9

> **TIP**
>
> You can tear off any panel and make it float by holding down **Ctrl** (**Cmd**) as you drag it away; I like to tear off the Render Queue panel and toggle it on and off via its shortcut (**Alt+Ctrl+0/ Opt+Cmd+0**).

Maximize the Screen

Which is best for After Effects, one big monitor or two smaller ones? Many After Effects artists like two HD-resolution displays side by side (**Figure 1.3**, top), although a single display can be optimal if it's large enough (**Figure 1.3**, bottom). However, you may notice that a floating panel (**Ctrl/Cmd-drag** the tab to make it float) lacks the Zoom button along the top to send the window to full screen. The shortcut **Ctrl+\ (Cmd+\)** maximizes and centers any window. Press it again and even the top menu bar toggles off, filling the entire screen.

If you're stuck with a single small display you can press the tilde key (~) to maximize a single panel and do a RAM preview in full-screen mode by checking the Full Screen box in the Preview panel.

Just to complete the workflow, you can render this composition as a work-in-progress. With the composition selected, Composition > Make Movie or **Ctrl+M (Cmd+M)** will bring up the Output Movie dialog the first time you use it; here you're asked to choose where to save the composition. You can also use **Ctrl+/ (Cmd+/)** to simply place it in the render queue without the dialog, or you can even drag the Composition icon to the Render Queue panel from the Project panel. Once you've specified at least a name and location, as well as any other parameters (covered later in this chapter), click Render and an output file is created. We've made it from start to finish in just a few steps with an After Effects project (**Figure 1.4**). We'll now spend the rest of the book refining that process.

Figure 1.3 The preferred After Effects monitor setup seems to be a pair of 2K or larger displays (top), although a single 30-inch display at a high resolution (bottom), used with the tilde key to zoom panels to full screen, is also quite luxuriant.

Figure 1.4 You don't even have to start with source footage, as we've done here, but for effects compositing work it's typical to at least begin with a foreground and background, work with them in a comp, and render that as a new moving image.

Organization

Now let's proceed more deliberately through the workflow, considering more variables at each step and reducing the extra steps you may take many, many times in a normal After Effects workday.

Import and Organize Source

Getting a source file into After Effects so you can use it is no big deal. You can choose File > Import > File (or Multiple Files), or just drag footage directly from the Explorer or Finder into the Project panel. You can also double-click in an empty area of the Project panel.

Image sequences have a couple of specific extra rules but there are benefits that make them more reliable than QuickTime movies:

▶ An image sequence is less fragile than a QuickTime movie; if there is a bad frame in a sequence, it can be replaced, but a bad frame will corrupt an entire movie.

> **TIP**
>
> Prefer your workspace customizations to the defaults? Choose New Workspace in the Workspace menu and enter a new name to overwrite it; now After Effects will reset to your customized version.

> ► You can interrupt and restart an image sequence render without then having to splice together multiple movies.

> ► QuickTime in particular has its own form of color management that isn't entirely compatible even with Apple's own applications, let alone the Adobe color management pipeline (explained in depth in Chapter 11).

Unfortunately, none of the Adobe applications has ever become "smart" about recognizing sequences, let alone playing them back the way an application like Iridas Frame-Cycler (a version of which is included with Nuke) can.

Any single image sequence in a folder can simply be dragged in, if you're certain its frame rate is correct at the top of the Project panel (if not, see the sections on settings later in this chapter for the fix). If you instead intend to bring in that folder's contents as individual files, hold down the **Alt** (**Opt**) key as you drag it in.

Things get more complicated if you are dealing with multiple image sequences in a single folder. With the Import dialog, it doesn't matter which specific image in a sequence you select; they are all imported, provided you select only one. By holding the **Shift** or **Ctrl** (**Cmd**) key as you select more than one frame, however, you can

> ► specify a subset of frames to be imported instead of an entire sequence

> ► select frames from more than one sequence in the same folder; a Multiple Sequences check box appears as an option below to make certain this is really what you want to do

> ► specify sets of frames from multiple sequences (a combination of the above two modes)

This is, in many ways, a work-around for the fact that the After Effects importer doesn't group a frame sequence together the way other compositing applications do.

By default, if a sequence has missing frames (anywhere the count doesn't increment by 1), a color bar pattern is inserted with the name of the file presumed missing, which helps you track it down (see "Missing Footage" later in this chapter).

SCRIPT

Immigration by Lloyd Alvarez (http://aescripts.com/immigration) transforms the process of importing or substituting image sequences from a pain into an absolute breeze. It is particularly good at incrementing new versions of multiple sequences all at once, selecting subsets of frames, and finding multiple sequences in a single folder.

The Force Alphabetical Order check box in the Import dialog is for cases in which the frame does not increment by 1. Suppose you render "on twos," creating every other frame from a 3D application; check this box and you avoid color bars on every other frame.

Want to be rehired repeatedly as a freelancer or be the hero on your project? Make it easy for someone to open your project cold and understand how it's organized. On a more ambitious project, it's worth organizing a project template so that items are easy to find in predictable locations. Chapter 4 offers suggestions.

Context-Clicks (and Keyboard Shortcuts)

As you advance in your skills, by all means avoid the bar like a recovered alcoholic—the top menu bar, that is. I often refer to *context-clicking* on interface items. This is "right-clicking" unless you're on a Mac laptop or have an ancient one-button mouse, in which case you can hold down **Ctrl**. Here's what happens when you context–click on

- a **layer in the Timeline**: access to the full Layer menu, minus a few less useful items, such as the Adobe Encore submenu; useful additional items include Reveal Layer Source in Project and Reveal Expression Errors
- a **layer in a Composition** viewer: Many of the same items appear, plus the Select option at the bottom of the menu displays a list of all of the items below your pointer (**Figure 1.5**)
- a **panel tab**: The Panel menu (also found at the upper right) houses a bunch of options that even advanced users hardly know exist can be found, such as the View Options that allow you to, for example, show only motion tangents
- an **item in the Project panel**: Besides the File menu, you can reveal a file in the Explorer or Finder, the system counterpart to the Project panel

Keep these options right under your cursor and you may find yourself more focused as you work.

TIP

Waiting for a long 3D render from Maya or Cinema 4D? Render the first and last 3D frames only, with their correct final sequence numbers, and import them using the Import dialog with Force Alphabetical Order unchecked. You now have a placeholder of the correct length that is fully set up as soon as the file is rendered.

Figure 1.5 One of the biggest productivity boosts in After Effects comes from using the context menus that exist throughout After Effects and are always right under your cursor. This Layer context menu contains everything you'd want from the Layer menu, plus a couple of extra Timeline-specific commands. Display context menus by right-clicking the mouse (Windows) or Ctrl-clicking (Mac).

TIP

If source needs replacing with an element that's not yet available, note a couple of extra options under the Replace Footage menu item, including Placeholder, which inserts color bars.

NOTES

The icon shown for an item in the Project panel indicates its source application.

Missing Footage

After Effects links to any source footage file that can be located on your system or network. Any source can become unlinked if it moves or changes its name or location (**Figure 1.6**). To re-link an item, find it in the Project panel and double-click it (or **Ctrl+H/Cmd+H**), or context-click and choose Replace Footage > File.

If instead, you need only to reload or update a source, context-click and choose Reload Footage (**Ctrl+Alt+L/Cmd+Opt+L**). You can even edit a file in its source application and update it automatically in After Effects with Edit > Edit Original (**Ctrl+E/Cmd+E**), as long as you don't try anything tricky like saving it as a new file.

Sometimes it's difficult to locate a missing file or frame in your project. You may have used the Find Missing Footage check box in older versions, and you may wonder where it has gone. You're not alone.

Figure 1.6 Missing Footage displays the telltale color bars.

To search for particular types of footage in your project, including missing source, use the search field (**Ctrl+F/Cmd+F**) in the Project panel and the following commands (**Figure 1.7**):

▶ `missing` is the replacement for the Find Missing Footage check box.

▶ `unused` gets you all of the source that isn't in any composition.

▶ `used` is, self-evidently, just what it says.

▶ text strings that appear in the Project panel (say, `tif` or `Aug 26`).

The date column in the Project panel may be hidden by default; context-click to reveal it, then type in yesterday's date using a three-letter month abbreviation; the Project panel now displays only the items that were introduced or updated yesterday.

Because every project is likely to be moved or archived at some point (you *are* making backups, right?), it's best to keep all source material in one master folder. This helps After Effects automatically re-link all of the related files it finds there at once, thus avoiding a lot of tedium for you.

Figure 1.7 Missing footage is replaced with color bars, both in the Project thumbnail and anywhere the footage appears in the project. You can reveal all missing files in a Project by typing the word "missing" in the Project search field, highlighted in yellow.

Move, Combine, and Consolidate Projects

At some point you probably will need to

▶ move an entire After Effects project, including its source, or archive it

▶ merge or combine two projects

▶ clean up a project, getting rid of unused files or extra instances of a single file

To move or archive a project with only its linked sources, choose File > Collect Files. This command allows you to create a new folder that contains a copy of the project and all of its source files. The source files are reorganized with a directory structure identical to that of the Project panel (**Figure 1.8**).

Figure 1.8 Collect Files resaves all source files from your project using the same organization and hierarchy as the project itself.

Let the computer do what it does best and automate a cleanup of your sources. Choose Collect Source Files > For Selected Comps; After Effects collects only the footage needed to create that composition. If you check Reduce Project as well, the unused source is also removed from the collected project.

Select the master compositions in your project and choose File > Reduce Project; After Effects eliminates project items not used in the selected compositions. You even get a warning dialog telling you how many items were removed—not from the disk, only from your project.

You can also reduce only the source footage (keeping compositions and solids) with File > Remove Unused Footage, which deletes from the project any footage that hasn't made its way into a composition. If the same clips have been imported more than once, File > Consolidate All Footage looks for the extra instances and combines them, choosing the first instance, top to bottom, in the project. File > Remove Unused Footage rids a project of footage not included in any composition (but the files do remain on your drive).

Need to combine two or more projects? Import one into the other (just drag it in), or drag several into a new project. The imported project appears in its own folder labeled with the source name.

Advanced Save Options

After Effects projects are saved and overwritten completely separate from the elements they contain. They tend to be small, making it easier to save often so that you don't lose your work.

File > Increment and Save attaches a version number to your saved project or increments whatever number is already there, at the end of the filename. It helps the automation process if you make a habit of naming files with the version number at the end, right before the .aep extension.

Preferences > Auto-Save fills in the spaces between incremented versions; toggle it on and you'll never lose more than the number of minutes you specify (Save Every 20 Minutes is the default), along with whatever number of most recent versions you prefer (**Figure 1.10**).

If the projects being combined are organized using the same set of subfolders, you can merge them with Redefinery's Merge Projects script, which is included on the book's disc (**Figure 1.9**).

Figure 1.9 Load the highly useful rd_MergeProjects.jsx script from the scripts folder on the book's disc into Adobe After Effects CS5 > Scripts > ScriptUI Panels, and you can then reveal it at any time from the bottom of the Window menu. This script takes nested folders with the same name as those closer to the root and merges them, while consolidating duplicate footage. It's great for importing a project and maintaining a tidy structure.

Use Increment and Save when you reach a point where you're happy with a project and ready to move on to the next step; you can then choose File > Revert to get back there in one step instead of using a series of undos.

Figure 1.10 Auto-Save must be enabled (in Preferences > Auto-Save) in order for a folder to be created adjacent to the project that will contain the most recent saves of the project—you specify the number and gap between saves.

Take Control of Settings

After Effects includes a bunch of settings that you must understand in order to avoid getting in a fight with them. These have to do with essentials such as how time, color depth, transparency, pixel aspect ratio, and field data are handled. It's not necessarily fun—but it's the law.

Project Settings

As shown in **Figure 1.11,** the Project Settings dialog (**Ctrl+Alt+Shift+K/Cmd+Opt+Shift+K**) contains three basic sections:

▶ Display Style determines how time is displayed—predominantly whether a composition's frame count is kept in integers (frames) or in timecode (hours, minutes, seconds, and frames). Broadly, film projects tend to work in frames, broadcast video projects in timecode. This won't affect the frame rates of your footage or compositions.

▶ The Color Settings section includes the project-wide color depth (8, 16, or 32 bits per channel), as well as color management and blend settings. Chapter 11 covers this in ample depth.

▶ Audio Settings affects only previews; lowering the rate can save RAM. I never touch this.

If you're displaying timecode, you'll almost never want to change the default Auto setting unless you're working with footage containing more than one frame rate and need to conform everything to a particular standard.

If you're working with frames, it's often most helpful to start numbering them at 1, although the default is 0. This applies to imported image sequences, not compositions. Numbering in a composition is determined by the Start Frame number in Composition Settings (**Ctrl+K/Cmd+K**).

TIP

Instead of opening Project Settings, change Display Style by Ctrl- or Cmd-clicking on the timecode indicator in the timeline; change color depth by Alt- or Opt-clicking the bpc indicator in the Project panel.

Figure 1.11 When getting started, be certain to set Display Style and Color Depth the way you want them. The other Color Settings are elucidated in Chapter 11.

Interpret Footage

This book generally eschews the practice of walking through After Effects menus, but a well-designed UI helps you think, so focusing on the material in this section allows access to the best analytical tools. Decisions about how footage is interpreted are both vital and somewhat tedious. This makes the Interpret Footage dialog (**Figure 1.12**), where you can specify details for any source clip, even more vital as a preflight checklist for source footage. Here you'll determine

- Alpha interpretation
- Frame Rate
- Fields and Pulldown
- Pixel Aspect Ratio (under Other Options)
- Color Management (under More Options with certain file types and the Color Management tab)

Figure 1.12 The Interpret Footage dialog is a checklist for getting footage settings correct before you ever assemble a composition. Alpha determines transparency settings, Frame Rate is essential with an image sequence, Fields and Pulldown and Pixel Aspect Ratio (under Other Options) convert footage optimized for playback. The Color Management tab (purple) gets a complete treatment in Chapter 11.

The Interpret Footage icon in the Project panel ▣ is the easiest way to open the Interpret Footage dialog. Select a clip in the Project panel and click it, or press **Ctrl+Shift+G** (**Cmd+Shift+G**). Or, you can context-click and select Interpret Footage > Main.

Alpha

Effective compositing requires a thorough understanding of alpha channels, but only when something goes wrong with them. **Figure 1.13** shows the most visible symptom of a misinterpreted alpha channel: fringing.

You can easily avoid these types of problems:

▶ If the alpha channel type is unclear, click Guess in the mini Interpretation dialog that appears when importing footage with alpha. This often (not always) yields a correct setting.

Figure 1.13 It's not hard to distinguish a properly interpreted (left) from an incorrect (right) alpha channel. The giveaway is the contrasting fringe, caused in this case by the failure to remove the black background color premultiplied into edge pixels. The left image is unmultiplied; the right is not.

▶ Preferences > Import contains a default alpha channel preference, which is fine to set on a project with consistent alpha handling. If you are in any doubt about that, set it to Ask User to avoid forgetting to set it properly.

More information on alpha channels and how they operate is found in Chapter 3.

Frame Rate

I have known many experienced artists to be bitten by careless errors with frame rate, myself included. Misinterpreted frame rate is typically an issue with image sequences only, because unlike in QuickTime, the files themselves contain no embedded frame rate (not even formats like .dpx, which have this capability). You can also override the QuickTime frame rate, which is exactly what After Effects does with footage containing any sort of pulldown (see next section).

The following two statements are both true:

▶ After Effects is flexible in allowing you to mix clips with varying frame rates and to change the frame rate of a clip that's already in a composition.

▶ After Effects is *precise* about how those timing settings are handled. If your true frame rate is 23.976 fps or 29.97 fps, don't round those to 24 and 30, or strange things are bound to happen: motion tracks that don't stick, steppy playback, and more.

The current frame rate and duration as well as other interpretation information is displayed at the top of the Project panel when you select a source clip (**Figure 1.14**).

TIP

After Effects does not interpret an alpha unless you specifically click Guess; if you merely clear the dialog (**Esc**) it uses the previous default.

TIP

You can change the default Frames Per Second setting for Sequence Footage under Preferences > Import. This should be among the first things you check when you are starting a new project so you don't have to continually change it.

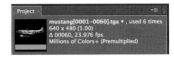

Figure 1.14 Useful information about any selected item appears atop the Project panel. The caret to the right of the filename reveals specific compositions in which it is used.

Why an Image Sequence?

Movie formats, which these days usually means QuickTime (.mov), have the following flaws compared with image sequences:

▶ A bad frame in a rendered image sequence can typically be quickly isolated and replaced; a bad frame will sink an entire QuickTime movie, sometimes costing hours of rework.

▶ It's easy to update a section of an image sequence precisely by overwriting a subset of frames instead of re-rendering the whole movie, cutting and pasting, or opening a nonlinear editor.

▶ Still image formats have more predictable color management settings than QuickTime. If QuickTime is fast food—convenient but potentially bad for the health of your project, causing bloat and slowness—then image sequences are a home-cooked meal, involving more steps but offering more control over how they are made and consumed.

It's not always practical, particularly when making quick edits to video footage, to convert everything to image sequences, which don't play back so easily on your system or in your nonlinear editor. However, on larger or longer-form projects, they will preserve your work more effectively.

Fields, Pulldown, and Pixel Aspect Ratio

One surprise for the novice is that video images are not typically made up of whole frames containing square pixels like stills. A video frame, and in particular one shot for broadcast, is often interlaced into two *fields*, and its pixels are stored nonsquare, for the purpose of faster and more efficient capture and delivery.

A frame combines two fields by *interlacing* them together, vertically alternating one horizontal line of pixels from the first with one from the second. The result is half the image detail but twice the motion detail. **Figure 1.15** shows this principle in action.

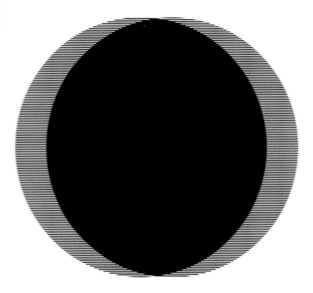

Figure 1.15 If a perfect ellipse were to travel horizontally at high speed, the interlaced result would look like this on a single frame. This contains two fields' worth of motion, alternating on vertical pixels of a single frame. If you see something like this in your composition, interlacing hasn't been removed on import.

If you're doing any compositing, transformation, paint/masking, or distortion—pretty much anything beyond basic color correction—match the Separate Fields setting to that of the footage, causing After Effects to recognize the interlaced frame as two separate frames of video.

Pulldown allows 24-fps film footage to play smoothly at 29.97 fps by repeating one field every five frames (**Figure 1.16**). This creates a pattern that After Effects

NOTES

To see interlaced footage in action with clips that contain interlacing, check out 01_interlaced_footage on the book's disc.

can accurately guess if there is sufficient motion in the first few frames of the footage. If not, the backup option (which still works) is trial-and-error. Do the following:

▶ Create a 23.976 composition with the source file in it.

▶ Try each initial pattern listed under Remove Pulldown until the field artifacts disappear.

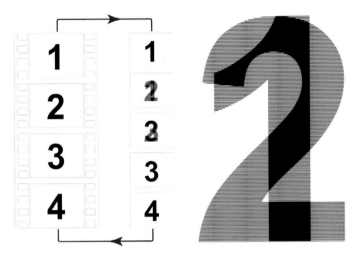

Figure 1.16 Pulldown allows 24-fps footage, the film frame rate, and enables it to play smoothly at 30 fps; without interleaving it into fields in this manner, the motion stutters, as it does if you try to go straight from 30 fps (no pulldown) to 24.

There are two basic types of pulldown (3:2 and 24 Pa), each with five potential initial patterns, so if none of these works to remove interlacing, there is some other problem with the footage.

Pixel aspect ratio (PAR) is another compromise intended to maximize image detail while minimizing frame size. The pixels in the image are displayed nonsquare on the broadcast monitor, with extra detail on one axis compensating for its lack on the other.

Your computer monitor, of course, displays square pixels, so any clip with a nonsquare PAR will look odd if displayed without compensating for the difference. Therefore, After Effects includes a toggle () below the viewer panels to stretch the footage so that its proportions preview correctly (**Figure 1.17**) although the footage or composition itself isn't changed.

NOTES

3:2 pulldown is the traditional format designed to make footage that originated at 24 fps play smoothly at 29.97 fps; telecine conversions from film to television use this. 24P Advance Pulldown was introduced to reduce field artifacts by grouping 24 whole frames with 6 interlaced frames, which are essentially filler and can be discarded on removal (see the diagram in Figure 1.16).

Figure 1.17 Think all of your problems with Pixel Aspect Ratio are gone with the demise of standard definition? Think again. DVCPRO HD footage with Pixel Aspect Ratio Correction on (left) and off (right) via the toggle (circled in red). If subjects look anamorphic—long and skinny—toggle this, and if it looks OK, After Effects is handling it for you; no need to render a square pixel version.

With some digital formats such as DV, field order and pixel aspect are standardized and set automatically in After Effects. With other formats, you may need to know the correct field order and pixel aspect as specified by the camera or software that generated the image.

Source Formats

After Effects is capable of importing and exporting a wide array of footage formats, yet only a small subset of these occur regularly in production. **Table 1.1** contains a rundown of common raster image formats and some advantages and disadvantages of each. Which formats will you use most? Probably TIFF or DPX for source and JPEG (with a Quality setting of 7 or higher) for temporary storage when file space is at a premium.

TIFF offers lossless LZW compression, giving it an advantage over Adobe Photoshop format, especially when you consider that TIFF can even store multiple layers, each with its own transparency. Other formats with lossless compression, such as TGA, don't support multiple bit depths and layers like TIFF does. PNG is more limited and slower, but the file sizes are smaller.

NOTES

One oddity of the PNG format is that it specifies that an alpha channel is saved and interpreted as Straight, with no explicit option to change the default, although After Effects lets you override this.

TABLE 1.1 Raster Image Formats and Their Advantages

Format	Bit Depth	Lossless Compression	Lossy Compression	Alpha Channel	Output Format
TIFF	8/16/32	Y	N	Y (multiple via layers)	Y
PNG	8/16	Y	N	Y (straight only)	Y
CIN/DPX	10	N	N	N	Y (Cineon 4.5 or DPX; see Cineon settings)
CRW	12	N	N	N	N
EXR	16/32	Y	N	Y	Y
JPG	8	N	Y	N	Y

For film and computer graphics, it is normal to pass around CIN and DPX files (essentially the same format) and EXR, designed (and open-sourced) by ILM specifically to handle high-dynamic-range (HDR) renders with multiple channels of data (and these can be customized to contain useful information such as Z depth and motion data). More on these formats is found in Chapters 11 and 12, which also include information on working with camera raw CRW images.

> **NOTES**
>
> After Effects includes EXR tools, which are highlighted in Chapter 12.

Photoshop Files

Although the PSD format does not offer any type of compression, it has a few unique advantages when used with After Effects. Specifically, PSD files can

▶ be imported directly as virtually *identical* After Effects compositions, with blending modes, layer styles, and editable text. In the Import File dialog, choose Composition or Composition-Retain Layer Sizes using the Import As pop-up menu (**Figure 1.18**)—you get a second chance in the Photoshop dialog that appears in After Effects itself after you click Import.

▶ be created from After Effects (File > New > Adobe Photoshop File or even Layer > New > Adobe Photoshop File).

▶ include moving footage. More about why you might want to work with video in Photoshop (for its paint tools) is included in Chapter 7.

Figure 1.18 Composition-Retain Layer Sizes means "just like in Photoshop. "The other option, Composition, reframes everything to the image area (all with the same center point)—and crops any pixels that fall outside frame. Choose Retain Layer Sizes to ensure that each layer has its own unique anchor point—and is *not* cropped.

A 2K plate is the minimum typical horizontal film resolution: approximately 2000 pixels, or more precisely 2048 pixels in width. HD video is 1920 pixels horizontal resolution.

▶ include Live Photoshop 3D layers: 3D models with lighting, material, and surface characteristics created in Photoshop that can be manipulated in After Effects. More about this feature is found in Chapter 9.

Once your source footage is imported and organized (Chapter 4), the next step is to place it in a composition.

Composition Settings

My advice is to begin with your *plate*: the main footage, whether a background shot or a foreground yet to be keyed. To ensure that composition settings are exactly as they should be with the least effort, try one of the following:

▶ Use a prebuilt project template that includes compositions whose settings match the intended output; you can even create and save your own (see Chapter 4).

▶ Create a new composition by dragging the plate footage (often the background plate) to the Create a New Composition icon 🖼. This automatically matches pixel dimensions, Pixel Aspect Ratio, Frame Rate, and Duration, all of which are crucial.

Composition Settings also contains an Advanced tab. This pertains to temporal and spatial settings (Chapter 4) and motion blur and 3D (Chapter 9).

View Panels and Previews

How exactly does a professional work with footage in After Effects? I've noticed some good habits that experienced pros tend to share.

Resolution and Quality

First, keep in mind that you might never work at full resolution, but you should almost always leave layers set to Best quality. There are several effective ways to speed up previews and interactivity without ever setting a layer to Draft quality, which creates inaccurate previews by rounding off crucial values.

In rough order of preference, you can

▶ lower viewer Resolution to Half, or in extreme cases, Quarter (see Note)

▶ set Region of Interest (ROI) to isolate only the area that needs to be previewed

▶ use Shift+RAM Preview to skip frames (the default setting of 1 skips every second frame—details in "Caching and Previewing," later in this chapter)

Half resolution allows four times as much data to fill a RAM preview, and Shift+RAM Preview can reduce overhead further by skipping every nth frame (according to the Skip setting in the Preview panel). The default setting of 1 plays every other frame (**Figure 1.19**).

To quickly change the display resolution in the Composition panel, use the keyboard shortcuts shown in **Table 1.2**.

TABLE **1.2** Display Resolution/Size Shortcuts

RESOLUTION/SIZE	KEYBOARD SHORTCUT
Full	Ctrl+J or Cmd+J
Half	Ctrl+Shift+J or Cmd+Shift+J
Quarter	Ctrl+Shift+Alt+J or Cmd+Shift+Opt+J
Fit in viewer	Shift+/
Fit up to 100%	Alt+/ or Opt+/

Activate the Hand tool (H, spacebar, or middle mouse button) to move your view of a clip around. To zoom in and out, you can use

▶ **Ctrl+=** (**Cmd+=**) and **Ctrl+-** (**Cmd+-**)

▶ Zoom tool (**Z**) and **Alt** (**Opt**) **Z**

▶ comma and period keys

▶ a mouse with a scroll wheel, or scrolling options on a track pad or tablet

Ever notice yourself focusing only on a particular section of a huge image? Use the Region of Interest (ROI) tool (**Figure 1.20**) to define a rectangular preview region. Only the layer data needed to render that area is calculated and buffered, lengthening RAM previews.

The Auto setting under the Resolution menu in the Composition panel downsample the image so that resolution is never higher than magnification.

Figure 1.19 Shift+RAM Preview is a secondary previewing option with unique settings. The default difference is a Skip setting of 1, which previews every other frame but can be changed to the pattern of your preference. To set a preview this way, either press Shift+0 (on the numerical keypad) or switch to Shift+RAM Preview in the Preview panel.

With the cursor over a specific area of the frame, hold the **Alt** (**Opt**) key as you zoom to keep that point centered.

Figure 1.20 Region of Interest crops the active view region. Want to keep this view? Crop Comp to Region of Interest (in the Composition menu).

Figure 1.21 Disabling Live Update and enabling Caps Lock could be seen as desperation moves when interactivity becomes unacceptable, but the former is rarely necessary (you can do it temporarily with **Alt/Opt**) and the latter can actually be a handy way to do setup as quickly as possible without worrying about previews. The frame goes black as soon as you make an adjustment.

TIP

OpenGL in After Effects can have undesirable side effects; most power users tend to leave it off most of the time.

Responsiveness

Has your After Effects UI slowed to a crawl as you work on a big shot? Here's a quick triage you can try:

▶ **Deactivate Live Update (Figure 1.21).** On by default, this toggle (▣) enables real-time update in the viewers as you adjust controls. Deactivate it and updates occur only when you release the mouse.

▶ **Hold Alt (Opt) as you make adjustments.** With Live Update on, this toggle prevents views from updating. Deactivate Live Update and the behavior is inverted; the modifier keys instead enable real-time updates.

▶ **Activate Caps Lock.** If you don't mind working "blind" for periods of time, pressing the Caps Lock key on your keyboard prevents updates to any viewer.

▶ **Enable OpenGL.** Preferences > Previews includes the Enable OpenGL option, off by default (and unavailable with older graphics cards). Enable it, and OpenGL-Interactive mode in a viewer panel is accelerated in certain cases, for example, when positioning layers in 3D space. There are two OpenGL options, Interactive and Always On; the former will help you with fast scene setup, especially in a complicated 3D scene, and the latter will give you the look of OpenGL at all times as you work.

In general, the more responsive you can make your user interface, the better will be the result because you can make more decisions in a shorter period of time. Just leave time to double-check the result if you are in the habit of disabling screen viewers.

Multiprocessing

Multiprocessing, which allows After Effects to use all of the processor cores on your system, is disabled by default. This does not mean that After Effects doesn't use all of your processors, just that by default it doesn't work on more than one frame at a time, and thus doesn't maximize usage of your system. CS5 is the first version of After Effects for which I would wholeheartedly recommend you go into Preferences > Memory & Multiprocessing and enable Render Multiple Frames Simultaneously if you're running a system with more than the barest of resources. Ideally, your system should have more than a couple of processors and at least 4 GB of physical memory (RAM).

The great thing about multiprocessing in a 64-bit application is that it actually works. Gone are the days when this option tied up your system while it started and created a bunch of render cores that locked up system resources, forcing a restart. Today, not only can this option be enabled on the fly, but in most cases it will speed your RAM previews and renders significantly. Try it yourself—preview a processor-intensive animation with this option off, then on, and notice the difference when you click 0 on the numeric keypad or with the render time required. You now don't even need to restart the application.

There are a couple of other adjustments you can make to tune this option. Since it's likely these days that you are running a system with eight or more cores, reserve a couple of them for other applications by setting CPUs Reserved for Other Applications in that same Preferences panel. Ideally, you can assign 2 GB per background CPU and still have a few GB of memory to reserve for other applications, as in **Figure 1.22**.

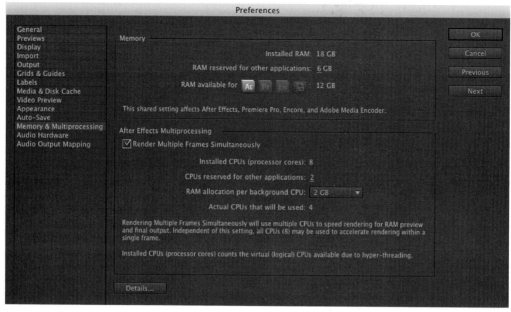

Figure 1.22 This dynamic Preferences panel contains useful information about how After Effects can use the resources on your specific system. Refreshingly, there's little here you need to adjust, other than enabling Render Multiple Frames Simultaneously and then optionally adjusting the amount of memory and number of processors reserved for other applications.

TIP

Initial results show that After Effects actually runs faster with fewer than the full number of cores on a system with eight or more cores. Reserve two for other applications and see if you get a speed boost.

Note that few other Adobe applications share the same protected memory pool as After Effects. Premiere Pro, Encore, and Adobe Media Encoder don't count as "other applications" but have been tuned to cooperate using the same settings you give After Effects, so you can work between these memory-hungry applications, editing and encoding simultaneously to compositing, without the need for further adjustments.

For more information on how the application is using your system resources you can click the Details button at the bottom of Preferences > Memory & Multiprocessing. It won't monitor all of your applications, just the four that fall into its managed pool: the CS5 versions of Premiere Pro, Encore, and Media Encoder.

Caching and Previewing

After Effects automatically caches footage as you navigate from frame to frame (**Page Up/Page Down**) or load a RAM preview (**0** on the numeric keypad). The green line atop the Timeline panel shows which frames are stored for instant playback. You can extend the cache from physical memory (RAM) to physical media (ideally a high-speed local drive) by enabling Disk Cache in Preferences > Memory & Cache. This locks away a portion of your drive for use only by After Effects. A blue line shows frames loaded in the Disk Cache (**Figure 1.23**).

Disk Cache saves the time required to re-render a frame but doesn't necessarily deliver real-time playback and often is not invoked when you might think it should be. The cache is not saved between After Effects sessions.

Figure 1.23 Enable Disk Cache and you may see your previews extended; the blue areas of the timeline have been cached to disc in addition to the green areas cached into physical memory (RAM).

Preview Settings

Here are some cool customizations to a RAM preview:

▶ **Loop options** (Preview panel). Hidden among the playback icons atop Preview is a toggle controlling how previews loop. Use this to disable looping, or amaze your friends with the ping-pong option.

▶ **From Current Time** (Preview panel). Tired of resetting the work area? Toggle this on and previews begin at the current time and roll through to the end of the composition.

▶ **Full Screen** (Preview panel). Self-explanatory and rarely used, but a cool option, no?

▶ **Preferences > Video Preview** lets you specify the output device and how it is used. If you have an external video device attached with its own monitor, you can use it to preview. Third-party output devices, such as Kona and Blackmagic cards, are supported as well.

If refined motion is not critical, use Shift+RAM Preview—this skips frames according to whatever pattern is set in the Preview panel under the Shift+RAM Preview Options menu.

TIP

To update an external preview device, press /.

TIP

The shortcut for Shift+RAM Preview is, naturally enough, **Shift+0** (on the numeric keypad). To set the Work Area to the length of any highlighted layers, use **Ctrl+Alt+B (Cmd+Opt+B)**.

Backgrounds

You need to see what you're doing, and when you use a contrasting background it's like shining a light behind layer edges. You can customize the background color of the Composition viewer right in Composition > Compositing Settings or toggle the Transparency Grid icon ▨ beneath the Composition panel to evaluate edges in sharp relief.

You can even insert background or reference footage or a custom gradient background that you created (**Figure 1.24**). If it's set as a Guide Layer ▤(Layer > Guide Layer or context-click the layer), it does not show up when rendered or nested in another composition.

Several other modes and toggles are available in the viewer panels. Some are familiar from other Adobe applications:

▶ **Title/Action Safe overlays** determine the boundaries of the frame as well as its center point. **Alt-** or **Opt**-click on the Grid & Guide Options icon ▦ to toggle it.

▶ **View > Show Grid** (**Ctrl+"/Cmd+"**) displays an overlay grid.

▶ **View > Show Rulers** (**Ctrl+R/Cmd+R**) displays not only pixel measurements of the viewer, but allows you to add guides as you can in Photoshop.

All of these are toggled via a single menu beneath the viewer panel (the one that looks like a crosshair). To pull out a guide, choose Show Rulers and then drag from either the horizontal or vertical ruler. To change the origin point (0 on each ruler), drag the crosshair from the corner between the two rulers.

TIP

To create a basic gradient background, apply the Ramp effect to a solid layer.

TIP

Use Preferences > Grids & Guides to customize the Safe Margins in the Title/Action Safe overlay or the appearance of grids and guides.

Figure 1.24 If the gradient behind a matted object is made a guide layer, you can clearly see the edge details of the foreground, but the gradient doesn't show up in any subsequent compositions or renders.

Masks, keyframes, and motion paths can get in the way. You can

▶ hide them all using View > Hide Layer Controls (**Ctrl+Shift+H**/**Cmd+Shift+H**)

▶ use the Toggle Mask and Shape Path Visibility button at the bottom of the Composition panel

▶ customize what is shown and hidden with View > View Options (**Ctrl+Alt+U**/**Cmd+Opt+U**)

Beginning in Chapter 5 you'll be encouraged to study images one color channel at a time. The Show Channel icon exists for this purpose (keyboard shortcuts **Alt+1** [**Opt+1**] through **Alt+4** [**Opt+4**] map to R, G, B, and A, respectively). An outline in the color of the selected channel reminds you which channel is displayed (**Figure 1.25**).

Figure 1.25 The green border indicates that only the green channel is displayed. (Image courtesy of Mark Decena, Kontent Films.)

Effects: Plug-ins and Animation Presets

After Effects contains about 200 default effects plug-ins, and third parties provide plenty more. Personally, I use less than 20 percent of these effects around 80 percent of the time, and you probably will too. So my opinion is that you don't need to understand them all in order to use the most powerful ones. And even cooler, once you thoroughly understand the core effects, you can use them together to do things with After Effects that you might have thought required third-party plug-ins.

SCRIPT

Opened a project only to discover a warning that some effects are missing, and wondering which ones, and where to find them? The script pt_EffectSearch by Paul Tuersley (http://aescripts.com/pt_effectsearch/) helps you locate missing plug-ins and where they are used.

Figure 1.26 Type the word **blur** in the Effects & Presets search field and only effects with that text string in the name appear. You can also choose to display only effects with higher bit depths (when working at 16 or 32 bits per channel—see Chapter 11 for more on that).

TIP

Convert raw footage by dragging it directly to the Render Queue panel, no composition required (one is made for you). This is a quick and easy way to convert an image sequence to a QuickTime movie, or vice versa.

To apply an effect to a layer, my advice is to avoid the Effect menu and either context-click that layer, then use the Effect context menu, or double-click it in the Effects & Presets panel. The Effects & Presets panel helps beginners and pros alike by displaying effects alphabetically (without their categories) as well as offering a search field to help you look for a specific effect by name or for all the effects whose names include a specific word, such as "blur" or "channel" (**Figure 1.26**).

Animation presets allow you to save specific configurations of layer properties and animations, including keyframes, effects, and expressions, independent of the project that created them. Save your own by selecting effects and/ or properties and choosing Animation > Save Animation Preset. Save to the Presets folder (the default location) and your preset will show up when After Effects is started.

Output and the Render Queue

As you know, the way to get a finished shot out of After Effects is to render and export it. Here are a few things you might not already know about the process of outputting your work.

To place an item in the render queue, it's simplest either to use a shortcut (**Ctrl+M** or **Cmd+M**, or **Ctrl+Shift+/** or **Cmd+Shift+/**) or to drag items from the Project panel.

Each Render Queue item has two sets of settings: Render Settings (which controls how the composition itself is set when generating the source image data) and Output Module (which determines how that image data is then written to disk).

Render Settings: Match or Override the Composition

Render Settings breaks down to three basic sections (**Figure 1.27**):

▶ **Composition** corresponds directly to settings in the Timeline panel; here you choose whether to keep or override them. The more complex options, such as Proxy Use, are described in Chapter 4.

Figure 1.27 The Composition area of the Render Settings dialog gives details on how an individual frame is rendered while the Time Sampling section determines the timing of the whole sequence.

▶ **Time Sampling** gives you control over the timing of the render; not just frame rate and duration but the ability to add pulldown and fields—say, when rendering a 24-fps film composition for 29.97 video—as well as motion blur and frame blending (Chapter 2).

▶ **Options** contains one super-important feature: Skip Existing Files, which checks for the existence of a file before rendering it. This is useful for splitting image sequences between sessions (see Chapter 4 for details on how to use this feature).

If you find that rendered output doesn't match your expectations, Render Settings is generally the place to look (unless the problem involves color management, compression, or audio). The output modules handle writing that output to a file.

TIP

Need to render several items to one location? Set up one item, then add the rest. The location of the first becomes the default.

Output Modules: Making Movies

Output modules convert the rendered frame into an actual file. The main decisions here concern

▶ **format**—what file type is being created?

▶ **size**—should the pixel dimensions of the output differ from those of the composition being rendered?

▶ **audio**—on or off, and in what format?

▶ **color management**—unavailable for some formats (QuickTime), essential for others (DPX and EXR)

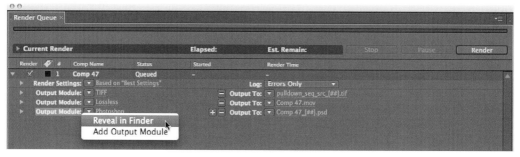

Figure 1.28 It's easy to miss that you can add multiple output modules to a single render queue item via Composition > Add Output Module or this context menu shown here. This is an immense time-saver, as each frame is rendered once and written as many times as you like.

Several elegant and easily missed problem-solving tools are embedded in output modules:

▶ Multiple output modules per render queue item avoid the need for multiple passes (**Figure 1.28**).

▶ Separate output modules can be changed at once by **Shift**-selecting the modules themselves (not the render queue items that contain them).

▶ A numbered image sequence can start with any number you like (**Figure 1.29**).

▶ Scaling can be nonuniform to change the pixel aspect ratio.

▶ Postrender actions automate bringing the result back into After Effects. Chapter 4 tells all.

▶ A numbered image sequence must contain a string in the format [###] somewhere within its name. Each # sign corresponds to a digit, for padding.

▶ The Color Management tab takes effect with many still image formats. Chapter 11 tells all.

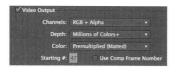

Figure 1.29 Custom-number a frame sequence here; no convoluted workarounds needed.

▶ Rendered files can include XMP metadata (if toggled on, as by default); this includes information that the file came from After Effects.

Save output modules early and often using the Make Template option at the bottom of the pop-up menu. If you intend to render with the same settings even once more, this will save time. Unfortunately, these cannot be easily sent to another user.

Optimized Output

Following are some suggested output settings (in Render Settings and Output Module) for specific situations:

▶ Final output should match the delivery format; it's usually an editor who decides this. Lossless, which is only 8 bit, is not sufficient if, for example, you've been working in 16 bpc to render a 10-bit final. For sending files internally, TIFF with lossless LZW compression is solid and can handle higher bit depths and color management.

▶ Low-loss output could be QuickTime with Photo-JPEG at around 75 percent. It works cross-platform and at 100 percent quality, it provides 4:4:4 chroma sampling, and at 75 percent, 4:2:2 (see Chapters 6 and 11 for details on what that means).

▶ Online review typically should be compressed outside of After Effects; such aggressive compression formats as H.264 are most successful on multiple passes.

Assemble the Shot

Seasoned visual effects supervisors miss nothing. Fully trained eyes do not even require two takes, although in the highest-end facilities, a shot loops for several minutes while the team picks it apart.

This process, though occasionally hard on the ego, makes shots look good. A Chinese proverb in an earlier edition of this book read, "Men in the game are blind to what men looking on see clearly." That may even go for women, too, who knows?

Naming Conventions

Part of growing a studio is devising a naming scheme that keeps projects and renders organized. It's generally considered good form to:

▶ Use standard Unix naming conventions (replacing spaces with underscores, intercaps, dashes, or dots).

▶ Put the version number at the end of the project name and the output file, and make them match. To add a version number to a numbered sequence, you can name the image sequence file something like foo_bar_[####]_v01.tif for version 1.

▶ Pad sequential numbers (adding zeros at the beginning) to keep things in order as the overall number moves into multiple digits.

And remember, After Effects itself doesn't always handle long filenames and paths particularly well, so a system that is concise makes key information easier to find in the Project panel.

Chapter 4 tells more about how to send your project to Adobe Media Encoder for multipass encoding; this requires Adobe CS5 Production Premium.

After Effects offers a number of output formats and can be useful for simple file conversion; you need only import a source file and drag it directly to Render Queue, then add settings and press Render.

Working with QuickTime

QuickTime is the most ubiquitous and universal playback format among video professionals, despite the fact that it is proprietary. There are design decisions behind QuickTime that don't change unless Apple decides to change them. Some of these amount to a gotcha:

▶ Color management of QuickTime remains (at this writing) a moving target, with MOV files appearing differently when they are moved from one platform, application, or even monitor, to another. "Application" includes those from Apple itself, which has not always been consistent on how to display the format.

▶ High Quality in QuickTime Player is unchecked by default. Direct your unhappy client to Window > Show Movie Properties > Video Track > Visual Settings and the little toggle to the lower right.

▶ There's no reliable way to rescue a QuickTime movie with a corrupt frame.

On the other hand, QuickTime is a great review and delivery format that benefits from having been well designed at its inception and having stood the test of time. One great integration with After Effects: If you've rendered a QuickTime movie and wonder what project was used to create it, import the rendered QuickTime file and select Edit > Edit Original (**Ctrl+E/Cmd+E**). If the project can still be found on the available drives, it will open in the source After Effects project.

You can and should scrutinize your shot just as carefully in After Effects. Specifically, throughout this book I encourage you to get in the following habits:

▶ Keep an eye on the Info panel (**Figure 1.30**).

Figure 1.30 By moving the cursor over the area that appears black and examining the pixel values (here shown as Percentage), it becomes apparent that the black levels are not pure 0 percent black.

▶ Loop or rock-and-roll previews (or as Adobe likes to say, ping-pong previews).

▶ Zoom in to the pixel level, especially around edges.

▶ Examine footage and compositions channel by channel (Chapter 5).

▶ Turn the Exposure control in the Composition viewer up and down to make sure everything still matches (Chapter 5).

▶ Assume there's a flaw in your shot; it's the only way around getting too attached to your intentions.

▶ Approach your project like a computer programmer and minimize the possibility of bugs (careless errors). Aspire to design in modules that anticipate what might change or be tweaked.

This list may not mean a lot you on the first read-through, I suggest you check out the rest of the book and come back to it as your work continues to progress.

2

The Timeline

The right word may be effective, but no word was ever as effective as a rightly timed pause.

—Mark Twain

The Timeline

The Timeline panel is something like After Effects' killer application within the overall app. More than any other feature, the Timeline panel extends the unique versatility of After Effects to a wide range of work, and differentiates it from less flexible node-based compositing applications. With the Timeline panel at the center of the compositing process, you can time elements and animations precisely while maintaining control of their appearance.

The Timeline panel is also a user-friendly part of the application that is full of hidden powers. By mastering its usage, you can streamline your workflow a great deal, setting the stage for more advanced work. One major subset of these hidden powers is the Timeline panel's set of keyboard shortcuts and context menus. These are not extras to be investigated once you're a veteran but small productivity enhancers that you can learn gradually as you go.

If this chapter's information seems overwhelming on first read, I encourage you to revisit often so that specific tips can sink in once you've encountered the right context in which to use them.

Organization

The goal here isn't to keep you organized but to get rid of everything you don't need and put what you *do* need right at your fingertips.

Column Views

You can context-click on any column heading to see and toggle available columns in the Timeline panel, or you can start with the minimal setup shown in **Figure 2.1** and then augment or change the setup with the following tools:

Figure 2.1 This most basic Timeline panel setup is close to optimal, especially if space is tight; it leaves everything you need within a single click, such as Toggle Switches/Modes. No matter how big a monitor, every artist tends to want more space for the keyframes and layers themselves.

- ▶ Lower-left icons : Most (but not quite all) of the extra data you need is available via the three toggles found at the lower left of the Timeline panel.

- ▶ Layer switches and transfer controls are the most used; if you have plenty of horizontal space, leave them both on, but the F4 key has toggled them since the days when 1280 x 960 was an artist-sized display.

- ▶ Time Stretch toggles the space-hogging timing columns. The one thing I do with this huge set of controls is stretch time to either double speed or half speed (50% or 200% stretch, respectively), which I can do by context-clicking Time > Time Stretch.

- ▶ Layer/Source (**Alt** or **Opt** key toggles): What's in a name? Nothing until you customize it; clear labels and color (see Tip) boost your workflow.

- ▶ Parent: This one is often on when you don't need it and hidden when you do (see "Spatial Offsets" later in this chapter); use **Ctrl+Shift+F4** (**Cmd+Shift+F4**) to show or hide it.

- ▶ I can't see why you would disable AV Features/Keys; it takes effectively no space.

The game is to preserve horizontal space for keyframe data by keeping only the relevant controls visible.

Color Commentary

When dissecting something tricky, it can help to use

- ▶ solo layers to see what's what
- ▶ locks for layers that should not be edited further
- ▶ shy layers to reduce the Timeline panel to only what's needed
- ▶ color-coded layers and project items
- ▶ tags in the comments field

TIP

To rename an item in After Effects, highlight it and press **Enter** (**Return**) instead of clicking and hovering.

TIP

To change the visibility (rather than the solo state) of selected layers, choose Layer > Switches > Hide Other Video.

TIP

I prefer to use solo switches only for previewing, and often set the Solo Switches menu to All Off in my default Render Settings to ensure I don't leave them activated by accident.

Figure 2.2 Shy layers can greatly reduce clutter in the Timeline panel, but if they ever trick you, study the Index numbers; if any fall out of sequence, there's a hidden shy layer.

SCRIPT

Comments are generally the least-used column in the Timeline panel, but that could change if more people start using a script called Zorro—The Layer Tagger by Lloyd Alvarez (http://aescripts.com/zorro-the-layer-tagger/). This script manages the process of adding tags to layers and using them to create selection sets.

Solo layers make other layers that are not solo invisible. They allow you to temporarily isolate and examine a layer or set of layers, but you can also keep layers solo when rendering (whether you intend to or not).

It can make a heck of a lot of sense to lock (**Ctrl+L/Cmd+L**) layers that you don't want "nudged" out of position, such as adjustment layers, track mattes, and background solids (but once they're locked, you can't adjust anything until you unlock them). If you're a super-organized person, you can use layer locks effectively to check layers in and out, with the locked ones completed—for now.

Shy layers are a fantastic shortcut in an often-cluttered Timeline panel. Layers set to Shy are hidden from the layer stack (once the Timeline panel's own Shy toggle is enabled) but remain visible in the Composition viewer itself (**Figure 2.2**). Even if you keep the number of layers in a composition modest (as you must for effective visual effects compositing work—see Chapter 4 for more on how), a composition containing an imported 3D track from such software as SynthEyes or Boujou may arrive with hundreds of null layers. I tend to make these shy immediately, leaving only the camera and background plate ready for compositing.

Colors are automagically assigned to specific types of layers (like cameras, lights, and adjustment layers) according to Preferences > Label. I often apply unique colors to track matte layers so I remember not to move them. On someone else's system, the colors may change according to local user preferences, although they will correspond overall.

Layer and composition markers can hold visible comments. You can add a layer marker for a given point in time with the asterisk (*) key on your numeric keypad, meaning you can add them while looping up a RAM preview in real time. Composition markers are added using **Shift** and the numbers atop your keyboard or using the asterisk key with nothing selected. I sometimes double-click them to add short notes.

Navigation and Shortcuts

Keyboard shortcuts are essential for working speedily and effortlessly in the Timeline panel.

Time Navigation

Many users—particularly editors, who know how essential they are—learn time navigation shortcuts right away. Others primarily drag the current time indicator, which quickly becomes tedious. See if there are any here you don't already know:

▶ **Home**, **End**, **PgUp**, and **PgDn** correspond to moving to the first or last frame of the composition, one frame backward or one frame forward, respectively.

▶ **Shift+PgUp** and **Shift+PgDn** skip ten frames backward or forward, respectively.

▶ **Shift+Home** and **Shift+End** navigate to the work area In and Out points respectively, and the **B** and **N** keys set these points at the current time.

▶ **I** and **O** keys navigate to the beginning and end frames of the layer.

▶ Press **Alt+Shift+J** (**Opt+Shift+J**) or click on the current time status at the upper left of the Timeline panel to navigate to a specific frame or timecode number. In this dialog, enter +47 to increment 47 frames or +−47 to decrement the same number; if you entered −47, that would navigate to a negative time position instead of offsetting by that number.

Layers Under Control

We were reviewing film-outs of shots in progress from *The Day After Tomorrow* at the Orphanage when my shot began to loop; it looked out a window at stragglers making their way across a snow-covered plaza and featured a beautiful matte painting by Mike Pangrazio. About two-thirds of the way through the shot came a subtle but sudden shift. At some point, the shot had been lengthened, and a layer of noise and dirt I had included at approximately 3% transparency (for the window itself) had remained shorter in a subcomposition. Gotcha!

TIP

Laptop users in particular may prefer **Ctrl+Left Arrow** *or* **Right Arrow** (**Cmd+Left Arrow** *or* **Right Arrow**) as an alternative to **PgUp** and **PgDn**.

NOTES

Don't bother with punctuation when entering time values into a number field in After Effects. 1000 is ten seconds (10:00) when in Timecode mode.

TIP

The increment/decrement method, in which you can enter + 47 to increase a value by 47 or + −417 to reduce it by 417, operates in most number fields throughout After Effects (including Composition Settings).

After Effects allows you to time the entrance and exit of layers in a way that would be excruciating in other compositing applications that lack the notion of a layer start or end. To avoid the accompanying gotcha where a layer or composition comes up short, it's wise to make elements way longer than you ever expect you'll need—overengineer in subcompositions and trim in the master composition.

To add a layer beginning at a specific time, drag the element from the Project panel to the layer area of the Timeline panel; a second time indicator appears that moves with your cursor horizontally. This determines the layer's start frame. If other layers are present and visible, you can also place the layer in order by dragging it between them.

Here are some other useful tips and shortcuts:

▶ **Ctrl+/** (**Cmd+/**) adds a layer to the active composition.

▶ **Ctrl+Alt+/** (**Cmd+Opt+/**) replaces the selected layer in a composition (as does **Alt**-dragging or **Opt**-dragging one element over another—note that this even works right in the Project panel and can be *hugely* useful).

▶ **J** and **K** navigate to the previous or next visible keyframe, layer marker, or work area start or end, respectively.

▶ **Ctrl+Alt+B** (**Cmd+Opt+B**) sets the work area to the length of any selected layers. To reset the work area to the length of the composition, double-click it.

▶ Numeric keypad numbers select layers with that number.

▶ **Ctrl+Up Arrow** (**Cmd+Up Arrow**) selects the next layer up; **Down Arrow** works the same way.

▶ **Ctrl+]** (**Cmd+]**) and **Ctrl+[** (**Cmd+[**) move a layer up or down one level in the stack. **Ctrl+Shift+]** and **Ctrl+Shift+[** move a layer to the top or bottom of the stack.

▶ Context-click > Invert Selection to invert the layers currently selected. (Locked layers are not selected, but shy layers are selected even if invisible.)

▶ **Ctrl+D** (**Cmd+D**) to duplicate any layer (or virtually any selected item).

TIP

The keyboard shortcut **Ctrl+/** (**Cmd+/**) adds selected items as the top layer(s) of the active composition.

TIP

To trim a composition's duration to the current work area, choose Composition > Trim Comp to Work Area.

- **Ctrl+Shift+D** (**Cmd+Shift+D**) splits a layer; the source ends and the duplicate continues from the current time.

- The bracket keys [and] move the In or Out points of selected layers to the current time. Add **Alt** (**Opt**) to set the current frame as the In or Out point, trimming the layer.

- The double-ended arrow icon over the end of a trimmed layer lets you slide it, preserving the In and Out points while translating the timing and layer markers (but *not* keyframes).

- **Alt+PgUp** or **Alt+PgDn** (**Opt+PgUp** or **Opt+PgDn**) nudges a layer and its keyframes forward or backward in time. **Alt+Home** or **Alt+End** (**Opt+Home** or **Opt+End**) moves the layer's In point to the beginning of the composition, or the Out point to the end.

Timeline Panel Views

After Effects has a great keyframe workflow. These shortcuts will help you work with timing more quickly, accurately, and confidently:

- The semicolon (**;**) key toggles all the way in and out on the Timeline panel: single frame to all frames. The slider at the bottom of the Timeline panel zooms in and out more selectively.

- The scroll wheel moves you up and down the layer stack.

- **Shift**-scroll moves left and right in a zoomed Timeline panel view.

- **Alt**-scroll (**Opt**-scroll) zooms dynamically in and out of the Timeline panel, remaining focused around the cursor location.

- The backslash (\) key toggles between a Timeline panel and its Composition viewer, even if previously closed.

- The Comp Marker Bin contains markers you can drag out into the Timeline panel ruler. You can replace their sequential numbers with names.

- X scrolls the topmost selected layer to the top of the Timeline panel.

NOTES

For those who care, a preference controls whether split layers are created above or below the source layer (Preferences > General > Create Split Layers Above Original Layer).

TIP

It can be annoying that the work area controls both preview and render frame ranges because the two are often used independent of one another. Dropping your work composition into a separate "Render Final" composition with the final work area set and locked avoids conflicts between working and final frame ranges and settings.

TIP

Hold down the **Shift** key as you drag the current time indicator to snap the current time to composition or layer markers or visible keyframes.

Keyframes and the Graph Editor

Transform controls live under every layer's twirly arrow. There are keyboard shortcuts to each Transform property. For a standard 2D layer these are

- ▶ **A** for Anchor Point, the center pivot of the layer
- ▶ **P** for Position, by default the center of the composition
- ▶ **S** for Scale (in percent of source)
- ▶ **R** for Rotation (in revolutions and degrees)
- ▶ **T** for Opacity, or if it helps, "opaci-T" (which is not technically spatial transform data but is grouped here anyhow because it's essential)

Once you've revealed one of these, hold down the **Shift** key to toggle another (or to hide another one already displayed). This keeps only what you need in front of you. A 3D layer reveals four individual properties under Rotation to allow full animation on all axes.

Add the **Alt** (**Opt**) to each of these one-letter shortcuts to add the first keyframe; once there's one keyframe, any adjustments to that property at any other frame generate another keyframe automatically.

There are selection tools to correspond to perform Transform adjustments directly in the viewer:

- ▶ **V** activates the Selection tool, which also moves and scales in a view panel.
- ▶ **Y** switches to the Pan-Behind tool, which moves the anchor point.
- ▶ **W** is for "wotate"—it adjusts Rotation. Quite the sense of humor on that After Effects team.

Once you adjust with any of these tools, an Add Keyframe option for the corresponding property appears under the Animation menu, so you can set the first keyframe without touching the Timeline panel at all.

Graph Editor

The project 02_bouncing_ball.aep in the accompanying disc's examples folder contains a simple animation, bouncing ball 2d, which can be created from scratch;

Figure 2.3 The Graph Editor is enabled in the Timeline panel instead of default Layer view. There is no option to see them together.

you can also see the steps below as individual numbered compositions.

To enable the Graph Editor, click its icon in the Timeline panel or use the shortcut **Shift+F3**. Below the grid that appears in place of the layer stack are the Graph Editor controls (**Figure 2.3**).

Show Properties

By default, if nothing is selected, nothing displays in the graph; what you see depends on the settings in the Show Properties menu . Three toggles in this menu control how animation curves are displayed in the graph:

▶ Show Selected Properties displays whatever animation property names are highlighted.

▶ Show Animated Properties shows everything with keyframes or expressions.

▶ Show Graph Editor Set displays properties with the Graph Editor Set toggle enabled.

Show Selected Properties is the easiest to use, but Show Graph Editor Set gives you the greatest control. You decide which curves need to appear, activate their Graph Editor Set toggle, and after that it no longer matters whether you keep them selected.

To begin the bouncing ball animation, include Position in the Graph Editor Set by toggling its icon. **Alt+P** (**Opt+P**) sets the first Position keyframe at frame 0; after that, any changes to Position are automatically keyframed.

TIP

To work in the Graph Editor without worrying about what is selected, disable Show Selected Properties and enable the other two.

TIP

The other recommended change prior to working through this section is to enable Default Spatial Interpolation to Linear in Preferences > General (**Ctrl+Alt+;** or **Cmd+Opt+;**). Try this if your initial animation doesn't seem to match that shown in Figure 2.4.

Figure 2.4   The layer travels across the frame like a bouncing ball, going up and down.

Basic Animation and the Graph View

Figure 2.4 shows the first step: a very basic animation blocked in using Linear keyframes, evenly spaced. It won't look like a bouncing ball yet, but it's a typical way to start when animating, for new and experienced animators alike.

To get to this point, do the following:

▶ Having set the first keyframe at frame 0, move the ball off the left of the frame.

▶ At frame 24, move the ball off the right of the frame, creating a second keyframe.

▶ Create a keyframe at frame 12 (just check the box, don't change any settings).

▶ Now add the bounces: At frames 6 and 18 move the ball straight downward so it touches the bottom of the frame.

This leaves five Position keyframes and an extremely unconvincing-looking bouncing ball animation. Great—it always helps to get something blocked in so you can clearly see what's wrong. Also, the default Graph Editor view at this point is not very helpful, because it displays the speed graph, and the speed of the layer is completely steady at this point—deliberately so, in fact.

To get the view shown in Figure 2.4, make sure Show Reference Graph is enabled in the Graph Options menu ▣. This is a toggle even advanced users miss, although it is now on by default. In addition to the not-very-helpful speed graph you now see the value graph in its X (red) and Y (green) values. However, the green values appear upside-down! This is the flipped After Effects Y axis in action; 0 is at the top of frame so that 0,0 is in the top-left corner, as it has been since After Effects 1.0, long before 3D animation was even contemplated.

Ease Curves

The simplest way to "fix" an animation that looks too stiff like this is often to add eases. For this purpose After Effects offers the automated Easy Ease functions, although you can also create or adjust eases by hand in the Graph Editor.

Select all of the "up" keyframes—the first, third, and fifth—and click Easy Ease (**F9**). When a ball bounces, it slows at the top of each arc, and Easy Ease adds that arc to the pace; what was a flat-line speed graph now is a series of arcing curves (**Figure 2.5**).

Figure 2.5 Easy Ease is applied (top) to the mid-air keyframes; Layer view (bottom) also shows the change from linear to Bezier with a changed keyframe icon.

NOTES

Auto Select Graph Type selects speed graphs for spatial properties and value graphs for all others.

WARNING

Mac users beware: The F9 key is used by the system for the Exposé feature, revealing all open panels in all applications. You can change or disable this feature in System Preferences > Dashboard & Exposé.

Technically, you could have applied Easy Ease Out ![icon] (**Ctrl+Shift+F9**/**Cmd+Shift+F9**) to the first keyframe and Easy Ease In ![icon] (**Shift+F9**) to the final one, because the ease in each case only goes in one direction. The "in" and "out" versions of Easy Ease are specifically for cases where there are other adjacent keyframes and the ease should only go in one direction (you'll see one in a moment). In this case it's not really necessary.

Meanwhile, there's a clear problem here: The timing of the motion arcs, but not the motion itself, is still completely linear. Fix this in the Composition viewer by pulling Bezier handles out of each of the keyframes you just eased:

1. Deselect all keyframes but leave the layer selected.

2. Make sure the animation path is displayed (**Ctrl+Shift+H**/**Cmd+Shift+H** toggles).

3. Click on the first keyframe in the Composition viewer to select it; it should change from hollow to solid in appearance.

4. Switch to the Pen tool with the **G** key; in the Composition viewer, drag from the highlighted keyframe to the right, creating a horizontal Bezier handle. Stop before crossing the second keyframe.

5. Do the same for the third and fifth keyframes (dragging left for the fifth).

The animation path now looks more like you'd expect a ball to bounce (**Figure 2.6**). Preview the animation, however, and you'll notice that the ball crudely pogos across the frame instead of bouncing naturally. Why is that?

Separate XYZ

The Graph Editor reveals the problem. The red X graph shows an unsteady horizontal motion due to the eases. The problem is that the eases should be applied only to the vertical Y dimension, whereas the X animation travels at a constant rate.

New to After Effects CS4 was the ability to animate X and Y (or, in 3D, X, Y, and Z) animation curves separately. This allows you to add keyframes for one dimension only at a

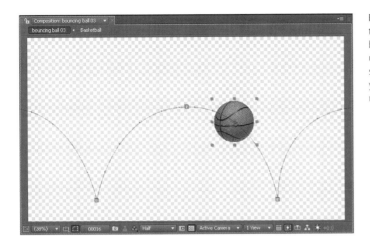

Figure 2.6 You can tell from the graph that this is closer to how a bouncing ball would look over time. You can use **Ctrl+Shift+H** (**Cmd+Shift+H**) to show and hide the animation path, or you can look in the Composition panel menu > View Options > Layer Controls.

given point in time, or to add keyframes in one dimension at a time.

Select Position and click Separate Dimensions . Where there was a single Position property, there are now two marked X Position and Y Position. Now try the following:

1. Disable the Graph Editor Set toggle for Y Position so that only the red X Position graph is displayed.

2. Select the middle three X Position keyframes—you can draw a selection box around them—and delete them.

3. Select the two remaining X keyframes and click the Convert Selected Keyframes to Linear button .

Now take a look in the Composition viewer—the motion is back to linear, although the temporal eases remain on the Y axis. Not only that, but you cannot redraw them as you did before; enabling Separate Dimensions removes this ability.

Instead, you can create them in the Graph Editor itself.

1. Enable the Graph Editor Set toggle for Y Position, so both dimensions are once again displayed.

2. Select the middle Y Position keyframe, and you'll notice two small handles protruding to its left and right. Drag each of these out, holding the Shift key if necessary to keep them flat, and notice the corresponding change in the Composition viewer (**Figure 2.7**).

TIP

Show Graph Tool Tips displays values of whatever curve is under the mouse at that exact point in time.

Figure 2.7 If Separate Dimensions is activated, pull out the handles to create the motion arcs right in the Graph Editor; the handles are no longer adjustable in the Composition viewer.

3. Select the first and last Y Position keyframes and click Easy Ease; the handles move outward from each keyframe without affecting the X Position keyframes.

4. Drag the handles of the first and last Y Position keyframes as far as they will go (right up to the succeeding and preceding keyframes, respectively).

Preview the result and you'll see that you now have the beginnings of an actual bouncing ball animation; it's just a little bit too regular and even, so from here you give it your own organic touch.

Transform Box

The transform box lets you edit keyframe values in all kinds of tricky or even wacky ways. Toggle on Show Transform Box and select more than one keyframe, and a white box with vertices surrounds the selected frames. Drag the handle at the right side to the left or right to change overall timing; the keyframes remain proportionally arranged.

So, does the transform box help in this case? Well, it could, if you needed to

▸ scale the animation timing around a particular keyframe: Drag the anchor to that frame, then **Ctrl**-drag (**Cmd**-drag)

▸ reverse the animation: **Ctrl**-drag/**Cmd**-drag from one edge of the box to the other (or for a straight reversal, simply context-click and choose Keyframe Assistant > Time-Reverse Keyframes)

▸ diminish the bounce animation so that the ball bounces lower each time: **Alt**-drag (**Opt**-drag) on the lower-right corner handle (**Figure 2.8**)

TIP

Separate Dimensions does not play nicely with eases and cannot easily be round-tripped back, so unfortunately you're best to reserve it for occasions when you really need it.

NOTES

There is a whole menu of options to show items that you might think are only in Layer view: layer In/Out points, audio waveforms, layer markers, and expressions.

NOTES

The Snap button snaps to virtually every visible marker, but not—*snap!*—to whole frame values if Allow Keyframes Between Frames is on .

Figure 2.8 How do you do that? Add the **Alt** (**Opt**) key when dragging a corner of the transform box; this adjustment diminishes the height of the ball bounces proportionally over time.

If you **Ctrl+Alt**-drag (**Cmd+Opt**-drag) on a corner that will taper values at one end, and if you **Ctrl+Alt+ Shift**-drag (**Cmd+Opt+Shift**-drag) on a corner, it will skew that end of the box up or down. I don't do that kind of stuff much, but with a lot of keyframes to scale proportionally, it's a good one to keep in your back pocket.

Holds

At this point you may have a fairly realistic-looking bouncing ball; maybe you added a little Rotation animation so the ball spins forward as it bounces, or maybe you've hand-adjusted the timing or position keys to give them that extra little organic unevenness. Hold keyframes won't help improve this animation, but you could use them to go all *Matrix*-like with it, stopping the ball mid-arc before continuing the action. A Hold keyframe 🔲 (**Ctrl+Alt+H/ Cmd+Shift+H**) prevents any change to a value until the next keyframe.

Drag all keyframes from the one at the top of the middle arc forward in time a second or two. Copy and paste that mid-arc keyframe (adding one for any other animated properties or dimensions at that point in time) back to the original keyframe location, and toggle it to a Hold keyframe (**Figure 2.9**).

Figure 2.9 Where the graph line is flatlined, the bounce stops mid-air—the result of Hold keyframes, which have the benefit of ensuring no animation whatsoever occurs until the next keyframe.

Beyond Bouncing Balls

In the (reasonably likely) case that the need for a bouncing ball animation never comes up, what does this example show you? Let's recap:

▶ You can control a Bezier motion path in the Composition viewer using the Pen tool (usage detailed in the next chapter).

▶ Realistic motion often requires that you shape the motion path Beziers and add temporal eases; the two actions are performed independently on any given keyframe, and in two different places (in the viewer and Timeline panel).

Animation can get a little trickier in 3D, but the same basic rules apply (see Chapter 9 for more).

Three preset keyframe transition types are available, each with a shortcut at the bottom of the Graph Editor: Hold , Linear , and Auto Bezier . Adjust the handles or apply Easy Ease and the preset becomes a custom Bezier shape.

Copy and Paste Animations

Yes, copy and paste; everyone knows how to do it. Here are some things that aren't necessarily obvious about copying and pasting keyframe data:

▶ Copy a set of keyframes from After Effects and paste them into an Excel spreadsheet or even an ordinary text editor, and behold the After Effects keyframe format, ready for hacking.

▶ You can paste from one property to another, so long as the format matches (the units and number of parameters). Copy the source, highlight the target, and paste.

▶ Keyframes respect the position of the current time indicator; the first frame is always pasted at the current time (useful for relocating timing, but occasionally an unpleasant surprise).

▶ There's a lock on the Effect Controls tab to keep a panel forward even when you select another layer to paste to it.

TIP

You can use an Excel spreadsheet to reformat underlying keyframe data from other applications; just paste in After Effects data to see how it's formatted, and then massage the other data to match that format (if you have Excel skills, so much the better). Once done, copy and paste the data back into After Effects.

Roving Keyframes

Sometimes an animation must follow an exact path, hitting precise points, but progress steadily, with no variation in the rate of travel. This is the situation for which Roving keyframes were devised. **Figure 2.10** shows a before-and-after view of a Roving keyframe; the path of the animation is identical, but the keyframes proceed at a steady rate.

Figure 2.10 Compare this graph with the one in Figure 2.5 (top); the speed graph is back to a flat-line because the animation runs at a uniform pace. You may not want to bounce a ball, but the technique works with any complex animation, and it maintains eases on the start and end frame.

▶ Copy and paste keyframes from an effect that isn't applied to the target, and that effect is added along with its keyframes.

Pay close attention to the current time and what is selected when copying, in particular, and when pasting animation data.

Layer vs. Graph

To summarize the distinction between layer bar mode and the Graph Editor, with layers you can

▶ block in keyframes with respect to the overall composition

▶ establish broad timing (where Linear, Easy Ease, and Auto-Bezier keyframes are sufficient)

The Graph Editor is essential to

▶ refine an individual animation curve

▶ compare spatial and temporal data

▶ scale animation data, especially around a specific pivot point

▶ perform extremely specific timing (adding a keyframe in between frames, hitting a specific tween point with an ease curve)

In either view you can

▶ edit expressions

▶ change keyframe type (Linear, Hold, Ease In, and so on)

▶ make editorial and compositing decisions regarding layers such as start/stop/duration, split layers, order (possible in both views, easier in Layer view)

By no means, then, does the Graph Editor make Layer view obsolete; Layer view is still where the majority of compositing and simple animation is accomplished.

You must enable Allow Keyframes Between Frames in the Graph Editor or they all snap to exact frame increments. However, when you scale a set of keyframes using the transform box, keyframes will often fall in between frames whether or not this option is enabled.

Timeline Panel Shortcuts

The following keyboard shortcuts have broad usage when applied with layers selected in the Timeline panel:

▶ **U** toggles all properties with keyframes or expressions applied.

▶ **UU** (U twice in quick succession) toggles all properties set to any value besides the default; or every property in the Timeline panel that has been edited.

▶ **E** toggles all applied effects.

▶ **EE** toggles all applied expressions.

The term "toggle" in the above list means that not only do these shortcuts reveal the listed properties, they can also conceal them, or with the **Shift** key, they can be used in combination with one another and with many of the shortcuts detailed earlier (such as the Transform shortcuts **A**, **P**, **R**, **S**, and **T** or the Mask shortcuts **M**, **MM**, and **F**). You want all the changes applied to masks and transforms, not effects? **UU**, then **Shift+E**. Lose the masks? **Shift+M**.

The **U** shortcut is a quick way to find keyframes to edit or to locate a keyframe that you suspect is hiding somewhere. But **UU**—now *that* is a full-on problem-solving tool all by itself. It allows you to quickly investigate what has been edited on a given layer, is helpful when troubleshooting your own layer settings, and is nearly priceless when investigating an unfamiliar project.

Highlight all the layers of a composition and press **UU** to reveal all edits. Enable Switches, Modes, Parent, and Stretch columns, and you see everything in a composition, with the exception of

▶ contents of nested compositions, which must be opened (**Alt/Opt**-double-click) and analyzed individually

▶ locked layers

▶ shy layers (disable them atop the Timeline panel to show all)

▶ composition settings themselves, such as motion blur and frame rate

In other words, this is an effective method to use to understand or troubleshoot a shot.

Dissect a Project

If you've been handed an unfamiliar project and need to make sense of it quickly, there are a couple of other tools that may help.

Composition Mini-Flowchart, aka Miniflow (with the Timeline panel, Composition panel, or Layer panel active, press the Shift key; see **Figure 2.11**, bottom) quickly maps any upstream or downstream compositions and allows you to open any of them simply by clicking on one.

If you're looking for a whole visual map of the project instead, try Flowchart view (**Ctrl+F11/Cmd+F11** or the tree/node icon in the Composition viewer). You have to see it to believe it: a nodal interface in After Effects (**Figure 2.11**, top), perhaps the least nodal of any of the major compositing applications.

Figure 2.11 The tree/node interface in Flowchart (top) is a diagnostic rather than a creative tool. The gray nodes are compositions, the red source clips, and the yellow is an effect, but there is no way to apply or adjust an effect in this view. Its usage has largely been superseded by the new Miniflow (bottom), which focuses interactively on the current composition.

Nerd-Based Compositing

Flowchart, the After Effects nodal view, reveals the truth that all compositing applications are, at their core, nodal in their logic and organization. However, this particular tree/node view is diagnostic and high-level only; you can delete but not create a layer.

If keyframes are "hiding" outside the Timeline panel—you know they're there if the keyframe navigation arrows stay highlighted at the beginning or end—select all of them by clicking the Property Name, **Shift-drag** a rectangular selection around those you can see, and delete the rest.

This view shows how objects (layers, compositions, and effects) are used, and in what relationship to one another. The + button above a composition reveals its components; for the cleanest view, toggle layers and effects off at the lower left. Click the ⬚ icon to switch the view to flow left to right, which fits well on a monitor, or **Alt**-click (**Opt**-click) it to clean up the view. You can't make any edits here, but you can double-click any item to reveal it where you can edit it—back in the Timeline panel, of course.

Keyframe Navigation and Selection

Although no shortcut can hold a candle to the all-encompassing überkey, there are several other useful essentials:

▶ **J** and **K** keys navigate backward and forward, respectively, through all *visible* keyframes, layer markers, and work area boundaries; hide the properties you don't want to navigate.

▶ Click *Property Name* to select all keyframes for a property.

▶ Context-click keyframe > Select Previous Keyframes or Select Following Keyframes to avoid difficult drag selections.

▶ Context-click keyframe > Select Equal Keyframes to hit all keyframes with the same setting.

▶ **Alt+Shift+***Transform shortcut*, or **Opt+Shift+***Transform shortcut* (**P**, **A**, **S**, **R**, or **T**), sets a keyframe; no need to click anywhere.

▶ Click a property stopwatch to set the first keyframe at the current frame (if no keyframe exists), or delete all existing keyframes.

▶ **Ctrl**-click (**Cmd**-click) an effect stopwatch to set a keyframe.

▶ **Ctrl+Alt+A** (**Cmd+Opt+A**) selects all visible keyframes while leaving the source layers, making it easy to delete them when, say, duplicating a layer but changing its animation.

▶ **Shift+F2** deselects keyframes only.

Read on; you are not a keyframe Jedi—yet.

Keyframe Offsets

To offset the values of multiple keyframes by the same amount in Layer view, select them all, *place the current time indicator over a selected keyframe* (that's important), and drag the setting; all change by the same increment. If instead you type in a new value, or enter an offset, such as +20 or +-47, with a numerical value, all keyframes take on the (identical) new value.

With multiple keyframes selected you can also

▶ **Alt+Right Arrow** or **Alt+Left Arrow** (**Opt+Right Arrow** or **Opt+Left Arrow**) to nudge keyframes forward or backward in time.

▶ Context-click > Keyframe Assistant > Time-Reverse Keyframes to run the animation in reverse without changing the duration and start or end point of the selected keyframe sequence.

▶ **Alt**-drag (**Opt**-drag) the first or last selected keyframe to scale timing proportionally in Layer view (or use the transform box in the Graph Editor).

Spatial Offsets

3D animators are familiar with the idea that every object (or layer) has a pivot point. In After Effects, there are two fundamental ways to make a layer pivot around a different location: Change the layer's own anchor point, or parent it to another layer.

After Effects is generally designed to preserve the appearance of the composition when you are merely setting up animation, toggling 3D on, and so forth. Therefore, editing an anchor point position with the Pan Behind tool triggers the inverse offset to the Position property. Parent a layer to another layer and the child layer maintains its relative position until you further animate either of them. If you set up your offsets and hierarchy before animating, you may find fewer difficulties as you work—although this section shows how to go about changing your mind once keyframes are in place.

Keyframe multiselection in standard Layer view (but not Graph Editor) is inconsistent with the rest of the application: you **Shift**-click to add or subtract a single frame from a group. **Ctrl**-clicking (**Cmd**-clicking) on a keyframe converts it to Auto-Bezier mode.

The 02_parent_offset_setup folder and project on the disc contain relevant example comps.

To simply frame your layers, Layer > Transform (or context-click a layer > Transform) includes three methods to fill a frame with the selected layer:

▶ **Ctrl+Alt+F** (**Cmd+Opt+F**) centers a layer and fits both horizontal and vertical dimensions of the layer, whether or not this is nonuniform scaling.

▶ **Ctrl+Alt+Shift+H** (**Cmd+Opt+Shift+H**) centers but fits only the width.

▶ **Ctrl+Alt+Shift+G** (**Cmd+Opt+Shift+G**) centers but fits only the height.

Those shortcuts are a handful; context-clicking the layer for the Transform menu is nearly as easy.

Anchor Point

The Pan Behind tool (**Y**) repositions an anchor point in the Composition or Layer viewer (and offsets the Position value to compensate). This prevents the layer from appearing in a different location on the frame in which you're working.

The Position offset is for that frame only, however, so if there are Position keyframes, the layer may appear offset on other frames if you drag the anchor point this way. To reposition the anchor point without changing Position:

▶ Change the anchor point value in the Timeline panel.

▶ Use the Pan Behind tool in the Layer panel instead.

▶ Hold the **Alt** (**Opt**) key as you drag with the Pan Behind tool.

Any of these options lets you reposition the anchor point without messing up an animation by changing one of the Position keyframes.

You can also animate the anchor point, of course; this allows you to rotate as you pan around an image while keeping the view centered. If you're having trouble seeing the anchor point path as you work, open the source in the Layer panel and choose Anchor Point Path in the View pop-up menu (**Figure 2.12**).

Figure 2.12 Switch the default Masks to Anchor Point Path for easy viewing and manipulation of the layer anchor point. For the bouncing ball, you could move the anchor point to the base of the layer to add a little cartoonish squash and stretch, scaling Y down at the impact points.

Parent Hierarchy

Layer parenting, in which all of the Transform settings (except Opacity, which isn't really a Transform setting) are passed from parent to child, can be set up by revealing the Parent column in the Timeline panel. There, you can choose a layer's parent either by selecting it from the list or by dragging the pick whip to the parent layer and using the setup as follows:

▶ Parenting remains valid even if the parent layer moves, is duplicated, or changes its name.

▶ A parent and all of its children can be selected by context-clicking the parent layer and choosing Select Children.

▶ Parenting can be removed by choosing None from the Parent menu.

▶ Null Objects (**Ctrl+Alt+Shift+Y**/**Cmd+Opt+Shift+Y**) exist only to be parents; they are actually 100 x 100 pixel layers that do not render.

You probably knew all of that. You might *not* know what happens when you add the **Alt** (**Opt**) key to Parent settings:

▶ Hold **Alt** (**Opt**) as you select the None option and the layer reverts to the Transform values it had before being parented (otherwise the offset at the time None is selected remains).

▶ Hold **Alt** (**Opt**) as you select a Parent layer and its Transform data at the current frame is applied to the child layer prior to parenting.

This last point is a very cool and easily missed method for arraying layers automatically. You duplicate, offset, and parent to create the first layer in a pattern, then duplicate that layer and **Alt+Parent** (**Opt+Parent**) it to the previous duplicate. It behaves like the Duplicate and Offset option in Illustrator (**Figure 2.13**).

Figure 2.13 Until you know the trick, setting up a series of layers as an array seems like a big pain. The trick is to create the first layer, duplicate, and offset; now you have two. Duplicate the offset layer and—this is the key—**Alt**+Parent (**Opt**+Parent) the duplicate to the offset. Repeat this last step with as many layers as you need; each one repeats the offset.

Blurred Vision

Motion blur occurs in your natural vision, although you might not realize it—stare at a ceiling fan in motion, and then try following an individual blade around instead and you will notice a dramatic difference. There is a trend in recent years to use extremely high-speed electronic shutters, which drastically reduce motion blur. It gives the psychological effect of excitement or adrenaline by making your eye feel as if it's tracking motion with heightened awareness.

Motion Blur

Motion blur is clearly essential to a realistic shot with a good amount of motion. It is the natural result of movement that occurs while a camera shutter is open, causing objects in the image to be recorded at every point from the shutter opening to closing. The movement can be from individual objects or the camera itself. Although it essentially smears layers in a composition, motion blur is generally desirable; it adds to persistence of vision and relaxes the eye. Aesthetically, it can be quite beautiful.

The idea with motion blur in a realistic visual effects shot is usually to match the amount of blur in the source shot, assuming you have a reference; if you lack visual reference, a camera report can also help you set this correctly. Any moving picture camera has a *shutter speed* setting that determines the amount of motion blur. This is not the camera's frame rate, although the shutter does obviously have to be fast enough to accommodate the frame rate. A typical film camera shooting 24 fps (frames per second) has a shutter that is open half the time, or $\frac{1}{48}$ of a second.

Decoding After Effects Motion Blur

The Advanced tab of Composition Settings (**Ctrl+K/ Cmd+K**) contains Motion Blur settings (**Figure 2.14**):

▶ **Shutter Angle** controls shutter speed, and thus the amount of blur.

Figure 2.14 These are the default settings; 16 is really too low for good-looking blur at high speed, but a 180-degree shutter and –90 degree shutter angle match the look of a film camera. Any changes you make here stick and are passed along to the next composition, or even the next project, until you change them.

▶ **Shutter Phase** determines at what point the shutter opens.

▶ **Samples Per Frame** applies to 3D motion blur and Shape layers; it sets the number of slices in time (samples), and thus, smoothness.

▶ **Adaptive Sample Limit** applies only to 2D motion blur, which automatically uses as many samples as are needed up to this limit (**Figure 2.15**).

Figure 2.15 The low default 16 Samples Per Frame setting creates steppy-looking blur on a 3D layer only; the same animation and default settings in 2D use the higher default Adaptive Sample Limit of 128. The reason for the difference is simply performance; 3D blur is costlier, but like many settings it is conservative. Unless your machine is ancient, boost the number; the boosted setting will stay as a preference.

Figure 2.16 The 180-degree mechanical shutter of a film camera prevents light from exposing film half the time, for an effective exposure of 1/48 of a second. In this abstraction the dark gray hemi-circular shutter spins to alternately expose and occlude the aperture, the circular opening in the light gray plate behind it.

NOTES

The 02_motion_blur folder and project on the disc contains relevant example comps. The 02_shutter_angle_diagram project contains the graphics used to create Figure 2.16.

Here's a bit of a gotcha: The default settings that you see in this panel are simply whatever was set the last time it was adjusted (unless it was never adjusted, in which case there are defaults). It's theoretically great to reuse settings that work across several projects, but I've seen artists faked out by vestigial extreme settings like 2 Samples Per Frame or a 720-degree blur that may have matched perfectly in some unique case.

Shutter Angle refers to an angled mechanical shutter used in older film cameras; it is a hemisphere of a given angle that rotates on each frame. The angle corresponds to the radius of the open section—the wedge of the whole pie that exposes the frame (**Figure 2.16**). A typical film shutter is 180 degrees—open half the time, or $\frac{1}{48}$ of a second at 24 frames per second.

Electronic shutters are variable but refer to shutter angle as a benchmark; they can operate down in the single digits or close to a full (mechanically impossible) 360 degrees. After Effects motion blur goes to 720 degrees simply because sometimes mathematical accuracy is not the name of the game, and you want more than 360 degrees.

If you don't know how the shutter angle was set when the plate was shot, you can typically nail it by zooming in and matching background and foreground elements by eye (**Figure 2.17**). If your camera report includes shutter speed, you can calculate the Shutter Angle setting using the following formula:

shutter speed = 1 / frame rate * (360 / shutter angle)

This isn't as gnarly as it looks, but if you dislike formulas, think of it like this: If your camera takes 24 fps, but Shutter Angle is set at 180 degrees, then the frame is exposed half the time (180/360 = ½) or $\frac{1}{48}$ of a second. However, if the shutter speed is $\frac{1}{96}$ per second with this frame rate, Shutter Angle should be set to 90 degrees. A $\frac{1}{1000}$ per second shutter would have a 9-degree shutter angle in order to obey this rule of thumb.

Shutter Phase determines how the shutter opens relative to the frame, which covers a given fraction of a second beginning at a given point in time. If the shutter is set to 0, it

Figure 2.17 The white solid tracked to the side of the streetcar has been eye-matched to have an equivalent blur by adjusting Shutter Angle; care is also taken to set Shutter Phase to −50% of Shutter Angle so that the layer stays centered on the track.

opens at that point in time, and the blur appears to extend forward through the frame, which makes it appear offset.

The default −90 Shutter Phase setting (with a 180-degree shutter angle) causes half the blur to occur before the frame so that blur extends in both directions from the current position. This is how blur appears when taken with a camera, so a setting that is −50% of shutter angle is essential when you're adding motion blur to a motion-tracked shot. Otherwise, the track itself appears offset when motion blur is enabled.

Enhancement Easier Than Elimination

Although software may one day be developed to resolve a blurred image back to sharp detail, it is much, much harder to sharpen a blurred image elegantly than it is to add blur to a sharp image. Motion blur comes for free when you keyframe motion in After Effects; what about when there is motion but no blur and no keyframes, as can be the case in pre-existing footage?

If you have imported a 3D element with insufficient blur, or footage shot with too high a shutter speed, you have the options to add the effect of motion blur using

▶ Directional Blur, which can mimic the blur of layers moving in some uniform X and Y direction

▶ Radial Blur, which can mimic motion in Z depth (or spin)

▶ Timewarp, which can add motion blur without any retiming whatsoever

Yes, you read that last one correctly. There's a full section on Timewarp later in this chapter, but to use it to add procedural motion blur

▶ set Speed to 100

▶ toggle Enable Motion Blur

▶ set Shutter Control to Manual

Now raise the Shutter Angle and Shutter Samples (being aware that the higher you raise them, the longer the render time). The methodology is similar to that of Reel Smart Motion Blur (RE:Vision Effects); try the demo version on the book's disc and compare quality and render time.

Timing and Retiming

After Effects is more flexible when working with time than most video applications. You can retime footage or mix and match speeds and timing using a variety of methods.

Absolute (Not Relative) Time

After Effects measures time in absolute seconds, rather than frames, whose timing and number are relative to the number per second. If frames instead of seconds were the measure of time, changing the frame rate on the fly would pose a much greater problem than it does.

Figure 2.18 The bounce animation remains the same as the composition frame rate changes; keyframes now fall in between whole frames, the vertical lines on the grid.

Change the frame rate of a composition and the keyframes maintain their position in actual time, so the timing of an animation doesn't change (**Figure 2.18**), only the position of the keyframes relative to frames. Here's a haiku:

keyframes realign
falling between retimed frames
timing is unchanged

Likewise, footage (or a nested composition) with a mismatched frame rate syncs up at least once a second, but the intervening source frames may fall in between composition frames. Think of a musician playing 3 against 4; one second in After Effects is something like the downbeat.

Time Stretch

Time Stretch lets you alter the duration (and thus the speed) of a source clip—but it doesn't let you animate the retiming itself (for that, you need Time Remap or Timewarp). The third of the three icons at the lower left of the Timeline panel reveals the In/Out/Duration/Stretch columns.

I mostly change the Stretch value and find the inter-related settings of all four-columns redundant. I also never use a Time Stretch setting that is anything but an integer multiple or division by halves: 300%, 200%, 50%, or 25%. You can do without the columns altogether using the Time Stretch dialog (context-click > Time > Time Stretch). **Ctrl+Alt+R** (**Cmd+Opt+R**) or Layer > Time > Time-Reverse Layer sets the Stretch value to –100%. The layer's appearance alters to remind you that it is reversed (**Figure 2.19**).

Figure 2.19 The candy striping along the bottom of the layer indicates that the Stretch value is negative and the footage will run in reverse.

Layer > Time > Freeze Frame applies the Time Remap effect with a single Hold keyframe at the current time.

Frame Blend

Suppose you retime a source clip with a Stretch value that doesn't factor evenly into 100%; the result is likely to lurch in a distracting, inelegant fashion. Enable Frame Blend for the layer and the composition, and After Effects averages the adjacent frames together to create a new image on frames that fall in between the source frames. This also works when you're adding footage to a composition with a mismatched frame rate. There are two modes:

The 02_frame_blend folder and project on the disc contain relevant example comps.

▸ Frame Mix mode overlays adjoining frames, essentially blurring them together.

▸ Pixel Motion mode uses optical flow techniques to track the motion of actual pixels from frame to frame, creating new frames that are something like a morph of the adjoining frames.

Figure 2.20 The Frame Blend switches for the composition and layer (the overlapping filmstrips to the right of frame). Just because Pixel Motion mode uses the same icon as Best in the Quality switch, to the left, doesn't mean it's guaranteed to be the best choice.

Confusingly, the icons for these modes are the same as Draft and Best layer quality, respectively (**Figure 2.20**), yet there are cases where Frame Mix may be preferable instead of merely quicker. Pixel Motion can often appear too blurry, too distorted, or contain too many noticeable frame artifacts, in which case you can move back to Frame Mix, or move up to the Timewarp effect, with greater control of the same technology (later in this chapter).

Nested Compositions

Time Stretch (or Time Remap) applies the main composition's frame rate to a nested composition; animations are not frame-blended; instead the keyframe interpolation is resliced to this new frame rate. If you put a composition with a lower frame rate into a master composition, the intention may be to keep the frame rate of the embedded composition. In such a case, go to the *nested* composition's Composition Settings > Advanced panel and toggle Preserve Frame Rate When Nested or in Render Queue (**Figure 2.21**). This forces After Effects to use only whole frame increments in the underlying composition, just as if the composition were pre-rendered with that frame rate.

Figure 2.21 The highlighted setting causes the subcomposition to use its own frame rate instead of resampling to the rate of the master composition, if they are different from one another.

Time Remap

For tricky timing, Time Remap trumps Time Stretch. The philosophy is elusively simple: A given point in time has a value, just like any other property, so it can be keyframed, including eases and even loops — it operates like any other animation data.

Ctrl+Alt+T (**Cmd+Opt+T**) or Layer > Time > Enable Time Remapping sets two Time Remap keyframes: at the beginning and one frame beyond the end of the layer. Time remapped layers have a theoretically infinite duration, so the final Time Remap frame effectively becomes a Hold keyframe; you can then freely scale the layer length beyond that last frame.

Beware when applying Time Remap to a layer whose first or last frame extends beyond the composition duration; there may be keyframes you cannot see. In such a case, I tend to add keyframes at the composition start and end points, click Time Remap to select all keyframes, Shift-deselect the ones I can see in the Timeline panel, and delete to get rid of the ones I can't see.

Timewarp

The Foundry's sophisticated retiming tool known as Kronos provides the technology used in Pixel Motion and Timewarp. Pixel Motion is an automated setting described earlier, and Timewarp builds this up by adding a set of effect controls that allow you to tweak the result. Timewarp uses optical flow technology to track any motion in the footage. Individual, automated motion vectors describe how each pixel moves from frame to frame. With this accurate analysis it is then possible to generate an image made up of those same pixels, interpolated along those vectors, with different timing. The result is new frames that appear as if in between the original frames. When it works, it has to be seen to be believed.

What's the difference between Time Remap, which requires little computational power, and the much more complex and demanding Timewarp? Try working with the keyed_timewarp_source sequence on the disc (02_timewarp folder) or open the associated example project where it's already done. **Figure 2.22** shows the basic difference between Frame Mix and Pixel Motion.

So flipping the Frame Blend toggle in the Timeline panel (Figure 2.20) to Pixel Motion with Time Stretch or Time Remapping gets you the same optical flow solution as

TIP

There is also a Freeze Frame option in After Effects; context-click a layer, or from the Layer menu choose Time > Freeze Frame, which sets Time Remap (if not already set) with a single Hold keyframe.

NOTES

The Foundry's Kronos tool is now available as a stand-alone plug-in which among other features uses the GPU to outperform Timewarp. A demo version can be found on the book's disc.

Figure 2.22 Frame Mix (left) simply cross-dissolves between adjacent whole frames, where as Pixel Motion (right) analyzes the actual pixels to create an entirely new in-between frame.

NOTES

To transfer Time Remap keyframes to Source Frame mode in Timewarp, enable an expression (Chapter 10) for Source Frame and enter the following:

```
d = thisComp.
➥frameDuration
timeRemap * 1/d
```

Timewarp with the same Pixel Motion method. What's the difference?

▶ All methods can be used to speed up or slow down footage, but only Time Remapping and Timewarp dynamically animate the timing with keyframes.

▶ All methods can access all three Frame Blending modes (Whole Frames, Frame Mix, and Pixel Motion).

▶ Time Remapping keyframes can even be transferred directly to Timewarp, but it requires an expression (see note) because Timewarp uses frames and Time Remapping seconds.

Timewarp is worth any extra trouble in several ways:

▶ It can be applied to a composition, not just footage.

▶ It includes the option to add motion blur with the Enable Motion Blur toggle.

▶ The Tuning section lets you refine the automated results of Pixel Motion.

To apply Timewarp to the footage, enable Time Remapping and extend the length of the layer when slowing footage down—otherwise you will run out of frames. Leave Time Remapping with keyframes at the default positions and Timewarp will override it.

The example footage has been pre-keyed, which provides the best result when anyone (or anything) in the foreground is moving separate from the background. Swap in the gs_timewarp_source footage and you'll see some errors. Add the keyed_timewarp_source layer below as a reference, set it as the Matte Layer in Timewarp, and the errors should once again disappear, with the added benefit of working with the full unkeyed footage.

You can even further adjust the reference layer and precomp it (for example, enhancing contrast or luminance to give Timewarp a cleaner source), and then apply this precomposed layer as a Warp Layer—it then analyzes with the adjustments but applies the result to the untouched source.

The Tuning section is where you trade render time and accuracy, but don't assume that greater accuracy always yields a better result—it's just not so. These tools make use of Local Motion Estimation (LME) technology, which is thoroughly documented in the Furnace User Guide, if you ever want to fully nerd out on the details.

Now try a shot that needs more tuning and shows more of the flaws of Pixel Motion, and how Timewarp can help solve them. The footage in the 02_rotoSetup_sk8rboi folder on the disc features several planes of motion—the wheels of the minivan, the van itself, the skater—and at the climatic moment where the skater pulls the 360 flip, the board utterly lacks continuity from one frame to the next, a classic case that will break any type of optical flow currently available (**Figure 2.23**).

Here are a few tweaks you can try on this footage, or your own:

▶ While raising Vector Detail would seem to increase accuracy, it's hard to find anywhere in this clip where it helps. Not only does a higher number (100) drastically increase render time, it simply increases or at best shifts artifacts with fast motion. This is because it is analyzing too much detail with not enough areas to average in.

▶ Smoothing relates directly to Vector Detail. The Foundry claims that the defaults, which are balanced,

NOTES

Roto Brush (see Chapter 7) is a highly effective tool to create a foreground Matte Layer for Timewarp. This helps eliminate or reduce motion errors where the foreground and background move differently.

work best for most sequences. You can raise Global Smoothness (all vectors), Local Smoothness (individual vectors), and Smoothing Iterations in order to combat detail noise, but again, in this case it changes artifacting rather than solving it.

▶ During the skateboard ollie itself, the 360 flip of the board is a tough one because it changes so much from frame to frame. Build From One Image helps quite a bit in a case like this—instead of trying to blend two nonmatching sets of pixels, Timewarp favors one of them. The downside is that sudden shifts occur at the transition points—the pixels don't flow.

Figure 2.23 Timewarp's excellent super slow-mo capabilities work best with continuous motion, such as the torso and legs of the skater; the board itself and his hands move much more unpredictably from frame to frame, causing more difficulty. The best fix is to rotoscope to separate these areas from the background.

▶ There's no need in this clip to enable Correct Luminance Changes —it's for sudden (image flicker) or gradual (moving highlights) shifts in brightness.

▶ Error Threshold evaluates each vector before letting it contribute; raise this value and more vectors are eliminated for having too much perceived error.

▶ Block Size determines the width and height of the area each vector tracks; as with Smoothing, lower values generate more noise, higher values result in less detail. The Foundry documentation indicates that this value should "rarely need editing."

▶ Weighting lets you control how much a given color channel is factored. As you'll learn in Chapter 5, the defaults correspond to how the eye perceives color to produce a monochrome image. If one channel is particularly noisy—usually blue—you can lower its setting.

▶ Filtering applies to the render, not the analysis; it increases the sharpness of the result. It will cost you render time, so if you do enable it, wait until you're done with your other changes and are ready to render.

The biggest thing you could do overall to improve results with a clip like sk8rboi is to use Roto Brush (see Chapter 7) to separate out each moving element—the van, skater, and background.

NOTES

Twixtor (RE:Vision Effects) is a third-party alternative to Timewarp; it's not necessarily better but some artists—not all—do prefer it. A demo can be found on the disc.

TIP

Did you notice back in the Motion Blur section that Timewarp can be used to generate procedural motion blur without retiming footage (**Figure 2.24**)?

Figure 2.24 Footage that is shot overcranked (at high speed, left) typically lacks sufficient motion blur when retimed. Timewarp can add motion blur to speed up footage; it can even add motion blur to footage with no speed-up at all, in either case using the same optical flow technology that tracks individual pixels. It looks fabulous.

So Why the Bouncing Ball Again?

Some computer graphics artists are also natural anima-tors; others never really take to it. After Effects is more animation-ready than most compositing applications, and many compositors don't need to get much into animation. The exercises in this chapter could tell you in an hour or two which camp you fall into, and along the way, cover just about every major Timeline panel animation tool. If you take the trouble to try the animations and learn the short-cuts, you will find yourself with a good deal more control over timing and placement of elements—even if you never find yourself bouncing any virtual balls.

CHAPTER

3

Selections:
The Key to Compositing

There is no abstract art. You must always start with something. Afterward you can remove all traces of reality.

—Pablo Picasso

Selections: The Key to Compositing

A particle physicist works with atoms, bakers and bankers each work with their own form of dough, and compositors work with selections—many different types of selections, even thousands, each derived one at a time.

If compositing were simply a question of taking pristine, perfect foreground source A and overlaying it onto perfectly matching background plate B, there would be no compositor in the effects process; an editor could accomplish the job before lunchtime. Instead, compositors break sequences of images apart and reassemble them, sometimes painstakingly, first as a still frame and then in motion. Often, it is one element, one frame, or one area of a shot that needs special attention. By the clever use of selections, a compositor can save the shot by taking control of it.

This chapter focuses on how a layer merges with those behind it. Then Section II of the book, "Effects Compositing Essentials" (in particular Chapters 6 and 7), examines specific ways to refine selections, create high-contrast mattes, and pull color keys (aka greenscreen mattes).

Methods to Combine Layers

You may already be familiar with all of the ways to create layer transparency or the effect of one layer blended with another, but it's worth a look just to be certain you're clear on all of the options in After Effects to begin with.

Mattes

In his book *CG 101: A Computer Graphics Industry Reference*, author Terrence Masson defines a matte as "a grayscale single-channel image used to hold out a portion of a composite element when it is placed over a background plate... The pixel values of a matte channel therefore represent the opacity of the corresponding image data."

As you know, After Effects uses a layer-based metaphor similar to that of Photoshop (and of the two, After Effects had them first). Many users of both apps are first introduced to mattes by beginning with elements that have mattes already included; they can also be created by keying out the green background from a visual effects shoot (**Figure 3.1**), but there are other ways to procedurally generate a matte, such as a high-contrast or hi-con matte using carefully manipulated luminance data. Chapter 6 goes into depth about these processes; for now, this overview offers a basic working understanding.

Figure 3.1 This split-screen image shows a blue-screen shoot (left) and the resulting matte.

Alpha Channel

An alpha or transparency channel is a specific type of matte that can be contained within an imported image; with computer-generated images the alpha channel is generated as part of the rendering process itself. After Effects

Figure 3.2 A computer-generated baseball's color and alpha channels.

NOTES

The built-in assumption of unmultiplied edge pixels can, in some cases, make life more difficult should things not go as planned. The "Alpha Channels and Edge Multiplication" section later in this chapter offers the lowdown on changing edge multiplication midstream.

Figure 3.3 This split-screen view shows the garbage matte mask that was added to remove areas of the stage not covered by the blue screen.

itself can, of course, also create alpha and transparency channels in rendered images (**Figure 3.2**).

Like Photoshop but unlike many other compositing applications, After Effects has a persistent concept of a fourth alpha or transparency channel alongside three channels of color data. After Effects assumes (also unique from other compositing apps) that edge premultiplication is automatically removed before image combination or manipulation is begun. Internally then, all alphas in After Effects are processed as straight (see Chapter 1 for a review of how interpretation is determined on import). This is natural enough, but can occasionally become inflexible to anyone who actually comprehends transparency and edge multiplication and wants to manage them directly.

Mask

A mask in After Effects is a shape made up of points and vectors (**Figure 3.3**). As a vector shape, it can be infinitely scaled without losing any definition, but as it is generally drawn by hand, hand-animating the selection (a process known as *rotoscoping*, detailed in Chapter 7) is much more involved than generating a matte procedurally.

There are also now several automated methods (**Figure 3.4**) to create animated selections by tracking raster data (pixel values):

▶ **Roto Brush**—this much talked-about feature added to After Effects CS5 can automatically generate and track an animated mask. The advantages are that it works well and can be automatically tracked; however, it is far from perfect and the result is its own effect-based selection instead of a standard After Effects mask. You'll read more about this in Chapter 7.

Figure 3.4 Before the introduction of Roto Brush (top), which analyzes pixels from user-generated brushstrokes, the closest thing to automatic mask generation in After Effects was Auto-trace, which uses simple luminance criteria to generate masks—lots of them, as is apparent from all the colored outlines (bottom).

▶ **mocha shape**—a shape tracked in mocha for After Effects can be brought in and applied using the mocha Shape plug-in. It is capable of automatically generating a mask that can include per-vertex feathering in many (but by no means all) situations. Mocha shape is also an effect-based selection tool incompatible with the standard After Effects mask. More on this in Chapters 7 and 8.

▶ **mocha-AE Copy/Paste**—it's also possible to copy a shape tracked in mocha-AE and paste it directly into After Effects as a mask shape. This offers most of the advantages of mocha shape (other than per-vertex feathering), and because it is applied as mask data it integrates with all of the many effects and plug-ins that rely on selections in that format. More on this in Chapters 7 and 8.

▶ **Layer > Auto-trace**—While technically impressive, Auto-trace is problematic as a selection tool because it typically creates dozens of masks on any but the simplest live-action shot. It also offers less control than the other methods, so there are only benefits if you want to do something stylized (motion graphics) with those masks. If this has a use for effects compositing, I haven't found it.

Blending Modes

Blending modes (Add, Screen, Multiply, Difference, and so on) do not, by and large, generate alpha channel transparency; most apply a specific mathematical formula to the compositing operation of a given layer. They are essential to re-create the phenomena of real-world optics.

For example, when compositing an element that is made up more of light or shadows than reflective surfaces, such as fire shot in a blackout environment, it is vital to use blending modes instead of a luminance matte—don't try keying out the black (see Chapter 14 for more details). You can, of course, use selections combined with blending modes to get the best of both worlds. Blending modes—which to ignore, which are essential, and how to use them—are discussed in depth later in this chapter.

Effects

Effects and plug-ins can also generate transparency: some (such as Levels and Curves) by offering direct adjustment of the alpha channel, others (in the Channel folder) by creating or replacing the alpha channel. Some even generate images from scratch that may include an alpha channel (**Figure 3.5**).

Figure 3.5 The Checkerboard effect is one of a few that is generated in the alpha channel (displayed here) by default.

Combined Selection Techniques

An ordinary effects shot may use more than one, or even all, of the above techniques. Suppose you have greenscreen footage (say a stylish Ford GT40) and want to replace the number on the side. You might key out the greenscreen to create a matte channel for the car, import the number decal via a Photoshop or Illustrator file with an alpha channel or other transparency data already included, create masks for the areas you couldn't key (such as where the wheels make contact with the floor), blend in some smoke coming out of the exhaust with layers using Add and Multiply modes, and create some heat ripple using a Displacement Map effect (Chapter 14).

The art is in knowing which approach to apply in a given situation, and for this there is no substitute for knowledge of how they operate.

Close-Up: The Compositing Formula

The act of laying one object on top of another is so natural—A over B—it's hard to remember that re-creating this phenomenon on a computer means that something mathematically sophisticated occurs wherever there is transparency. The foreground pixel values are first multiplied by the percentage of transparency, which, if not fully opaque, reduces their value. The background pixels are multiplied by the percentage of opacity (the inverse of the foreground layer's transparency), and the two values are added together to produce the composite. Expressed as a formula, it looks like

$(Fg * A) + ((1-A)*Bg) = Comp$

With real RGB pixel data of R: 185, G: 144, B: 207 in the foreground and R: 80, G: 94, B: 47 in the background, calculating only one edge pixel would look like

$[(185, 144, 207) 3 .6] + [.4 3 (80, 94, 47)] = (143, 124, 143)$

The result is a weighted blend between the brightness of the foreground and the darker background.

Other effects compositing programs, such as Nuke or Shake, do not take this operation for granted the way that After Effects and Photoshop do. You can't simply drag one image over another in a layer stack—you must apply an Over function to create this interaction.

This is not a disadvantage of After Effects—it actually makes basic compositing simpler and faster—but it can obscure important related details such as edge pixel premultiplication (detailed later in this chapter).

Optics and Edges

What exactly is happening in a simple A over B composite? In After Effects, it seems nearly as natural as laying one object on top of another does in the real world. In most other compositing applications even A over B is an individualized compositing *operation,* and that is closer to the truth—a truth that After Effects obscures in order to make the process easier. Not only that, but there is more to what is going on than might be obvious, because of the phenomena of optics. The four stages of image gathering and viewing—the physical world itself, camera optics, human vision, and the display device and its environment—exhibit phenomena that are interdependent.

As a compositor, you are not supposed to re-create actual reality, but instead the way the camera (and the eye) gathers visual data from the world. This affects something even so fundamental as how the edges of objects should look in order for the eye to accept them as believable.

Bitmap Alpha

A *bitmap* can be defined as an image made up of pure white or black pixels (ones and zeroes, if you will), and a bitmap selection is made up of pixels that are either fully opaque or fully transparent. This is the type of selection generated by the old Magic Wand tool in Photoshop. You can feather or blur the resulting edge, but the initial selection contains no semitransparent pixels.

This type of selection may have an occasional use, but it truly belongs to the world of primitive computers, not complex nature (or optics). An edge made up of pixels that are either fully opaque or invisible cannot describe a curve or angle smoothly, and even a straight line looks unnatural in a natural image if it completely lacks edge thresholding (**Figure 3.6**).

Feathered Alpha

Although it's easy enough to see that a bitmap edge does not occur in nature, it's hard to imagine that hard objects should have transparent, feathered edges. Look around you at the edges of hard-surface items; they appear sharp.

But study an image of the same thing more closely, and you'll find some degree of edge softness. Adding softness, threshold, or "feather" to an edge approximates this softness in the hard digital world of single pixels, which are square and either on or off. Properly feathered edges can

Figure 3.6 This bitmap image contains no threshold pixels. Compare this result with that of Figure 3.7 to see how your monitor displays a curved shape.

▶ approximate organic curves (**Figure 3.7**); we're used to this in *raster images*—digital images made up of pixels

▶ mimic the natural behavior of optics; edges rarely are 100% sharp

Optics can be observed in any photo with no compositing whatsoever (**Figure 3.8**). Viewed close up, areas at the edge of objects become a fine wash of color combining the foreground and background. This is not due to inaccuracy in the camera; it is what happens to light as it travels around objects in the physical world and then through the lens of the camera (or your eye).

Figure 3.7 Zoom in far enough on a diagonal or curve and you see square pixels, yet further away your eye accepts the illusion.

Figure 3.8 Shallow depth of field causes most of the edges in this image to appear soft, but even where the subject is in perfect focus (inset) the edge displays surprising characteristics where it meets the defocused background. Lesson? A soft edge is not necessarily a mistake, since nature never makes any of those.

Opacity

Transparent foreground objects transmit light, and After Effects is designed to mimic the way they behave when layered together. Take two identical layers, with no alpha or transparency information for either layer. Set each layer to 50% opacity, and the result does not add up to 100%. Here's why.

Figure 3.9 shows light filtering through two overlapping sheets of paper. (No expense is spared bringing you these real-world simulations.) Let's suppose that each sheet is 75% opaque; 25% of the background light passes through. Add a second sheet and 25% of 25%—roughly 6%—passes through both layers. It's not a lot of light, but it's not zero; it would take a few more layers of paper to block out the light completely.

Figure 3.9 Although a single sheet of paper is more than 50% opaque, two sheets of paper layered one on top of another are not 100% opaque. This is how overlapping opacity is calculated in After Effects.

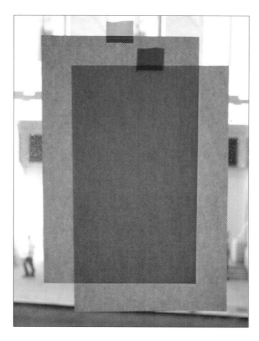

After Effects re-creates this behavior, adding fractional and not whole opacity values of two or more layers. It's Zeno's paradox—you are only getting a fraction of the way closer to the destination of 100% opacity when stacking layers whose opacity is less than 100.

Transparency: Alpha Channels and Edge Multiplication

One major source of confusion with After Effects has to do with its handling of alpha channels and edge multiplication against a unified background color, also known as premultiplication. After Effects has a persistent concept of the alpha channel as part of every image, and this channel is always expected to be unmultiplied within After Effects, whether it originated that way or not.

Any color multiplied into edge pixels is to be removed upon import (in the Alpha section of the Interpret Footage dialog), and reintroduced only on output. Provided those Alpha settings are correct, this works surprisingly well. At some point, however, you may need to better understand how to take control of edge multiplication within After Effects.

Premultiplication Illustrated

Premultiplication exists for one reason only: so that rendered images have realistic, anti-aliased edges *before they are composited*. **Figure 3.10** (left) shows an image rendered against black without edge multiplication; it just doesn't look very nice. **Figure 3.10** (right) looks more natural, but the edge pixels are now mixed with the background color and must effectively be un-composited from it before they are composited against some other image.

How Edge Multiplication Works

Imagine the background value to be 0,0,0 or solid black; an edge pixel is multiplied by 0 (making it pure black) and then added back to the source, in proportion to the amount of transparency in the alpha channel pixel. Removing edge multiplication with the Premultiplied setting subtracts this extra black from those edge pixels.

NOTES

The 02_edge_multiplication folder and project on the disc contain relevant example comps.

Figure 3.10 The purpose of premultiplication is principally so that images rendered against black, such as this motion-blurred basketball from Chapter 2 (left), appear natural by blending the semi-transparent edge pixels. You have the option to choose RGB Straight under the Channel menu and view the image the way After Effects works with it (right).

NOTES

Most computer-generated images are premultiplied, unless specific steps are taken to counteract the process. The Video Output section of the Output Module settings for items in the Render Queue includes a menu to specify whether you render with Straight or Premultiplied alpha; by default, it is set to Premultiplied.

NOTES

After Effects attempts to guess not only the setting but the background color of a premultiplied image; generally this is black or white, but watch out for situations where a 3D artist has become creative and rendered against canary yellow or powder blue. This is bad form, but it's also the reason there is an eyedropper adjacent to the Matted With Color setting (Figure 3.11).

Figure 3.11 Be careful here: Many experienced artists assume that After Effects has already made a guess (here, Straight) when it is merely using whatever was set the last time. It's better to find out what the correct setting is from the application (or artist) that created the image and set this yourself.

When you ask After Effects to "guess" how to interpret the footage (on import, by choosing Guess in the Interpret Footage dialog, or pressing **Ctrl+Alt+G/Cmd+Opt+G**), it looks for sections of uniform color that are mixed into edge pixels, indicating that the correct setting is Premultiplied.

Back in Chapter 1, Figure 1.13 presented the same foreground image with two alpha interpretations, one interpreted correctly, the other not. A misinterpreted alpha either fails to remove the background color from the edge pixels or does the opposite, removing shading that should actually be present.

You may find that fringing appears in your comps despite your careful managing of the alpha channel interpretation on import. This does not indicate some bug in After Effects, but rather a mystery you must solve. There are two basic ways it can occur:

▶ An alpha channel is misinterpreted in Interpret Footage.

▶ Edge multiplication can materialize within After Effects, probably unintentionally, when a matte is applied to a layer that has already been comped against black.

Unfortunately, artists who misunderstand the underlying problem will resort to all sorts of strange machinations to fix the black edge, ruining what may be a perfectly accurate edge matte.

Get It Right on Import

Preferences > Import > Interpret Unlabeled Alpha As determines what happens when footage with an unlabeled alpha channel is imported; the default is Ask User.

The Ask User dialog has three choices, one of which is checked, and a Guess button (**Figure 3.11**). This is confusing, as it seems as if After Effects has already guessed, when it has not: *It is merely using whatever was set the previous time.*

The Guess option is not accurate 100% of the time; if the foreground and background are similar, it can be fooled.

Ideally you will work on a project whose images are consistent (in terms of edge multiplication and background color); in that case, you can set an Import preference. Typically, however, it's best to be able to find out from whoever created it whether the source contains edge multiplication and what settings to use.

When that's not possible, examine the image and look for the symptoms of a misinterpreted alpha: dark (or bright) fringing in the semi-opaque edges of the foreground.

Solve the Problem Internally

The really gnarly fact is that premultiplication errors can be introduced within a composition, typically by applying a matte to footage that is already somehow blended—multiplied—with a background.

If you see fringing in your edges, you can try the Remove Color Matting effect (**Figure 3.12**). This effect has one setting only, for background color, because all it does is apply the unpremultiply calculation (the antidote to premultiplication) in the same manner that it would be applied in Interpret Footage.

TIP

RGB Straight **(Alt+Shift+4/ Opt+Shift+4** or use the Show Channel menu at the bottom of a viewer panel) displays the image in straight alpha mode, as After Effects views it internally.

Figure 3.12 The plane was matted against a white background, but transparency has been applied via a track matte (the equivalent of a straight alpha), so white fringing appears against black (top). Remove Color Matting, with Color set to pure white, corrects the problem (bottom), but only when applied to a precomp of the image and matte.

TIP

The Remove Color Matting effect will not work properly on a layer with a track matte; be sure to precompose the layer and its track matte prior to applying Channel > Remove Color Matting.

NOTES

Shape layers are directly related to masks; they are drawn with the same tools. If a layer that can receive a mask is selected, then After Effects draws a mask; otherwise, it creates a new Shape layer.

An even better option in cases where you have an element against black and no alpha channel is to use the Channel Combiner effect, with Max RGB as the From value and Alpha Only as the To value. Follow this with the Remove Color Matting effect. This one-two punch uses black areas of the image to create transparency and removes the multiplied black from the resulting transparent pixels. You can save it by choosing Animation > Save Animation Preset.

Mask Modes

Masks in After Effects are an available part of any layer (provided it's not a camera, light, or null object); just twirl down the layer in the Timeline and there they are. These are vector shapes that you draw by hand, and they are the fundamental method used to hand-animate a selection. There are five basic shapes (the **Q** key cycles through them) and the Pen tool (**G**) for drawing free-form.

You can draw a mask in either the Composition or Layer viewer. In Layer viewer the source image persists in its default view; there is a Render toggle next to the Masks selection in the View menu to disable all mask selections. Artists may want to see a masked layer in the context of the comp but find it difficult to adjust the mask in that view—in such a case, the Layer and Composition views can be arranged side by side (**Figure 3.13**).

Figure 3.13 With the Composition and Layer panels side by side, you can leave the mask enabled in the Composition panel but uncheck Render in the Layer panel.

When you draw a mask directly in the Composition viewer, a selection is created as soon as the shape is closed (which is how it begins unless you create it point by point with the Pen tool). This allows you to examine the selection in situ, but it conceals anything you might have missed. If the layer is rotated in 3D space, the mask shape is also rotated.

If you cannot see what you're doing in the Composition viewer, switch to the Layer viewer and, if necessary, uncheck Render at the bottom to disable the mask in this view (but not in the comp itself). When using any mask shape tool it's possible to

- double-click the tool (in the Tools panel) to set the boundaries of the mask shape to match those of the layer
- press **Shift** to constrain proportions when drawing or scaling
- use **Ctrl** (**Cmd**) to draw from the center (with the Rectangle, Rounded Rectangle, and Ellipse tools)
- click Shape under Mask Path (**M**) in the Layer Switches column to open the Mask Shape dialog; here you can enter exact mask dimensions
- double-click the shape with the Selection tool to activate Free Transform mode, then
    - **Shift**-drag on a corner to scale the mask proportionally
    - **Shift**-drag an outside corner to snap rotation to 45-degree increments
    - **Shift**-drag anywhere else to transform on one axis only
- press the **M** key twice, rapidly, to reveal all Mask options for the selected layer
- press the **F** key to solo the Mask Feather property— feather is applied everywhere equally on the mask, equidistant inward and outward from the mask shape
- use the Mask Expansion property to expand or (given a negative value) contract the mask area; two masks can be used together, one contracted, one expanded, to create an edge selection

TIP

Mask shapes can be edited to create more precise custom shapes; for example, you can make a half-circle by deleting one vertex and adjusting two vertices of an ellipse.

NOTES

Easter egg alert! *Simpsons* fans, try this: Hold **Ctrl+Alt+Shift** (**Cmd+Opt+Shift**) and click on Mask Expansion. The property disappears. Now enter **MM** for a humorous reference to Season 3, Episode 13.

Chapter 7 offers more specifics about drawing precise masks; big, soft masks are referenced throughout the book for all kinds of lighting, smoke, and glow effects (**Figure 3.14**).

Figure 3.14 A series of layers with soft masks can be used to create depth in cloud cover; these clouds are made up of a series of overlapping masked layers, and each mask has a Feather value of 200–500 pixels.

Bezier Masks

By default, the Pen tool creates Bezier shapes; learn the keyboard shortcuts and you can fully edit a mask without ever clicking anywhere except right on the mask.

I like to start by placing points at key transitions and corners, without worrying about fine-tuning the Beziers. Or, as a point is drawn, it is possible to

- **Shift**-hold and drag to move the vertex
- hold and drag out a Bezier tangent

before drawing the next point. Once I've completed a basic shape, I can activate the Pen tool (**G**) ✒ and

✒- click a point to delete it

✒+ click a segment between points to add a point

⌐ (**Alt**-click or **Opt**-click) on a point to enable the Convert Vertex tool, which toggles Bezier handles; drag a point with no handles to create them, or click a point with handles to delete them

⌐ click a Bezier handle to break the handles and adjust them independently

➤ press the **Shift** key with the mouse still down to pull out Bezier handles

Ctrl-click (**Cmd**-click) to toggle the Selection tool temporarily (to move a point)

▶ press the **V** key to activate the Selection tool (pressing the **G** key switches back to the Pen)

▶ press **F2** or **Ctrl+Shift+A** (**Cmd+Shift+A**) to deselect the current mask and start a new one without switching tools, leaving the Pen tool active

Context-click on a mask path to change settings in the Mask submenu. This includes all settings from the Timeline as well as Motion Blur settings just for the mask (optionally separate from the Layer). The Mask and Shape Path submenu contains special options to close an open shape, set First Vertex (more on this later in this chapter) and toggle RotoBeziers (Chapter 7).

Shape Layers

Shape layers add functionality from Adobe Illustrator directly into After Effects. The same tools can be used to draw either a mask or a Shape layer. Here's how they differ:

▶ Create a star, polygon, or rounded rectangle as a mask and its vertices can be edited as normal Beziers. Shapes offer a different type of control in the Timeline over properties such as number of points and inner and outer roundness.

▶ Shapes can include effects such as Pucker & Bloat, Twist, and Zig Zag that procedurally deform the entire shape.

▶ Shapes display with two optional characteristics: Fill and Stroke. With a shape active, **Alt**-click (**Opt**-click) on Fill and Stroke in the toolbar to cycle through the options (also available in the Timeline).

▶ Shapes can be instanced and repeated in 2D space; **Alt**-drag (**Opt**-drag) to duplicate (as in Illustrator) or use a Repeater operation to instance and array a shape.

Consider shapes when you need a repeatable pattern of some type, as in **Figure 3.15**. Using the Repeater, you only have to adjust a single shape to edit all instances of it and how it is arrayed.

For the time being, there is no option to array shapes in 3D.

Figure 3.15 Shapes are not mere eye candy fodder, are they? The sprocket holes in this film were made with a Rounded Corner shape and a Repeater. (I even added an Inner Shadow Layer Style to give a little feeling of depth and dimension.)

NOTES

The 03_blend_mode_stills folder and project on the disc contain relevant example comps.

TIP

Preferences > User Interface Color > Cycle Mask Colors assigns a unique color to each new mask. Enable it.; it makes masking better and is disabled by default.

Combine Selections

By default, all masks are drawn in Add mode, meaning that the contents of the mask are added to the layer selection and the area outside all of the masks is excluded.

▶ The Add mode masks contents to the image as a whole (**Figure 3.16**).

▶ Subtract masks contents from displayed areas of the image (**Figure 3.17**).

▶ Intersect masks contents to show only areas overlapping with masks higher in the stack (**Figure 3.18**).

▶ Difference masks contents to hide areas overlapping with masks higher in the stack (**Figure 3.19**).

▶ None disables the mask (**Figure 3.20**).

The Inverted toggle next to Add mode selects the areas outside the mask to be added; combined with Subtract it causes the areas outside the mask to be subtracted, and so on.

The Mask Opacity property (**TT**) attenuates the strength of a mask; setting any mask other than the first one to 0% disables it. This control works differently for the first (top) mask. A single Add mask set to 0% Mask Opacity causes the entire layer to disappear, inside or outside the mask.

Figure 3.16 Add mode combines the luminance values of overlapping masks.

Figure 3.17 Subtract mode is the inverse of Add mode.

Figure 3.18 Intersect mode adds only the overlapping areas of opacity.

However, if you set the first mask to Subtract, and Mask Opacity to 50%, it does just that—instead of the area inside the mask reappearing, the rest of the scene becomes 50% transparent. It's the same result as Add > Inverted. It will behave as it should if you set another full-frame mask at the default Add mode (just double-click the rectangle mask), *then* add the Subtract mask as the second (or later).

To keep multiple masks organized

▸ enable Preferences > User Interface Color > Cycle Mask Colors to assign a unique color to each new mask

▸ press the **Enter** (**Return**) key with a mask selected, then type in a unique name

▸ click Mask Color swatch (to the left of the name) to make it more visible or unique

▸ context-click > Mask > Locked, Mask > Lock Other Masks, or Mask > Hide Locked Masks to keep masks you no longer wish to edit out of your way

Overlap Transparent Density

"Density" is a film term describing how dark (opaque or "dense") the frame of film is at a given area of the image: the higher the density, the less light is transmitted. Masks and alpha channels are also referred to in terms of "density," and when two masks or mattes overlap, density can build up when it should not (with masks) or fail to build up when it should (with mattes).

Figure 3.19 The inverse of Intersect, Difference mode subtracts overlapping areas.

Figure 3.20 With None mode, the mask is effectively deactivated.

> **NOTES**
>
> Chapter 7 demonstrates how effective rotoscoping involves multiple simple masks used in combination instead of one big complex mask.

Figures 3.21 and **3.22** show the simple solution to a common problem; the Darken and Lighten mask modes prevent any pixel from becoming more dense than it is in the semi-transparent areas of either matte. These modes should be applied to the masks that are below overlapping masks in the stack in order to work.

Figure 3.21 A Darken mask (left) uses only the darker (lower) value where threshold (semi-opaque) pixels overlap. It prevents two masks from building up density as in Intersect mode (right).

Figure 3.22 A Lighten mask (left) uses only the lighter (higher) value where threshold (semi-opaque) pixels overlap. It prevents two masks from building up density as in Add mode (right).

Overlap Inverted Layers Seamlessly

Suppose it's necessary to break out a selection into segments and adjust each segment as a separate layer, then combine them in the final result. A gap will appear along the threshold areas of the matte for the reasons explained in the Opacity section earlier; two overlapping 50% opaque pixels do not make a 100% opaque combined pixel.

Just as the name implies, the Alpha Add blending mode directly adds transparent pixels, instead of scaling them proportionally (**Figure 3.23**). You can cut out a piece of a layer, feather the matte, and apply the inverted feathered matte to the rest of the layer. Recombine them with Alpha Add applied to the top layer, and the seam disappears.

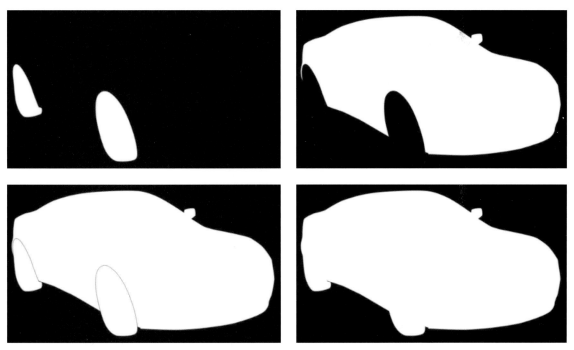

Figure 3.23 Comp a layer with matte A (upper left) over one with matte B (upper right) and you get a halo along the overlapping, inverted threshold edge pixels—around the wheels (bottom left). Alpha Add does just what the title implies, adding the alpha values together directly (bottom right).

Animated Masks

Following are some basics to put a mask in motion. **Alt+M (Opt+M)** sets a mask keyframe to all unlocked layer masks. Mask movement can be eased temporally, but there are no spatial curves; each mask point travels in a completely linear fashion from one keyframe to the next. An arced motion requires many more keyframes.

You can only adjust a mask point on one keyframe at a time, even if you select multiple Mask Path keyframes before adjusting. If you must arc or offset the motion of an entire mask animation, one workaround is to duplicate the masked layer and use it as an alpha track matte for the source layer, then keyframe the track matte like any animated layer.

Move, Copy, and Paste Masks

Copy a mask path from any compatible source, whether it's

▶ a Mask Path property from a separate mask or layer

▶ a Mask Path keyframe from the same or a separate mask

▶ a mask path from a separate Adobe application such as Illustrator or Photoshop

and paste it into an existing Mask Path channel, or paste it to the layer to create a new mask. If there are any keyframes, they are pasted in as well, beginning at the current time; make sure they don't conflict with existing keyframes in the mask shape.

To draw an entirely new shape for an existing, keyframed mask path, use the Target menu along the bottom of the Layer panel to choose the existing mask as a target, and start drawing. This replaces the existing shape (**Figure 3.24**).

KeyTweak by Mathias Möhl (http://aescripts.com/keytweak/) achieves the seemingly impossible: Edit a keyframed mask globally simply by adjusting points on one or two mask keyframes, and the rest are automagically changed accordingly. It works not just for Mask Shape keys but for any keyframed property. This means it can be used, for example, to correct a drifting track.

If a pasted mask targets a layer with dimensions unique from the source, the mask stretches proportionally.

Figure 3.24 This pop-up menu along the bottom of the Layer panel makes it easy to create a new mask path that replaces the shape in the target mask. If the target mask has keyframes, After Effects creates a new keyframe wherever the new shape is drawn.

First Vertex

When pasting in shapes or radically changing the existing mask by adding and deleting points, you may run into difficulty lining up the points. Hidden away in the Layer > Mask (or Mask context) menu, and available *only with a single vertex of the mask selected*, is the Set First Vertex command.

If your mask points twist around to the wrong point during an interpolation, setting the First Vertex to two points that definitely correspond should help straighten things out. This also can be imperative for effects that rely on mask shapes, such as Reshape (described in Chapter 7).

Composite With or Without Selections: Blending Modes

After Effects includes 38 blending modes, each created with a specific purpose, but as with anything, for visual effects work the 80/20 rule is in full effect—a few of them, featured in this section, do most of the work, while Pin Light or Dancing Dissolve may be used only for motion graphics styling, if that. The goal is to help you understand how each option actually operates and in what situations it's useful.

NOTES

Window > Mask Interpolation is designed to smooth transitions between radically different shapes.

SCRIPT

ReverseMaskPath by Charles Bordenave (http://aescripts.com/reversemaskpath/) reverses the direction of selected masks without altering the shape, which is useful in any situation where point direction matters, including with effects that use open mask shapes such as Stroke and Trapcode 3D Stroke.

Figure 3.25 The panel menu for Info has more than one mode, and you can choose whichever you like. Whichever mode you select also carries over to the Adobe Color Picker and all other color controls within After Effects.

CLOSE-UP

Normalized Pixel Values

Most digital artists become used to color values in the 8 bpc range of 0 to 255, but the internal math of compositing is all done with pixel values normalized to 1. This means that a pure monitor white value of 255 is expressed as 1, and black is 0. Chapter 11 shows how values above 1 and below 0 are also possible; these operations also make much more sense when working with values normalized to 1, which is an optional mode in the After Effects Info panel—and all associated color controls—no matter the bit depth (**Figure 3.25**).

NOTES

Traditional optical compositing—covering all movies made prior to the 1990s—was capable of bi-packing (multiplying) and double-exposing (adding) two source frames (layers). Many sophisticated effects films were completed using only these two "blending modes."

To help you understand what the various blending modes are doing, **Figure 3.26** features text with a soft (large threshold) edge over a grayscale gradient, blended with a color gradient, while **Figure 3.28** uses the same text over a single contrasting color. Contextual examples using these blending modes follow in the next section. (The 03_blend_mode_stills folder and project on the disc contain the examples shown.)

Figure 3.26 Check out the example containing the word "normal" to see the basic elements: soft text in a grayscale box on the top layer that will have the blending mode, and a simple blue (primary) to yellow (secondary, in a digital additive color world) color gradient behind.

Add and Screen

Add and Screen modes both effectively brighten the lighter areas of the layer where they overlap with light areas of the image behind them. They also subdue darker pixels such that the blacks are not factored. Screen mode yields a subtler blend than Add mode in normal video color space, but Add is preferred with linear blending (details in Chapter 11).

An Add blending mode is every bit as simple as it sounds; the formula is

```
newPixel = A + B
```

where A is a pixel from the foreground layer and B is a background pixel. The result is clipped at 1 for 8- and 16-bit pixels.

Add is incredibly useful with what After Effects calls a linearized working space, where it perfectly re-creates the optical effect of combining light values from two images, as with a film double-exposure (if that analog reference has any resonance in this digital era). It is useful for laying fire and explosion elements shot in negative space (against black) into a scene, adding noise or grain to an element, or any other element that is made up of light and texture, as in **Figure 3.26**.

Screen mode yields a result similar to Add, but via a slightly different formula. The pixel values are inverted and multiplied together, and the result is inverted back in order to prevent clipping (pushing values above 1, which is the upper limit in 8 or 16 bpc):

```
newPixel = 1-((1-A) * (1-B))
```

Once you discover the truth about working linearized with a 1.0 gamma, you understand that Screen is a workaround, a compromise for how colors blend in normal video space. Screen is most useful in situations where Add would blow out the highlights too much—glints, flares, glow passes, and so on; check out the subtle but clear difference in Figure 3.26.

Multiply

Multiply is another mode whose math is as elementary as it sounds; it uses the formula

```
newPixel = A * B
```

Keep in mind that this formula normalizes color values between 0 and 1 (see the earlier sidebar "Normalized Pixel Values"). Multiplying two images together, therefore, typically has the effect of reducing midrange pixels and

NOTES

Linear Dodge is Photoshop's name for Add. The two blending modes are identical.

NOTES

In Screen mode, fully white pixels stay white, fully black pixels stay black, but a midrange pixel (0.5) takes on a brighter value (0.75), just not as bright as it would be with Add (1).

NOTES

The difference between Add and Screen is more fully illuminated in the discussion of a linearized working space in Chapter 11.

darkening an image overall, although pixels that are fully white in both images remain fully white, because 1 x 1 = 1.

Multiply or Add has the inverse effect of Screen mode, darkening the midrange values of one image with another. It emphasizes dark tones in the foreground without replacing the lighter tones in the background, useful for creating texture, shadow, or dark fog, as in Figure 3.26 (which features that type of foreground element generated with simple Fractal Noise—as you'll see in Chapter 13—instead of fire).

Overlay and the Light Modes

Overlay uses the Screen or Multiply formula, depending on the background pixel value. Above a threshold of 50% gray (or .5 in normalized terms), a Screen operation is used, and below the threshold, Multiply is used. Hard Light does the exact same thing but bases the operation on the top layer, so the two have an inverse effect.

These modes, along with Linear and Vivid Light, can be most useful for combining a layer that is predominantly color with another layer that is predominantly luminance, or contrast detail, as in Figure 3.26. I can add the firsthand anecdote that much of the lava texturing in the Level 4 sequence of *Spy Kids 3-D* was created by using Hard Light to combine a hand-painted color heat map with moving fractal noise patterns (for that videogame look).

Difference

Difference inverts a background pixel in proportion to the foreground pixel. I don't use it as much in my actual comps as I do to line up two identical layers (**Figure 3.27**).

NOTES

Overlay and the various Light modes do not work properly with values above 1.0, as can occur in 32 bpc linearized working spaces (see Chapter 11).

NOTES

Reversing layer order and swapping Overlay for Hard Light yields an identical result.

Figure 3.27 This layer is Difference matted over itself—in this image it is offset just slightly, creating contrasting outlines where the edges don't match up. When two layers with identical image content become completely black in Difference mode, you know they are perfectly aligned.

HSB and Color Modes

The Hue, Saturation, and Brightness modes each combine one of these values (H, S, or B) from the foreground layer with the other two from the background layer. Color takes both the hue and saturation from the top layer, using only the luminance (or brightness) from the underlying background (**Figure 3.28**).

These modes are often useful at an Opacity setting below 100% to combine source HSB values with ones that you choose.

Figure 3.28 Color modes are not intuitive at first, but once you see what they do, you are likely to find uses for them.

NOTES

Stencil Alpha and Silhouette Alpha are useful to create custom edge mattes (a technique detailed in Chapter 6) as well as a light wrap effect, demonstrated in Chapter 12.

Stencil, Silhouette, and Preserve Transparency

Commonly overlooked, Stencil and Silhouette blending modes operate only on the alpha channel of the composition. The layer's alpha or luminance values become a matte for all layers below it in the stack. Stencil makes the brightest pixels opaque, and Silhouette the darkest.

Suppose you have a foreground layer that is meant to be opaque only where the underlying layers are opaque, as in **Figure 3.29**. The small highlighted toggle labeled Preserve Underlying Transparency makes this happen, much to the amazement of many who've wished for this feature and not realized it was already there.

Luminescent Premultiply

Luminescent Premultiply is one method you can use to remove premultiplication on the fly from source footage, retaining bright values in edge pixels that are otherwise clipped. Premultiplication over black causes all

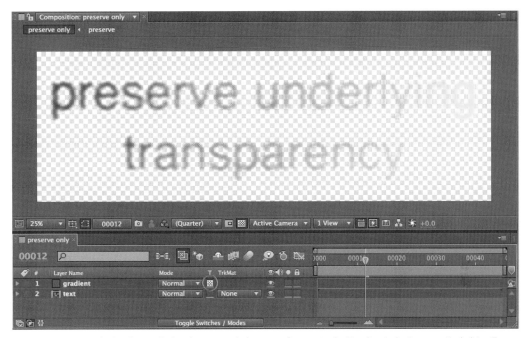

Figure 3.29 Among the hardest-to-find and most-easily-forgotten features in the Timeline is the Preserve Underlying Transparency toggle, circled. This re-creates behavior familiar to Photoshop users, where a layer's own transparency only applies where it intersects with that of the underlying layer. Here the same gradient is simply placed over a text layer; without this mode, the gradient would fill the frame as a solid.

semitransparent pixels to become darker; removing it can cause them to appear dimmer than they should.

Luminescent Premultiply is used to remove premultiplication (for cases in which edges have somehow become multiplied within After Effects). In **Figure 3.30**, the source text over black has been matted using the same layer—white text over black—as a luma matte, which means that black remains multiplied into the background unless this mode is set.

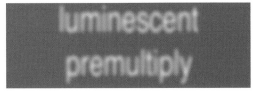

Figure 3.30 Did you create edge multiplication by luma matting a layer against black with itself (left)? Luminescent Premultiply (right) fixes this.

CLOSE-UP

Adjustment Layers and Blending Modes

Here's something I didn't used to know, and you may not either—when you apply a blending mode to an Adjustment layer, that layer's effects are first applied and then the result is comped over the underlying layers with that mode applied. In other words, if you create an Adjustment layer with a Levels effect in Add mode, the Levels effect is applied to underlying layers and that result is then added to them. Leave Levels at the default in this scenario and the area defined by the Adjustment layer—usually the entire underlying image—is added to itself.

Figure 3.31 The alpha of layer 1 is set as the alpha of layer 2 via the circled pop-up menu. The small icons to the left indicate which is the image and which is the matte.

Track Mattes

Track mattes allow you to use the alpha or luminance information of one layer as the transparency of another layer (**Figure 3.31**). It's a simple enough concept, yet one that is absolutely fundamental as a problem-solving tool for complex composites.

The perceptual difference between an alpha channel and a track matte isn't, for the most part, too difficult to grasp. In both cases, you have pixels with an 8-bit value between 0 and 255, whether derived from a grayscale alpha matte or the grayscale average of three channels of color, a luma matte. With color, the three channels are simply averaged together to make up a single grayscale alpha. With 16 and even 32 bpc, it's finer increments in the same range.

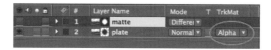

To set a track matte, place the layer that contains the transparency data directly above its target layer in the Timeline and choose one of the four options from the Track Matte pop-up menu:

▶ **Alpha Matte**: The alpha channel of the track matte layer is the alpha

▶ **Alpha Inverted Matte**: Same but the black areas are opaque

▶ **Luma Matte**: Uses the average brightness of red, green, and blue as the alpha

▶ **Luma Inverted Matte**: Same but the black areas are opaque

By default, the visibility of the track matte layer is disabled when you activate it from the layer below by choosing one of these four modes. This is generally desirable. Some clever uses of track mattes leave them on. For example, by matting out the bright areas of the image and turning on the matte, and setting it to Add mode, you could naturally brighten those areas even more.

Track mattes solve a lot of compositing problems. They also help overcome limitations of After Effects. Chapter 7 describes more uses for them.

Gotchas

Even an advanced user has to pay attention when working in a composition with track mattes. Unlike parented layers, track mattes do not stay connected with their target if moved around; they must occupy the layer directly above in order to work.

After Effects does help manage changes in certain ways. Duplicate a layer (**Ctrl+D/Cmd+D**) with a track matte activated and it moves up two layers, above the track matte layer. Include the track matte when you duplicate and it also moves up two layers, so layer order is preserved (**Figure 3.32**).

Share a Matte

Node-based compositing programs make it easy for a single node to act as a selection for as many others as needed without being duplicated. The way to do this in After Effects is using the Set Matte effect, detailed below, which has the disadvantage of having no visible reference in the Timeline or Flowchart views. The standard way in After Effects to provide one-to-many operation is to precomp the matte being shared and then duplicate the nested comp layer as needed, but this complicates dynamic adjustments such as animating the matte layer in the master composition.

Figure 3.32 Select and duplicate two layers that are paired to make use of a track matte (as in Figure 3.31), and the two duplicate layers leapfrog above to maintain the proper image and matte relationship.

There is a workaround that allows a matte layer to be anywhere in the Timeline, but it offers its own perils. Effect > Channel > Set Matte not only lets you choose any layer in the comp as a matte, it keeps track if that layer moves to a different position. It also offers a few custom matte-handling options regarding how the matte is scaled and combined. However, nothing you add to the other layer, including Transform keyframes, is passed through; these would need to be added in a precomp.

Chapter 9 focuses on 3D compositing; for now, keep in mind that while you might want to use a 2D layer as a track matte for a 3D layer, or even a 3D layer to matte a 2D layer, rarely will you want to matte a 3D layer with another 3D layer. The reason is that the matte is applied to the underlying layer and then any animation is added to both layers—so it becomes a double 3D animation (or possibly a glimpse into the ninth dimension, we can't be sure—either way it doesn't usually look right).

NOTES

Combine a track matte and an image with an alpha channel, and the selection uses an intersection of the two.

NOTES

If you're not certain whether your edits to the matte are being passed through, save the project and try cranking them up so it's obvious. Then undo or revert. If it's not working, precomp the matte layer.

This brings us to render order with track mattes. In most cases, adjustments and effects that you apply to the matte layer are calculated prior to creating the target matte. To see how this can break, however, try applying a track matte to another track matte. It works… sometimes, but not often enough that it should become something you try unless you're willing to troubleshoot it.

Right Tool for the Job

The goal of this chapter is to give you a comprehensive look at your options for creating a selection in After Effects and some hints as to where you might ideally use each of them. In many cases you have more than one viable option to create a given composite, and this is where you must learn to look a little bit into the future. Which approach offers the most flexibility and overall control given what may evolve or be changed or even deleted? Which can be done with the fewest steps? Which is most lucid and easily understandable to anyone else who might work with your project?

Now that we've covered selections in some detail, the next chapter looks in depth at solving specific workflow issues, including those that pertain to render order; you'll begin to see how to use the Timeline as a visual problem-solving tool for such situations.

4

Optimize Projects

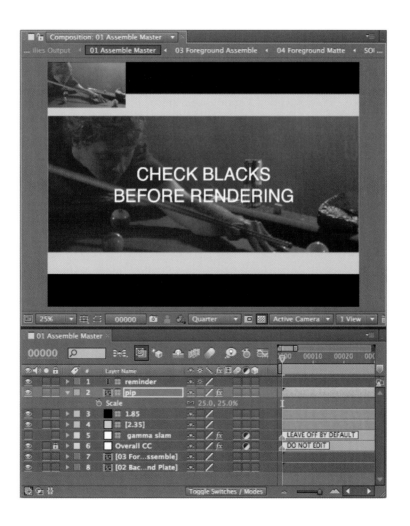

*Build a system that even a fool can use and only a fool
will want to use it.*

— George Bernard Shaw

Optimize Projects

This chapter examines how image data flows through
an After Effects project in close detail. It's full of the kind
of information that will help you make the most of After
Effects.

Sometimes you take the attitude of a master chef—you
know what can be prepped and considered "done" before
the guests are in the restaurant and it's time to assemble
the pièce de résistance. At other times, you're more like a
programmer, isolating and debugging elements of a project, even creating controlled tests to figure out how things
are working. This chapter helps you both artistically and
technically (as if it's possible to separate the two).

Once you

- ▶ understand how to use multiple compositions
- ▶ know when to precomp (and when it's safe to avoid it)
- ▶ know how to optimize rendering time

you may find the After Effects experience closer to what you
might consider "real time." This type of efficient rendering
depends not only on optimized software and a speedy workstation, but on well-organized compositions and the ability
to plan for bottlenecks and other complications.

Nested Comps, Multiple Projects

It's easy to lose track of stuff when projects get complicated. This section demonstrates

- ▶ how and why to work with some kind of project
  template
- ▶ how to keep a complex, multiple-composition pipeline
  organized

▶ shortcuts to help maintain orientation within the project as a whole

These tips are especially useful if you're someone who understands compositing but sometimes finds After Effects disorienting.

Precomping and Composition Nesting

Precomping is often regarded as the major downside of working in After Effects, because vital information is hidden from the current comp's timeline in a nested comp. Artists may sometimes let a composition become unwieldy, with dozens of layers, rather than bite the bullet and send a set of those layers into a precomp. Yet precomping is both an effective way to organize the timeline and a key to problem solving and optimization in After Effects.

Typically, precomping is done by selecting the layers of a composition that can sensibly be grouped together, and choosing Precompose from the Layer menu (keyboard shortcut **Ctrl+Shift+C**/**Cmd+Shift+C**). Two options appear (the second option grayed out if multiple layers have been selected): to leave attributes (effects, transforms, masks, paint, blending modes) in place or transfer them into the new composition.

Why Precomp?

Precomping prevents a composition from containing too many layers to manage in one timeline, but it also lets you do the following:

▶ Reuse a set of elements and manage them from one place.

▶ Fix render order problems. For example, masks are always applied before effects in a given layer, but a precomp can contain an effect so that the mask in the master comp follows that effect in the render order.

▶ Organize a project by grouping elements that are interrelated.

▶ Specify an element or set of layers as completed (and even pre-render them, as discussed later in this chapter).

NOTES

Precomping is the action of selecting a set of layers in a master composition and assigning it to a new subcomp, which becomes a layer in the master comp. Closely related to this is *composition nesting*, the act of placing one already created composition inside of another.

rd: Pre-compose by Jeff Almasol (http://aescripts.com/rd-pre-compose/) displays a dialog box to precomp one or more layers, just like the regular After Effects dialog, but adds the ability to trim the precomp to the selected layer's duration, including trim handles.

The 04_comp_templates folder and project on the disc contain relevant example comps.

Many After Effects artists are already comfortable with the idea of precomping but miss that last point. As you read through this, think about the advantages of considering an element finished, even if only for the time being.

The Project Panel: Think of It as a File System

How do you like to keep your system organized—tidy folders for everything or files strewn across the desktop? Personally, I'm always happiest with a project that is well organized, even if I'm the only one likely ever to work on it. When sharing with others, however, good organization becomes essential. The Project panel mirrors your file system (whether it's Explorer or Finder), and keeping it well organized and tidy can clarify your thought process regarding the project itself.

I know, I know, eat your vegetables, clean your room.

Figure 4.1 shows a couple of typical project templates containing multiple compositions to create one final shot, although these could certainly be adapted for a group of similar shots or a sequence. When you need to return to a project over the course of days or weeks, this level of organization can be a lifesaver.

Figure 4.1 A complex project such as a shot for a feature film might be generically organized (left) to include numbering that reflects pipeline order and multiple output comps with no actual edits, just the necessary settings. At minimum (right), you should have Source and Precomps folders, as well as a Reference folder, to keep things tidy.

Here are some ideas to help you create your own comp template:

- **Create folders,** such as Source, Precomps, and Reference, **to group specific types of elements.**
- **Use numbering to reflect comp and sequence order** so that it's easy to see the order in the Project panel.
- **Create a unique Final Output comp** that has the format and length of the final shot, particularly if the format is at all different from what you're using for work (because it's scaled, cropped, or uses a different frame rate or color profile).
- **Use guide layers and comments** as needed to help artists set up the comp (**Figure 4.2**).

TIP

If nothing else, a locked, untouchable Final Output comp prevents losing a render to an incorrectly set work area (because you were editing it for RAM previews).

Figure 4.2 Here is a series of non-rendering guide layers to define action areas and color.

- **Organize Source folders** for all footage, broken down as is most logical for your project.
- Place each source footage clip into a precomp. Why? Unexpected changes to source footage—where it is replaced for some reason—are easier to handle without causing some sort of train wreck.

The basic organization of master comp, source comp, and render comp seems useful on a shot of just about any complexity, but the template can include a lot more than that: custom expressions, camera rigs, color management settings, and recurring effects setups.

Manage Multiple Comps from the Timeline

Ever had that "where am I?" feeling when working with a series of nested comps? That's where Mini-Flowchart, or Miniflow, comes in. Access it via 🔲 in the Timeline panel, or simply press the **Shift** key with the Timeline panel forward to enable it.

SCRIPT

Arrange Project Items into Folders (http://aescripts.com/arrange-project-items-into-folders/) looks for project items with a matching prefix and groups them together in a folder. Load Project or Template at Startup (http://aescripts.com/load-project-at-startup/) loads a project or template each time you start After Effects—this can really help if you need several people in a studio to follow a certain organizational style. Both scripts are by Lloyd Alvarez.

By default, the comp order is shown flowing right to left. The reason for this is probably that if you open subcomps from a master comp, the tabs open to the right; however, you may want to choose Flow Left to Right in Miniflow's panel menu instead.

Miniflow shows only the nearest neighbor comps (**Figure 4.3**), but click on the flow arrows at either end and you navigate up or down one level in the hierarchy. Click on any arrows or items in between the ends and that level is brought forward. You're even free to close compositions as you're done editing them (**Ctrl+Alt+W/Cmd+Opt+W**) and reopen only the ones you need using this feature.

Figure 4.3 Mini-Flowchart view is a navigable pop-up showing dependent comps above and below (right and left of) the current comp in the hierarchy.

The Always Preview This View toggle lets you work entirely in a precomp but switch automatically to the master comp (if this is toggled in that comp) when previewing. Use it if you're only interested in how changes look in your final.

What about cases where you'd like to work in the Timeline panel of a subcomp while seeing the result in the master comp? The Lock icon at the upper left of the Composition viewer lets you keep that Composition viewer forward while you open another composition's Timeline panel and close its view panel. Lock the master comp and double-click a nested comp to open its Timeline panel; as you make adjustments, they show up in the master comp.

Ctrl+Alt+Shift+N (**Cmd+Opt+Shift+N**) creates two Composition viewers side by side, and locks one of them, for any artist with ample screen real estate who wants the best of both worlds.

To locate a comp in the Project panel, you can

▶ select an item in the Project panel; adjacent to its name by the thumbnail at the top of the panel is a small pull-down caret, along with the number of times, if any, the item is used in a comp (**Figure 4.4**)

Figure 4.4 Click the caret next to the total number of times an item is used to see a list of where it is used.

▶ context-click an item in the Project panel and choose Reveal in Composition; choose a composition and that comp is opened with the item selected (**Figure 4.5**)

Figure 4.5 Context-click any item, and under Reveal in Composition, choose from a list, if applicable; that timeline opens with the item selected.

▶ context-click a layer in the timeline and choose Reveal Layer Source in Project to highlight the item in the Project panel (**Figure 4.6**)

Figure 4.6 Context-click any footage item in the timeline and you can choose to reveal it either in the Project panel or in Flowchart view.

▶ context-click in the empty area of a timeline—and choose Reveal Composition in Project to highlight the comp in the Project panel (**Figure 4.7**)

Figure 4.7 Find the empty area below the layers in the timeline and context-click; you can reveal the current comp in the Project panel.

▶ type the name of the comp in the Project panel search field

Ways to Break the Pipeline

Precomping solves problems, but it can also create more problems—or at least inconveniences. Here are a few ways that render order can go wrong:

▶ Some but not all properties are to be precomped, others must stay in the master comp? With precomping it's all-or-nothing, leaving you to rearrange properties manually.

▶ Changed your mind? Restoring precomped layers to the master composition is a manual (and thus error-prone) process, due to the difficulty of maintaining proper dependencies between the two (for example, if the nested comp has also been scaled, rotated, and retimed).

▶ Do the layers being precomped include blending modes or 3D layers, cameras, or lights? Their behavior changes depending on the Collapse Transformations setting (detailed below).

▶ Is there motion blur, frame blending, or vector artwork in the subcomp? Switches in the master composition affect their behavior, as do settings on each individual nested layer, and this relationship changes depending on whether Collapse Transformations is toggled.

TIP

You may already know that a double-click opens a nested comp, and **Alt**–double-click (**Opt**–double-click) reveals it in the Layer viewer.

SCRIPT

The script preCompToLayerDur.jsx from Dan Ebberts (found on the book's disc) starts a precomped layer at frame 1 even if the layer to be precomped is trimmed to a later time.

- Layer timing (duration, In and Out points, frame rate) and dimensions can differ from the master comp. When this is unintentional, mishaps happen: Layers end too soon or are cropped inside the overall frame, or keyframes in the precomp fall between those of the master, wreaking havoc on, for example, tracking data.

- Are you duplicating a comp that contains subcomps? The comp itself is new and completely independent, but the nested comps are not (see Script at right).

No wonder people avoid precomping. But there is hope if you recognize any difficulty and know what to do, so that inconveniences don't turn into deal-killers.

Boundaries of Time and Space

Each composition in After Effects contains its own fixed timing and pixel dimensions. This adds flexibility for animation but if anything reduces it for compositing; most other compositing applications such as Nuke and Shake have no built-in concept of frame dimensions or timing and assume that the elements match the plate, as is often the case in visual effects work.

Therefore it is helpful to take precautions:

- Make source compositions longer than the shot is ever anticipated to be, so that if it changes, timing is not inadvertently truncated.

- Enable Collapse Transformations for the nested composition to ignore its boundaries (**Figure 4.8**).

- Add the Grow Bounds effect if Collapse Transformations isn't an option (see sidebar on next page).

Collapse Transformations is the most difficult of these to get your head around, so it's worth a closer look.

Collapse Transformations

In After Effects, when a comp is nested in another comp, effectively becoming a layer, the ordinary behavior is for the nested comp to render completely before the layer is animated, blended, or otherwise adjusted (with effects or masks) in the master comp.

True Comp Duplicator (http://aescripts.com/true-comp-duplicator/) was created by Brennan Chapman to address the biggest bugbear of working with nested comps in After Effects—in a node-based app, you can duplicate an entire nested tree and all of the components are unique, but duplicate a comp in After Effects and its subcomps are the same as in the source. This script can reside in a panel ready to create an entire new hierarchy. Highly recommended.

Figure 4.8 The nested comp has a blue background and the leg of the letter "p" extends outside its boundaries (top); a simple quick fix is to enable Collapse Transformations, and the boundaries of the nested comp are ignored (bottom).

The 04_collapse_transformations folder and project on the disc contain relevant example comps.

115

Grow Bounds

Sometimes enabling Collapse Transformations is not desirable—for example, if you set up 3D layers with a camera in a subcomp and don't want their position to be changed by a camera in the master comp. The Grow Bounds effect overcomes one specific (and fairly rare) problem (in which the embedded layer is too small for an applied effect), but it is also useful in cases where other effects create a comp boundary that leads visual data to appear cropped.

However, there are immediate exceptions. Keyframe interpolations, frame blending, and motion blur are all affected by the settings (including frame rate and timing) of the master comp—they are calculated according to its settings (which can become tricky; see the next section). 3D position data and blending modes, on the other hand, are not passed through unless Collapse Transformations is enabled. Enable the toggle and it is almost as if the pre-composed layers reside in the master comp—but now any 3D camera or lighting in the subcomp is overridden by the camera and lights in the master comp.

Not only that, but layers with Collapse Transformations lose access to blending modes—presumably to avoid conflicts with those in the subcomp. Now here comes the trickiest part: Apply any effect to the layer (even Levels with the neutral defaults, which doesn't affect the look of the layer) and you force After Effects to render the collapsed layer, making blending modes operable. It is now what the Adobe developers call a *parenthesized* comp. Such a nested comp is both collapsed and not: You can apply a blending mode, but 3D data is passed through (**Figure 4.9**).

Thus, if you want to collapse transformations but not 3D data, applying any effect—even one of the Expression Controls effects that don't by themselves do anything—will parenthesize the comp. It's a good trick to keep in your pocket. Will you run into this exact situation? It may be a while before that ever happens, but it's a case study to help you sort out exactly what is going on when you precomp and collapse transformations.

Nested Time

After Effects is not rigid about time, but digital video itself is. You can freely mix and change frame rates among compositions without changing the timing, as has been shown. However, because your source clips always have a very specific rate, pay close attention when you

TIP

Annoyed to find sequences importing at the wrong frame rate? Change the default Sequence Footage Frames per Second under Preferences > Import.

▸ import an image sequence

▸ create a new composition

▸ mix comps with different frame rates

Figure 4.9 Shown is the simplest example I could devise of the most complicated precomping situation. The nested comp (left) is a 3D box made up of solids, each with a Multiply blending mode. In the master comp (right) a Levels (effect with no adjustment) is set, allowing an Add mode to be applied, yet the box can still be rotated in 3D—those values are passed through.

In the first two cases you're just watching out for careless errors. But you might want to maintain specific frame rates in subcomps, in which case you must set them deliberately on the Advanced tab of the Composition Settings dialog.

Advanced Composition Settings

In addition to the Motion Blur settings introduced in Chapter 2 and covered in detail in Chapter 8, Composition Settings > Advanced contains two Preserve toggles that influence how time and space are handled when one composition is nested into another.

Preserve Frame Rate maintains the frame rate of the composition wherever it goes—into another composition with a different frame rate or into the render queue with different frame rate settings. So if a simple animation cycle looks right at 4 frames per second (fps), it won't be expanded across the higher frame rate, but will preserve the look of 4 fps.

TIP

The Posterize Time effect will force any layer to the specified frame rate.

Preserve Resolution When Nested controls what is called *concatenation.* Typically, if an element is scaled down in a precomp and the entire composition is nested into another comp and scaled up, the two operations are treated as one, so that no data loss occurs via quantization. This is concatenation, and it's usually a good thing. If the data in the subcomp is to appear pixilated, as if it were scaled up from a lower-resolution element, this toggle preserves the chunky pixel look.

Adjustment and Guide Layers

Two special types of layers, adjustment and guide layers, offer extra benefits that might not be immediately apparent, and are thus underused by less-experienced After Effects artists.

Adjustment Layers

Adjustment layers are the most natural thing in the world to anyone working with nodal compositing; they are a way of saying "at this point in the compositing process, I want these effects applied to everything that has already rendered." Because render order is not readily apparent in After Effects until you learn how it works, adjustment layers can seem trickier than they are.

Figure 4.10 The highlighted column includes toggle switches, indicating an adjustment layer. Any layer can be toggled but the typical way to set it is to create a unique layer. An adjustment layer created under Layer > New > Adjustment Layer (or via the shortcuts) is a white, comp-sized solid.

The *adjustment layer* is itself invisible, but its effects are applied to all layers below it. It is a fundamentally simple feature with many uses. To create one, context-click in an empty area of the Timeline panel, and choose New > Adjustment Layer (**Ctrl+Alt+Y**/**Cmd+Opt+Y**) (**Figure 4.10**).

Adjustment layers allow you to apply effects to an entire composition without precomping it. That by itself is pretty cool, but there's more:

▶ Move the adjustment layer down the stack and any layers above it are unaffected, because the render order in After Effects goes from the lowest layer upward.

▶ Shorten the layer and the effects appear only on frames within the adjustment layer's In/Out points.

▶ Use Opacity to attenuate any effect; most of them work naturally this way. Many effects do not themselves include such a direct control, even when it makes perfect sense to "dial it back 50%," which you can do by setting Opacity to 50%.

▶ Apply a matte to an adjustment layer to hold out the effects to a specific area of the underlying image.

▶ Add a blending mode and the adjustment layer is first applied and then blended back into the result (**Figure 4.11**).

It's a good idea 99% of the time to make sure that an adjustment layer remains 2D and at the size and length of the comp, as when applied. It's rare that you would ever want to transform an adjustment layer in 2D or 3D, but it is possible, so don't let it happen by accident. If you enlarge the composition, you must resize the adjustment layers as well.

NOTES

Alpha channel effects change the alphas of the layers below, not of the adjustment layer itself.

Figure 4.11 The basic setup in these two examples is identical: An adjustment layer uses the image itself as a luma matte so that it works only with the highlights, to which it applies a Box Blur (for a defocused look) and a Levels adjustment (to bring a glow to the highlights), as seen in the top figure. But applying Add mode to the adjustment layer (bottom) causes the adjusted image to be added to the original, giving it a subtle extra pop (that can be seen in the brighter highlights) in one simple step.

Guide Layers

Like adjustment layers, *guide layers* are standard layers with special status. A guide layer appears in the current composition but not in any subsequent compositions or the final render (unless it is specifically overridden in Render Settings.) You can use this for

▶ foreground reference clips (picture-in-picture timing reference, aspect ratio crop reference)

▶ temporary backgrounds to check edges when creating a matte

▶ text notes to yourself

▶ adjustment layers that are used only to check images (described further in the next chapter); a layer can be both an adjustment and a guide layer

Any image layer can be converted to a guide layer either by context-clicking it or by choosing Guide Layer from the Layer menu. (**Figure 4.12**).

Figure 4.12 Check out all the guide layers that won't render but help you work: One pushes up gamma to check blacks, and two provide crops for different aspects (1.85:1 and 2.35:1, the common cinematic formats). A picture-in-picture layer shows timing reference from the plate, along with a text reminder that does not render, either. None of this is visible in another composition, or in the render.

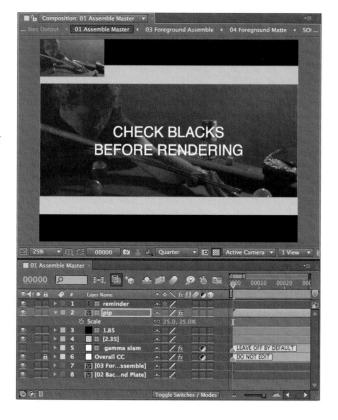

Faster! Control the Render Pipeline

The *render pipeline* is the order in which operations happen; by controlling it, you can solve problems and overcome bottlenecks. For the most part render order is plainly displayed in the timeline and follows consistent rules:

▶ 2D layers are calculated from the bottom to the top of the layer stack—the numbered layers in the timeline.

▶ Layer properties (masks, effects, transforms, paint, and type) are calculated in strict top-to-bottom order (twirl down the layer to see it).

▶ 3D layers are instead calculated based on distance from the camera; coplanar 3D layers respect stacking order and should behave like 2D layers relative to one another.

So to review: In a 2D composition, After Effects starts at the bottom layer and calculates any adjustments to it in the order that properties are shown, top to bottom. Then, it calculates adjustments to the layer above it, composites the two of them together, and moves up the stack in this manner (**Figure 4.13**).

Figure 4.13 2D layers render starting with the bottom layer, rendering and compositing each layer above in order. Layer properties render in the order shown when twirled down; there is no direct way to change the order of these categories.

Although effects within a given layer generally calculate prior to transforms (except in the case of continuously rasterized vector layers), an adjustment layer above a layer guarantees that its effects are rendered after the transforms of all layers below it.

Track mattes and blending modes are applied last, after all other layer properties (masks, effects, and transforms) have been calculated, *and* after their own mask, effect, and transform data are applied. Therefore, you don't generally need to pre-render a track matte simply because you've added masks and effects to it.

Faster!

Have you heard of a "real-time" compositing system? No such thing actually exists. The ones that claim to be real-time cleverly pre-render and cache elements so that they don't have to be recalculated as each frame is displayed. You can do this in After Effects, too—you're just left more to your own devices to set it up.

As I work, I try to organize any portions of my master comp that I consider finished into a subcomp, and if it is render-intensive, I pre-render it. Failure to commit to decisions—keeping options open—costs time and efficiency. It's as true in After Effects as it is in life as a whole. Pre-rendering a subcomp does, however, lead to another decision about how it behaves after you render it.

Post-Render Options

Tucked away in the Render Queue panel, but easily visible if you twirl down the arrow next to Output Module, is a menu of three post-render actions. After the render is complete, you can use

▶ **Import** to simply **bring** the result back into the project

▶ **Import & Replace Usage** to replace the usage of the source comp in the project without blowing it away

▶ **Set Proxy** to add a proxy to the source (the most elegant solution, but the most high-maintenance)

The latter two options even let you use the pick whip icon adjacent to the menu to connect whatever item in the Project panel needs replacement. If you've already created a pre-render or proxy, you can target that (**Figure 4.14**).

Proxies and Pre-Renders

Any image or clip in your Project panel can be set with a *proxy*, which is an imported image or sequence that stands in for that item. Its pixel dimensions, color space, compression, and even length can differ from the item it replaces. For example, you can use a low-resolution, JPEG-compressed still image to stand in for a full-resolution moving-image background.

TIP

Preferences > Display > Show Rendering Progress in Info Panel and Flowchart shows what is happening on your system. It is disabled by default because it requires some extra processing power, but I would argue you get that time back from the ability to spot and solve an obvious bottleneck.

TIP

If you choose Import & Replace Usage and then need to change back, **Alt**-drag (**Opt**-drag) the source comp over the replacement clip in the Project panel to globally replace its usage.

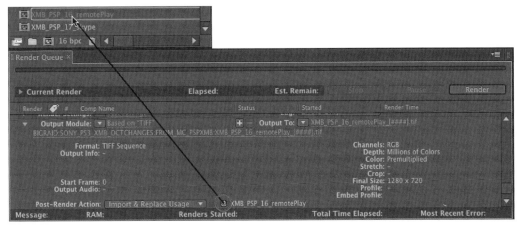

Figure 4.14 Virtually any project item can be the target for replacement or a proxy; click and drag the pick whip icon to choose the item to be replaced by the render.

To create a proxy, context-click an item in the Project panel and choose Create Proxy > Movie (or Still). A render queue item is created and automatically renders at Draft quality and half-resolution; the Output Module settings create a video file with alpha, so that transparency is preserved and Post-Render Action uses the Set Proxy setting.

Figure 4.15 shows how a proxy appears in the Project panel. Although the scale of the proxy differs from that of the source item, transform settings within the comps that use this item remain consistent with those of the source item so that it can be swapped in for the final at any time. This is what proxies were designed to do, to allow a low-resolution file to stand in, temporarily and nondestructively, for the high-resolution final.

Figure 4.15 The black square icon to the left of an item in the Project panel indicates that a proxy is enabled; a hollow square indicates that a proxy is assigned but not currently active. Both items are listed atop the Project panel, the active one in bold.

There's another use for proxies. Instead of creating low-res temp versions, you can generate final quality pre-rendered elements. With a composition selected, choose Composition > Pre-render and change the settings to Best quality, full resolution, making certain that Import and Replace Usage is set for Output Module. If, for example, you've completed the greenscreen key on a source, pre-render it so that you don't waste time continuing to redo a decision that is already finalized.

By default, the source file or composition is used to render unless specifically set otherwise in Render Settings > Proxy Use. Choosing Use Comp Proxies Only, Use All Proxies, or Current Settings options (**Figure 4.16**) allows proxies to be used in the final render. To remove them from a project, select items with proxies, context-click (or go to the File menu), and choose Set Proxy > None.

Chapter 1 contains more information on multiprocessing, caching, and previewing.

Figure 4.16 I typically set Proxy Use to Current Settings, but Use Comp Proxies Only lets you set low-res stand-ins for footage and full-res pre-renders for comps, saving gobs of time.

Background Renders

Rendering from the render queue ties up the application and most of the machine's processing power for as long as is needed to output footage. On a modern system with multiple processors, you can do much better than that.

aerender

Background rendering allows a render to occur without the user interface, allowing you to continue working with it. The aerender application is found alongside the After Effects CS5 application itself on your system but runs via the command line (in Terminal Unix shell on a Mac, or the DOS shell in Windows). You can drag it into the shell window to run it, or press **Enter** (**Return**) to reveal its Unix manual pages (if you're into that sort of thing). Shown are its arguments, the variables that can be added in quotes to the command *aerender*, and the location string of the project file.

But that's all such geeky gobbledygook when there's a panel to do it, thanks to the BG Render script, which is so good I almost never use the render queue anymore.

Network Rendering

The *aerender* command is also used by third-party rendering solutions that go beyond what BG Render can do by distributing your render across multiple machines on a network. These programs run scripts that manage the process of running aerender on multiple machines and are capable of far more than just straight-ahead renders; you can, for example, have a render wait until a certain time or until another one completes before commencing, and you can automatically re-queue renders that fail for any reason. All of the third-party rendering options—Rush Render Queue, Qube!, Smedge, Muster—also support other terminal-friendly applications such as Maya and Nuke.

Be forewarned, however, that at this stage there is nothing like a one-button install for this type of software. Because of the need to coordinate resources across a network and make machines recognize one another and all file locations, a system administrator or equivalent technical expert is needed before those are up and running. However, if your facility is large enough to have dozens or hundreds of CPUs, it's worth the investment to implement and maintain such a system.

There is increasing interest these days in letting someone else manage a render network remotely and permit what is known as remote or "cloud" rendering, where you upload your source files and rendered output is returned to you. This makes plenty of sense for 3D animations, which often have small source files but require a lot of processing power. Big comps, however, usually have too much source data to make it worthwhile to even contemplate uploading it all. Plenty of smart people are working on improving this method, and once gigabit connections to the Internet are widely available, this approach is bound to take off.

BG Renderer by Lloyd Alvarez (http://aescripts.com/bg-renderer/) may be the most universally used After Effects script. Not only does it automatically set up a background render by creating the command line for you, but it offers you a user interface for extra variables you might miss that determine the priority and number of processors used to render (**Figure 4.17**).

Figure 4.17 BG Renderer uses ScriptUI, which means that it looks like it's part of the interface, and can remain in an open panel as you work. When you're ready to render, you can specify priority and number of processors; click the button and a terminal window opens that shows the render progress, line by line. You miss the progress bar of the render queue, but if you can live without that the benefit is that you can keep working while your machine renders.

Multiple After Effects Versions

You can open more than one After Effects on Mac or Windows. This is memory intensive and not ideal for rendering, but it lets you work with two projects at once.

On a Mac, locate Adobe After Effects CS4.app and duplicate it (**Cmd+D**); both will run. On Windows, go to the Start menu, choose Run, type cmd, and click OK. In the DOS shell that opens, drag in AfterFX.exe from your Programs folder and then add " –m" (that's a space, a dash, and m as in "multiple"). Voilà, a second version initializes. Write a .bat file, and you can do all of this with a double-click.

Suppose you just have one machine and a big render. You want it to keep running but shut down the system when it's done, and even notify you remotely that the render was a success. Render, Email, Save, and Shutdown by Lloyd Alvarez (http://aescripts.com/render-email-incremental-save-and-shutdown/) exists for this purpose; just queue up your render and fire one of them off.

Watch Folder

The myopic and slightly dotty granddaddy of network rendering on After Effects is Watch Folder. File > Watch Folder looks in a given folder for projects ready to be rendered; these are set up using the Collect Files option. The Adobe help topic "Network rendering with watch folders and render engines" page includes everything you need to know.

Watch Folder is OK on small, intimate networks, but it requires much more hands-on effort than dedicated render management software. With individual systems having become so powerful, it's easy to become lazy about taking the trouble required to set up a Watch Folder render, but if you're up against a deadline, don't have the dedicated software, and want to maximize multiple machines, it will do the trick.

Adobe Media Encoder

Delivering to the web or a DVD? Adobe Media Encoder is a dedicated render application that helps render certain video formats—including Flash video (FLV and F4V), H.264, and MPEG-2—that don't work well with the frame-by-frame rendering model of After Effects. For example, H.264 is a "long GOP" format that relies on keyframes with lots of image data surrounded by in-between frames with very little, and it requires all of the frames to be rendered before it can work its magic. Not only can Adobe Media Encoder collect frames to compress them, it can even render on multiple passes for higher quality.

Owners of Adobe Production Premium or Master Collection have the maximum render options, since Premiere Pro can dynamically link to After Effects comps and render to Adobe Media Encoder. Even if you own just After Effects CS5, Media Encoder is still included with your installation.

Instead of rendering from After Effects in an uncompressed format and then importing the result to Adobe Media Encoder, you can drag and drop an After Effects project to the application. This launches Dynamic Link, which peeks inside the project for renderable comps (**Figure 4.18**).

Most of the options from the After Effects Render Queue are here, albeit in a different configuration, so why go to the trouble to render this way? If you've ever tried creating an H.264, FLV, F4V, or MPEG-2 directly from After Effects, you know that it's virtually impossible to get a good-looking file at anything but the highest data rate, which defeats the purpose of using these formats. Adobe Media Encoder can hold more than one frame at a time prior to writing the output video file, and this can make all the difference with the right settings. Start with the presets and customize as needed.

Optimize a Project

To finish Section I of this book, let's take a final look at preferences that haven't come up previously, memory management settings, and what do to if After Effects crashes.

Setting Preferences and Project Settings

The preference defaults have changed in version CS5 and you may be happy with most of them. Here, however, are a few you might want to adjust that haven't been mentioned yet:

127

▶ **Preferences > General > Levels of Undo:** The default is 32, which may be geared toward a system with less RAM than yours. Raise it to the maximum value of 99 unless you're seriously short on RAM.

▶ **Preferences General:** Check the options Allow Scripts to Write Files and Access Network or certain scripts won't work; these are unchecked to protect against malicious scripts, and I've never heard of one. Toggle Default Spatial Interpolation to Linear (Chapter 2).

▶ **Preferences > Display:** Check all three boxes on any up-to-date system. If you do this, you don't need to wait for thumbnails to update from some network location each time you select a source file. I prefer it this way because I like to see rendering progress even though it costs processing time, and I have a good OpenGL card so I hardware-accelerate the UI.

▶ **Preferences > Appearance:** Toggle Cycle Mask Colors so that multiple masks applied to a layer vary automatically.

Hack Shortcuts, Text Preferences, or Projects

Some people are comfortable sorting through lines of code gibberish to find editable tidbits. If you're one of those people, After Effects Shortcuts and Preferences are saved as text files that are fully editable and relatively easy to understand—although if you're not comfortable with basic hacking (learning how code works by looking at other bits of code) I don't recommend it. The files are located as follows:

▶ Windows: [drive]:\Users\[user name]\AppData\Roaming\Adobe\After Effects\10.0

▶ Mac: [drive]:/Users/[user profile]/Library/Preferences/Adobe/After Effects/10.0/

The names of the files are

▶ Adobe After Effects 10.0-x64 Prefs.txt

▶ Adobe After Effects 10.0 Shortcuts

These can be opened with any text editor that doesn't add its own formatting and works with Unicode. Make a backup

TIP

Press **Alt+Ctrl+Shift (Opt+Cmd+Shift)** immediately after launching After Effects to reset Preferences. Hold **Alt (Opt)** while clicking OK to delete the shortcuts file as well.

copy before editing by simply duplicating the file (any variation in the filename causes it not to be recognized by After Effects). Revert to the backup by giving it the original filename should anything start to go haywire after the edit.

The Shortcuts file includes a bunch of comments at the top (each line begins with a # sign). The shortcuts themselves are arranged in a specific order that must be preserved, and if you add anything, it must be added in the right place. For example, if you don't like the fact that Go To Time was changed in CS3 (apparently to align it with other Adobe applications), search for `GoToTime` and make your changes to the shortcut in quotes after the = sign; `"(Alt+Shift+J)"` becomes `"(Ctrl+G)"` in Windows, `"(Opt+Shift+J)"` becomes `"(Cmd+G)"` on the Mac (and lose the Group shortcut until you change it to something else).

Be extra careful when editing Preferences—a stray character in this file can make After Effects unstable. Most of the contents should not be touched, but here's one example of a simple and useful edit (for studios where a dot is preferred before the number prefix instead of the underscore): Change

```
"Sequence number prefix" = "_"
```

to

```
"Sequence number prefix" = "."
```

This is the format often preferred by Maya, for example.

In other cases, a simple and easily comprehensible numerical value can be changed:

```
"Eye Dropper Sample Size No Modifier" = "1"
"Eye Dropper Sample Size With Modifier" = "5"
```

In many cases the value after the = is a binary yes/no value, expressed as 0 for no or 1 for yes, so if you're nostalgic for how the After Effects render chime sounded in its first several versions, find

```
"Play classic render chime" = "0"
```

and change the 0 to a 1. Save the file, restart After Effects, and invoke Proustian memories of renders past.

SCRIPT

A fantastic script for specifying your own modifier keys called KeyEd Up was developed specifically for After Effects by Jeff Almasol, author of other scripts included with this book. Find it on Adobe After Effects Exchange at http://tinyurl.com/6cu6nq

On the Mac: Force a Crash

When After Effects does crash, it attempts to do so gracefully, offering the option to save before it exits. The auto-save options, if used properly, further diminish the likelihood of losing project data. On OS X, an extra feature may come in handy when the application becomes unresponsive without crashing.

Open Activity Monitor and look for After Effects to get its PID number (**Figure 4.19**). Now open Terminal, and enter `kill -SEGV ###` where "###" is replaced by the After Effects PID value. This should cause the application to crash with a save opportunity.

XML

After Effects CS4 and CS5 projects can be saved as .aepx files. These are identical to use but are written in plain Unicode text; you can edit them with an ordinary text editor. Most of what is in these files is untouchable. What can you do with this format? Mostly, you can use it to locate and change file paths to swap footage sources without having to do so manually in the UI. If you're handy with scripting, or even text macros, you can automate the process when dozens or hundreds of files are involved.

This feature was added for one reason only: scriptability. Anyone capable of writing scripts to, say, swap source files procedurally (and you know who you are) has a method to edit this data without working in the application itself. We all look forward to gaining access to more editable stuff via XML in future versions of After Effects, but for now that's about it.

Figure 4.19 The Process ID for the nonresponding application is shown in the left column.

Batch Search-n-Replace Paths by Lloyd Alvarez (http://aescripts.com/batch-search-n-replace-paths/) may save you the need to dig around in an .AEPX file to change footage source locations; it also makes use of regular expressions to make the matching process more sophisticated than what is possible with an ordinary text editor.

Memory Management

Chapter 1 included advice about running After Effects with multiprocessing enabled on a system with multiple cores and a good deal of physical memory. Although more effective handing of memory is the number one addition to After Effects CS5, it doesn't necessarily mean all of your memory troubles are over forever, particularly if your system is more limited.

If you see your system's wait icon come up—the hourglass in Windows, the spinning ball on a Mac—that means there is a fight going on somewhere for system resources. In addition to following Chapter 1's advice to leave memory available for outside applications, you may have to quit any application that is both resource intensive and outside the memory pool managed by After Effects (in other words, any app besides Premiere Pro, Encore, or Adobe Media Encoder).

But overall, the most effective way to improve memory handling on a 64-bit system is to provide the system with more physical memory, since it can be used so much more effectively. As a rule of thumb, 2 GB of RAM per processor core is not a bad guide; you can go below this to, say, 1.5 GB per core, but much lower and your system will be less efficient unless you also limit the number of cores being used (in Preferences > Memory & Multiprocessing).

Conclusion

You've reached the end of Section I (if you're reading this book linearly, that is) and should now have a firm grasp on getting the most out of the After Effects workflow. Now it's time to focus more specifically on the art of visual effects. Section II, "Effects Compositing Essentials," will teach you the techniques, and Section III, "Creative Explorations," will show you how they work in specific effects situations.

Here comes the fun part.

Although the RAM cache is less likely to become full or fragmented with 64-bit processing, Throttle-n-Purge by Lloyd Alvarez (http://aescripts.com/throttle-n-purge/) provides a UI panel with a one-button solution to clear all caches and get maximum efficiency out of a preview render (**Figure 4.20**). It also lets you switch bit depths, which while easily enough done in the Project panel is more obvious here, and it lets you turn multiprocessing on and off without opening Preferences.

Figure 4.20 Throttle-n-Purge exposes controls to help you manage memory usage as well as offering a one-button option to purge all caches (undos and image buffers) and start over.

SECTION II

Effects Compositing Essentials

CHAPTER

5

Color Correction

Color is my obsession, joy and torment…one day, at the deathbed of a dear friend, I caught myself in the act of focusing on her temples, analyzing the succession of appropriately graded colors which death imposed on her motionless face.

—Claude Monet

Color Correction

When you picture a compositor, you may think of an artist at a workstation busily extracting greenscreen footage, but if I had to name the number one compositing skill, it would be color matching. This ability to authoritatively and conclusively take control of color, so that foreground and background elements seem to inhabit the same world, shots from a sequence are consistent with one another, and their overall look matches the artistic direction of the project, is more than anything what would cause you to say that a comper has a "good eye."

The compositor, after all, is often the last one to touch a shot before it goes into the edit. Inspired, artistic color work injects life, clarity, and drama into standard (or even substandard) 3D output, adequately (or even poorly) shot footage, and flat, monochromatic stills. It draws the audience's attention where it belongs, away from the artifice of the shot.

So whether or not you think you already possess a "good eye," color matching is a skill that you can practice and refine even with no feel for adjusting images—indeed, even if you're color-blind. And despite the new color tools that appear each year to refine your ability to dial in color, for color matching in After Effects, three color correction tools are consistently used for most of the heavy lifting: Levels, Curves, and Hue/Saturation (and in many ways, Levels and Curves overlap in functionality). These have endured from the earliest days of Photoshop because they are stable and fast, and they will get the job done every time.

A skeptic might ask

- ▶ why these old tools when there are so many cool newer ones?
- ▶ why not use Brightness & Contrast to adjust, you know, brightness and contrast, or Shadow and Highlight if that's what needs adjustment?
- ▶ what do you mean I can adjust Levels even if I'm color-blind?

This chapter holds the answers to these questions and many more. First, we'll look at optimizing a given image using these tools, and then we'll move into matching a foreground layer to the optimized background, balancing the colors. The goal is to eliminate the need to hack at color work and to build skills that eliminate a lot of the guesswork.

This chapter introduces topics that resound throughout the rest of the book. Chapter 11 deals specifically with HDR color, and then Chapter 12 focuses on specific light and color scenarios, while the rest of Section III describes how to create specific types of effects shots using these principles.

Color Correction for Image Optimization

What constitutes an "optimized" clip? What makes a color-corrected image correct? Let's look at what is typically "wrong" with source footage levels and the usual methods for correcting them, in order to lay the groundwork for color matching. As an example, let's look at brightness and contrast of a *plate* image, with no foreground layers to match.

Levels

Levels may be the most-used tool in After Effects. It consists of five basic controls—Input Black, Input White, Output Black, Output White, and Gamma—each of which can be adjusted in five separate contexts (the four individual image channels R, G, B, and A, as well as all three color channels, RGB, at once). There are two different ways to adjust these controls: via their numerical sliders or by dragging their respective caret sliders on the histogram (which is the more typical method).

NOTES

The term *plate* stretches back to the earliest days of optical compositing (and indeed, of photography itself) and refers to the source footage, typically the background onto which foreground elements will be composited. A related term, *clean plate*, refers to the background with any moving foreground elements removed.

Figure 5.1 The CS5 version of Levels displays each channel of the histogram in color. The small round icons at the right of the histogram (left) toggle between this and the traditional black and white histogram, which can be easier to read. (Image from the film *Dopamine*, courtesy of Mark Decena, Kontent Films.)

Contrast: Input and Output Levels

Four of the five controls—Input Black, Input White, Output Black, and Output White (**Figure 5.1**)—determine brightness and contrast, and combined with the fifth, Gamma, they offer more precision than is possible with the Brightness & Contrast effect.

Figure 5.2 shows a Ramp effect applied to a solid using the default settings, followed by the Levels effect. Move the black caret at the lower left of the histogram—the Input Black level—to the right, and values below its threshold (the numerical Input Black setting, which changes as you move the caret) are pushed to black. The further you move the caret, the more values are "crushed" to pure black.

Figure 5.2 Levels is applied to a layer containing a Ramp effect at the default settings, which creates a smooth gradient from black to white. The spikes occur simply because the gradient height does not have an exact multiple of 256 pixels.

Move the Input White caret at the right end of the histogram to the left, toward the Input Black caret. The effect is similar to Input Black's but inverted: More and more white values are "blown out" to pure white (**Figure 5.3**).

Figure 5.3 Raising Input Black and lowering Input White has the effect of increasing contrast at either end of the scale; at an extreme adjustment like this, many pixels in an 8-bpc or 16-bpc project are pushed to full white or black or "crushed."

Either adjustment effectively increases contrast, but note that the midpoint of the gradient also changes as each endpoint is moved in. In Figure 5.3, Input Black has been adjusted more heavily than Input White, causing the horizon of the gradient to move closer to white and the shadows to darken. You can re-create this adjustment with Brightness & Contrast (**Figure 5.4**), but there's no direct control of the midpoint (gamma) of the image (**Figure 5.5**).

Figure 5.4 This gradient with Brightness & Contrast applied shows the midpoint clearly sliding toward brighter values, and the effect contains no gamma control to influence this side effect.

Figure 5.5 Interiors with exterior windows present a classic lighting and color challenge (left). A well-shot image from a powerful enough camera can resolve detail in both. However, Brightness & Contrast doesn't let you adjust the midpoint (gamma) and thus forces you to choose between resolving the background (Brightnesss –45, Contrast –8; middle) and the foreground (Brightness 30, Contrast 30; right).

> **TIP**
>
> You can reset any individual effect control (any property that has its own ⏱ icon) by context-clicking it and choosing Reset. You know it's an individual effect if it has its own stopwatch.

Reset Levels (click Reset at the top of the Levels effect controls) and try adjusting Output Black and Output White, whose controls sit below the gradient. Output Black specifies the darkest black that can appear in the image; adjust it upward and the minimum value is raised.

Lowering Input White is something like dimming the image, cutting off the maximum white value at the given threshold. Adjust both and you effectively reduce contrast in the image. Bring them alongside one another, and the gradient becomes a solid gray (**Figure 5.6**).

Figure 5.6 Raising Output Black and lowering Output White reduces contrast in the dark and light areas of the image, respectively; it doesn't produce such a beautiful image in this case, but comes into play in the Matching section.

So Input and Output controls have inverse effects. But you will find situations where you might use them together, first balancing the image, then reducing contrast in the whites, blacks, or both.

As is the case throughout After Effects, the controls operate in the order listed in the interface. In other words, raising the Input Black level first raises black density, and a higher Output Black level raises all of the resulting black levels together (**Figure 5.7**). If you've crushed the blacks with Input Black they remain crushed, and they all just appear lighter (unless you work in 32 bpc—Chapter 11 has the details on that).

If you're thinking, "So what?" at this point, just stay with this until we move to a situation in which to apply it.

Figure 5.7 Black and white levels crushed by adjusting the Input controls aren't then brought back by the Output controls. Instead, Output simply limits the overall dynamic range of the image (bottom), raising the darkest possible black level and lowering the brightest possible white.

Brightness: Gamma

As you adjust the Input Black and White values, you may have noticed the third caret that maintains its place between them. This is the Gamma control, affecting midtones (the middle gray point in the gradient) without

What Is Gamma, Anyway?

It would be nice but inaccurate simply to say, "Gamma is the midpoint of your color range" and leave it at that. The more accurate the discussion of gamma becomes, the more purely mathematical it becomes. Plenty of artists out there understand gamma intuitively and are able to work with it without knowing the math behind it—but here it is anyway.

Gamma adjustment shifts the midpoint of a color range without affecting the black or white points. This is done by taking a pixel value and raising it to the inverse power of the gamma value:

`newPixel = pixel (1/gamma)`

You're probably used to thinking of pixel values as fitting into the range 0 to 255, but this formula works with values *normalized* to 1. 0 is 0, 255 is 1, and 128 is 0.5—which is how the math "normally" operates behind the scenes in computer graphics.

Gamma operates according to the magic of logarithms: Any number to the power of 0 is 1, any number to the power of 1 is itself, and any fractional value (less than 1) raised to a higher power approaches 0 without ever reaching it. Lower the power closer to 0 and the value approaches 1, again without ever reaching it. Not only that, but the values distribute proportionally, along a curve, so the closer an initial value is to pure black (0) or pure white (1) the less it is affected by a gamma adjustment.

touching the white and black points. Adjust gamma of the gradient image and notice that you can push the grays in the image brighter (by moving it to the left) or darker (by moving it to the right) without changing the black and white levels.

Many images have healthy contrast, but a gamma boost gives them extra punch. Similarly, an image that looks a bit too "hot" may be instantly adjusted simply by lowering gamma. As you progress through the book, you will see that gamma plays a crucial role not only in color adjustment but also in how an image is displayed and how your eye sees it (more on that in Chapter 11).

In most cases, the image itself rather than the histogram offers the best clue as to whether the gamma needs adjustment (see the upcoming section "Problem Solving Using the Histogram," as well as **Figure 5.8**). So what is your guideline for how much to adjust gamma, if at all? I first learned always to go too far before dialing back, which is especially helpful when learning. An even more powerful gamma adjustment tool that scares novices away is Curves (coming up).

By mixing these five controls together, have we covered Levels? No—because there are not, in fact, five basic controls in Levels (Input and Output White and Black plus Gamma), but instead, five times five (RGB, Red, Green, Blue, and Alpha).

Individual Channels for Color Matching

Many After Effects artists completely ignore the pop-up menu at the top of the Levels control allowing adjustment of the five basic Levels controls on an individual channel, but this is where its powers for color matching lie. Let's take a look at these controls on the gradient image to reveal what exactly is going on.

Reset any Levels effect applied to the Ramp gradient. Pick Red, Green, or Blue in the Channel pop-up menu under Levels and adjust the Input and Output carets. The grayscale image takes on color. With the Red channel selected, move Red Output Black inward to tint the darker areas of the image red. Adjust Input White inward to make the

Figure 5.8 Proper shooting with a low-dynamic-range digital video camera such as a DSLR requires that you shoot a flat-looking image with low contrast and then bracket the histogram's white and black points, as it's always possible to add contrast to optimize an image but not possible to remove it without losing detail. The only difference between the left and right sides of the image is a Levels adjustment transforming the flat source, left, into the richer image on the right.

midtones and highlights pink (light red). If, instead, you adjust Input Black or Output White inward, the tinting moves in the opposite direction—toward cyan—in the corresponding shadows and highlights.

As you probably know, each primary on the digital wheel of color (red, green, or blue) has an opposite (cyan, magenta, or yellow, respectively). As your color skills progress you will notice when your method of, say, reducing green spill has made flesh tones too magenta, but when you're starting out it's enough simply to be aware that adjustments to each color channel proportionally affect its opposite (**Figure 5.9**). See the file Motionworks_ levels_and_curves. pdf, in the additional resources folder on the book's disc for a reference on color adjustments to channels.

Figure 5.9 These charts were devised by John Dickinson at Motionworks (www.motionworks.com.au) after he read an earlier edition of this book; it shows the relationship of each color to its opposite when adjusting the Levels Effect.

Gradients are one thing, but the best way to make sense of this with a real image is to develop the habit of studying footage on individual color channels as you work. This is the key to effective color matching.

Along the bottom of the Composition panel, all of the icons are monochrome by default save one: the Show Channel menu. It contains five selections: the three color channels as well as two alpha modes. Each one has a shortcut that, unfortunately, is not shown in the menu: **Alt+1** through **Alt+4** (**Opt+1** through **Opt+4**) toggle each color channel. A colored outline around the edge of the composition palette reminds you which channel is displayed (**Figure 5.10**); toggling the active channel returns the image to RGB.

Try adjusting a single channel of the gradient in Levels while displaying only that channel. The effect of brightness and contrast adjustment on a grayscale image is readily apparent. This is the way to work with individual channel adjustments, especially when you're just beginning or if you have difficulty distinguishing colors. As you work with actual images instead of gradients, the histogram can offer valuable information about the image.

Figure 5.10 Four Views mode is generally intended for 3D use, but it can also be used to show RGB and individual red, green, and blue channels. This becomes extremely useful for color matching. Note differences in the three channels and the colored outline showing which is which.

Levels: Histograms and Channels

You might have noticed the odd appearance of the histogram for an unadjusted gradient. If you were to try this setup on your own, depending on the size of the layer to which you applied Ramp, you might see a histogram that is flat along the top with spikes protruding at regular intervals (**Figure 5.11**).

Figure 5.11 Strange-looking histograms: A colored solid (top) shows three spikes, one each for the red, green, and blue values, and nothing else. With Ramp (bottom) the distribution is even, but the spikes at the top are the result of the ramp not being an exact multiple of 255 pixels, causing certain pixels to recur more often than others.

The histogram is exactly 256 pixels wide; you can think of it as a bar chart made up of 256 bars, each one pixel in width and corresponding to one of the 256 possible levels of luminance in an 8-bpc image. These levels are displayed below the histogram, above the Output controls. In the case of a pure gradient, the histogram is flat because of the even distribution of luminance from black to white. If the image height in pixels is not an exact multiple of 256, certain pixels double up and spike.

In any case, it's more useful to look at real-world examples, because the histogram is useful for mapping image data that isn't plainly evident on its own. The point is to help you assess whether any color changes are liable to improve or harm the image. There is in fact no single typical or ideal histogram—they can vary as much as the images themselves, as seen back in Figure 5.8.

Despite that fact, you can try a simple rule of thumb for a basic contrast adjustment. Find the top and bottom end of the RGB histogram—the highest and lowest points where there is any data whatsoever—and bracket them with the Input Black and Input White carets. To "bracket" them means to adjust these controls inward so each sits just outside its corresponding end of the histogram. The result stretches values closer to the top or bottom of the dynamic range, as you can easily see by applying a second Levels effect and studying its histogram.

Try applying Levels to any image or footage from the disc and see for yourself how this works in practice. First densify the blacks (by moving Input Black well above the lowest black level in the histogram) and then pop the whites (moving Input White below the highest white value). Don't go too far, or subsequent adjustments will not bring back that detail—unless you work in 32-bpc HDR mode (Chapter 11). Occasionally a stylized look calls for crushed contrast, but generally speaking, this is bad form.

Black and white are not at all equivalent in terms of how your eye sees them. Blown-out whites are ugly and can be a dead giveaway of an overexposed digital scene, but your eye is much more sensitive to subtle gradations of low black levels. These low, rich blacks account for much of what makes film look like film, and they can contain a surprising amount of detail, none of which, unfortunately, shows up on the printed page. Look for it in the images themselves.

The occasions on which you would optimize an image by raising Output Black or lowering Output White controls are rare, as this lowers dynamic range and the overall contrast. However, there are many uses in compositing for lowered contrast, to soften overlay effects (say, fog and clouds), high-contrast mattes, and so on. Examples follow in this chapter and throughout the rest of the book.

TIP

Auto Levels serves up a result similar to bracketing Input White and Input Black to the edges of the histogram. If that by itself isn't enough to convince you to avoid using Auto Levels, or really any "Auto" correction, consider also that they are processor intensive (slow) and resample on every frame. The result is not consistent from frame to frame, like with auto-exposure on a video camera—reality television amateurism.

TIP

Footage is by its very nature dynamic, so it is essential to leave headroom for the whites and foot room for the blacks until you start working in 32 bits per channel. You can add contrast, but once the image blows out, that detail is gone.

NOTES

LCD displays, as a whole, lack the black detail that can be captured on film. The next time you see a movie in a cinema, notice how much detail you can see in the shadows and compare.

amazon.com°

Your order of September 3, 2011 (Order ID 105-0826754-6351415)

Qty.	Item	Item Price	Total
1	**Adobe After Effects CS5 Visual Effects and Compositing Studio Techniques** Christiansen, Mark --- Paperback (** P-1-D141B440 **) 032171962X	$37.79	$37.79

Subtotal		$37.79
Order Total		$37.79
Paid via credit/debit		$37.79
Balance due		$0.00

V4

This shipment completes your order.

Have feedback on how we packaged your order? Tell us at www.amazon.com/packaging.

2/Dt4cmqmRR/-1 of 1-//1S5/second/6692022/0906-15:30/0904-03:36/tkeme

Problem Solving Using the Histogram

You may have noticed that the Levels histogram does not update as you make adjustments. After Effects lacks a panel equivalent to Photoshop's Histogram palette, but you can, of course, apply a Levels effect just to view the histogram (as in Figure 5.11).

The histogram reveals a couple of new wrinkles in the backlit shot from Figure 5.5, now adjusted with Levels to bring out foreground highlights (**Figure 5.12**). Spikes at the end of the second histogram (which is there just to evaluate the adjustment of the first) indicate clipping at the ends of the spectrum, which seems necessary for the associated result. Clipping, then, is part of life.

Figure 5.12 Adjusted to emphasize the foreground as in Figure 5.5 (top), the values below midgray are stretched, resulting in clear gaps in a second histogram that indicate loss of detail. Those same gaps appear, to a lesser extent, with the more modest adjustment to emphasize the background (bottom).

Note also the gaps that appear in the second histogram. Again, the net effect is a loss of detail, although in this case, the gaps are not a worry because they occur among a healthy amount of surrounding data. In more extreme

Figure 5.13 Push an adjustment far enough and you may see quantization, which appears as banding in the image. Those big gaps in the histogram are expressed as visible bands on a gradient. Switching to 16 bpc from 8 bpc is an instant fix for this problem in most cases.

cases, in which there is no data in between the spikes whatsoever, you may see a prime symptom of overadjustment, *banding* (**Figure 5.13**).

Banding is typically the result of limitations of 8-bpc color. 16-bpc color mode was added to After Effects 5.0 specifically to address this problem. You can switch to 16 bpc by **Alt**-clicking (**Opt**-clicking) on the bit-depth identifier along the bottom of the Project panel (**Figure 5.14**) or by changing it in File > Project Settings. Chapter 11 explains this in more detail.

Figure 5.14 An entire project can be toggled from the default 8-bpc color mode to 16-bpc mode by **Alt**-clicking (**Opt**-clicking) the project color depth toggle in the Project panel; this prevents the banding seen in Figure 5.13.

Curves: Gamma and Contrast

Curves rocks. I heart Curves. The Curves control is particularly useful for gamma correction.

▶ Curves lets you fully (and visually) control how adjustments are weighted and roll off.

▶ You can introduce multiple gamma adjustments to a single image or restrict the gamma adjustment to just one part of the image's dynamic range.

▶ Some adjustments can be nailed with a single well-placed point in Curves, in cases where the equivalent adjustment with Levels might require coordination of three separate controls.

It's also worth understanding Curves controls because they are a common shorthand for how digital color adjustments are depicted; the Curves interface recurs in most color correction toolsets.

Curves does, however, have drawbacks, compared with Levels:

▶ It's not immediately intuitive and can easily yield hideous results if you don't know what you're doing. There are plenty of artists who aren't comfortable with it.

▶ Unlike Photoshop, After Effects doesn't offer numerical values corresponding to curve points, making it a purely visual control that can be hard to standardize.

▶ In the absence of a histogram, you may miss obvious clues about the image (making Levels more suitable for learners).

The most daunting thing about Curves may be its interface, a simple grid with a diagonal line extending from lower left to upper right. There is a Channel selector at the top, set by default to RGB as in Levels, and there are some optional extra controls on the right to help you draw, save, and retrieve custom curves. To the novice, the arbitrary map is an unintuitive abstraction that you can easily use to make a complete mess of your image. Once you understand it, however, you can see it as an elegantly simple description of how image adjustment works. You'll find a project containing the equivalent Curves graph to the previous Levels corrections on the book's disc.

Figure 5.15 shows the more fully featured Photoshop Curves, which better illustrates how the controls work.

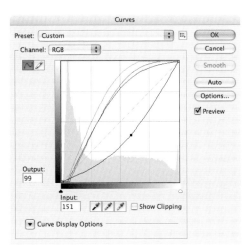

Figure 5.15 Photoshop's more deluxe Curves includes a histogram, built-in presets, displays of all channels together, and fields for input and output values for a given point on the curve.

Figures 5.16 shows some basic Curves adjustments and their effect on an image. **Figure 5.17** uses linear gradients to illustrate what some common Curves settings do. I encourage you to try these on your own.

Figure 5.16 What you see in an image can be heavily influenced by gamma and contrast. **A.** The source image. **B.** An increase in gamma above the shadows. **C.** A decrease in gamma. **D.** Both corrections combined.

Figure 5.17 This array of Curves adjustments applied to a gradient shows the results of some typical settings. **A.** The default gradient and Curves setting. **B.** An increase in gamma. **C.** A decrease in gamma. **D.** An increase in brightness and contrast. **E.** Raised gamma in the highlights only. **F.** Raised gamma with clamped black values.

Most interesting are the types of adjustments that only Curves allows you to do—or at least do easily. I came to realize that most of the adjustments I make with Curves fall into a few distinct types that I use over and over.

The most common adjustment is to simply raise or lower the gamma with Curves, by adding a point at or near the middle of the RGB curve and then moving it upward or downward. **Figure 5.18** shows the result of each. This produces a subtly different result from raising or lowering the Gamma control in Levels because of how you control the roll-off (**Figure 5.19**).

Figure 5.18 Two equally valid gamma adjustments via a single-point adjustment in the Curves control. Fine tuning follows in Figure 5.21.

Figure 5.19 Both the gradient itself and the histogram demonstrate that you can push the gamma harder, still preserving the full range of contrast, with Curves rather than with Levels, where you face a choice between losing highlights and shadows somewhat or crushing them.

Figure 5.20 The classic S-curve adjustment: The midpoint gamma in this case remains the same, directly crossing the midpoint, but contrast is boosted.

The classic S-curve adjustment, which enhances brightness and contrast and introduces roll-offs into the highlights and shadows (**Figure 5.20**), is an alternative method to get the result of the double curves in the image labeled D in Figure 5.16.

Some images need a gamma adjustment only to one end of the range—for example, a boost to the darker pixels, below the midpoint, that doesn't alter the black point and doesn't brighten the white values. Such an adjustment requires three points (**Figure 5.21**):

▶ one to hold the midpoint

▶ one to boost the low values

▶ one to flatten the curve above the midpoint

Figure 5.21 The ultimate solution to the backlighting problem presented back in Figure 5.5: Adding a mini-boost to the darker levels while leaving the lighter levels flat preserves the detail in the sky and brings out detail in the foreground that was previously missing.

A typical method for working in Curves is to begin with a single-point adjustment to adjust gamma or contrast, then to modulate it with one or two added points. More points quickly become unmanageable, as each adjustment changes the weighting of the surrounding points. Typically, I will add a single point, then a second one to restrict its range, and a third as needed to bring the shape of one section back where I want it.

Hue/Saturation: Color and Intensity

The third of three essential color correction tools in After Effects is Hue/Saturation. You can use this one to

▶ desaturate an image (or add saturation)

▶ colorize a monochrome image

▶ shift the overall hue of an image

▶ de-emphasize or remove an individual color channel (for example, to reduce green spill; see Chapter 6)

The Hue/Saturation control allows you to do something you can't do with Levels or Curves, which is to directly control the hue, saturation, and brightness of an image. The HSB color model is merely an alternate slice of RGB color data. All "real" color pickers include RGB and HSB as two separate but interrelated modes that use three values to describe any given color.

Thus you could arrive at the same color adjustments using Levels and Curves, but Hue/Saturation is more directly effective. To desaturate an image is essentially to bring the red, green, and blue values closer together, reducing the relative intensity of the strongest of them; a saturation control lets you do this in one step, without guessing.

Often colors are balanced but too "juicy" (not a strictly technical term), and lowering the Saturation value somewhere between 5 and 20 can be a direct and effective way to pull an image adjustment together (**Figure 5.22**). It's essential to understand the delivery medium as well, because film and even images from the web on your phone can be more tolerant and friendly to saturated images than television.

The other quick fix with Hue/Saturation is a shift to the hue of the whole image or of one of its component channels. The Channel Control menu for Hue/Saturation has red, green, and blue as well as their chromatic opposites of cyan, magenta, and yellow. In RGB color, these secondary colors work in direct opposition, so that lowering blue gamma effectively raises yellow gamma, and vice versa.

NOTES

Chapter 12 details why Tint or Black and White, not Hue/Saturation, is appropriate to convert an entire image to grayscale.

TIP

When in doubt about the amount of color in a given channel, try boosting its Saturation to 100%, blowing it out—this makes the presence of tones in that range very easy to spot.

Figure 5.22 Boosting a saturated image's contrast can make its saturation a bit too juiced up with color (top); if you recognize this, a simple and modest pullback in overall Saturation is a quick solution.

The HSB model includes all six individual channels, which means that if a given channel is too bright or oversaturated, you can dial back its Brightness & Saturation levels, or you can shift Hue toward a different part of the spectrum without unduly affecting the other primary and secondary colors. This can even be an effective way to reduce green or blue spill (Chapter 6).

Color Look Development

There are lots of ways to adjust the color levels of an image, with new ones emerging all the time, but most rely to some extent on these same basic component tools. Alternatives used to create a specific look are explored in Section III of this book.

Color Finesse and Three-Way Color

Colorists define the look of contemporary film and television. Make your way into the suite of a high-end colorist, and whether he or she is working with Lustre, Scratch, DaVinci Resolve, or even Apple Color you will find the

TIP

One alternative usage of these basic color correction tools is to apply them via an adjustment layer, because you can then dial them back simply by adjusting the layer's opacity or hold them out from specific areas of the image using masks or track matte selections.

same three or four color pots and accompanying wheeled surface controllers. This is also known as a three-way color corrector, and it has been the major missing color tool in the shipping version of After Effects until now. Synthetic Aperture's Color Finesse version 3, now included with After Effects, fills this gap.

Although Color Finesse is a full color correction application that has been included with After Effects for many years, major upgrades to the version 3 included with CS5 finally make it a toolset that I am comfortable putting front and center in this book, for two basic reasons. First, it now has a simple interface that runs in the Effect Controls panel, which provides three-way color correction and more. Second, the full Color Finesse application now offers a full complement of features, allowing you to navigate through time and save your color work in the form of a LUT.

What does all of this mean? Apply the SA Color Finesse 3 effect and twirl down the Simplified Interface. Now play with the hue offsets; for a typical modern color look, try dragging the point at the center of Shadows toward the cobalt blue 4:00 and Highlights in the opposite direction, toward the orangey 10:00. Gently nudge the midtones toward 2:00 or so for a warm look, or more like 8:00 for the Matrix (**Figure 5.23**).

Figure 5.23 The simplified interface of Color Finesse delivers color pots to After Effects, here used to take the image in a cooler direction.

Note the other controls right here in the Effect Controls—Curves properties with identical control to the Curves effect, but a friendlier multichannel interface, as well as HSL and RGB controls corresponding to Hue/Saturation and Levels, respectively. These are broken down to correspond to all four color wheels: Master, Highlights, Midtones, and Shadow effects. In other words, without having ever clicked Full Interface, you have one toolset that equates everything covered in this chapter so far. This is not to say that you'll never want to use the basic After Effects color tools—but you now have many more options.

You could perform all of your color corrections here, without opening the full Color Finesse interface, but when you do open it, you'll find more ways to take complete control of the color look (**Figure 5.24**). In the lower left are slider controls for all four color modes: HSL, RGB, its opposites CMY and the YCbCr controls of analog video, along with full Curves and Levels controls (with histogram), a Levels alternate called Luma Range, and a Secondary control for particular colors you might want to isolate and change.

Figure 5.24 Color Finesse brings scopes into—or at least makes them available to—After Effects CS5.

The top half of Color Finesse contains most of the professional modes of viewing and analyzing a digital video image for color. Parade, vectorscope, histogram, and tone curve slices of the image as well as a split view, a reference image toggle, and a luma range view to look only for areas that might be blown out or crushed.

Finally, note that under the File menu of Color Finesse, you can choose Export and t format, and the application will create a file containing a 3D color lookup table that can be saved for use in After Effects or used in most of the world's leading compositing and color correction applications, including those you see on the list: Autodesk Lustre and Smoke, LUTher, Scratch, and Truelight Cube, among others.

Color Matching

Now, having laid the groundwork with the toolset, it's time for the bread-and-butter work of compositing: to match separate foreground and background elements so that the scene appears to have been shot all together, at once. You can learn this skill and produce measurable, objective results. The process obeys such strict rules that you can do it without an experienced eye for color. You can satisfactorily complete a shot on a monitor that is nowhere near correctly calibrated, and the result would not even suffer from color-blindness on your part.

How is that possible?

It's simply a question of breaking down the problem. In this case, the job of matching one image to another obeys rules that can be observed channel by channel, independent of the final, full-color result.

Of course, compositing goes beyond simply matching color values; in many cases that is only the first step. Observation of nature plays a part. And even with correctly matched colors, any flaws in edge interpretation (Chapter 3), a procedural matte (Chapter 6), lighting (Chapter 12), camera view (Chapter 9), or motion (Chapter 8) can sink an otherwise successful shot.

These same basic techniques can also be used to match clips from a source precisely—for example, color correcting a sequence to match a *hero* shot (usually based on facial skin tones and other essentials), a process also sometimes known as *color timing*.

The Fundamental Technique

Integration of a foreground element into a background scene often follows the same basic steps:

1. **Match overall contrast** without regard to color, using Levels (and likely examining only the Green channel). Align the black and white points, with any necessary adjustments for variations in atmospheric conditions.

2. Next, study each color channel individually as a grayscale image and use Levels to **match the contrast of each channel.**

3. **Align midtones (gamma)**, also channel by channel, using Levels or Curves. This is sometimes known as *gray matching* and is easiest when foreground and background contain areas that are something like a colorless midgray.

4. **Evaluate the overall result** for other factors influencing the integration of image elements—lighting direction, atmospheric conditions, perspective, and grain or other ambient movement (all of which follow as specific topics later in this book). Here you get to work a bit more subjectively, even artistically.

This uncomplicated approach propels you to make adjustments your brain doesn't necessarily understand because of its habit of stereotyping based on assumptions. An image that "looks green" may have a good deal of blue in the shadows but yellowish highlights, but a less experienced eye might not see these (and even a veteran can miss them). The choices are bolder than those derived from noodling around, and the results can be stunning (as we'll see on a subtle example here, followed by a couple of radical ones thereafter).

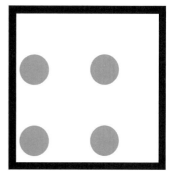

Figure 5.25 There are no yellow dots in the image at left, and no blue dots in the middle image; the four dots shown in the image at right are identical to their counterparts in the other two images.

Truthfully, even an experienced artist can be completely fooled by the apparent subjectivity of color because of how human vision works. **Figure 5.25** shows an example in which seeing is most definitely *not* believing. Far from some sort of crutch or nerdy detail, channel-by-channel analysis of an image provides fundamental information as to whether a color match is within objective range of what the eye can accept.

Ordinary Lighting

We begin with a simple example: comp a neutrally lit 3D element into an ordinary exterior day-lit scene. **Figure 5.26** shows a simple A over B result in which the two layers are close enough in color range that a lazy or hurried compositor might be tempted to leave it as is, other than adding a bit of motion blur to match the car entering the frame. For an inexperienced comper, this shot is a bit of a challenge, as it may be difficult with the naked eye to say exactly how or why the color doesn't match.

To begin, make certain that you are working in 16-bpc mode (**Alt**- or **Opt**-click on the indicator at the bottom of the Project panel to toggle). This prevents banding and enhances accuracy when adjusting color of low-dynamic-range images. Now reveal the Info panel, and choose Decimal (0.0 - 1.0) under the panel menu at the upper right to align with the settings used in this section. If you like, tear off the Info panel by **Ctrl**-dragging (**Cmd**-dragging) it over the Composition viewer.

> **NOTES**
>
> For simplicity's sake, the example on the disc uses still images only, but a multi-pass render of the plane and a full background plate are included to allow you to complete the shot. For more info on working with multi-pass source, see Chapter 12.

Figure 5.26 An unadjusted foreground layer (the plane) over a day-lit background.

This example can be found on the disc in the 05_color_match_01_ basic folder.

This particular background plate helps us a lot, as it's filled with monochromatic elements: a concrete landscape and a silver car, black shadows and car tires, little white details such as a sign, license plate, reverse lights, and the stripe of a loading zone. The foreground aircraft is also predominantly monochromatic, with many black details and white highlights. For this exercise we use a single 8-bpc image, although the full animation with multiple passes will be used later in the book for more precision adjusting.

The first step is to match overall contrast with the Levels effect, so apply that to the foreground layer. This adjustment can be performed while viewing regular RGB but it may be easier with only the green channel displayed (**Alt+2/Opt+2**, or select from the ▨ menu). Move the cursor over the highlight areas along the top of the plane (or just look at the Levels histogram) and you'll notice that some of the highlights are clipped to 1.00 on all three color channels, as are highlights. Clipping is part of life and not necessarily a bad thing unless those highlights need to be recovered for some reason; in this case, let's suppose we don't need to worry about Levels and just want to match the clipped foreground to the clipped background.

Figure 5.27 Just because the Info panel and histogram clearly indicate clipping in the foreground doesn't mean you can't clip highlights further if it helps properly match it to the background. Shadows appear to match reasonably well on the green channel.

Here, the white foreground contrast doesn't appear hot enough for the outdoor lighting of the background. Even the road surface blacktop is close to pure white in the direct sunlight, so clearly the highlights on the plane should, if anything, be pushed further. Lower Input White to at least the top of the visible histogram, around 0.82 (**Figure 5.27**).

Black contrast areas, the shadows, are at least as subjective. Again the histogram indicates that some blacks are already clipped; the question is whether the shadows, for example, under the back wing, need to be deeper (or lighter). Move the cursor to the shadows underneath the cars and they are clearly deeper—as low as 0.04. But higher up on the building, reflected light from the surface lightens the shadows under the overhangs to something like we see under the wings, in the range between 0.2 and 0.3 on all channels. Subjectively, you can try raising Output Black slightly to get more of the effect of shadows lightened by reflected light, or you can crush the shadows more with Input Black to match those under the cars. Try each before leaving them close to neutral.

Having aligned contrast, it's time to balance color by aligning contrast on each channel. Move your cursor back over shadow areas and notice that although the foreground plane's shadows are neutral, the background shadows are approximately 20% more intense in the blues than greens,

> **TIP**
>
> The human eye is most sensitive to green, so we begin by matching overall RGB contrast while viewing the green channel, then adjusting the other two channels to accommodate that adjustment.

and around 20% less intense in red versus green. The goal is not so much to match the blacks to the exact levels of the background as to match these proportions on the red and blue channels.

Place the cursor under the big plane wing and notice that the green value of that shadow is around 0.2. Switch Levels to Red under the Channel menu and raise Red Input Black just a hint, to something like 0.025, until the red value under the wing is approximately 0.18, or 20% lower than green. Now switch Levels to Blue; this time you'll raise Blue Output Black to lift the darkest blue shades slightly (maybe even just 0.015, **Figure 5.28**). Double-check with your cursor under the wing; the red, green, and blue proportions are now similar to those of the background blacks.

Now for the whites. Take a look at the RGB image again, and notice the silver car left of frame and the difference between it and the plane. It's not clear that they should be the exact same shade, but let's assume that they are both neutral gray and should be made much more similar, which can be accomplished by adjusting just white contrast on all three channels.

Starting with the Blue channel, notice that the plane looks a little dull overall compared with the car. Bring Blue Input White down to at least 0.95 while viewing the blue channel (**Alt+3/Opt+3**) and see if it doesn't appear to be a better match. Switch the view and Levels control to Red, and

Figure 5.28 Black levels for Red and Blue in the foreground are taken just a hint in opposite directions, raising the effective black level in blue and lowering it in red (left). These adjustments are a little too subtle in this case to perform with the naked eye, so they were arrived upon using values shown in the Info panel.

Figure 5.29 Compare this integration to that of Figure 5.26.

notice that, conversely, the side of the plane looks bright compared to the car. Bring Red Output White down about the same amount, to 0.95. A final look at green shows that the same adjustment there, of Green Output White to 0.95, helps the match. Notice that these edits influence not just the highlights, but also midtones, so there's no need to adjust gamma directly.

Et voilá, back to RGB—you'll see the result, which you can compare with the source image from Figure 5.26 simply by toggling Levels, in **Figure 5.29**. Motion blur can be roughed in by adding Fast Blur, setting Blur Dimensions to Horizontal, and raising Blurriness to approximately 100.0 to match the car entering frame right. The plane is now more effectively integrated into the scene, and these subtle changes make a huge difference (toggle the before and after to see for yourself).

Dramatic Lighting

If you're working with a daring cinematographer shooting in available light, or heed the advice in the Foreword, you'll be happy to know that this matching technique is even more impressive with strong lighting.

This example can be found on the disc in the 05_color_match_02_bridge folder.

Figure 5.30 Not only is it clear that the can does not belong in the color environment of the background, the mismatch is equally apparent on each color channel. (Plate courtesy of Shuets Udono via Creative Commons license.)

The composite in **Figure 5.30** clearly does not work; the foreground element does not contain the scene's dominant color and is white-lit. That's fine; it will better demonstrate the effectiveness of the following technique.

It helps that both the foreground and the background elements have some areas that you can logically assume to be flat gray. The bridge has concrete footings for the steel girders along the edges of the road, while the can has areas of bare exposed aluminum.

The steps to color-match a scene like this are as follows:

1. Apply Levels to the foreground layer.

2. Switch the view in the Composition panel to Green (**Alt+2/Opt+2**). Not only is this the dominant color in this particular scene, but it is dominant in human vision, so green-matching is the first step in most scenes, not just this one.

NOTES

This section discusses colors expressed as percentages; to see the same values in your Levels effect, use the wing menu of the Info palette to choose Percent for the Color Display.

3. Begin as if you are looking at a black-and-white photograph, and match the element to this dark contrasty scene using Levels in the RGB channel. If the element needs more contrast in the shadows and highlights, as this one does, raise Input Black and lower Input White; if it needs less, adjust the Output controls instead. Finally, adjust the gamma; in this scene, should it come down to match the darkness of the scene or up so the element stands out more? The result should look like a monochrome photo whose elements match believably (**Figure 5.31, part A**).

4. Switch the view (**Alt+1/Opt+1**) and the Levels control to the Red channel and repeat the grayscale matching process. Clearly, the foreground element is far too bright for the scene. Specifically, the darkest silver areas of the can are much brighter than the brightest areas of the concrete in the background. Therefore, adjust the gamma down (to the right) until it feels more like they inhabit the same world. Now have a look at the highlights and shadows; the highlights look a little hot, so lower Red Output White (**Figure 5.31, part B**).

5. Now move over to Blue in the view (**Alt+3/Opt+3**) and in Levels. In this case, there is almost no match whatsoever. The can is much brighter and more washed out than the background. Raise Input Blue and bring gamma way down. Now the can looks believably like it belongs there (**Figure 5.31, part C**).

It's strange to make all of these changes without ever looking at the result in full color. So now, go ahead and do so. Astoundingly, that can is now within range of looking like it belongs in that scene; the remaining adjustments are subjective. If you want the can to pick up a little less green from the surroundings as I did, lower Green Input White. Back in the RGB channel, adjust Gamma according to how much you want this element to pop. And of course, finish the composite: Defocus slightly with a little fast blur, add a shadow, and you may start to buy it (**Figure 5.32**).

A

B

C

Figure 5.31 It's fun and satisfying to pull off an extreme match like this channel by channel. The Levels settings come from looking for equivalent black/white/midpoints in the image and just analyzing whether the result looks like a convincing black-and-white image on each channel.

Figure 5.32 The result of all your previous efforts includes a subtle shadow that has been color-matched as well as a final adjustment to the white contrast.

No Clear Reference

Life doesn't always cooperate and provide nice white, black, and midgray references in foreground and background source; the world is much more interesting than that.

Figure 5.33 contains a scene so strongly lit with one color, it's hard to tell what anything besides the glass would look like under white light, and even that is suspect.

The basic technique still works in this case, but it requires a bit more artistry. Instead of carefully matching specific values, this time you must go channel by channel and simply make each image look plausible in grayscale black and white.

NOTES

This example can be found on the disc in the 05_color_match_03_red_interior folder.

Figure 5.33 Sometimes a source scene will have completely crazy lighting. Once you are confident about how to match it, you may say to an image that is blown out and over-balanced in one direction, "Bring it on." This one requires as much intuition as logic, but the channel-by-channel approach works.

This time, begin with the red, not the green, channel, because it is clearly dominant. The foreground needs little adjustment to RGB to work in Red; just a slight reduction in Output White, to 0.85, and it looks pretty good. (We'll address matching the strong grain in Chapter 9.)

Move over to the green channel and it's a whole different story. Were it not for the light of the candle this channel might be black, and matching the foreground clearly means bringing Green Output White way, way down (as low as 0.15). Now it's hard to tell what's even happening, so raise the exposure control in the viewer until the scene is somewhat illuminated (up as high as 10.0), and the foreground looks washed out compared with the extreme contrast of the background. Crush black and white contrast by raising Green Input Black up toward 0.3 and lowering Green Input White down to about 0.55. Great, but now the black level needs to be lifted just a touch, to 0.005 (you'd never notice it except that it's so overexposed). Click the exposure control icon to reset that and it's looking pretty good.

Blue is the same story only more so, and yowza, is there a lot of grain here. Similar Blue Output White and Blue Input Black levels to green will work, but there's no clear reason to increase white contrast in this channel, so leave Blue Input White where it is, and likewise Blue Output Black. Flashing with the exposure control reveals all.

Now for the moment of truth: Toggle back to RGB to reveal a darned good color match happening here. With grain and maybe a little specular kick on the side, this element could look as though it had been there all along.

So even in cases where it's not really possible to be scientific about matching color, there are clear procedures to follow that allow you to make confident, bold, even radical color adjustments in composites.

Direction and Position

An element generated in 3D software ideally contains multiple passes for more control. Even with that, if the lighting direction and perspective of an element are wrong, there's no practical way to make it match (**Figure 5.34**).

NOTES

It can be a good idea to take a break when attempting fine color adjustment. Upon return, a clear first impression can save you a lot more noodling.

On the other hand, compositing frees artists from hanging around trying to solve everything in 3D software. **Figure 5.35** shows the simplest solution to the previous problem: Match the camera angle and basic lighting by observing what's in the scene. From looking at the pool balls and shadows, it seems apparent that there are a couple of overhead lights nearby and that the one off camera right is particularly strong.

The angle can be matched by placing the background shot into the background of the 3D software's camera view, making sure that there are a couple of lights roughly matched to that of the scene to produce the correct shading and specular highlights. This element does not match perfectly, but I am done with what I need to do in 3D.

More complex and dynamic perspective, interactive lighting, animation, and other variables certainly can be done in 3D, yet at the end of the day, the clever computer graphics artist moves a scene over to 2D as soon as the elements are within shooting distance (**Figure 5.36**).

Gamma Exposure Slamming

True story: *Return of the Jedi* had its debut on national television in the '80s, and when the emperor appeared, black rectangular garbage mattes could clearly be seen dancing around his head, inside the cloak. All of this happened prior to the digital age, and these optical composites clearly worked fine on film—they were done at ILM by the best optical compositors in the business—but on video, those blacks were flashed and the illusion broke.

Don't lose your illusion, Axl, use it. Now that you know how to match levels, put them to the test. *Slam the gamma exposure* of the image: Just adjust the Exposure control at the lower right of the viewer upward. Slamming (**Figure 5.37** on the next page) exposes areas of the image that might have been too dark to distinguish on your monitor; if the blacks still match with the gamma exposure slammed up, you're in good shape. Everything must match whether the image is blown out or dimmed way down.

This example can be found on the disc in the 05_color_match_04_pool_interior folder.

Figure 5.34 All of the 2D compositing trickery in the world can't change the fact that this element is angled wrong. It is also lit from the wrong side. (Source clip from *Jake Forgotten*, courtesy of John Flowers.)

Figure 5.35 The angle and lighting have been roughly matched in 3D; rather than tweaking it further there, work on getting a quicker and more accurate result in 2D.

Figure 5.36 The color-matched final includes a shadow.

Figure 5.37 Slamming gamma is like shining a bright light on your scene. In this case it reveals a mismatch in the shadow color and the need for grain.

Get into this habit anywhere that you find subtle discrepancies of contrast; you can use it to examine a color key, as you'll learn in the next chapter, or a more extreme change of scene lighting. Any reputable effects studio typically examines footage this way before it's sent for final.

Conclusion

This chapter has covered some of the basics for adjusting and matching footage. Obviously there are exceptions that occur all of the time: depth cueing, changes in lighting during the shot, backlighting, interactive light, and shadow. There are even cases in which you can, to some degree, relight a shot in After Effects, introducing light direction, exchanging day for night, and so on. You'll discover more in Chapter 12, and on your own.

6

Color Keying

Slow down, I'm in a hurry.

— Franz Mairinger (Austrian equestrian)

Color Keying

Color keying was devised in the 1950s as a clever means to combine live-action foreground footage with backgrounds that could come from virtually anywhere. What was once a fragile and expensive proposition is now fully mainstream; whole films have come to rely on this technique, while *The Colbert Report* invites anyone with a computer—and more than likely, a copy of After Effects—to try the "Greenscreen Challenge" (and it runs entries from none less than John Knoll).

The process goes by many names: color keying, bluescreening, greenscreening, pulling a matte, color differencing, and even chroma keying—a term from analog color television, the medium defined by chroma and heavily populated with weather forecasters.

The purpose of this chapter is to help you not only with color keying of bluescreen and greenscreen footage, but with all cases in which pixel values (hue, saturation, and brightness) stand in for transparency, allowing compositors to effectively separate the foreground from the background based on color data.

All of these methods extract luminance information that is then applied to the alpha channel of a layer (or layers). The black areas become transparent, the white areas opaque, and the gray areas gradations of semi-opacity. Here's an overall tip: It's the gray areas that matter.

Procedural Mattes

A *procedural matte* is generated by making adjustments to controls, instead of *rotoscoping* it by hand. You could say that the selection is generated mathematically rather than manually. Each artist has a threshold of tolerance to

Example footage and comps for this chapter are all gathered together in the 06_keying folder on the disc.

For those reading nonlinearly, this chapter extends logically from fundamental concepts about mattes and selections in Chapter 3.

Figure 6.1 The background influences what you see. Against black, almost no detail is visible (left). Checkerboard reveals shadows (middle), but flaws in the matte are clearest with a bright, solid, contrasting background (right). (Source footage courtesy of Pixel Corps.)

continue to solve a matte procedurally or rotoscope it. My own threshold is high—I tend to avoid roto at all costs—so I have learned many methods to make the procedural approach work, and share as many as possible here.

Following is some top-level advice to remember when creating any kind of matte.

▶ **Create contrast for clarity.** Use a bright, saturated, contrasting background (**Ctrl+Shift+B**/**Cmd+Shift+B**) such as yellow, red, orange, or purple (**Figure 6.1**). If the foreground is to be added to a dark scene, a dark shade is OK, but in most cases bright colors better reveal matte problems. Solo the foreground over the background you choose.

▶ **Protect edges at all costs.** This is the name of the game (and the focus of much of this chapter); the key to winning is to isolate the edges as much as possible and focus just on them to avoid crunchy, chewy mattes (**Figure 6.2**).

▶ **Keep adjustments as simple as possible, even starting over if necessary to simplify.** Artists spend hours on keys that could be done more effectively in minutes, simply by beginning in the right place. There are many complex and interdependent steps involved with creating a key; if you're hung up on one, it may be time to try a different approach.

Figure 6.2 A "chewy" matte like this is typically the result of clamping the foreground or background (or both) too far.

▶ **Keep dancing: Check adjacent frames and zoom into detail.** When possible, start with the trickiest area of a difficult frame; look for motion blur, fine detail, excessive color spill, and so on, and keep looking around with a critical eye for what needs improvement (**Figure 6.3**).

Figure 6.3 A glimpse of the alpha channel can reveal even more problems, such as faint holes in the foreground, which should be solid white.

▶ **Break it down.** This is the single most important concept novices miss. Most mattes will benefit from separate garbage, core, and edge passes—a process detailed later in this chapter—and in many cases it helps to create a separate pass just for delicate edges: hair, a translucent costume, motion blur, and so on.

I encourage you to review this list again once you've explored the rest of the chapter.

Linear Keyers and Hi-Con Mattes

There are cases in which edge detail is less of a factor because the matte is used to adjust, not simply composite, an element; for example, you could hold out the highlight areas of an image for adjustment using a *high-contrast* (*hi-con*) matte. You might create this matte with a *linear keyer*.

Linear keyers are relatively simple and define a selection range based only on a single channel. This could be red, green, or blue, or just overall luminance. They're useful in a wide variety of cases outside the scope of bluescreen and greenscreen shots, although similar principles apply with Keylight. (Keylight is covered later in this chapter.)

The most useful linear keyers, Extract and Linear Color Key, are unfortunately less intuitively named than the keyers to avoid at all costs—Luma Key and Color Key. The latter two are limited to a bitmap (black and white) selection; only by choking and blurring the result with Edge Thin and Edge Feather controls can you add threshold adjustment. It's a little unfortunate that Adobe hasn't let these ancient effects go into the bin marked "obsolete" since the other, less intuitively named effects supersede them (and yet those not in the know naturally reach for the ones with the obvious titles).

Extract and Linear Color Key

The Extract effect is useful for *luminance (luma) keying*, because it uses the black-and-white points of an image or any of its individual channels. Linear Color Key is a more appropriate tool to use to isolate a particular color (or color range).

CLOSE-UP

Linear Color Key vs. Roto Brush

In Chapter 7 we'll take a look at Roto Brush, which goes beyond what can be done with a simple linear key by combining many criteria (beyond luminance) for what makes up a selection. It is powerful enough that it may seem to supersede linear keying, but keep in mind that Roto Brush is always more expensive (in terms of processing power and setup). Sometimes a luminance key is all you need.

Extract

If you're comfortable with the Levels effect, then Extract is no problem. It includes a histogram and sliders over a gradient. Try working with the chimp clip. Before adjusting the effect, take a look at all three color channels (**Alt+1, 2, 3/Opt+1, 2, 3**). One of the three typically has the best initial contrast, while the default luminance channel is merely an average of the three and not as strong a choice. In this case, the blue channel has the most uniformly dark subject area, so in the Channel menu of Extract, choose that (**Figure 6.4**).

The Extract histogram gives you a strong clue as to the likely white or black thresholds on each channel. To set these, drag the upper right pair of square controls at the

Figure 6.4 Extract the luminance channel and you get all three channels blended together—but first examine those channels and it's easy to see that the foreground figure is most consistently dark in the blue channel. A gentle slope with Softness set to 75 (bottom) retains some of the softness and fine detail of the hair, and it certainly helps to comp over a light background.

white end of the gradient, below the histogram. Watch the image itself and the histogram; just like with Levels, you're bracketing the area where the foreground image data is held but stopping short of clipping—which in this case causes holes in the foreground.

The only way to decide how far to go is to add the target background. If you're removing a white set wall, the hope is that whatever is replacing it is also quite bright. If not, you may have to choke the edges more than is ideal to avoid white fringing. A bright sky behind this subject is much simpler than trying to make this matte work against black.

Once you've found the lowest white point setting that yields a nice edge (and if there are small holes in the foreground, don't worry too much about them yet), soften it by dragging the lower box in that pair of square controls to the right, raising White Softness. This adds threshold pixels to the matte naturally, by tapering between the fully opaque values at the white point and the transparent background.

If there are holes in the matte, duplicate the layer, and then in the duplicate, raise the White Point value so that the holes disappear. Now protect the edge by adding a Simple Choker effect on that duplicate layer and raising the Choke Matte value until you can toggle this layer on and off without seeing any effect on the edge. This is a core matte, and it will be essential with color keying, ahead.

Linear Color Key

The Linear Color Key offers direct selection of a key color using an eyedropper tool. It's useful in cases where Keylight won't work, because the color being selected is not one of the digital primaries (red, green, or blue) that Keylight relies on for its fundamental operations. You may never come up with a situation in which you need to key out a background made of up some secondary color, so this key can also be useful to select a certain range of color in an image for adjustment. The default 10% Matching Softness setting is arbitrary and defines a rather loose range. I often end up setting it closer to 1%.

CLOSE-UP

All Channels Are Not Created Equal

If you set an RGB image as a luma matte, the red, green, and blue channels are averaged together to determine the luminance of the overall image. However, they are not weighted evenly, because that's not how the eye sees them. Details about how to work with this fact can be found in Chapter 12.

If you find yourself wanting to use a particular channel as a luma matte, use Effect > Channel > Shift Channels; set Take Alpha From as Full On and the other three channels to whichever channel—red, green, or blue—is most effective.

Figure 6.5 Suppose you want to make a change to the distant, out-of-focus area of this shot. By selecting a prominent object in the foreground, the sweater, and adjusting the selection (bottom), you can create a matte that separates the foreground and background. (Image courtesy of Eric Escobar.)

Note that there are, in fact, three eyedropper tools in the Linear Color Key effect. The top one defines Key Color, and the other two add and subtract Matching Tolerance. I tend not to use these eyedroppers because they don't work in the Comp viewer; the main Key Color eyedropper and the Matching sliders work for me (**Figure 6.5**).

There's a hidden trick to getting better results with Linear Color Key. Because it is linear, it will pick up hues that seem unrelated. To reduce the effect of these, you can add a second instance of Linear Color Key. Under Key Operation, changing the default Key Colors setting to Keep Colors does nothing if it's the first instance except annul the effect. On the second instance, Keep Colors is unaffected by the first instance and can bring back hues that were already keyed. The one-two punch will often deliver the best result (**Figure 6.6**).

Figure 6.6 By using Linear Color Key set to Keep Colors again (left), I'm able to get rid of the extra selection areas in the background, apply the matte, and add a glow effect to just the background.

Figure 6.7 I was hoping to grab just the shadows on the floor with a difference matte applied to the image on the left using the middle image as a Difference layer. Unfortunately, subtle stuff like that tends to be indistinguishable from noise, even with clean, low-grain source.

Difference Mattes

The difference matte is a little like Santa Claus. It would be nice to believe in it because it would give so much if it really existed, but it is mostly just a fantasy that a computer can compare two images, one with a foreground figure, one without, and extract that figure cleanly. It sounds like the kind of thing computers were made to do. But not only does this require a completely locked-off shot, you'd be shocked at how much one pixel of one frame that should be identical can vary due to compression grain and subtle variations of light. Low-lit areas, in particular, tend to gray out in a way that foils this technique, which works best with saturated, differentiated color. **Figure 6.7** amply demonstrates the problem and shows that Difference keying may be useful for the crudest type of isolation, but not much more.

Color Keying: Greenscreen, Bluescreen

And now, ladies and gentlemen, the main event. Past editions of this book have taken a high-level approach to explaining the art of keying along with specific advice about Keylight, the powerful keyer from the Foundry included with After Effects, but this time around, the two are combined in a practical example of a challenging key.

Keylight is useful in keying situations beyond studio-created bluescreen or greenscreen shots. For example, you can use Keylight for removal of a blue sky (**Figure 6.8**). You wouldn't use Keylight to pull a luminance key, however, or when you're simply trying to isolate a certain color range within the shot; it really is only effective at making one of the three primary colors transparent.

Figure 6.8 Can a bright blue sky serve as an effective bluescreen? On the right day, why yes, it certainly can.

Keylight is most typically used on footage shot against a uniform, saturated, primary color background, where preservation of edge detail is of utmost importance.

To get started, make a new comp containing the blue-Scrn_mcu_HD clip. At first glance this does not look like it will be a difficult shot to key: The background is a uniform, well-lit, and fully saturated blue, and the talent is well lit, with some nice warm edge lighting. The hair is edge-lit in a contrasting color from the left, contains wispy details to preserve, and the hands move quickly, creating motion blur (**Figure 6.9**).

Figure 6.9 The plate is well-shot and contains the kind of challenges that are fun to work with: nice hair details and beautiful motion blur.

Nowadays it has become somewhat unusual to see blue-screen shots, which had their heyday in the pre-digital optical compositing era. Green is favored for digital shoots for several reasons, predominantly that it is the dominant color in the visual spectrum and therefore most cameras are able to resolve it with far more image data than is found in the blue channel, which typically has less luminance and more noise.

Oddly enough, I've always preferred blue to green. For one thing, a nicely lit blue background is soothing to the eye, whereas digital green—the hue that is pure, luminant green, a specialty color not found at any ordinary paint store—is actually the most jarring color in the spectrum, one that has become a favorite of emergency services crews and warning signs around the world. The phenomenon known as "greenscreen psychosis," in which talented actors and directors struggle on a greenscreen set, has to partly do with it being such an empty environment, but I'm willing to bet it also has something to do with the vibe of that awful color.

The following steps apply to virtually any key, with specifics about this shot:

1. **Garbage matte** any areas of the background that can easily be masked out. "Easily" means you do not have an articulated matte (you don't animate individual mask points). As a rule of thumb, limit this to what you can accomplish in about 20 minutes or less (**Figure 6.10**).

Figure 6.10 Even a quick-and-dirty garbage matte as simple as this isolates the action and eliminates the darker blue values in the corners.

This shot doesn't seem to need a garbage matte, but notice that the talent's action of raising her arms does not cover all areas of the frame, including at about 100 pixels from the left edge of the frame, 200 pixels from the right edge, and 100 pixels at the top. Notice also the slight vignette effect at the edges of the frame; move your cursor to the upper-right corner, for example, and take a look at the Info panel as you do so— you'll notice values are 10% to 15% lower in luminance than those along the edge of the talent.

If you didn't bother with a simple garbage matte in this case, you've already compromised the matte. The game is to key only the essential pixels, and those are the ones along the edge of the moving figure. Lazily keying the full frame compromises those edges by overweighting background pixels that don't matter, even on a shot as clean as this one. Draw a rectangular mask around the area containing the action as in Figure 6.10 and step through all frames of the clip to make sure no elbows are clipped out.

2. Use a side-by-side Composition and Layer view to create the **first pass** of the key with no extra adjustments.

This is a slightly new approach to this most essential step in Keylight—sampling the Screen Colour (that "u" gives away its British heritage). Before you even apply the effect, create a new workspace as follows: choose Minimal from View > Workspace (resetting it if necessary to get back to just a Timeline and a Composition viewer), and double-click the bluescreen clip in the timeline to open it in Layer view. Drag the Layer tab to one side or the other of the panel to create a new panel, so that you have two views of the clip side-by-side. Add an Effect Controls panel next to the timeline (**Figure 6.11**).

Go to a frame with some clear motion blur as well as hair detail in it, such as frame 5. Now try this. In Keylight, choose Status from the View menu. Both images will turn white, showing a solid alpha channel. In the Layer panel, toggle off the Render check box to bring back the source image. Now click the Screen Colour eyedropper and, holding down the **Alt** (**Opt**) key, drag around the blue background in the Layer view and notice what happens in the other viewer.

TIP

The side-by-side layout is so useful, you should save it as a workspace named Keying or Matte.

Figure 6.11 This layout looks redundant right now, but just wait.

Figure 6.12 You can't see it in a still figure, but by **Alt**-dragging (**Opt**-dragging) around the blue area of Layer view on the right, which is set to not render, a real-time update of Status view on the left allows you to discover the optimum background color.

Status view is an exaggerated view of the alpha channel matte. Opaque pixels are displayed as white, transparent pixels are black, and those containing any amount of transparency are gray (**Figure 6.12**). It's an easy way to see how well the background is keying (turning black) on the first pass and whether any significant holes (in gray) appear in the foreground subject.

It's suddenly apparent that what looked like a straightforward shot will be a challenging key. Although it is possible, with a little patience, to find a spot in the background that turns most of the background pixels black as in Figure 6.12, the dark areas of the shirt and the hair are nowhere near solid white. Still, having carefully chosen the best Screen Colour, you are free to move on and refine this matte.

3. Gently **refine the matte** and **preview** the result at full resolution, in full motion, against a contrasting color.

In previous editions of this book, I dutifully explained and made recommendations about the controls below Screen Colour: Screen Gain and Balance, Despill and Alpha Bias, and Screen Pre-blur. There's more information about these later in the chapter, but on the whole my advice is, don't touch these. They all have one thing in common—they change the way the matte itself is calculated—and I have come to believe that manipulating them does more harm than good.

Skip down to Screen Matte and twirl down those controls. From here down, all of the Keylight controls are working with the matte after it has already been generated. In other words, adjusting these controls is no different than applying a separate effect after Keylight to refine its matte, and that's a good thing in this case.

Raise Clip Black by dragging to the right across the value to bring it upward. Stop when you see all of the gray pixels in the background turn black in Status view. (Even though you'll also see some of the gray pixels around the hair—the ones you want to keep gray—turn black as well. We'll deal with those next.) In my attempt, I ended up with a value of 26.0, and as a rule of thumb, anything above 20 is a bit high—another reason to take more care with this matte than just pulling the key in one pass.

Now lower Clip White by dragging to the left across that value to bring it downward. Here you may find that you have to go pretty far—like down into the 50s—in order to see all of the gray or green pixels in the torso become white. I ended up with a value of 57.0. You'll also see some green pixels remaining around the edges of the figure, particularly around the wisps of hair.

The green pixels in Status view are Keylight's signal that the color values of those pixels have changed in the keying process. Focus on the wisps of hair on the light side, and switch between Final Result and Intermediate Result in the View menu. The former suppresses that blue spill that you see in the latter to the natural hair color as part of the keying process.

Intermediate Result shows the source footage with the matte applied as an alpha channel but no alteration to the RGB pixels at all, while Final Result adds color suppression as a natural by-product of Keylight's method of removing the background color. Final Result seems to be the one you want, but there's an unfortunate side effect to watch out for: It can dramatically enhance graininess in the result. **Figure 6.13** shows a before and after in which the suppression process clearly pushes pixels to a much contrastier shade even though the source is well lit footage from the RED camera. For this reason, don't let Keylight do your spill suppression for you.

Figure 6.13 Flashing the image with the exposure control at the lower right reveals a horrific amount of grain in Final Result view of this Keylight operation (left). Intermediate Result (right) omits any alteration to the source color, revealing that the original image, even flashed like this, is nicely shot, with smooth, tolerable grain.

Spill suppression will have to wait until after we're done with this key, and at this point, we're not even close. Getting that shirt to key has ruined the detail in the hair and motion of the hands. Had the talent been wearing a different costume and not moved around as much, the steps taken to this point might have resulted in a completed key, but with anything more complicated—and most effects shots seem to be much more complicated—it's now necessary to break this operation into component parts (or be painted into a corner.) Neither holes in the matte nor crunchy edges on the hair are acceptable, and right now the two are fighting one another (**Figure 6.14**).

4. This is the moment to **separate the plate for multiple passes**. In every case there are two basic ways to do this.

Figure 6.14 Closing all those little gaps in the foreground will mean destroying that hair detail if this matte is attempted in one pass.

▶ Separate one part of the foreground from the rest with a mask or other selection. For example, in this case you could rotoscope a mask around the hair, and possibly another one around the moving hands.

▶ Create multiple passes of the same matte: one as a garbage matte (or gmatte), one as a core matte (or cmatte), and the final one featuring only the isolated edge.

In this case, we know that there are prominent holes in the foreground, so the latter approach—to create at least a core matte so that the interior areas are isolated from the all-important edge—is the way to go.

This method of breaking down the shot would work with any software keyer, but we're sticking with Keylight, as it is the most powerful keyer included with After Effects and this maximizes what it can do.

a. Duplicate the layer to be keyed.

At this point, our bluescreen shot has a garbage mask and an instance of Keylight applied to it. Leave these on the upper of the two layers, rename that layer "edge matte," and turn off its visibility—we'll deal with it later.

b. Rename the lower layer "cmatte" and refine the core matte (Figure 6.15).

To begin, reset Clip Black by right-clicking on that property in the Effect controls and choosing Reset.

We're keeping our Screen Colour selection, but will now crush the matte. Switch back to Status view and lower Clip White until the torso and hair are completely filled in with white (around 66.0 may work). Now raise Clip Black all the way to one unit below the Clip White value (65.0 if the previous value was as specified).

You now have the worst matte possible, with no edge subtlety whatsoever. What possible good is this?

Switch to Intermediate Result. Yep, horrible matte. Now close the Keylight controls and apply the Simple Choker effect. Toggle Alpha Channel view in the Composition viewer (**Alt+4/Opt+4**) and take a snapshot (**Shift+F5** or **F6**, **F7**, or **F8** all work).

Raise the Choke Matte value into the low double digits—say, around 15.00. The matte shrinks. Press F5 to toggle back and forth with the un-choked matte, and make sure that all of the choked matte's edges are several pixels inside that of the unchoked matte. This is important: There must be no edge pixels in the core matte that overlap with those of the edge matte.

Figure 6.15 A heavily choked source matte, turning all areas of the alpha channel either white or black, makes a good core matte to sit behind the edge matte.

TIP

Switch a RAM preview to Alpha Channel view (**Alt+4/Opt+4**) and the cache is preserved; you can watch a real-time preview of the alpha channel without re-rendering the preview.

Figure 6.16 This isn't how the actual comp looks; it's showing the core matte as the white center with the plate translucently revealing that nicely isolated edge, where all efforts are to be focused.

Figure 6.17 Blue matte line around the edges.

This matte may behave better if it's softer—for now, you can take my word for that, since we're not yet putting it into use. As an extra precaution, apply Channel Blur and raise Alpha Blurriness to 15.0. This provides an extra threshold between the chunky core and the fine edge (**Figure 6.16**).

c. Kill the spill.

Leaving the View on Intermediate Result is great for avoiding side effects such as enhanced graininess, but the layer almost always then requires some sort of spill suppression. More often than not, you have to do this anyway.

There's a Spill Suppressor effect in After Effects; how great it would be if all you had to do was sample the color, change Color Accuracy from Faster to Better, leave Suppression at 100, and be done. But heck, you can crank Suppression up to 200 if you want (who knew?) and still see your talent looking green (or in this case, blue) around the gills (**Figure 6.17**).

You could also use the Edge Colour Correction in Keylight, but it has no effect other than in Final Result mode, and—gotcha—that's likely to mess with your footage too much, remember?

Spill suppression is a big enough deal that it merits its own section below. The key (please excuse the pun) is not to simply suppress or desaturate it but in fact to bring it back around to its natural hue. For that you need an effect a lot like Hue/Saturation and the skills to use it (coming up).

5. Evaluate the shot in full motion.

How are the details holding up? And how does the foreground look in the actual composite? It's easy to get so wrapped up in creating the perfect matte that you forget that some problems are harder to spot against some backgrounds. If she's headed for a bluish environment, why trouble yourself too much with spill suppression? Would more blending of the background into the foreground (later in this chapter in the "Edge Selection" section) or even light wrap help sell this composite (**Figure 6.18**)?

Figure 6.18 At this stage, prior to any color matching, the detail is well preserved but the matte lines along the torso and arms, in particular, remain.

6. **Isolate and refine further.**

Do you need to isolate the hair for its own keying pass? How about those motion-blurred hands? Are there holes in the matte, or problems with the core pass? Does the talent, heaven forbid, make direct contact with the background, for example lying down on the colored floor?

For these types of issues, create *holdout mattes*.

Keylight for Color Keying

The core of Keylight is *screen matte* generation, and as mentioned, the most essential step is choosing the exact color to key. From that, Keylight makes weighted comparisons between its saturation and hue and that of each pixel, as detailed in **Table 6.1**. From this, you see that the ideal background is distinct and saturated.

CLOSE-UP

Holdout Matte

A *holdout matte* isolates an area of an image for separate treatment. I recommend that you think of a color key as an isolated edge matte surrounded by two holdout mattes: one for the core, one for the background. Details on creating these can be found ahead in the "Fine Tuning and Problem Solving" section.

TABLE 6.1 How Keylight Makes Its Key Decisions

COMPARED TO SCREEN COLOR, PIXEL IS	KEYLIGHT WILL
of a different hue	consider it foreground, making it opaque
of a similar hue and more saturated	key it out completely, making it transparent
of a similar hue but less saturated	subtract a mathematically weighted amount of the screen color and make it semitransparent

The controls atop Keylight (from Screen Colour down to Screen Preblur) alter the actual generation of the matte. Everything from Screen Matte down adjusts the result of that first step.

My current advice is to leave all other top controls in Keylight alone, but in case you're curious about them, following is a bit of extra information on how each works.

Screen Gain

The ideal Screen Gain setting is 100, no change from the default. This adjustment is compensation for a poorly lit matte or a foreground contaminated with background color. While raising it may make the matte channel look better, you are also likely to see increased color grain and lost edge detail with values above the default. The alternative with fewer side effects is to raise Clip Black.

Screen Gain boosts (or reduces) the saturation of each pixel before comparing it to the screen color. This effectively adds more desaturated background pixels into the keyed color range.

Screen Balance

Keylight relies on one of the three RGB color values being the dominant background color. It is even more effective when it knows whether one of the two remaining colors is more prevalent in the background, and which one. Screen Balance makes use of a dominant secondary background color.

The software automatically sets a balance of 95% with bluescreens (which typically contain a good deal of green) and leaves it at 50% for greenscreens (which tend to be more monochromatic). If you want to try adjusting it yourself, try alternate settings of either 5.0 or 95.0 to take it close to one or the other secondary color.

A Rosco Ultimatte Blue screen contains quite a bit of green—much more than red, unless improperly lit. Ultimatte Green screens, meanwhile, are nearly pure green (**Figure 6.19**).

Figure 6.19 The Rosco colors: Ultimatte Blue, Ultimatte Green, and Ultimatte Super Blue. Blue is not pure blue but double the amount of green, which in turn is double the amount of red. Ultimatte Green is more pure, with only a quarter the amount of red and no blue whatsoever. Lighting can change their hue (as does converting them for print in this book).

Bias

The Bias settings color-correct the image by scaling the primary color component up or down (enhancing or reducing its difference from the other two components). The Foundry recommends that in most cases you leave Alpha Bias at the default and that you click the Despill Bias eyedropper on a well-lit skin tone to be preserved; despill pivots around this value.

Bias has the unpleasant side effect of significantly increasing graininess. If this happens to your footage, try other despill methods discussed later in this chapter.

Refinement

When you spot an area that looks like a candidate for refinement, save (to hold an undo point should you need to use File > Revert), zoom in, and create a region of interest around the area in question.

Now take a look at the tools provided by Keylight to address some common problems.

Clip White, Black, Rollback

The double-matte method (core and edge) eliminates a lot of the tug of war that otherwise exists between a solid foreground and subtle edges. Even with this advantage, both mattes may require adjustments to the Clip White or Clip Black controls.

Keep the largest possible difference (or *delta*, if you prefer) between these two settings, as this is where all of the gray, semitransparent alpha pixels live. The closer the two numbers get, the closer you are to a bitmap alpha channel, in which each pixel is pure black or white—a very bad thing indeed (**Figure 6.20**).

If you push too far, restore back toward the initial matte with Clip Rollback. Its value is the number of pixels from the edge that are rolled back relative to the original, unclipped screen matte. So if your edges were subtle but sizzling on the first pass, and removing noise from the matte hardened them, then this tool may restore subtlety.

TIP

Hold down **Alt** (**Opt**) to center a zoom around your cursor.

Figure 6.20 Here's how the hair looks without a separated edge matte. Not nice.

**Chroma Subsampling:
The 411 on 4:1:1, 4:2:2, and 4:2:0**

Video images are RGB on your computer, but video devices themselves use Y'CrCb, the digital equivalent of YUV. Y' is the luminance or brightness signal (or "luma"); Cr and Cb are color-difference signals (roughly corresponding to red-cyan and blue-yellow)—you could call them chrominance or "chroma."

It turns out that the human eye is much more particular about gradations in luma than chroma, as is amply demonstrated in **Figure 6.21**.

The standard types of digital video compression take advantage of this fact. **Figure 6.22** shows the difference between straight RGB and 4:2:2 compression, which is common to popular formats including DVCPRO HD and DVCPRO50, ProRes 422 and cameras such as the Sony F900, as well as 4:1:1, which is used by DVCPRO and NTSC DV. Almost as bad for keying purposes is 4:2:0, the MPEG-2 (DVD), HDV, and PAL DV format.

As you might imagine, chromatic compression is far less than ideal for color keying (**Figure 6.23**), hence the workarounds in this section.

Figure 6.21 The source (top left) can be converted to YUV with Channel Combiner and the UV (chroma) or Y (luminance) blurred individually, then round-tripped back to RGB with Channel Combiner again. With heavy blur to the color data (top right) the image is still clear, albeit stylized, if the luminance is untouched, but blur the luminance and leave the color and the result is far less recognizable (lower left).

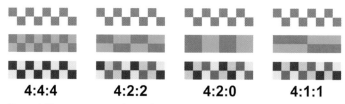

Figure 6.22 4:4:4 is just pixels, no chroma subsampling, where 4:2:2 and 4:1:1 group the nearest neighboring pixels, giving them identical luminance according to the patterns shown here.

Figure 6.23 Key a 4:1:1 image (left) and Keylight's Status view (right) clearly shows the horizontal blocks associated with that type of chroma subsampling (images are shown at 400%).

Noise Suppression

For seriously sizzling mattes, Keylight includes a Screen Pre-blur option that I would reserve for footage with a clearly evident noise problem, such as heavy compression. Blurring source footage before keying adds inaccuracy and is something of a desperation move. The footage itself does not appear blurred, but the matte does.

A better alternative for a fundamentally sound matte is Screen Softness, under the Screen Matte controls. This control blurs the screen matte itself, so it has a much better chance of retaining detail than a pre-blur approach. As shown in Chapter 3, edges in nature are slightly soft, and a modest amount of softness is appropriate even with a perfectly healthy matte.

The Despot cleanup tools are meant to fill matte holes, but at high levels they add blobbiness, so they are rarely useful. An alternative approach, particularly with DV formats (which, by the way, are guaranteed to add compression noise and are not recommended for bluescreen and greenscreen work), is to do as follows:

1. Convert the footage to YUV using Channel Combiner (the From pop-up menu). This will make the clip look very strange, because your monitor displays images as RGB. Do not be alarmed (**Figure 6.24**).

Figure 6.24 This is how an image converted to YUV should look on an RGB monitor—weird. The point is not how YUV looks, but what you can do to adjust it before using Channel Combiner to round-trip it back to RGB.

2. Apply Channel Blur to the green and blue channels only, at modest amounts. To gauge this, examine each channel as you work—press **Alt+2** (**Opt+2**) or **Alt+3** (**Opt+3**) while zoomed in on a noisy area. Make sure Repeat Edge Pixels is checked.

3. Round-trip back from YUV to RGB, using a second instance of Channel Combiner.

4. Apply Keylight.

Matte Choke

Besides mismatched lighting, fringing (excess edge opacity) and choking (lost edge detail) are the most common tells of a greenscreen comp. Screen Grow/Shrink deals with this issue directly. Don't be afraid to use it, gently (a setting of around 1.0, or one pixel, won't do your matte much harm, especially if combined with a bit of matte softness).

This is not the last resort for choking and spreading a matte; alternatives follow in "Fine Tuning and Problem Solving."

Spill Suppression

Keylight suppresses *color spill* (foreground pixels contaminated by reflected color from the background) as part of the keying operation when displaying the final result. Thus spill-kill can be practically automatic if you pull a good initial key.

There are a surprising number of cases in which Keylight's spill suppression is not what you want, for the following reasons:

▶ Dramatic hue shifts occur to items whose colors are anywhere near green (for example, cyan) or opposite green (for example, magenta). It's challenging enough to keep green off of a green set, let alone its neighboring and opposite hues.

▶ These hue shifts can also add graininess, even to footage that was shot uncompressed and has little or no source grain.

In **Figure 6.25**, notice how the whole shape of the girl's face seems to change due to the removal of highlights via spill suppression.

Figure 6.25 Her face doesn't even look the same without the highlights reflected with the green. Even worse, at this magnification, it's easy to see that the amount of grain noise has increased significantly (right). It's a definite case for pulling the matte on one pass and applying spill suppression separately.

Should Keylight's spill suppression become unwieldy or otherwise useless for the preceding reasons, there is an easy out: Ordinarily, the View is set to Final Result, but set it to Intermediate Result for the matte applied to the alpha without any change to RGB. The CC Composite effect does the same thing, eliminating all RGB changes from preceding effects but keeping the alpha.

Keylight itself also includes spill suppression tools, under Edge Colour Correction, that influence only the edge pixels. Enable its check box and adjust the controls below, softening or growing the edge as needed to increase the area of influence. Sometimes adjusting Luminance or Saturation of edges is a quick fix.

The next section, which goes beyond this tool, describes better ways to kill spill.

Fine Tuning and Problem Solving

The key here is to break it down. The above steps apply to most ordinary keying situations, but extraordinary ones happen all the time. The trick is to find the areas that are closer to ordinary, deal with those, and isolate the extraordinary stuff separately. In this section we focus on how to break apart a key with various types of holdout mattes and keep procedural keys effective.

Although each shot is different, there are really only a few challenges that consistently come up with a color matte:

▶ Lighting: If the shot was not lit properly, everything that follows will be much more difficult.

▶ Image quality: Bluescreen and greenscreen keys put footage quality to the test, and the worst cameras are those that lose the most data right at the time of capture. Mini DV cameras used to be the main culprits, but nowadays it is sadly the mighty DSLR that is most often inappropriately used to shoot effects plates.

These two points are determined at the shoot itself; for more about that, see the next section, "Shoot for the Perfect Matte."

▶ Fine detail such as hair, motion, or lens blur (**Figure 6.26, top row**).

▶ Costume contamination: shiny, reflective, or transparent subjects, or those simply containing colors close to that of the background, can present a fun keying challenge but can also turn out to be more of a nightmare (**Figure 6.26, bottom left**).

▶ Set contact is always a huge challenge, whether simply a full-body shot including feet or talent interacting with objects painted green, sitting on a green stool, or lying on the green floor.

Figures 6.26 Fun challenges you may encounter when pulling a color key include wispy hair (top left), motion blur (top right), contamination of foreground elements by the background color (bottom left), and shadows (bottom right).

▶ Shadows are typically all or nothing—one either carefully lights to keep them or needs to be prepared to remove them, despite that they are by their very nature areas of low contrast and difficult to key (**Figure 6.26, bottom right**).

These require separate holdout passes in order to be keyed, and the really stubborn situations may even require roto (Chapter 7).

Holdout Matte

Check out grnScrn_mcu_HD on the book's disc—this time it's the yellow stripes in the shirt that wreak havoc due to their similarity to green. There's no way to get a good key of the hair without pulling that key on a separate pass—so how exactly is that done?

Create a garbage matte—a mask—around all the hair edges only, carefully animating it so that they are fully isolated and nothing is missed. This layer then gets its own key using the same criteria and steps as you would use to derive the main matte. The Clip White and Black settings are much more mild than for the overall matte, allowing more detail.

That's clear enough—the place where artists sometimes get confused is then combining this with the main matte. Once this matte is complete, copy its mask and all keyframes and paste them on the main matte layers, but choose Subtract so that they hold out the inverse area. Now—and this is the step that's easily missed—switch the hair matte layer's blending mode to Alpha Add. This causes the mask and its inverse to blend together seamlessly without leaving a gap along the semitransparent edges (**Figure 6.27**).

Procedural Garbage Matte

Often the background is anything but uniform and the action is fast, so making a garbage matte to isolate the edge is quite a chore. In such cases, the same process that was used to create the core matte above can also be used to create a garbage matte, or gmatte, without drawing more than an elementary mask.

TIP

If a key requires several holdout mattes, this can become a bit heavy to manage. You do have the option to link Mask Shape properties with an expression (Chapter 10) so that if you change the mask animation in the holdout matte you don't have to remember to recopy the keyframes.

Figure 6.27 The mask is applied to the top layer to hold out the hair for a separate pass (top left), and the master layer has the same mask, inverted (or in Subtract mode). A telltale hairline appears where the two mattes overlap (top right) until the upper layer is set to Alpha Add mode (lower left).

The clip from Figure 6.27 can be garbage matted procedurally in this manner. Just as with the cmatte, create a hard, chewy matte that pushes all of the background pixels to black and the foreground to white. Now spread that matte using one of the following methods.

Simple Choker allows you to spread the alpha channel using a negative number. You can push it hard and even use more than one instance if the 100-pixel limit gets in your way, as it can with garbage mattes.

Minimax is the choice if Simple Choker isn't effective enough. It provides a quick way to spread or choke pixel data, even without alpha channel information, and it has a powerful effect. It can also operate on individual channels of luminance.

Matte Choker sounds more pro than Simple Choker but it's really just unnecessarily complicated.

Now comes the part you won't like: Create three duplicates of the plate and label them, top to bottom as gmatte, edge-matte and cmatte, then precomp them. The reason for this is that the next step requires it.

Set the blending mode of that gmatte you just spread, the top layer, to Stencil Alpha. The layer disappears but its alpha channel cuts all the way through the comp, like—a stencil! **Figure 6.28** shows why it's necessary to precomp; otherwise, the stencil operates on the background as well.

Figure 6.28 This is a great way to isolate an edge without hand-animating the garbage matte. The top layer is another crushed dirty matte that has been spread with Simple Choker with a value of −100.00. If it's not enough you can use two instances of Simple Choker or Minimax. Stencil Alpha blend mode then applies the result to the layers below.

Now once you refine the core matte according to the Color Keying section above, the edge matte pass is truly as isolated as it can be, leading to a much more effective result or your money back. Actually, if you're not done at that point, it must mean you need holdout passes for specific areas of frame. Keep breaking it down.

Figure 6.29 Mind the gaps; choking and spreading a matte, or using tools to do so automatically, such as the third-party Key Correct tools, is likely to close small gaps.

Close Holes

Suppose you can't close a hole in the core matte using just Keylight. You can close them by choking, then spreading the matte as follows:

1. Choke (garbage matte) or Spread (core matte) the holes until they disappear.

2. Spread or Choke (the opposite of the previous step) an equivalent or greater amount.

This will of course destroy any edge subtlety, which is why it only works well on a core or garbage matte. It will also cause small gaps near an outside edge to close (**Figure 6.29**), in which case you have to rotoscope. It can help to use the Roto Brush (Chapter 7) or track in a paint stroke (Chapter 8).

Edge Selection

Sometimes it's simpler to just select the edge and subtly blur the blend between foreground and background using that selection. **Figure 6.30** shows a comp in which it would be simpler to soften matte lines rather than choke the matte, and add subtle light wrap.

Here's how it's done:

1. **Apply Shift Channels**. Set Take Alpha From to Full On and all three color channels to Alpha.

2. **Apply Find Edges** (often mistaken for a useless psychedelic effect because, as with Photoshop, it appears in the Stylize menu and many goofy artists of the early 1990s thought it would be cool to apply it to an entire color image). Check the Invert box for an edge highlighted in white.

Minimax can help choke or spread this edge matte since it's luminance data, not an alpha channel. The default setting under Operation in this effect is Maximum, which spreads the white edge pixels by the amount specified in the Radius setting. Minimum chokes the edge in the same manner. If the result appears a little crude, an additional Fast Blur will soften it (Figure 6.30).

TIP

A useful third-party alternative to Minimax is Erodilation from ObviousFX (www.obviousfx.com). It can help do heavier choking (eroding) and hole filling (dilating), and its controls are simple and intuitive (choose Erode or Dilate from the Operation menu and the channel—typically Alpha).

Figure 6.30 An edge matte can be used to blur background and foreground together, or to match the intensity and saturation to the background. The matte can itself be softened with a blur, Minimax, set to Maximum and Color, can be used to grow the matte by increasing the Radius setting.

3. **Apply the result via a luma matte to an adjustment layer.** You should not need to precomp before doing so.

You can then use Fast Blur to soften the blend area between the foreground and background, which often works better than simply softening a chewy matte. A Levels adjustment will darken or brighten the composited edge to better blend it. Hue/Saturation can be used to desaturate the edge, similar to using a gray edge replacement color in Keylight.

Color Spill

I promised earlier to share an alternative to the tools that simply suppress color spill to gray, using the Hue/Saturation effect as follows.

1. Apply Effect > Color > Hue/Saturation.

2. Under Channel Control, choose the background primary (Greens or Blues).

3. This will sound odd, but raise the Saturation value for that channel to 100.0.

4. Adjust the Channel Range sliders until all spill is pushed to 100.0 saturation (**Figure 6.31**).

Figure 6.31 By maxing saturation in the Greens, it's easier to adjust the range to encompass the green spill on the side of the shirt but leave out most of the yellow stripes.

5. Now try some mixture of the following to eliminate spill:

   ▶ Lower the Saturation (still on the individual color channel) somewhere from −40.0 to −80.0.

   ▶ Shift the Hue between about 30 and 50 degrees in the warmer direction of skin tones. Positive values (clockwise) produce a bluescreen; negative values (counter-clockwise) produce a greenscreen.

This combination of desaturation and hue shift with a carefully targeted range should do the trick once you get the hang of using the Channel Range, which is why it helps to crank Saturation at first. The inside rectangular sliders are the core range, the outside, triangular sliders determine the threshold area between the two sliders on each end. It's usually a good idea to give the selection range a good bit of thresholding (**Figure 6.32**).

There will be cases where it is impossible not to contaminate some part of the costume or set with spill suppression; for example, a cyan-colored shirt will change color when the actor is corrected for green. The above method is a better work-around than most of the automated tools (especially Keylight itself), but there are cases where you might have to add some loose roto to isolate the contaminated bits and adjust them separately.

Shoot for the Perfect Matte

Here are a few steps to take to ensure a good matte if you happen to be on set or, even better, involved in preproduction.

The Camera

Not all digital cameras are ideal for shooting a greenscreen or bluescreen, and with the recent advent of the DSLR, we have a prime example of a camera that can shoot a lovely looking image that does not hold up so well for effects work. Since the last version of this book, hundreds of thousands of DSLR cameras have entered the world, and they are capable of shooting high-definition video that can look incredibly cinematic and gorgeous, if well shot.

The reason DSLR footage looks so good has mostly to do with the optics. Pair this camera with a high-quality lens and the lens resolves an excellent image, which the sensor is able to capture at full HD—but not without throwing away every other line of data, trashing data that is essential to a clean edge. While a still photo from a DSLR such as the Canon 5D or 7D is a dream to key, the sensor is not capable of streaming video at 24 or more fps without drastically reducing the amount of data being produced before it ever leaves the sensor.

Someday, a camera like this will be available that won't simply melt down when shooting a lightly compressed HD clip. Meanwhile, there are other video cameras that produce much better effects footage if it's well lit and shot. RED and the new (as of this writing) Arri Alexa are two cameras that create effects plates you would use on a movie of any budget. You can rent these cameras inexpensively.

After Effects CS5 even has the means to work natively with RED .r3d files so you can key them in their full source color space at full 4K (or more) resolution. The previous version of After Effects could import an .r3d, but any attempt to key it natively would inevitably run into the memory limit that is no longer applicable in a 64-bit application. By keying an .r3d file natively at full resolution, you get the best possible matte even in the likely case that you will scale the plate down to a more reasonable HD size later on.

The bottom line about cameras is to choose the least compressed recording format possible and to work with someone (or *be* someone) who has created effects footage on that camera before and knows how to light for it.

On Set

If you have the opportunity to supervise on set, I highly recommend it. Be careful to bring a good bedside manner and refrain from disrupting the proceedings, develop the best possible relationship with the director of photography, and discreetly take as many reference images and clips with your DSLR as you can. It's pretty great to get out from behind the desk and have an adventure.

A hard *cyclorama*, or *cyc* (rhymes with "like") is far preferable to soft materials such as paper or cloth, especially if the floor is in shot. If you can't rent a stage that has one, the next best thing might be to invest in a roll of floor covering and paint it, to get the smooth transition from floor to wall, as in **Figure 6.33** (assuming the floor is in shot).

Regarding the floor, don't let anyone walk across it in street shoes, which will quickly contaminate it with very visible dust. There are white shoe-cover booties often used specifically to avoid this, and you can also lay down big pieces of cardboard for the crew to use setting up. Be pedantic about this if you're planning to key shadows.

NOTES

If you end up being handed DSLR footage for effects usage, don't despair. The image quality is still far above Mini DV, which was as ubiquitous just a few short years ago.

Figure 6.33 On a set with no hard cyclorama, you can create the effect of one—the curve where the wall meets the floor—using a soft bluescreen instead. It doesn't behave as well (note the hotspot on the curve), but it will certainly do in a pinch and is preferable to removing the seam caused by the corner between the wall and floor.

Lighting is, of course, best left to an experienced director of photography (DP) and gaffer (bonus points if they've shot effects before and understand the process even a little), and any kind of recommendations for a physical lighting setup are beyond the scope of this book. Because you'll spend more time examining this footage than anyone else, here are a few things to watch for on set:

Figure 6.34 The larger the set, the more diffuse white lights you'll see in the grid, to eliminate hotspots in the background.

▶ Light levels on the foreground and background must have matching intensity, within a stop or so of one another. A spot light meter tells you if they do.

▶ Diffuse lights are great for the background (often a set of large 1K, 2K, or 5K lights with a silk sock covering them, **Figure 6.34**), but fluorescent Kino Flo lights have become increasingly popular as they've become more flexible and powerful. With fluorescents you may need more instruments to light the same space, but they consume relatively low power and generate very little heat.

▶ Maintain space, along with separate lighting setups, between the foreground and background. Ten feet as a minimum is a good rule of thumb.

▶ Avoid unintentional shadows, but by all means light for shadows if you can get them and the floor is clean. Note that this works only when the final shot also has a flat floor. Fill lights typically mess up floor shadows by creating extras.

The Right Color?

The digital age lets shooters play fast and loose with what they consider a keyable background. You will likely be asked (or attempt) to pull mattes from a blue sky, from a blue swimming pool (like I did for *Pirates of the Caribbean*), or from other monochrome backgrounds. However, you're probably asking for trouble if you paint your blue or green background with a can of paint from the hardware store; they're generally designed to be more neutral—grayer and less saturated. Rosco and Composite Components designs paints specifically for the purpose of color keying, and those are the ones to go with if when painting a set.

How different must the background color be from the foreground? The answer is, not as much as you probably think. I have had little trouble keying a girl in a light blue dress or a soldier in a dress blue uniform. This is where it can be hugely helpful to have any type of capture device on set—even a point-and-shoot camera—to pull a test matte.

Shoot a lot of reference of the set, including anything and everything you can think of. If you plan to recreate the lighting, it's also a great idea to take HDR images using bracketed exposures—the same image shot at various f-stops. Photoshop includes the File > Automate > Merge to HDR function to combine these into a 32 bpc linear light image.

▶ Where possible, avoid having talent sit, kneel, or lie down directly on the floor or any other keyable surface; not only does an astonishing wash of shadow and reflection result, but there is no realistic interaction with the surface, which is especially noticeable if they are to end up on carpet, grass, or the beach. If possible, use real sets and furniture in these cases.

▶ Here's a novel idea: Shoot exteriors outside where possible, forgoing the set and controlled lighting environment for chromatic tarps and the sun, which is a hard lighting source to fake.

▶ Record as close to uncompressed as possible. Even "prosumer" HD cameras such as the Sony EX-3 often have an HDMI port that outputs live, uncompressed signal; pair this with a workstation or laptop containing a video capture card and high-speed storage and you can get 4:2:2 or better practically for free.

▶ Shoot clean plate: a few frames of the set only, particularly on a locked-off shot and each time a new setup occurs.

In this day and age of quick camera to laptop transfer, it's great to have the means on the set to pull test comps; they not only help ensure that the result will key properly, they give the Director of Photography (DP) and talent a better idea of where they are, and where they can lead to more motivated light from the DP and more motivated action from the talent, who otherwise must work in a void.

Conclusion

Not even mentioned in this chapter is Red Giant's Primatte Keyer, most certainly my favorite Keylight alternative. Particularly for cases where the matte is uneven or of a non-standard color, Primatte (demo on the disc) is worth a look.

The next chapter offers hands-on advice for situations where procedural matte generation must be abandoned in favor of hand matte generation, also known as rotoscoping. There are also situations where rotoscope techniques, and in particular the Roto Brush tool, can be used to augment a difficult key.

Rotoscoping and Paint

It's a small world, but I wouldn't want to paint it.

—Steven Wright

Rotoscoping and Paint

Effective rotoscoping has always been about combining a variety of techniques, and Roto Brush is, in After Effects CS5, a novel addition to the conventional bag of tricks. *Rotoscoping* (or roto) is simply the process of adjusting a shot frame by frame (generally with the use of masks, introduced in Chapter 3). Cloning and filling using paint tools are variations on this task.

After Effects is not exactly famed as a bread-and-butter rotoscoping tool, yet many artists use it effectively for just that purpose. Combine paint and roto with tracking and keying, or let the software do so for you with Roto Brush, and you have in After Effects a powerful rotoscoping suite.

Here are some overall guidelines for roto and paint:

▶ Your basic options are as follows, from most automated and least difficult to the higher-maintenance techniques:

   ▶ Roto Brush

   ▶ keying (color and contrast)

   ▶ motion-tracked masks and paint

   ▶ hand-animated masks (conventional roto)

   ▶ paint via individual brushstrokes

▶ Paint is generally the last resort, although it can in certain cases be most expedient.

▶ Keyframe deliberately: My own ideal is to use as few keyframes as possible. Some artists keyframe every frame. Either approach is valid for a given mask or section, depending mostly on whichever seems less challenging in that instance.

▶ Review constantly, and keep your system and project as responsive as possible to support this process.

NOTES

Rotoscoping was invented by Max Fleischer, the animator responsible for bringing Betty Boop and Popeye to life, and patented in 1917. It involved tracing over live-action movement, a painstaking form of motion capture. The term has come to stand for any frame-by-frame manipulation of a moving image.

▶ Notice opportunities to switch approaches, and combine strategies, as none of them is perfect.

It can be satisfying to knock out a seamless animated matte, and once you have the tools under your fingertips it can even be pleasant to chill out and roto for a few hours, or perhaps even as a full-time occupation.

Roto Brush

Wouldn't it be great if your software could learn to roto so effectively that you never had to articulate a matte by hand again? That's the lofty goal of Roto Brush. Although the version making its debut in After Effects CS5 doesn't quite deliver at that level, once you get the hang of it you may find it a useful component of the matting process, reducing rather than omitting the need to roto by hand. It may also lead you generally to create and use articulated selections more often for tasks where complete isolation isn't needed. This tool can't magically erase the world's rotoscoping troubles, but it opens new possibilities for using selections that you might not otherwise consider.

To get a feel for how Roto Brush works, let's work with a fairly challenging clip that shows strengths and limitations of this tool. Create a new composition containing the "gatoraid" clip found in the 07_roto_gator folder on the book's disc, which is 23.976 in the nonsquare DVCPRO HD 720 format. Make sure that you're at full resolution (**Ctrl+J/Cmd+J**) and view the clip with Pixel Aspect Ratio Correction on ▦ (head back to Chapter 1 if you are confused about pixel aspect ratios).

Double-click to open the layer in the Layer viewer. If you haven't previewed the footage already, scrub through it and notice what a challenge procedural removal of the gator from the water presents. For example, you can flip through the color channels (**Alt+1**, **2**, **3/Opt+1**, **2**, **3**) and notice how little contrast there is in any of them. That neutral-colored gator is well camouflaged in neutral greenish water. In no way could a luma or color key help here.

Go to a frame somewhere in the middle of the clip, such as frame 57. Click the Roto Brush tool ▨ in the toolbar to make it active. Scale the brush if necessary by **Ctrl**-dragging (**Cmd**-dragging) the brush in the Layer panel. Make it about 50% of the size of the nose to stay well within the gator's boundaries (**Figure 7.1**, left).

Now comes the strange part: Paint the skeletal form of he head, never touching its edges. Travel down the mouth and loop back to the forehead, like you're sketching the shape of the head within its boundaries (**Figure 7.1**, middle). As soon as you release, the tool shows the *segmentation boundary* in pink, its first guess as to where the foreground boundaries may be. Notice that some areas of the head were missed on this first pass, a little bit of the water may have also been inadvertently selected, and it's a little unclear where the head disappears in the water (**Figure 7.1**, right).

Now improve upon the initial selection just on this one frame by adding to and subtracting from it. First fill any areas of the snout, head, and neck by painting those in. You can travel closer to the edge this time, but if you paint into the background at all, undo before painting any more strokes and try again. Eliminate any other background included in the original boundary by **Alt**- or **Opt**-swiping those areas, again being careful not to cross

TIP

The idea when swiping with Roto Brush is explicitly not to paint along the outline to refine the edge. If it's a human figure being roto-brushed, paint the appropriate form of a stick figure. If it's a head, draw a circle; if a car, just draw along the center of its structure, around its wheels, and so on.

Figure 7.1 Size the Roto Brush by **Ctrl**- or **Cmd**-dragging (left), then paint the form of the foreground inside its boundaries (middle) to get an initial segmentation boundary, outlined in pink (right).

the foreground edges. The result on this frame may look lumpy and bumpy, but it should at least be reasonably complete (**Figure 7.2**) within a pixel or two of the actual edge.

Thoroughly defining the shape on this base frame gives you the best chance of holding the matte over time without an inordinate number of corrections. Press the spacebar and watch as the matte updates on each frame. Watch closely as more of the body emerges from the water. Roto Brush adapts to these changes but you have to add the detail that emerges from out of the water at the back of the neck, somewhere after frame 60. Add that detail on a couple of consecutive frames, until you see it picked up on the following frames.

Work your way backward in time from the base frame and you'll notice that the head remains selected; the only trouble seems to be the highlight areas of the waves that ripple along the edges (**Figure 7.3**). Leave these alone until they propagate over more than a single frame, picking up a whole section of water. Any details that simply come and go on a single frame are best handled with Refine Matte settings described in the next section.

As errors do occur and propagate, *look for the frame closest to the base frame*, where the first errors occur. Any fixes you make there will affect the following frames, but it doesn't work in the other direction. So if, for example, you fixed the boundary way out at frame 75, you would then also need to go back and fix the preceding frames, because the changes only propagate in one direction, outward from the base frame (backward and forward in time).

By frame 75, where the gator fully emerges from the water for the tasty snack, the segmentation is definitely off target, as the mouth is now open and the edges heavily motion-blurred (**Figure 7.4**). When a shape changes this fundamentally, it's probably time to create a new span, that set of light gray adjacent frames, by creating a new base frame. It's the appropriate thing to do as a figure radically changes its profile. Drag the end frame of the span to wherever you want it, just as you would the end frame of a layer, and create a new base frame at the point that contains the clearest and most exposed frame of the next

Figure 7.2 Carefully **Alt**- or **Opt**-paint any areas where the segmentation boundary includes background.

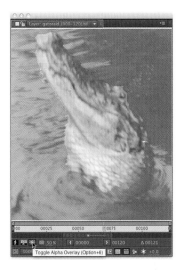

Figure 7.3 Moving a few frames ahead, and viewing in Alpha Overlay mode, it's apparent that reflections in the water are creeping in and darker areas of the head are being masked out. Instead of fixing these, wait and see how they improve with Refine Matte settings.

Figure 7.4 By this frame the figure is so different from the source that it is probably time to limit the previous span and begin again with a new base frame.

SCRIPT

Purview is included on the book's disc in the scripts folder and via download from Adobe Exchange. It places the Alternate RAM Preview setting right in a UI panel so you can change the number of preceding frames previewed without digging into Preferences. You might create a workspace for Roto Brush with this panel open and the Layer panel prominent.

section of action—perhaps frame 78, in this case. It probably goes without saying that the spans do extend in both directions from the base frame.

RAM preview shortcuts have been augmented for the purpose of working with Roto Brush spans. **Alt+0 (Opt+0)** (on the numeric keypad) begins the preview a specific number of frames before the current one—the default 5 frame setting can be changed in Preferences > Previews.

Strengths & Limitations

Because Roto Brush isn't a one-trick pony relying on anything so simple as contrast (like a luma or extract matte), color (like Linear Color Key or Keylight), or even automated tracking of pixels (Timewarp), it can offer surprising success in situations where other tools fail completely.

Move forward in the example clip and you hit the type of section that gives Roto Brush the greatest trouble. The gator's mouth snaps rapidly open and shut as the body turns, causing heavy motion blur and small details (the teeth) and a gap between the jaws to emerge. All of these—rapid changes of form, blur, fine detail, and gaps—are difficult for this tool to track (**Figure 7.5**).

Figure 7.5 Even on the base frame, the blurred edges of the lower jaw and the gap in the mouth are not easy to define within a pixel or two of the edge, and on the following frame (right), that gap and the ends of the snout lose detail.

Once you have as much of the segmentation boundary as possible within a couple pixels of the foreground boundary (**Figure 7.6**), you can improve the quality of the resulting selection quite a bit by enabling Refine Matte under the

Figure 7.6 The unrefined matte can look pretty rough, but don't waste time fixing it with more brushstrokes; instead, work on the Refine Matte settings for a much better result (right) with the exact same outline.

Roto Brush controls in the Effect Controls. The effect is set automatically as soon as you paint a stroke, but the refine setting is off because it takes longer to calculate and actually changes the segmentation boundary. Work with it off; preview with it on.

It's easy to miss the Propagation settings at the top of the Roto Brush effect, but it's worth working with these, as they change how the matte itself is calculated. There's a huge difference between changing Edge Detection from Balanced to either Favor Predicted Edges (which uses data from the previous frame) or Favor Current Edges (which works only with the current frame). Neither is absolute—there is always information used from previous and current frames—but predicted edges tend to work better in a case like this, where the contrast at the object boundary is weak.

The Smooth and Reduce Chatter settings are most helpful to reduce boiling edges; of course, there's only so much they'll do before you lose detail, but with a foreground subject that has few pointy or skinny edge details, you can increase it without creating motion artifacts. If you're trying to remove the object from its background entirely, edge decontamination is remarkably powerful and can be increased in power. And when it's time to render, you can enable Higher Quality under Motion Blur if your subject has this kind of motion (**Figure 7.7**).

TIP

The Use Alternate Color Estimation option can make a big difference in some cases as to how well Roto Brush holds an edge.

Figure 7.7 These settings resulted in the improvement shown in Figure 7.6.

The overall point about Roto Brush is as follows. Were you to rely on it to single-handedly remove the gator from the swamp in the example shot, you'd put in quite a bit of work and quickly reach a point of diminishing returns. But suppose you need merely to isolate the gator to, say, pop its exposure, contrast, and color to get it to stand out a bit, and for that, you can live with something less than a perfect extraction, which will be a much quicker process with this tool.

Even when a full extraction can take advantage of an automated or procedural approach, it often also requires a hand-articulated matte—good old roto—but even that can be greatly aided by enhanced techniques for creating and refining the matte.

How would you go about completing the extraction of this figure? Possibly by limiting the Roto Brush pass to the areas of the shot where it has more natural success, or possibly by abandoning the toolset altogether in this case. Either way, a hand-articulated matte is the reliable fix.

The Articulated Matte

An "articulated" matte is one in which individual mask points are adjusted to detail a shape in motion. For selections such as the one above that are only partially solved by Roto Brush, this is the complete solution. This method of rotoscopy is a whole skill set of its own and a legitimate artistic profession within the context of large-scale projects such as feature films. Many professional compositors have made their start as rotoscopers, and some choose to focus on roto as a professional specialty, whether as individuals or by forming a company or collective.

Hold the Cache Intact

Each adjustment made to an animated mask redraws the entire frame. That can waste time in tiny increments, like the proverbial "death by a thousand cuts." To roto-scope effectively you need to remain focused on details in motion. If you're annoyed at how After Effects deletes the cache with every small adjustment you make, try this:

1. Create a comp containing only the source plate.

2. Add a solid layer above the plate.

3. Turn off the solid layer's visibility .

4. Lock the plate layer .

5. Select the solid layer and draw the first mask shape, then press **Alt+Shift+M** (**Opt+Shift+M**) to keyframe it.

Now any changes you make to the masked solid have no effect on the plate layer or the cache; you can RAM preview the entire section and it is preserved, as is each frame as you navigate to it and keyframe it (**Figure 7.8**). When it comes time to apply the masks, you can either apply the solid as a track matte or copy the masks and keyframes to the plate layer itself. Genius!

Ready, Set, Roto

Following are some broad guidelines for rotoscoping complex organic shapes. Some of these continue with the gator shot as an example, again because it includes so many typical challenges.

▶ As with keying, approaching a complex shot in one pass will compromise your result. You can use multiple overlapping masks when dealing with a complex, moving shape of any kind (**Figure 7.9**).

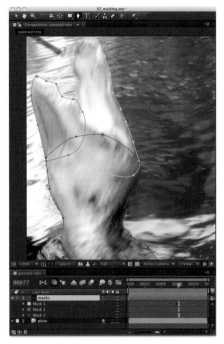

Figure 7.8 Multiple overlapping masks are most effective as parts of the figure move in distinct directions.

NOTES

There's one major downside to masking on a layer with its visibility off: You cannot drag-select a set of points (although you can **Shift**-select each of them).

Figure 7.9 It is crazy to mask a complex articulate figure with a single mask shape; the sheer number of points will have you playing whack-a-mole. Separated segments let you focus on one area of high motion while leaving another area, which moves more steadily, more or less alone.

TIP

Enable Cycle Mask Colors in Preferences > User Interface Colors to generate a unique color for each new mask. You can customize the color if necessary to make it visible by clicking its swatch in the timeline.

Suppose you drew a single mask around the gator's head, similar to the one created with Roto Brush in the previous set of steps. You're fine until the mouth opens, but at that point it's probably more effective to work instead with at least two masks: one for the top and bottom jaw.

It's not that you can't get everything with one mask, but the whole bottom jaw moves one direction as one basic piece, and the upper part of the head moves the opposite direction. By separating them you take advantage of the following strategies to be quick and effective.

▶ Begin on a frame requiring the fewest possible points or one with fully revealed, extended detail, adding more points as needed as you go. As a rule of thumb, no articulated mask should contain more than a dozen or so points.

Frame 77 is the frame with the most fully open mouth, so overlapping outlines on this frame for the upper and lower jaws, as well as the head and neck, can be animated backward and forward from here.

As recommended in the previous section, create a solid layer above the plate layer, turn off its visibility, and lock the plate. Now, with that layer selected, enable the Pen tool (shortcut **G**), click the first point, and start outlining the top jaw, dragging out the Bezier handles (keep the mouse button down after placing the point) with each point you draw, if that's your preference. You can also just place points and adjust Beziers after you've completed the basic shape.

NOTES

By default, After Effects maintains a constant number of points under Preferences > General > Preserve Constant Vertex Count when Editing Masks, so that if you add a point on one keyframe, it is also added to all the others.

In this particular case, the outline is motion-blurred, which raises the question of where exactly the boundary should lie. In all cases, aim the mask outline right down the middle of the blur area, between the inner core and outer edge, as After Effects' own mask feather operates both inward and outward from the mask vector.

The blur itself should be taken care of by animating the mask and enabling motion blur. For now, don't worry about it.

▶ Block in the natural keyframe points first, those which contain a change of direction, speed, or the appearance or disappearance of a shape.

You can begin the gator example with the frame on which the mouth is open at its widest. **Alt+M** (**Opt+M**) will set a Mask Path keyframe at this point in time, so that any changes you make to the shape at any time are also recorded with a keyframe. The question is where to create the next keyframe.

Some rotoscopers prefer straight-ahead animation, creating a shape keyframe on each frame in succession. I prefer to get as much as possible done with in-between frames, so I suggest that you go to the next extreme, or turning point, of motion—in this case, the mouth in its closed position to either side of the open position, beginning with frame 73.

▶ Select a set of points and use the Transform Box to offset, scale, or rotate them together instead of moving them individually (**Figure 7.10**). Most objects shift perspective more than they fundamentally change shape, and this method uses that fact to your advantage.

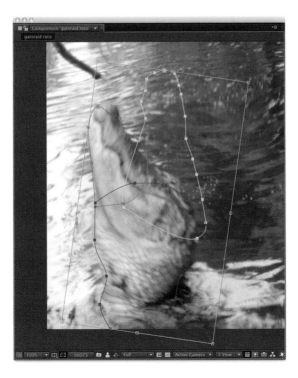

Figure 7.10 Gross mask transformations can be blocked in by selecting and double-clicking all, then repositioning, rotating, and scaling with the free-transform box, followed by finer adjustments to each mask.

At frame 73, with nothing but the layer containing the masks selected, double-click anywhere on one of the masks and a transform box appears around all of the highlighted points. With any points selected, the box appears around those points only, which is also useful; but in this case, freely position (dragging from the inside) and rotate (dragging outside) that transform box so that the end and basic contour of the snout line up.

This is a tough one! The alligator twists and turns quite a bit, so although the shape does follow the basic motion, it now looks as though it will require keyframes on each frame. In cases where it's closer, you may only need to add one in-between keyframe to get it right. Most animals move in continuous arcs with hesitation at the beginning and perhaps some overshoot at the end, so for less sudden movements, in-betweening can work better.

▶ Use a mouse—a pen and tablet system makes exact placement of points difficult.

▶ Use the arrow keys and zoom tool for fine point placement. The increments change according to the zoom level of the current view.

As you move the individual points into place one or more at a time, the arrow keys on your keyboard give you a finer degree of control and placement than dragging your mouse or pen usually does. The more you zoom in, the smaller the increment of one arrow-press, down to the subpixel level when zoomed above 100%.

▶ Lock unselected masks to prevent inadvertently selecting their points when working with the selected mask.

You may have inadvertently clicked the wrong mask at an area of the frame where two or more overlap. Each mask has a lock check box in the timeline, or you can right-click to lock either the selected mask or all other masks to prevent this problem.

▶ To replace a Mask shape instead of creating a new one, in Layer view, select the shape from the Target menu and start drawing a new one; whatever you draw

TIP

It's a little known fact that you can hide (or reveal) locked masks via a toggle in Layer > Masks (or right-clicking the layer), choosing one of the Lock/Unlock options at the bottom of the menu.

replaces the previous shape. Beware: The first vertex point of the two shapes may not match, creating strange in-between frames.

Rotobeziers

Rotobezier shapes are designed to animate a mask over time; they're like Bezier shapes (discussed in Chapter 3) without the handles, which means less adjustment and less chance of pinching or loopholes when points get close together (**Figure 7.11**). Rotobeziers aren't universally beloved, partly because it's difficult to get them right in one pass; adjoining vertices change shape as you add points.

Activate the Pen tool (**G** key) and check the Rotobezier box in the Tools menu, then click the layer to start drawing points; beginning with the third point, the segments are, by default, curved at each vertex.

The literal "key" to success with rotobeziers is the **Alt** (**Opt**) key. At any point as you draw the mask, or once you've completed and closed it by clicking on the first point, hold **Alt** (**Opt**) to toggle the Convert Vertex tool . Drag it to the left to increase tension and make the vertex a sharp corner, like collapsed Bezier handles. Drag in the opposite direction, and the curve rounds out. You can freely add or subtract points as needed by toggling the Pen tool (**G** key).

Look carefully at any mask, and you'll notice one vertex is bigger than the rest. This is the first vertex point. To set it, context-click on a mask vertex and choose Mask and Shape Path > First Vertex.

TIP

You can freely toggle a shape from Bezier to Rotobezier mode and back, should you prefer to draw with one and animate with the other.

Figure 7.11 Overlapping Bezier handles result in kinks and loopholes (left); switching the mask to Rotobezier (right) eliminates the problem.

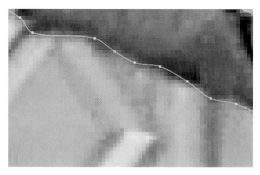

Figure 7.12 You can carefully avoid crossing handles with Beziers (left); convert this same shape to rotobeziers (right) and you lose any angles, direction, or length set with Bezier handles.

TIP

If the Selection tool (V) is active, **Ctrl+Alt (Cmd+Opt)** activates the Adjust Tension pointer.

The real advantage of the rotobezier is that it's impossible to kink up a mask as with long overlapping Bezier handles; other than that, rotobeziers are essentially what could be called "automatic" Beziers (**Figure 7.12**). By drawing enough Bezier points to keep the handles short, however, you may find that you don't need the handles.

Refined Mattes

OK, so you have the basics needed to draw, edit, and keyframe a mask, but perhaps you picked up this book for more than that. Here is a broad look at some easily missed refinements available when rotoscoping in After Effects.

▶ After Effects has no built-in method for applying a tracker directly to a mask, but there are now several ways to track a mask in addition to Roto Brush. See details below and more in Chapter 8, which deals specifically with tracking.

▶ Adding points to an animated mask has no adverse effect on adjacent mask keyframes. Delete a point, however, and it is removed from all keyframes, usually deforming them.

▶ There is no dedicated morphing tool in After Effects. The tools to do a morph do exist, though, along with several deformation tools described later in this chapter and again in Section III of the book.

▶ The Refine Matte tools within Roto Brush are also available as a separate Refine Matte effect that can be used on any transparency selection, not just those created with Roto Brush.

Details follow.

Tracking and Translating

You can track a mask in After Effects, and you can take an existing set of Mask Path keyframes and translate them to a new position, but neither is the straightforward process you might imagine. There's no way to apply the After Effects tracker directly to a mask shape, nor can you simply select a bunch of Mask Path keyframes and have them all translate according to how you move the one you're on (like you can with the layer itself).

You can track a mask using any of the following methods:

▶ Copy the mask keyframe data to a solid layer with the same size, aspect, and transform settings as the source, track or translate that layer, then apply it as a track matte.

▶ If movement of a masked object emanates from camera motion and occurs in the entire scene, you can essentially stabilize the layer, animate the mask in place, and then reapply motion to both. See Chapter 8 for details.

▶ Use Roto Brush to track a matte selection, as above.

▶ Use mocha-AE to track a shape and apply the tracked shape in After Effects via the mocha shape plug-in. Additional benefits to this approach are described in the next section on Mask Feather.

▶ Use mocha-AE to track a shape and copy and paste it as mask data in After Effects. Yes, you understood correctly—you can do that.

Mask shapes can be linked together directly with expressions. **Alt**-click (**Opt**-click) the Mask Path stopwatch, then use the pick whip to drag to the target Mask Path. Only a direct link is possible, no mathematical or logical operations, so all linked masks behave like instances of the first.

SCRIPT

Key Tweak by Matthias Möhl (http://aescripts.com/keytweak/) lets you translate a whole set of keyframes by translating just the start or end keyframe of a sequence.

Mask Feather & Motion Blur

An After Effects mask can be feathered (**F** key). This softening of the mask edge by the specified number of pixels occurs both inward and outward from the mask border in equal amounts and is applied equally all the way around the mask. This lack of control over where and how the feathering occurs can be a limitation, as there are cases where it would be preferable to, say, feather only outward from the edge, or to feather one section of the mask more than the others.

To work around the need to vary edge softness using the built-in mask tools requires compromises. Pressing the **MM** key on the keyboard on a layer with a mask reveals all mask tools, including Mask Expansion, which lets you move the effective mask boundary outward (positive value) or inward (using a negative value). The only built-in way to change the amount of feather in a certain masked area is to add another mask with a different feather setting. As you can imagine, that method quickly becomes tedious.

Instead, you can try creating a tracked mask with mocha-AE and adjusting the feather there. Although mocha-AE isn't really covered until Chapter 8, **Figure 7.13** shows how you can adjust a mask edge in that application to have varying feather and then import that mask into After Effects.

Animated masks in After Effects obey motion blur settings. Match the source's motion blur settings correctly (Chapter 2) and you should be able to match the blur of any solid foreground edge in motion by enabling motion blur for the layer containing the mask in motion. In other words, animate the mask with edges matching the center of the blurred edge, enable motion blur with the right settings, and it just works.

Refine Matte Effect

Among the most overlooked new features of After Effects CS5 is the Refine Matte effect. This is essentially the bottom half of the controls used to make the difference in the matte back in Figure 7.6.

Figure 7.13 Mocha-AE has the facility to set a feather region of a mask per vertex, and export the tracked result to After Effects via mocha shape.

Imagine being able to reduce chatter of roto created by hand, add feather or motion blur to an animated selection that was created without it, or decontaminate spill from the edges of an object that wasn't shot against a uniform green or blue.

This is what Refine Matte allows you to do, and it is more effective than some kludges you might have tried in the past to solve these problems. **Figure 7.14** shows a clearly defined matte line around the selected lamppost. Instead of choking the matte, apply Refine Matte in this situation and you are much closer to complete control of that matte.

Figure 7.14 Exaggerated for effect, this heavy matte line in (**a**) can be managed with an equally heavy Decontamination map to isolate the edges (**b**) and kill the background bleed in the edges (**c**), a built-in feature of Refine Matte.

A   B   C

Deformation

After Effects includes a number of effective tools to deform footage. These are related to rotoscoping and paint in as much as they can also involve selections, manual or tracked animation, and, in the case of Liquify, even paint strokes. Among the most useful:

▶ Corner Pin skews a 2D layer to make it appear aligned with a 3D plane, useful for billboard and screen replacement, among others. The After Effects tracker and, more usefully, mocha-AE can produce a Corner Pin track (Chapter 8).

▶ Mesh Warp covers the entire layer with a grid whose corners and vertices can be transformed to bend the layer in 2D. This is highly useful for animating liquid, smoke, and fire types of effects (Chapter 13).

▶ Displacement Map uses the luminance of a separate layer to displace pixels in X and Y space. It's great for creating heat ripple (Chapter 14).

▶ DigiEffects Freeform is the 3D version of both Mesh Warp and Displacement Map; it includes the main features from both, with the difference that its warps and displacements occur in Z-space for true 3D effects (Chapter 9).

▶ Liquify is a brush-based distortion effect (Chapter 13). You can choose a brush to smear, twirl, twist, or pinch the area you brush, and control the brush itself. This is great for smaller, more detailed instances of distorting liquids and gases, as an alternative to the full-frame Mesh Warp.

▶ Optics Compensation re-creates (or removes) lens distortion (Chapter 9).

▶ Turbulent Displace uses built-in fractal noise generators to displace footage, freeing you from setting up an extra noise source layer as with Displacement Map. This is great for making stuff just look wavy or wobbly.

▶ Reshape is specifically useful for morphing; it stretches the contents of one mask to the boundaries of another. A tutorial featuring Reshape's usage for morphing is included on the book's disc.

▶ Puppet is a pin-based distortion tool for instant character-animation type of deformation.

Puppet is an unusual tool; a version of it is included in Photoshop, but most other compositing and even animation software doesn't have a direct equivalent.

To get started with Puppet, select a layer (perhaps a foreground element with a shape defined by transparency, such as the lamppost shown in the example), and add the Puppet Pin tool (**Ctrl+P/Cmd+P**) simply by clicking points to add joints. Click two points, drag the third, and behold: The layer is now pliable in an organic, intuitive way (**Figure 7.15**).

NOTES

Puppet examples are found in the 07_burgher_rotobrush_puppet and 07_lamppost_refine_puppet folders on the disc.

Figure 7.15 The Puppet mesh in beige is the range of influence of the pins, in yellow; they are effectively the joints.

Here are the basic steps to continue:

1. No matter the source, use the Puppet Pin tool to add at least three pins to a foreground layer. Experimentation will tell you a lot about where to place these, but they're similar to the places you might connect wires to a marionette: the center, joints, and ends.

2. Move a point, and observe what happens to the overall image.

3. Add points as needed to further articulate the deformation.

4. To animate by positioning and timing keyframes: Expose the numbered Puppet Pin properties in the timeline (shortcut **UU**); these have X and Y Position values matching many other properties in After Effects.

5. To animate in real time: Hold **Ctrl** (**Cmd**) as you move the cursor over a pin, and a stopwatch icon appears; click and drag that pin, and a real-time animation of the cursor movement records from the current time until you release the mouse. You can specify an alternate speed for playback by clicking Record Options in the toolbar.

TIP

To animate an image from its initial position once you've already deformed it, create keyframes for the pins that have moved, go to the frame that should have the initial position, and click Reset for those pin properties. Only keyframes at the current time are reset.

Practice with the simple lamppost and you'll quickly get the feel for how Puppet is used. The basic usage is simple, but there are relatively sophisticated methods available to refine the result as needed.

In the toolbar is a toggle to show the mesh. The mesh not only gives you an idea of how Puppet actually works, it can be essential to allow you to properly adjust the result. There's no reason not to leave it on if it's helpful (**Figure 7.16**).

Figure 7.16 Wireframes are displayed when Show is enabled in the toolbar.

The Expansion and Triangles properties use defaults that are often just fine for a given shape. Raising Expansion can help clean up edge pixels left behind in the source. Raising Triangles makes the deformation more accurate, albeit slower. The default number of triangles varies according to the size and complexity of the source.

Starchy and Husk

The Puppet Pin tool does the heavy lifting, but wait, that's not all: **Ctrl+P** (**Cmd+P**) cycles through two more Puppet tools to help in special cases.

To fold a layer over or under itself requires that you control what overlaps what as two regions cross; this is handled by the Puppet Overlap tool. The mesh must be displayed to use Puppet Overlap, and the Overlap point is applied on the original, undeformed mesh shape, not the deformation (**Figure 7.17**).

Overlap is not a tool to animate (although you can vary its numerical settings in the timeline if the overlap behavior changes over time). Place it at the center of the area intended to overlap others and adjust how much "in front" it's meant to be as well as its extent (how far from the pin itself the overlap area reaches). If you add more than one overlap, raise the In Front setting to move the given selection closer to the viewer. Areas with no specified setting default to 0, so use a negative value to place the selection behind those. Play with it using multiple overlaps and you'll get the idea.

> **TIP**
>
> Pins disappeared? To display them, three conditions must be satisfied: The layer is selected, the Puppet effect is active, and the Puppet Pin tool is currently selected.

Figure 7.17 The Overlap tool gives full control over which areas are forward. It is displayed on an outline of the source shape, and with a positive setting, causes the top lamp to come forward.

The Starch 🖎 tool prevents an area from deforming. It's not an anchor—position it between regular puppet pins, preventing the highlighted area (expanded or contracted with the tool's Extent setting) from being squished or stretched (**Figure 7.18**).

Figure 7.18 Starch pins (in red) and the affected regions are designed to attenuate (or eliminate, depending on the Amount setting) distortion within that region.

Paint and Cloning

Paint is generally a last resort when roto is impractical, and for a simple reason: Use of this tool, particularly for animation, can be painstaking and more likely to show flaws than approaches involving masks. There are, of course, exceptions. You can track a clone brush more easily than a mask, and painting in the alpha channel can be a handy quick fix.

For effects work, then, paint controls in After Effects have at least a couple of predominant uses:

▶ Clean up an alpha channel mask by painting directly to it in black and white.

▶ Use Clone Stamp to overwrite an area of the frame with alternate source.

Once you fully understand the strengths and limitations of paint, it's easier to decide when to use it.

Paint Fundamentals

Two panels, Paint and Brush Tips, are essential to the three brush-based tools in the Tools palette: Brush 🖌, Clone Stamp 🖈, and Eraser 🩹. These can be revealed by choosing the Paint workspace.

The After Effects paint functionality is patterned after equivalent tools in Photoshop, but with a couple of fundamental differences. After Effects offers fewer customizable options for its brushes (you can't, for example, design your own brush tips). More significantly (and related), Photoshop's brushes are raster-based, while After Effects brushes are vector-based. Vector-based paint is more flexible, allowing you to change the character of the strokes—their size, feather, and so on—even after they're drawn.

Suppose that you have an alpha channel in need of a touch-up; for example, the matte shown in **Figure 7.19.** This is a difficult key due to tracking markers and shadows. With the Brush tool active, go to the Paint palette and set Channels to Alpha (this palette remembers the last mode you used); the foreground and background color swatches in the palette become grayscale, and you can make them black and white by clicking the tiny black-over-white squares just below the swatches.

Figure 7.19 Touch up an alpha channel matte (for example, to remove a tracking marker): In the Paint palette, select Alpha in the Channels menu, then display the alpha channel (**Alt+4/Opt+4**).

To see what you are painting, switch the view to Alpha Channel (**Alt+4/Option+4**); switch back to RGB to check the final result.

When using the paint tools keep in mind:

▶ Brush-based tools operate only in the Layer panel, not the Composition panel.

▶ Paint strokes include their own Mode setting (analogous to layer blending modes).

▶ With a tablet, you can use the Brush Dynamics settings at the bottom of the Brush Tips panel to set how the pressure, angle, and stylus wheel of your pen affect strokes.

▶ The Duration setting and the frame where you begin painting are crucial (details below).

▶ Preset brushes and numerical settings for properties such as diameter and hardness (aka feather) live in the Brush Tips panel.

For a more effective workflow experience, try the following shortcuts with the Brush tool active in the Layer viewer.

▶ Hold **Ctrl (Cmd)** and drag to scale the brush.

▶ Add the **Shift** key to adjust in larger increments and **Alt (Opt)** for fine adjustments.

▶ With the mouse button still held, release **Ctrl (Cmd)** to scale hardness (an inner circle appears representing the inside of the threshold, **Figure 7.20**).

▶ **Alt**-click (Opt-click) to use the eyedropper (with brushes) or clone source (with the clone brush).

By default, the Duration setting in the Paint menu is set to Constant, which means that any paint stroke created on this frame continues to the end of the layer. For cleaning up stray holes on given frames of an alpha channel, this is probably not desirable because it's too easy to leave the stroke active too long. The Single Frame setting confines your stroke to just the current frame on which you're painting, and the Custom setting allows you to enter the number of frames that the stroke exists.

Figure 7.20 Modifier keys (**Ctrl/Cmd** to scale, **Alt/Opt** to feather, all with the mouse button held) let you define a brush on the fly. The inner circle shows the solid core; the area between it and the outer circle is the threshold (for feathering).

TIP

There is a major gotcha with Constant (the default mode): Paint a stroke at any frame other than the first frame of the layer, and it does not appear until that frame during playback. It's apparently not a bug, but it is certainly an annoyance.

The other option, Write On, records your stroke in real time, re-creating the motion (including timing) when you replay the layer; this stylized option can be useful for such motion graphics tricks as handwritten script.

The Brush Tips panel menu includes various display options and customizable features: You can add, rename, or delete brushes, as well. You can also name a brush by double-clicking it if it's really imperative to locate it later; searching in the Timeline search field will locate it for you. Brush names do not appear in the default thumbnail view except via tooltips when the cursor is placed above each brush.

For alpha channel cleanup, then, work in Single Frame mode (under Duration in the Paint panel), looking only at the alpha channel (**Alt+4/Opt+4**) and progressing frame by frame through the shot (**Pg Dn**).

After working for a little while, your Timeline panel may contain dozens of strokes, each with numerous properties of its own. New strokes are added to the top of the stack and are given numerically ordered names; it's often simplest to select them visually using the Selection tool (**V**) directly in a viewer panel.

Cloning Fundamentals

When moving footage is cloned, the result retains grain and other natural features that still images lack. Not only can you clone pixels from a different region of the same frame, you can clone from a different frame of a different clip at a different point in time (**Figure 7.21**), as follows:

▶ **Clone from the same frame:** This works just as in Photoshop. Choose a brush, **Alt-click** (**Opt**-click) on the area of the frame to sample, and begin painting. Remember that by default, Duration is set to Constant, so any stroke created begins at the current frame and extends through the rest of the composition.

▶ **Clone from the same clip, at a different time:** Look at Clone Options for the offset value in frames. Note that there is also an option to set spatial offset. To clone from the exact same position at a different point in time, set the Offset to 0,0 and change the Source Time.

TIP

As in Photoshop, the **X** key swaps the foreground and background swatches with the Brush tool active.

NOTES

The Aligned toggle in the Paint panel (on by default) preserves 1:1 pixel positions even though paint tools are vector-based. Nonaligned clone operations tend to appear blurry.

Figure 7.21 Clone source overlay is checked (left) with Difference mode active, an "onion skin" that makes it possible to precisely line up two matching shots (middle and right images). Difference mode is on, causing all identical areas of the frame to turn black when the two layers are perfectly aligned.

TIP

To clone from a single frame only to multiple frames, toggle on Lock Source Time in the Paint panel.

NOTES

Clone is different from many other tools in After Effects in that Source Time Shift uses frames, not seconds, to evaluate the temporal shift. Beware if you mix clips with different frame rates, although on the whole this is a beneficial feature.

▶ **Clone from a separate clip:** The source from which you're cloning must be present in the current composition (although it need not be visible and can even be a guide layer). Simply open the layer to be used as source, and go to the current time where you want to begin; Source and Source Time Shift are listed in the Paint panel and can also be edited there.

▶ **Mix multiple clone sources without having to reselect each one:** There are five Preset icons in the Paint panel; these allow you to switch sources on the fly and then switch back to a previous source. Just click on a Preset icon before selecting your clone source and that source remains associated with that preset (including Aligned and Lock Source Time settings).

That all seems straightforward enough; there are just a few things to watch out for, as follows.

Tricks and Gotchas

Suppose the clone source time is offset, or comes from a different layer, and the last frame of the layer has been reached—what happens? After Effects helpfully loops back to the first frame of the clip and keeps going. This is dangerous only if you're not aware of it.

Edit the source to take control of this process. Time remapping is one potential way to solve these problems; you can time stretch or loop a source clip.

You may need to scale the source to match the target. Although temporal edits, including time remapping, render before they are passed through, other types of edits—even simple translations or effects—do not. As always, the solution is to precompose; any scaling, rotation, motion tracking, or effects to be cloned belong in the subcomposition.

Finally, Paint is an effect. Apply your first stroke and you'll see an effect called Paint with a single check box, Paint on Transparent, which effectively solos the paint strokes. You can change the render order of paint strokes relative to other effects. For example, you can touch up a green-screen plate, apply a keyer, and then touch up the resulting alpha channel, all on one layer.

The View menu in the Layer panel (**Figure 7.22**) lists, in order, the paint and effects edits you've added to the layer. To see only the layer with no edits applied, toggle Render off; to see a particular stage of the edit—after the first paint strokes, but before the effects, say—select it in the View menu, effectively disabling the steps below it. These settings are for previewing only; they will not enable or disable the rendering of these items.

You can even motion-track a paint stroke. To do so requires the tracker, covered in the next chapter, and a basic expression to link them.

Figure 7.22 Isolate and solo paint strokes in the View menu of the Layer panel.

Wire Removal

Wire removal and rig removal are two common visual effects needs. Generally speaking, *wire removal* is cloning over a wire (typically used to suspend an actor or prop in midair). *Rig removal*, meanwhile, is typically just an animated garbage mask over any equipment that appeared in shot.

After Effects has nothing to compete with the state-of-the-art wire removal tool found in the Foundry's Furnace plug-ins (which sadly are available for just about every compositing package except After Effects).

Photoshop Video

Photoshop offers an intriguing alternative to the After Effects vector paint tools, as you can use it with moving footage. The After Effects paint tools are heavily based on those brushes, but with one key difference: Photoshop strokes are bitmaps (actual pixels) and those from After Effects are vectors. This makes it possible to use custom brushes, as are common in Photoshop (and which are themselves bitmaps). You can't do as much overall with the stroke once you've painted it as in After Effects, but if you like working in Photoshop, it's certainly an option. After Effects can open but not save Photoshop files containing video. Render these in a separate moving-image format (or, if as Photoshop files, a .psd sequence).

Dust busting can be done rapidly with a clone brush and the Single Frame Duration setting in the Paint panel.

Silhouette is available as both a standalone application and a shape import/export plug-in for After Effects. The software is designed to rotoscope and generate mattes using the newest research and techniques. If you're curious about it, there is a demo you can try on the disc.

The CC Simple Wire Removal tool is indeed simple: It replaces the vector between two points by either displacing pixels or using the same pixels from a neighboring frame. There are Slope and Mirror Blend controls, allowing you a little control over the threshold and cloning pattern, and you can apply a tracker to each point via expressions and the pick whip (described in Chapter 10).

The net effect may not be so different from drawing a two-point clone stroke (sample the background by **Alt**- or **Option**-clicking, then click one end of the wire, and **Shift**-click the other end). That stroke could then be tracked via expressions.

Rig removal can very often be aided by tracking motion, because rigs themselves don't move, the camera does. The key is to make a shape that mattes out the rig, then apply that as a track matte to the foreground footage and track the whole matte.

Dust Bust

This is in many ways as nitty-gritty and low-level as rotoscoping gets, although the likelihood of small particles appearing on source footage has decreased with the advent of digital shooting and the decline of film. Most of these flaws can be corrected only via frame-by-frame cloning, sometimes known as *dust busting*. If you've carefully read this section, you already know what you need to know to do this work successfully, so get to it.

Alternatives

You would think that at the high end, there must be standard tools and all kinds of extra sophisticated alternatives to roto, but that's not entirely true. There are full-time rotoscope artists who prefer to work right in After Effects, and there are many cases where working effectively in After Effects is preferable to taking the trouble to exit to another application.

A lot of the more elegant ways to augment roto involve motion tracking, which is the subject of the next chapter.

8

Effective Motion Tracking

I'm sick of following my dreams. I'm just going to ask them where they're going and hook up with them later.

—Mitch Hedberg

Effective Motion Tracking

There is more to matchmoving than simply sampling the motion of one layer and applying it to another, even though that's fundamentally what motion tracking is. Because of the number of available tracking methods, whether standard or customized hacks, applications of the basic data go a bit beyond the obvious.

There's also more to motion tracking in After Effects than the built-in point tracker. Mocha-AE from Imagineer Systems is a planar tracker, a fundamentally different approach that solves a problem (corner pinning) that had been somewhere between difficult and impossible with the After Effects tracker. The latest version of mocha-AE adds shape tracking as an alternative to Roto Brush.

It is even possible to use third-party 3D tracking software to match real-world camera motion in After Effects. At this writing, the Foundry has released a plug-in to do just that, right in the software.

All of these automated trackers sample motion at a detail level that would be very difficult to replicate by hand. It's not a fully automated process, however, and so it helps to develop expertise in order to

- ▶ choose effective track regions to begin
- ▶ customize settings based on the particular scene or situation
- ▶ fix tracks that go astray
- ▶ work with blurred or soft selections

This chapter offers you a leg up. Once you grasp these, you can use tracking to go beyond the ordinary to

- ▶ match an entire scene using a single track applied once
- ▶ stabilize a handheld shot while preserving camera movement
- ▶ continue truncated tracks that leave the visible frame
- ▶ make use of 3D tracking data

There are many cases where effective tracking can help accomplish the seemingly impossible. The human eye, meanwhile, is extraordinarily sensitive to anomalies in motion, which is quite possibly related to some basic survival instinct.

Point Tracker

Step one for those learning to track is to lock in a good basic track right in After Effects. You may find your tracks going astray after reviewing the clear After Effects documentation on how to use the tracker. Here are some background fundamentals.

Tracking is a two-step process: The tracker analyzes the clip and stores its analysis as a set of layer properties that don't actually do anything. The properties are then applied to take effect. Both steps, setting the tracking target and applying the track, occur in the Tracker panel when matching or stabilizing motion in After Effects, although there are also ways to work with raw unapplied tracking data, typically with the use of expressions.

Choose a Feature

Success with the After Effects tracker relies on your ability to choose a feature that will track effectively (**Figure 8.1**).

Ideally, the feature you plan to track

- ▶ is unique from its surroundings
- ▶ has high-contrast edges—typically a corner or point—entirely within the feature region
- ▶ is identifiable throughout the shot
- ▶ does not have to compete with similar distinct features within the search region at any point during the track
- ▶ is close to the area where the tracked object or objects will be added

Figure 8.1 Objects with clear contours, definition, and contrast make the best track targets. The tracking markers on the wall were added for this purpose and could be used on a separate pass to track the distant background; the combination of tracking markers and foreground c-stands shown here creates the parallax needed for an effective 3D track.

TIP

Search and feature regions don't have to be square! Widen the feature region to match a wide, short target feature. With unidirectional motion—say, a right-to-left pan—widen and offset the search region in the direction of the pan.

Check out 08_01_track_basic. This shot was designed to be tracked, with c-stands left adjacent to the talent (but not overlapping, so as to be easily garbage matted out of the shot). Let's suppose that the scene to be added around the actors includes a set piece—say, a door frame or portal—coplanar to those stands. You can make a temporary one with a shape layer, as in **Figure 8.2.**

Figure 8.2 A crude portal drawn in simply with a shape layer helps visualize a layer that might replace the c-stands.

Right-click the plate layer, or under the Animation menu, choose Track Motion. This opens the Layer panel—where tracking is done in After Effects—and reveals the Tracker panel with a default tracker. Double-check that you're on the first frame (for simplicity), then carefully drag the middle of the feature region (the smaller square, identified in **Figure 8.3**) so that the whole control moves as one, and place it over the target feature. It's very easy to grab the wrong thing, so pay close attention to the icon under your cursor before you drag.

I suggest selecting one of the yellow joints on a stand as a target feature, because the detail is most consistent. If you choose a shinier detail on the chrome part of the stand, that specular detail will shift as the lighting angle shifts. The joints have a clearly definable shape that fits nicely in a modest-sized feature region, as in Figure 8.2, and doesn't change over the course of the shot.

Click ▶ in the Tracker panel and watch as After Effects tracks the feature from frame to frame. The Track Point icon only moves in whole pixel increments, so don't assume you have a bad track if you see it jittering a bit. Assuming you chose a well-defined feature with edges inside the feature region, you should quickly derive a successful track automatically.

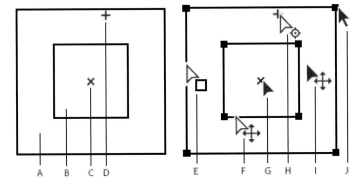

Figure 8.3 Many interactive controls are clustered close together in the tracker. Identified here are: **A.** Search region; **B.** Feature region; **C.** Keyframe marker; **D.** Attach point; **E.** Move search region; **F.** Move both regions; **G.** Move entire track point; **H.** Move attach point; **I.** Move entire track point; **J.** Resize region. Zoom in to ensure you're clicking the right one.

Now the only thing left to do is to apply it. Click the Apply button in the Tracker panel, then OK to the inevitable Motion Tracker Apply Options (to specify that this track does indeed apply to X and Y). Back in the Composition viewer, there are a couple of problems with this otherwise locked track: The object is shifted from its original position, and it doesn't scale up with the camera dolly. The next two sections solve these problems.

Before we move on, though, the main decisions when setting up a track regard the size and shape of the search and feature regions. Keep the following in mind:

▶ A large feature region averages pixel data, producing a smoother but possibly less accurate track (**Figure 8.4**).

▶ A small feature region may pick up noise and grain as much as trackable detail. This will lead to an accurate but jittery and therefore unusable track.

▶ The bigger the search region, the slower the track.

▶ The feature region doesn't have to contain the area of frame you want to match. One way to offset a track is to move the attach point—that little x at the center of the tracker. A better solution is to apply the track to a null, (discussed later).

Tracked features can often be unreliable, changing perspective, lighting, or color throughout the course of the

Figure 8.4 Thinking of tracking the entire c-stand? This will make the track smoother, because it averages more data, but less accurate (for the same reason). There's also the problem of the camera dolly in this shot, which will cause the whole stand to scale and change perspective quite a bit, a source of further inaccuracy.

shot. The following sections solve the initial difficulty experienced in this first attempt, and explain what to do when you don't have a constant, trackable feature exactly where you want the target to go, as was the case here.

Tweak the Tracker

There are five types of track listed under the Track Type menu in the Tracker panel. Before moving further one at a time, here is an overview of what each does. *Stabilize* and *Transform* tracks are created identically but applied uniquely. Edit Target shows the singular difference between them: Stabilize tracks are always applied to the *anchor point* of the tracked layer. Transform tracks are applied to the *position* of a layer other than the tracked layer (or the effect point control of any effect in any layer).

Using Stabilize, the animated anchor point (located at the center of the image by default) moves the layer in opposition to Position. Increasing the anchor point's X value (assuming Position remains the same, which it does when you adjust the Anchor Point value directly in the Timeline) moves the layer to the left, just as decreasing the Position value does.

Corner Pin tracks are very different; in After Effects these require three or four points to be tracked, and the data is applied to a Corner Pin plug-in to essentially distort the perspective of the target layer. Because these tracks are notoriously difficult and unreliable, the happy truth is that mocha-AE, which also generates data that can be applied to a corner pin, has more or less superseded Corner Pin tracking.

A *Raw track* generates track data only, graying out the Edit Target button. It's simply a track that isn't applied directly as Transform keyframes. What good is unapplied track data? For one thing it can be used to drive expressions or saved to be applied later. It's no different than simply never clicking Edit Target; the raw track data is stored within the source layer (**Figure 8.5**).

TIP

Keep in mind that you can track in reverse, for situations where the feature being tracked is larger, more prominent, or more clearly visible at the end of shot.

Figure 8.5 Tracker data is stored under the tracked layer, where it can be accessed at any time.

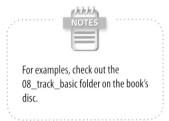

For examples, check out the 08_track_basic folder on the book's disc.

Position, Rotation, and Scale

You can't uncheck the Position toggle in the Tracker panel (thus avoiding the unsolvable riddle, what is a motion track without Position data?), but you can add Rotation and Scale. Enable either toggle, and a second track point is automatically added.

Additionally tracking rotation and scale data is straight-forward enough, employing two track points instead of one. Typically, the two points should be roughly equidis-tant from the camera due to the phenomenon of parallax (**Figure 8.6**).

Figure 8.6 A scale/rotation track will not succeed with two points that rest at completely different distances from the camera.

This, then, is the solution to one of the difficulties in the 08_01_track_basic example. Click Reset in the Tracker panel and check Scale, and there are two track points (the same occurs if you check Rotation, which isn't too applicable in this shot). The distance and angle between those points is used to determine rotation and/or scale, so they should be placed at two points that are equidistant from camera and far enough from one another to yield accurate data. The c-stands were clearly placed with this in mind, so choose similar features on each, retrack, and reapply. The target layer still shifts position, but it now scales with the movement of the shot. One down, one to go.

Solve Problems with Nulls

You may have already tried simply moving the target layer after tracking data was applied to it. Because there is a keyframe on each tracked frame, moving the object at any point moves only that keyframe, causing a jump. You can instead select all Position keyframes by clicking that property in the Timeline panel, then moving, but it's easy to forget to do this or for the keyframes to become deselected as you attempt it.

Choosing instead to apply track data to a null object layer and then parenting to apply the motion gains you the following advantages:

▶ Freely reposition tracked layers: It doesn't matter whether the track attach point is in the right location; the null picks up the relative motion, and any layer parented to it can be repositioned or animated on its own (**Figure 8.7**).

Figure 8.7 The null contains the applied motion data and is not touched. The foreground portal layer is parented and contains no keyframes, so you are free to move, scale, and rotate it without worrying about disrupting the track.

▶ Once a track is set you can lock the tracked layer so that it's not inadvertently nudged out of position.

▶ A Stabilization track can be used to peg multiple objects to a scene (next section).

▶ One set of motion data can be parented to another to build tracks, parenting one to the next.

To fully solve 08_01_track_basic, then, take the following steps:

1. Create a null object (under the Layer menu).

2. Track Position and Scale using equidistant points on either tracking target (the c-stands that are there for this purpose).

3. Click Edit Target to make certain the null is selected, then apply the track to the null.

4. Parent the layer to the null (**Shift+F4** toggles the Parent column in the timeline); then select the null as the target from the foreground object being tracked.

Track a Difficult Feature

A shot with rotation or scale of more than a few degrees typically requires that you track a feature that does not look at all the same within the Feature Region box from the start to the end of the frame (**Figure 8.8**). For just such situations, Tracker > Options contains the Adapt Feature on Every Frame toggle.

By default, the tracker is set to adapt the track feature if the Confidence setting slips below 80%. Adapt Feature on Every Frame is like restarting the track on each and every frame, comparing each frame to the previous one instead of the one you originally chose. For ordinary tracks this adds an unwanted margin of error, but in a case where a feature is in constant flux anyway, this can help.

Confidence

At the bottom of Motion Tracker Options is a submenu of options related to After Effects' mysterious Confidence settings. Every tracked frame gets a Confidence setting, an

Figure 8.8 To the naked eye, the pattern being tracked in these two frames is nearly identical, but to a point tracker, which does not understand context, the two might seem almost unrelated due to changes in angle, blur, and scale. The solution with a point that changes due to rotation, scale, blur, or light changes may be to toggle Adapt Feature on Every Frame and have the tracker stop each time Confidence goes below the default threshold of 80%.

TIP

Stopping and restarting a track resets Feature Region at the frame where you restart. Use this to your advantage by restarting a track that slips at the last good frame; it often works.

Figure 8.9 The Confidence graph clearly indicates where this track has lost its target.

evaluation of how accurate the track was at that frame. This may or may not be indicative of the actual accuracy, but my experience is that you're almost guaranteed to be fine with values above 90%, and real problems will cause this value to drop way, way down, to 30% or less (**Figure 8.9**).

Depending on this setting, you can

▶ continue Tracking. Power ahead no matter what happens!

▶ stop Tracking. Reset the tracker manually right at the problem frame.

▶ extrapolate Motion. Allow After Effects to guess based on the motion of previously tracked frames, for cases where the tracked item disappears for a few frames.

▶ adapt Feature. Change the reference Feature Region to the previous frame if Confidence is low.

Whichever you choose, you also have the option to go back to the frame where a track went wrong, reset Feature Region by hand, and restart the track.

Motion Blur

Motion blur is also essential to matchmoving. A good track won't look right until its motion blur also matches that of the background plate. If you don't know the shutter speed

TIP

To reveal the current track in the Timeline with the Track Controls active, use the **SS** (Show Selected) shortcut.

SCRIPT

TrackerViz by Charles Bordenave (http://aescripts.com/trackerviz/) originated as a tool to average motion data, so that several track attempts could be averaged together to make a single animation. Additional new features allow you to use mask shapes and tracker points interchangeably, or link a mask shape to the position of selected layers.

with which a shot was taken, you can match it by eye, most often zooming in to an area of the frame where it is apparent in both the foreground and background. If you know, for example, that the shutter speed was one-half of the frame rate (the standard setting for a cinematic look), use a 180-degree shutter, and be sure to set the Shutter Phase to –0.5 of that number, or –90.

Motion blur settings reside in Composition Settings (**Ctrl+K/Cmd+K**) > Advanced, and if you enable the Preview toggle at the lower left, you can see them update as you adjust them for eye matching. As described back in Chapter 2, adjust Shutter Angle and Shutter Phase until you see a good match, raising (or in the odd case, lowering) Samples per Frame and Adaptive Sample Limit to match (**Figure 8.10**).

Figure 8.10 Motion tracking can't work without matching motion blur (right). This shot uses the standard film camera blur: a 180-degree shutter angle, with a phase of –90.

If it's necessary to stabilize a scene that contains heavy motion blur, that's a bigger problem that needs to be avoided when shooting (even by boosting the shutter speed of the camera, where possible). **Figure 8.11** shows a case in which it's preferable to smooth camera motion rather than lock the stabilization (see "Smooth a Camera Move" later in this chapter for a shot that works much better).

Figure 8.11 If shooting with the intention of stabilizing later, raise the film shutter speed and reduce camera motion to minimize motion blur and a huge empty gutter around the image.. Otherwise, you end up with an image like this, which while fully trackable, won't look sharp enough completely stabilized.

The 08_stabilize_basic folder on the book's disc contains this simple tracking and stabilization example.

Track a Scene

In the real world, objects sit in an environment, and if that environment or the point of view changes, they remain in place. You knew this. You may not know how to make a 2D After Effects track re-create it.

The key is to stabilize the background layer and then parent a camera to that stabilization, restoring the motion. The motion of the source camera is captured and applied to a virtual camera so that any elements you add to the scene pick up on that motion. It's quite cool.

The AE Camera as a Tracking Tool

Suppose you have an arbitrary number of foreground layers to match to a background plate: not just objects, but color corrections, effects with holdout masks, you name it. Applying track data to each of those layers individually is a time-consuming headache, and even parenting them all to a tracked null may not work properly if there is rotation or scale data, as that null then becomes the center of those translations.

Instead, the following method allows you to stabilize the background scene, add static foreground elements, and then reapply the scene motion.

1. With the background layer selected, choose Stabilize Motion (either by context-clicking the layer or by choosing it from the Animation menu).

2. Stabilize the layer for Position, Rotation, and Scale, using two points equidistant from the camera.

3. The stabilized layer offsets and rotates in the frame (**Figure 8.12**). Return to the first frame of the track (quite possibly frame 0 of the comp). Turn on the stabilized layer's 3D switch.

Figure 8.12 Gaps open up around the edges of the image as the track points are held in place.

4. Add a 3D camera (context-click in an empty area of the Timeline panel); in the Camera Settings, give it a name like trackerCam, use the 50mm preset, and click OK.

5. Parent the camera layer to the stabilized layer (**Figure 8.13**).

NOTES

A 50 mm camera lens in After Effects offers a neutral perspective; toggle any layer to 3D and it should appear the same as in 2D.

Figure 8.13 The relevant Transform properties are copied and pasted to a null, to which the camera is then parented.

Everything now appears back to normal, with one intriguing twist: Any new item added to the scene picks up the scene motion as soon as you toggle its 3D switch. All you have to do is drop it in and enable 3D. Any layer that shouldn't follow the track, such as an adjustment layer, can remain 2D (**Figure 8.14**).

Figure 8.14 Extra layers for a new clock face and child's artwork along with a shadow are added as 3D layers, so they pick up the motion of the scene as captured by the tracked camera.

2.5D Tracking

You can even fake 3D parallax by offsetting layers in Z space. Any layer that is equidistant from the camera with the motion track points has a Z-depth value of 0. Offsetting layers is tricky as there is no frame of reference for where they should be placed in Z space—not even a grid (**Figure 8.15**).

NOTES

2.5D tracking will even stick foreground layers to a zoomed shot; the Scale stabilization scales the parented camera, making it appear to zoom.

This can be referred to as "2.5D tracking": a 3D camera paired with two-dimensional tracking points and layers. Any 3D offset derived from a 2D track is only approximately accurate, so this is a total hack. If your scene has areas of frame closer or further than the track points that you wish to match, guess where in 3D space to place a layer and you may just get lucky via a little trial and error.

If a shot tracks (the camera moves instead of zooming, creating changes in perspective), it probably requires a real 3D camera track (see "Try It Out for Yourself" at the end of this chapter).

Figure 8.15 Rotoscoped shapes can be tracked so that they "stick" in a scene; you don't have to animate the shape itself unless it is also a matte that needs to be articulated around a moving figure. Here it is even offset in 3D to match the parallax of the wall nearer camera.

Smooth a Camera Move

It's even possible to stabilize a shot in which the camera moves—handheld, aerial, crane, or dolly—smoothing bumps in the motion while retaining the move, although this feature is not built in to After Effects. Even if you don't have this immediate need—and with the number of shots these days coming from unstable DSLR cameras, I wouldn't be surprised if you do sometime soon—this exercise also contains some tips about tracking that apply elsewhere.

Figure 8.16 shows the panning action of a background plate shot that will be used in the final chapter of the book, in which the building depicted is set on fire. The camera was stabilized (suspended with a magic arm), but a small camera with a long lens is difficult to keep steady without a professional tripod while shooting lightly and guerrilla-style. The law where I live states that you only need a permit to shoot footage if you put down sticks (a tripod), offering an economical reason to set up this way and fix it in post.

All of the steps from the "AE Camera as a Tracking Tool" section apply here, with a couple of additions:

Figure 8.16 Notice that no part of the first frame of the sequence (top left) is contained in the end of the shot (bottom right). Check the shot itself and you'll see that its motion is as smooth as possible but jittery enough to be distracting.

For example footage and projects, try 08_stabilize_moving_camera and 08_aerial_stabilization.

1. To stabilize motion on this shot requires one extra step because, as shown in Figure 8.16, no one point appears in frame from start to finish.

   There is, however, a great solution for that. Try the following with 08_stabilize_moving_camera.aep from the book's disc:

   ▶ Track the shot starting at the beginning using a target in the upper-left corner (so that it will remain in frame through as much of the pan as possible). The multicolored lampshade above the fire escape is perfect. Be sure to enlarge the feature region and offset it down and to the right to cover the panning motion.

   ▶ The target reaches the edge of frame at frame 45. Go to the last good frame.

   ▶ Press **UU** to reveal keyframes for the layer, and then **Alt**-drag (**Opt**-drag) the tracker to a new target higher in frame (such as the green sofa).

   Notice that the Feature Center value changes in the timeline, but the Attach Point does not.

2. As in the previous "AE Camera as a Tracking Tool" section, set up the frame that has disappeared from view (**Figure 8.17**) to stabilize: Make the layer 3D, copy the anchor point animation to a null, and parent the camera to that null.

Figure 8.17 Stabilizing a layer with a full pan around that lamp in the upper-left corner causes it to leave frame completely, but this is only an interim step.

3. **Alt**-click (**Opt**-click) on the Anchor Point stopwatch of the layer to which the camera is parented. This sets the default expression transform.anchorPoint.

4. With the default expression (anchorPoint) still highlighted, go to the Expressions menu icon 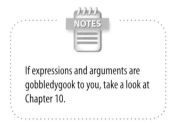, and under Property choose the smooth default: smooth(width = .2, samples = 5, t = time).

This works, but as a starting setting, I recommend discarding the third argument ("t = time") and the other hints ("width =" and "samples ="), then change the values to something like smooth(2, 48).

Next to the Anchor Point property is a toggle to graph the expression 📈, and under the graph type and options menu 🖿, you can choose Show Reference Graph and Show Expression Editor (**Figure 8.18**).

The expression works as follows: It gives a command (smooth()) followed by three settings known as *arguments*. The third one, time, is used only to offset the result, and

> **NOTES**
>
> If expressions and arguments are gobbledygook to you, take a look at Chapter 10.

Figure 8.18 The result of smoothing can be seen in the Graph Editor—there is a second red and green line for the new x and y, a white line down the middle of the white keyframe velocity graph, and the expression is shown at the bottom.

it's optional, so deleting it gets it out of the way. The hints for the other two (width = and samples =) are also not needed to make the expression work—they are there just to remind you of what they do.

Width determines how much time (before and after the current time) is averaged to create the result. A setting of 2 samples 2 seconds means 1 second before and 1 second after the current time. The samples argument determines how many individual points within that range are actually sampled for the result; generally, the more samples, the smoother the curve. A setting of 48 means that over 2 seconds, 48 individual frame values will be averaged (the maximum for 24-fps footage).

It's also possible to smooth rotation in this manner, although I find a lighter touch (fewer samples) works best with rotation. However, the best way to find out for your individual shot is by trying different settings, looking at how smooth the resulting curve (not to mention the actual motion) appears.

It's a little hard to imagine that you can smooth the motion data for the camera, causing it to go out of sync with the background, and not have a mismatch. What is actually happening, though, is that the scene motion is removed completely, then restored in a smoother state.

NOTES

The shot used in this example was taken with a high shutter speed, so there is very little motion blur, which is good for a handheld shot to be stabilized. However, check Chapter 2 for a tip on adding the appropriate amount of motion blur after the fact.

Planar Tracker: mocha-AE

There is, in fact, a more powerful option than the tracker built in to the After Effects UI, and it's included with every copy of After Effects CS5: mocha for After Effects, or mocha-AE, which is now in its own version 2. It is found adjacent to the After Effects application—standalone software designed to integrate directly with After Effects. It can be used to replace the functionality of the After Effects tracker, but it also adds capabilities not found with any point tracker.

Mocha is a planar tracker, which is truly and fundamentally different from a point tracker such as the one in After Effects. A planar tracker assumes that the area defined by the feature region is a plane in 3D space, and looks for that plane to change not only its position, rotation, and scale but its orientation while remaining a consistent surface. The result is 2D data that can be used to emulate 3D, in particular corner pin and shape tracks. A tracked plane can also be averaged to generate the same type of track data that the After Effects tracker creates.

Look around the environment where you are right now and you may notice numerous two-dimensional planes: walls, tabletops, the backs of chairs, the sides of hard-surface objects such as automobiles (**Figure 8.19**), even the trunk of a tree or a face. If you were sitting on the moon reading this book, the surface of Earth, though curved, would track more or less as a single unified plane as the camera passed across it.

NOTES

Imagineer also offers mocha, a standalone version of the same software designed to integrate with other compositing and animation applications besides After Effects.

Figure 8.19 A plane does not have to be flat and rectilinear in order for mocha to track it; look around and you will see many coplanar objects.

The plainest use for mocha-AE—pun very much intended—is Corner Pin tracking, replacement of a surface defined by a rectangle with another such surface. This type of track has long been the Achilles' heel of the After Effects tracker, whose use is now discouraged for this purpose, given the free availability of mocha-AE.

Mocha can, in fact, be used for just about any type of 2D tracking. The extra precision is often worth the extra steps of leaving the After Effects environment. I find nowadays that I rely on the After Effects tracker only for the most basic and foolproof tracks. As soon as I run into trouble, I look for a way to accomplish the shot in mocha-AE.

The Basics

Mocha is an application unto itself. Its manual is quite an easy read and longer than this entire chapter (just click Guide on the Mocha Welcome dialog). It's not a bad read. Because it's a new feature, here's an example with a few highlights.

1. Begin with a New Project by clicking at the upper left.

2. Choose the source clip, a TIFF sequence called 08_mocha_corner_pin_applied.

3. This is an image sequence, so be certain about setting the frame rate here and in After Effects. This footage was shot at 23.976 fps; if, for example, you instead choose 24, just make sure you do so in both applications (and remember that a new copy of After Effects defaults to 30).

4. Allow the clip to load, then drag the black time indicator below the viewer to some frame at the middle of the clip where you can clearly see the screen.

   In this shot, the camera pans on and off the screen, so it will be necessary to begin in the middle and track both forward and backward.

5. With the X-spline ⬚ tool (or if you prefer, Bezier splines ⬚), click four corner points in succession just outside the monitor's boundaries (**Figure 8.20**), and then press C to close the shape.

NOTES

The footage and projects used for this mocha AE example can be found in 08_mocha_corner_pin_basic on the book's disc.

Figure 8.20 Four corners are positioned outside the bounds of the item being tracked, without even taking the trouble to tighten the X-splines. The image on the monitor is washed-out enough that there's no need to hold that out (which would be done more carefully and is thoroughly explained in the mocha-AE manual).

Note that the boundaries don't really matter here. Capturing most of the foreground monitor, including its edges and even a bit of what's behind it, is fine.

6. Now track the shot, first forward to the end of the clip, then drag back to the beginning of the blue line of tracked frames and track backward to the opening of the shot.

   Note that mocha-AE has no trouble with motion blur, the moving content on the screen (because it's so faint in this case—see the mocha-AE manual for an example where it's necessary to hold out the screen), and most remarkably (compared with the After Effects tracker) it's no problem for the track area to exit frame.

7. Go back to the middle of the clip and enable the Surface button to the right of the viewer. Drag the four blue corners so that the shape aligns with the edges of the screen.

8. Click on the AdjustTrack tab below the viewer, then scrub or play the clip to see how well the corners hold.

9. Zoom Window picture-in-picture views helpfully appear (**Figure 8.21**) with a given corner selected; use the

Nudge controls under AdjustTrack to gently push them back into place anywhere you see them slipping, or simply try the Auto button at the center of those controls.

Figure 8.21 When it comes time to fine-tune the positions of the surface corners, mocha looks like a point tracker, but the crosshairs are only there to fine-tune the completed planar track.

10. Once you are satisfied that the surface is locked in place, click Export Tracking Data from the lower right of the UI. From the dialog that appears, choose After Effects Corner Pin [supports motion blur] and click Copy to Clipboard (**Figure 8.22**).

Figure 8.22 The most straightforward approach to an ordinary corner pin.

If you instead choose to save a text file, you can then copy and paste its data from an ordinary text editor.

11. Back in After Effects, at the same starting frame, paste the keyframes to the target layer to be added (if you don't have one, create a new solid or placeholder layer).

12. Enable Motion Blur for both the layer and the Composition in the Timeline.

This track now has everything you need: an entry, exit, and motion blur, and it even matches the skewing caused by the Canon 7D CMOS sensor (**Figure 8.23**).

SCRIPT

MochaImport by Mathias Möhl (http://aescripts.com/mochaimport/) simplifies the process of applying mocha-AE tracking data in After Effects. You can track or stabilize a layer without intermediate nulls or other steps, and even set up a scene track or camera move stabilization as shown earlier in this chapter.

Figure 8.23 Mocha-AE v2's use of position data makes corner pinning a heavily motion-blurred scene just work with the right settings.

Mocha is typically used for corner pinning, but you can instead choose to export After Effects Transform Data and use it like regular tracker data.

The Nitty-Gritty

It's normal for a track to be slightly more complicated than this, usually due to motion or perspective shifts within the track area. This can be the result of foreground objects passing across the track region or the appearance of the region itself changing over time.

Figure 8.24 shows an otherwise straightforward track—a screen, like the last one—with the following challenges: flares and reflections play across the screen, the hands move back and forth across the unit, and the perspective of the screen changes dramatically.

Figure 8.24 The tracking markers on the screen are not necessary for mocha to track this handheld unit for screen replacement; it's the reflective screen itself and the movement of the thumbs across it that present mocha with a challenge.

There are two standard solutions to any track that slips:

▶ Sudden slippage is often the result of foreground motion (or light shifts) changing the appearance of the tracked area; the solution is to mask out the area containing the disturbance.

▶ Small, gradual slippage is often the result of shifts in perspective and can be keyframed.

The clip shown in Figure 8.23 requires both techniques. A track of the entire face of the unit shifts slightly as it is tilted and it shifts a lot as the thumbs move across the track area and reflections play across the screen.

Big shifts in the track region are caused by changes in the track area, so I fix those first, adding an additional spline (or splines) containing the interruptive motion. The Add X-spline and Add Bezier Spline create a subtractive shape (or shapes) around the areas of the first region that contain any kind of motion. **Figure 8.25** shows that these can be oddly defined; they track right along with the main planar track.

Figure 8.25 Holdout masks are added to eliminate areas where the screen picks up reflections and the left thumb moves around. Notice that the tracking markers aren't even used; there is plenty of other detail for mocha to track without them.

Retracking with these additional holdout masks improves the track; all that is required to perfect this track is a single keyframe (at a point where the unit is tilted about 15 degrees toward camera), this time to the track mask itself, which creates a green keyframe along the main timeline. Mocha uses these keyframes as extra points of comparison, rather than simply averaging their positions.

In this example it's also helpful to check Perspective under Motion in the Track tab; this allows the change in proportions from the tilting of the screen to be included in the Corner Pin export.

Figure 8.26 The Red Giant Corner Pin effect not only includes a Mocha Import function, it allows "from" as well as "to" pins—so your Corner Pin content can be tracked from a moving source as well.

NOTES

The Red Giant Corner Pin effect included in the Warp collection (available on the book's disc) is designed specifically to be used with mocha-AE (**Figure 8.26**).

If you get into trouble, you'll want to know how to delete keys (under Keyframe Controls) or reference points (in the AdjustTrack tab). You also need to know a few new keyboard shortcuts, such as **X** for the hand tool and arrow keys to navigate forward and backward one frame.

Track Roto/Paint

Expressions and tracking data go together like Lennon and McCartney: harmoniously, sometimes with difficulty, but to great effect. You don't even have to apply raw tracking data in order to put expressions to use; the expressions pick whip can be used to link any property containing X and Y position data directly to the X and Y of a motion track.

For example, to track in a paint clone operation in a single layer:

1. Set up a track with the paint target as the feature center (the center of the feature region).

2. Move the attach point to the area from which you wish to clone.

CLOSE-UP

Shape Tracking

Mocha-AE version 2 also adds shape tracking via the new mocha shape effect. There are a couple of features that are unique to it:

▶ Shapes tracked in mocha-AE can be pasted into After Effects as mask shapes.

▶ Mocha shapes support adding feather to mask vectors (if applied with the mocha shape effect).

However, it has to be said that shape tracking is not the prime directive, if you will, of mocha-AE, and it can be challenging to set up the track (read the manual, as it involves linking shapes) and then to get the splines to conform to the actual contours of the item being tracked. Your mileage may vary.

3. Track motion; you can set Track Type to Raw or simply don't apply it.

4. Add a clone stroke with appropriate settings.

5. Pick whip Stroke Options > Clone Position to Attach Point and Transform: Clone 1 > Position to Feature Center.

This technique can just as easily be applied to any layer that can be placed within visible range for pick whipping.

Continue Loop

Sometimes a track point will disappear before the track is completed, either because it is obscured by a foreground object or because it has moved offscreen. As shown above, mocha-AE generally has no problem with this—any part of the tracked plane that remains in frame is tracked.

Nonetheless, there are many cases in which you'll want to continue a track or other motion-matched animation right in After Effects. First make certain there are no unwanted extra tracking keyframes beyond which the point was still correctly tracked; this expression uses the difference between the final two keyframes to estimate what will happen next.

Reveal the property that needs extending (Position in this case), and **Alt**-click (**Opt**-click) on its stopwatch. In the text field that is revealed, replace the text (`position`) by typing `loopOut("continue")`. Yes, that's right, typing; don't worry, you're not less of an artist for doing it (**Figure 8.27**).

This expression uses the delta (velocity and direction) of the last two frames. It creates matching linear motion (not a curve) moving at a steady rate, so it works well if those last two frames are representative of the overall rate and direction of motion.

Chapter 10 offers many more ideas about how to go beyond these simple expressions and to customize them according to specific needs.

NOTES

The techniques revealed earlier in the chapter to Track a Scene can also be used to place paint and roto, just as you would any comped and tracked object.

SCRIPT

Tracker2Mask by Mathias Möhl (http://aescripts.com/tracker-2mask/) uses tracker data to track masks without the need for a one-to-one correspondence between the tracked points and the mask points. This script is a fantastic roto shortcut for cases where a rigid body in the scene is changing position or perspective.

Figure 8.27 A continue loop is handy anywhere you have motion that should continue at the pace and in the direction at the first or last keyframe. Notice in this example that although it could help as the skater disappears behind the post, the loop doesn't do curves; motion continues along a linear vector.

3D Tracking

After Effects can make use of 3D tracking data. Many leading third-party motion tracking applications, including Pixel Farm's PF Track and SynthEyes, from Andersson Technologies, export 3D tracks specifically for After Effects. And CameraTracker, a new 3D tracking plug-in from the Foundry, make the process of incorporating a match-moved camera into an After Effects scene much more straightforward (**Figure 8.28**). The following discussion assumes you are not working with this plug-in, although much of the same information applies.

Generally, the 3D tracking workflow operates as follows:

1. Track the scene with a 3D tracking application. The generated 3D camera data and any associated nulls or center point can be exported as a Maya .ma file for After Effects.

Figure 8.28 The Foundry's CameraTracker looks set to bring real 3D tracking right into the After Effects Composition viewer.

You probably know that it's also possible to import Cinema 4D 3D data into After Effects via a Cinema 4D plug-in from Maxon, but using the pt_AEtoC4D script by Paul Tuersley (http://www.btinternet.com/~paul.tuersley/scripts/pt_AEtoC4D_v1.4.zip) you can also work the other direction with 3D camera animations, exporting them from After Effects to Cinema 4D.

After Effects can also extract camera data embedded in an RPF sequence (and typically generated in 3ds Max or Flame). Place the sequence containing the 3D camera data in a comp and choose Animation > Keyframe Assistant > RPF Camera Import.

2. Optionally, import the camera data into a 3D animation program and render 3D elements to be composited. Working with Maya, you can also create a 3D animation and camera data from scratch, and export that.

3. Import the camera data into After Effects; you'll see a composition with an animated 3D camera and nulls (potentially dozens if they haven't been managed beforehand). A 2D background plate with the original camera motion can be freely matched with 3D layers.

Figure 8.29 shows a shot that also began with a 3D track in Boujou. The fires that you see in the after shot are actually dozens of individual 2D fire and smoke layers, staggered and angled in 3D space as the camera flies over to give the sense of perspective. More on this shot and how to set up a shot like this is found in Chapter 14.

3D Tracking Data

After Effects can import Maya scenes (.ma files) provided they are properly prepped and include only rendering cameras (with translation and lens data) and nulls. The camera data should be "baked," with a keyframe at every frame (search on "baking Maya camera data" in the online help for specifics on this).

Figure 8.29 Just because you're stuck with 2D layers in After Effects doesn't mean you can't stagger them all over 3D space to give the illusion of depth, as with this fly-by shot. Tracking nulls from Boujou helped get the relative scale of the scene; this was important because the depth of the elements had to be to exact scale for the parallax illusion (right) to work. (Final fire image courtesy of ABC-TV.)

3D trackers operate a bit differently than the After Effects tracker. Generally you do not begin by setting tracking points with these; instead, the software creates a swarm of hundreds of points that come and go throughout the shot, and it "solves" the camera using a subset of them.

Besides Position and Rotation, Camera may also contain Zoom keyframes. Unless Sergio Leone has started making spaghetti westerns again, zoom shots are not the norm and any zoom animation should be checked against a camera report (or any available anecdotal data) and eliminated if bogus (it indicates a push or even an unstable camera). Most 3D trackers allow you to specify that a shot was taken with a prime lens (no zoom).

Work with a Maya Scene

A .ma scene is imported just like a separate .aep project; make sure it is named with the .ma extension. You may see one or two compositions: two in the case of nonsquare pixels (including a nested square pixel version). The camera may be *single-node* (in which case the camera holds all of the animation data) or *targeted*, in which case the transformation data resides in a parent node to which the camera is attached.

The first challenge is that any null object with the word "null" in its name is also imported. Unedited, the scene may become massive and cumbersome. Any composition

TIP

Because After Effects offers no proportional 3D grids in the viewers, nulls imported with a 3D scene are a huge help when scaling and positioning elements in 3D.

3D Tracking Software

The book's disc includes a demo of SynthEyes, a reasonably priced 3D tracker from Andersson Technologies which is no less accurate than more expensive options, provided you read the manual and learn how to use it beyond the big green tracking button (which often works even if you don't know much else).

The complex art of matchmoving is detailed in *Matchmoving: The Invisible Art of Camera Tracking* (Sybex Inc.) by Tim Dobbert.

with 500 layers of any kind is slow and unwieldy, so eliminate all but the nulls that correspond to significant objects in the scene. If possible, do this in the tracking software or 3D program so you never have to see the excess in After Effects.

If too many nulls make their way into After Effects, once you've selected the dozen or two useful ones, context-click on them and choose Invert Selection to select the potentially hundreds of other unused nulls. Delete them, or if that makes you nervous, at least turn off their visibility and enable them as Shy layers.

The next challenge is that nulls often come in with tiny values in the low single digits, which also means that they have 0, 0, 0 as a center point (standard in 3D but not in After Effects, which uses the coordinates at the center of the comp, such as 960, 540, 0).

Here's the honest truth: 0, 0, 0 is a much more sensible center point for anything 3D. If you think you can keep track of it and deal with the camera and other elements clustered around the upper-left corner in the orthographic views, it's more straightforward to handle a 3D scene with this center point and to reposition 2D layers to that point when they are converted to 3D.

This is also a way to tackle the problem of the tiny world of single-digit position values. Add a 3D null positioned at 0, 0, 0, then parent all layers of the imported Maya comp to it. Now raise the Scale values of the null. Once you have the scene at a healthier size, you can **Alt**-unparent (**Opt**-unparent) all of those layers, and the scaled values stick. This method will also invert a scene that comes in upside-down (as happens with After Effects, since its Y axis is centered in the upper-left corner and is thus itself upside-down).

3D matchmoving relies on the After Effects camera to track 3D data, and that feature and how it compares with the optics and behavior of a real-world camera is the subject of the next chapter.

9

The Camera and Optics

There is only you and your camera. The limitations in your photography are in yourself, for what we see is what we are.

— Ernst Haas

The Camera and Optics

Visual effects might seem to be all about realism, but that's not quite the goal; the compositor's actual job is more precisely to simulate the real world *as it appears through the lens of a camera.* The distinction is critical, because the photographed world looks different from the one you see with the naked eye and consider to be reality.

An understanding of cinematography is essential to compositing, because After Effects offers the opportunity to recreate and even change essential shooting decisions long after the crew has struck the set and called it a wrap. Your shot may be perfectly realistic on its own merits, but it will only belong in the story if it works from a cinematic point of view. Factors in After Effects that contribute to good cinematography include

▶ field of view

▶ depth of focus

▶ the shooting medium and what it reveals about the story (or if you like, the storyteller)

▶ planar perspective and dimensional perspective

▶ camera motion (handheld, stabilized, or locked) and what it implies about point of view

These seemingly disparate points all involve understanding how the camera sees the world and how film and video record what the camera sees. All of them transcend mere aesthetics, influencing how the viewer perceives the story itself.

Cameras: Virtual and Real

Our exploration of virtual cinematography begins with the After Effects camera, which relates closely to an actual motion picture camera without actually being anything like one. You can exploit the similarities as well as strong differences between 3D in After Effects and real-world counterparts: the camera, lighting and shading options.

See with the Camera

Toggle a layer to 3D and voilà, its properties contain three axes instead of two—but enabling 3D without a camera is a little bit like taking a car with a fully automatic transmission into a road race: You're fine until things get tricky, at which point you may hit the wall.

The Camera Settings dialog (**Figure 9.1**) includes a unique physical diagram to describe how settings in the 3D camera affect your scene.

Figure 9.1 The Camera Settings dialog provides a visual UI to elucidate the relationship between values. The 50 mm preset selected in the Preset menu is the neutral (default) setting; use it for neutral perspective.

Lens Settings

Although it is not labeled as such, and despite that After Effects defaults to any previous camera settings, the true neutral default After Effects lens is the 50 mm preset in Camera Settings. This setting (**Figure 9.2**) is neither wide (as with lower values, **Figure 9.3**) nor long (as with higher values, **Figure 9.4**), and it introduces no shift in perspective, in a scene that contains Z depth.

The folder 09_3d_lens_angles on the book's disc contains the cameras and 3D model used for the figures in this section.

Figure 9.2 The default lens (50 mm setting). If settings are at the defaults, with Z Position value the exact inverse of the Zoom value, the resulting camera does not shift the comp's appearance.

Figure 9.3 An extreme wide field of view does not distort in the "fish-eye" manner of a short glass lens, but it does radically alter the perspective and proportions of this 3D model imported into After Effects via Photoshop.

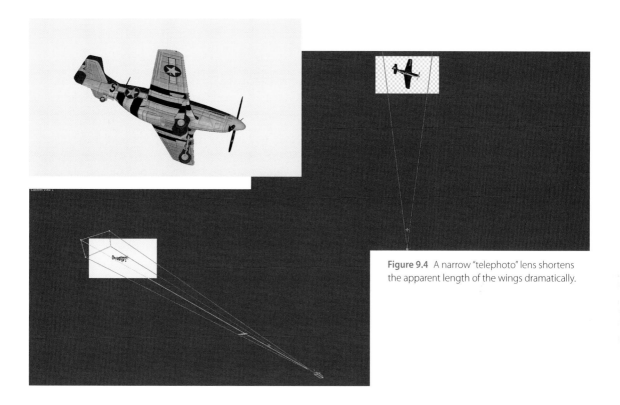

Figure 9.4 A narrow "telephoto" lens shortens the apparent length of the wings dramatically.

"50 mm" is literally meaningless, because virtual space doesn't contain millimeters any more than it contains kilograms, parsecs, or bunny rabbits. This is the median lens length of a 35 mm SLR camera, the standard professional still image camera.

Motion picture cameras are not so standardized. The equivalent lens on a 35 mm film camera shooting Academy ratio itself has a 35 mm length. A miniDV camera, on the other hand, has a tiny neutral lens length of around 4 mm. The length corresponds directly to the size of the backplate or video pickup, the area where the image is projected inside the camera.

Lens length, then, is a somewhat arbitrary and made-up value in the virtual world of After Effects. The corresponding setting that applies universally is Angle of View, which can be calculated whether images were shot in IMAX or HDV or created in a 3D animation package.

A fifth numerical field in Camera Settings, Focus Distance, is enabled by checking Enable Depth of Field; it corresponds to a camera's aperture setting.

Real Camera Settings

To understand the relationship of the After Effects camera to that of a real-world camera, look again at the Camera Settings diagram introduced in Figure 9.1. Four numerical fields—Film Size, Focal Length, Zoom, and Angle of View—surround a common hypotenuse.

A prime (or fixed) lens has static values for all four. A zoom lens allows Zoom and Focal Length to be adjusted, changing Angle of View. Either lens will resolve a different image depending on the size of the sensor (or film back, or in this case the Film Size setting). These four settings, then, are interrelated and interdependent, as the diagram implies. Lengthen the lens by increasing Focal Length and the Angle of View decreases proportionally.

Angle of View is the radius, in degrees, from one edge of the view to the other. If you have calculated this number in order to match it, note that Camera Settings lets you specify a horizontal, vertical, or diagonal measurement in the Measure Film Size menu.

In After Effects, the Zoom value is the distance of the camera, in pixels, from the plane of focus. Create a camera and its default Z Position value is the inverse of the Zoom value, perfectly framing the contents of the comp at their default Z Position, 0.0 (**Figure 9.5**). This makes for easy reference when measuring depth of field effects, and it lets you link camera position and zoom together via expressions (for depth of field and multiplane effects, discussed later).

Figure 9.5 The two exposed pulldown menus aren't available in the Timeline panel itself. The default position of a new camera corresponds to the Zoom value, which can be viewed here in pixels. A One-Node Camera has no point of Interest, like a real-world camera.

Emulate a Real Camera

Other considerations when matching a real-world camera include much of the material that follows in this chapter, such as

- **depth of field.** This is among the most filmic and evocative additions to a scene. Like any computer graphics program, After Effects naturally has limitless depth of field, so you have to re-create the shallow depth of real-world optics to bring a filmic look to a comp.

- **zoom or push.** A move in or out is used for dramatic effect, but a zoom and a push communicate very different things about point of view.

- **motion blur and shutter angle.** These are composition (not camera) settings; introduced in Chapter 2 and further explored here.

- **lens angle.** The perspective and parallax of layers in 3D space change according to the angle of the lens used to view them.

- **lens distortion.** Real lenses introduce curvature to straight lines, which is most apparent with wide-angle or "fish-eye" lenses. An After Effects camera has no lens, hence, no distortion, but it can be created or removed (see the section "Lens Distortion").

- **exposure.** Every viewer in After Effects includes an Exposure control ( ); this (along with the effect with the same name) is mathematically similar but different in practice from the aperture of a physical camera. Exposure and color range is detailed in Chapter 11.

- **boke, halation, flares.** All sorts of interesting phenomena are generated by light when it interacts with the lens itself. The appeal of this purely optical phenomenon in a shot is subjective, yet it can offer a unique and beautiful aesthetic and lend realism to a scene shot under conditions where we would expect to see it (whether we know it or not).

A *camera report* is a record of the settings used when the footage was taken, usually logged by the camera assistant (or equivalent).

The Camera Report

Maintaining an accurate camera report on a shoot (**Figure 9.6**) is the job of the second assistant camera operator (or 2nd AC). The report includes such vital information on a given scene and take as ASA and f-stop settings, as well as the lens used. Lens data is often vital to matching the scene with a virtual camera, although there are methods to derive it after the fact with reasonable accuracy. A great tip for a VFX supervisor is to take a shot of the camera itself on a given VFX shot so that there is visible reference of the lens and focal settings, in case they aren't recorded accurately.

Figure 9.6 This page from *The Camera Assistant's Manual* by David Elkins, SOC, shows the type of information typically recorded on a camera report, including lens and f-stop data for a given scene and take. The criteria are somewhat different when shooting digitally but fundamentally similar.

FILM CAMERA REPORT

LABORATORY		PAGE	OF

PROD. CO.	
PROD. TITLE	

DIRECTOR		D.P.	
1st AC		2nd AC	

DATE		PROD. #		CAMERA	
MAG #		ROLL #		FOOTAGE	
FILM TYPE		EMULSION #	

SCENE	TAKE	DIAL	FEET	LENS	F-STOP	REMARKS

☐ 16mm	☐ Super 16mm	☐ 35mm	☐ COLOR	☐ B & W	GOOD	
☐ PROCESS NORMAL		☐ ONE LIGHT PRINT		☐ BEST LIGHT PRINT	NO GOOD	
☐ PREP FOR TRANSFER		☐ TIME TO GRAY SCALE		☐ TIMED WORK PRINT	WASTE	
☐ PRINT ALL		☐ TIME TO THESE LIGHTS	___ — ___ — ___		SE	
☐ OTHER					TOTAL	

COMMENTS

The basic job of the visual effects supervisor is to record as much visual reference data as possible (typically using a DSLR camera) in addition to maintaining clear communications with the cinematographer, with whom the VFX supervisor is mutually dependent.

There are several other bits of data that can be of vital interest in postproduction, and these go beyond what is recorded in an ordinary camera report. Focal distance (a measurement from camera to subject), camera height, any angle to the camera if it is not level, and any start and end data on zooms or focus pulls might be missing from the standard camera report. When supervising, be sure to ask that these be included, particularly if any 3D tracking will be necessary.

With accurate information on the type of camera and the focal length of a shot, you know enough to match the lens of that camera with an After Effects camera.

Table 9.1 on the next page details the sizes of some typical film formats. If your particular brand and make of camera is on the list, and you know the focal length, use these to match the camera via Camera Settings (double-click the camera layer to reveal). The steps are as follows:

1. Set Measure Film Size to Horizontally. (Note that hFilmPlane in the expression stands for "Horizontal Film Plane.")

2. Set Units to millimeters.

3. Enter the number from the Horizontal column of the chart that corresponds to the source film format.

4. Enter the desired Focal Length.

Once the Angle of View matches the footage, tracked objects maintain position in the scene as the shot progresses. It's vital to get this right when re-creating a camera move, especially if a particularly wide or long lens was used, or things simply may not line up correctly. It's even more important for camera projection (discussed later).

NOTES

If lens data is missing for a given plate, it is possible to derive it if the vanishing point and a couple of basic assumptions about scale can be determined. Check the book's disc for a demonstration of how to do this courtesy of fxphd.com.

TIP

An alternative to the listed steps, for those who like using expressions, is to use the following expression on the camera's Zoom property:
FocalLength = 35 // change to your value, in mm
hFilmPlane = 24.892 // change to film size, in mm (horizontal); multiply values in inches by 25.4
this_comp.width*(Focal Length/hFilmPlane)

TABLE 9.1 Typical Film Format Sizes

Format	Horizontal (inches)	Vertical (inches)	Horizontal (mm)	Vertical (mm)
Full Aperture Camera Aperture	0.98	0.735	24.892	18.669
Scope Camera Aperture	0.864	0.732	21.9456	18.5928
Scope Scan	0.825	0.735	20.955	18.669
2:1 Scope Projector Aperture	0.838	0.7	21.2852	17.78
Academy Camera Aperture	0.864	0.63	21.9456	16.002
Academy Projector Aperture	0.825	0.602	20.955	15.2908
1.66 Projector Aperture	0.825	0.497	20.955	12.6238
1.85 Projector Aperture	0.825	0.446	20.955	11.3284
VistaVision Aperture	0.991	1.485	25.1714	37.719
VistaVision Scan	0.98	1.47	24.892	37.338
16 mm Camera Aperture	0.404	0.295	10.2616	7.493
Super-16 Camera Aperture	0.493	0.292	12.5222	7.4168
HD Full 1.78	0.378	0.212 (Full Aperture in HD 1.78)	9.6012	5.3848 (Full Aperture in HD 1.78)
HD 90% 1.78	0.34	0.191 (90% Safe Area used in HD 1.78)	8.636	4.8514 (90% Safe Area used in HD 1.78)
HD Full 1.85	0.378	0.204 (Full Aperture in HD 1.85)	9.6012	5.1816 (Full Aperture in HD 1.85)
HD 90% 1.85	0.34	0.184 (90% Safe Area used in HD 1.85)	8.636	4.6736 (90% Safe Area used in HD 1.85)
HD Full 2.39	0.3775	0.158 (Full Aperture in HD 2.39)	9.5885	4.0132 (Full Aperture in HD 2.39)
HD 90% 2.39	0.34	0.142 (90% Safe Area used in HD 2.39)	8.636	3.6068 (90% Safe Area used in HD 2.39)
APS-C (such as Canon 7D)	0.888	0.59	22.5552	22.225
Full-frame 35mm (such as Canon 5D)	1.42	0.945	36.068	24.003
RED One Mysterium	0.96	0.539	24.384	13.6906

Lens Distortion

A virtual camera with a wide-angle view (like the one back in Figure 9.2) has a dramatically altered 3D perspective but no actual lens. A virtual camera is only capable of gathering an image linearly—in a straight line to each object.

A physical lens curves light in order to frame an image on the flat back plate of the camera. The more curved the lens, the wider the angle of view it is able to gather and bend so that it is perpendicular to the back of the camera. A fish-eye view requires a convex lens a short distance from the plate or sensor in order to gather the full range of view.

At the extremes, this causes easily visible lens distortion; items in the scene known to contain straight lines don't appear straight at all but bent in a curve (**Figure 9.7**). The barrel distortion of a fish-eye lens shot makes it appear as if the screen has been inflated like a balloon.

Figure 9.7 The nearly psychedelic look of extreme lens distortion; the lens flare itself is extremely aberrated. You can create just as wide a lens with the 3D camera, but there would be no lens distortion because there is no lens.

As you refine your eye, you may notice that many shots that aren't as extreme as a fish-eye perspective contain a degree of lens distortion. Or you might find that motion tracks match on one side of the frame but slip on the opposite side, proportions go out of whack, or things just don't quite line up as they should (**Figure 9.8**).

Figure 9.8   The shot calls for the curb to be red, but a rectangular layer does not line up. Lens distortion is present in this shot.

Check out 09_lens_distort_ correction on the book's disc to try this for yourself.

The Optics Compensation effect is designed to mimic lens distortion. Increasing Field of View makes the affected layer more fish-eyed in appearance; the solution in this case is to apply that effect to the red rectangle layer. You can even remove fish-eye distortion (aka barrel distortion) by checking Reverse Lens Distortion and raising the Field of View (FOV) value, but the result is unnatural and the quantized pixels less aesthetically pleasing.

The setting is derived by eye, as follows.

1. Having identified lens distortion (Figure 9.8), create a new solid layer called Grid. If you like, make it 10% to 20% larger than the source comp so that even when distorted, it reaches the edges of frame.

2. Apply the Grid effect to the Grid layer. For a grid like the one in **Figure 9.9,** set Size From Width & Height and make the Width and Height settings equal, then give the grid the color of your choice (Figure 9.9).

Figure 9.9   The grid doesn't line up with the largely rectilinear background near the bottom and top of frame.

3. Apply Optics Compensation and raise the FOV value until the grid lines up with the background. If necessary, rotate either the grid or the background image so that they are horizontally level with one another.

4. Note that the vertical lines don't match up, because the camera was tilted up when the shot was taken. Correct for this by making the Grid layer 3D and adjusting the X Orientation value (or X Rotation—these are interchangeable). **Figure 9.10** shows a matched grid.

5. Copy Optics Compensation (and, if necessary, 3D rotation) settings to the foreground curb element and switch its blending mode to Color. It now conforms to the curb (**Figure 9.11**).

Figure 9.10 Optics compensation is applied to the grid, which is also rotated in 3D to account for camera tilt (left). Even the crazy shot from Figure 9.7 can be matched with the proper Optics Compensation setting.

Figure 9.11 The composited layer is distorted to match the curvature of the original background.

There's one unusual detail in this particular shot—study the distorted grid over the curb and notice that the curb curves away from it, and from the white lines out in the street. The curb has a curve of its own in z space, which we know for certain because we've corrected the lens distortion. You can freely edit the object for such details if necessary without compounding the problem by fighting lens distortion.

3D

At this writing 3D display technology is all the rage, thanks to box office records for *Avatar* and higher ticket prices for the privilege of wearing silly glasses in the movie theater. Up to this point in the chapter we've seen how accurate re-creation of 3D is useful throughout the compositing process even when not working in stereo.

There's an important distinction to be made between 3D input/output and the use of 3D in compositing. If you find yourself working with two simultaneous side-by-side images created for 3D stereo output, you'll find that After Effects doesn't offer much in the way of dedicated stereo tools. But even with 2D background footage being comped 2D, After Effects lets you freely mix 3D into your compositing process, as follows:

▶ A 2D background layer remains in place no matter what happens with the camera and 3D layers, which is key to 3D matchmoving to a 2D source clip.

▶ Standard 2D adjustment layers affect all layers below them, including 3D layers.

▶ 3D layers use standard blending modes (over 2D elements, they obey layer order, and with other 3D elements, Z-space depth).

But proceed with caution:

▶ When working with a track matte, the visible layer or the matte layer may be 3D, but in almost no case is it the right idea to make them both 3D with unique positions unless attempting to do something very strange.

▶ Paradoxically, plug-ins that work with After Effects 3D space typically reside on 2D layers (**Figure 9.12**).

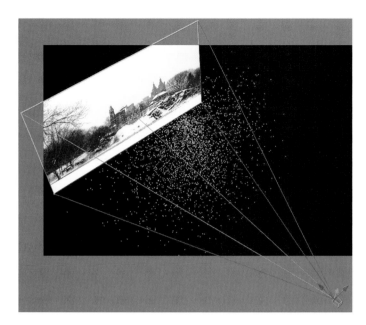

Figure 9.12 Particles generated by Trapcode Particular fill the volume of 3D space, as is evident in a perspective view, although the effect is applied to a 2D layer.

▶ Precomp a set of 3D layers and it's as if you have a single 2D view of them until you enable Collapse Transformations, at which point it's as if the layers are back in the main composition. Almost as if, that is—light and camera layers are not passed through, and strange things can happen as you mix 2D layers, effects, and 3D precomps.

If you come up against a setup that isn't working and doesn't make sense, be a little scientific and carefully test removing one variable at a time, then undoing, until you find the one that is confusing things.

Photoshop 3D Models

The views of the plane that appear in Figures 9.2 through 9.4 were indeed rendered in After Effects. Unlike ordinary 3D layers, also known as "postcards in space," this is a full 3D mesh with geometry, shading, and textures. Photoshop provides the means to open 3D models in specific formats—this one came in as an .obj with a few texture images—and save them as Photoshop .psd files. These files can then be imported into After Effects.

But is it worth the trouble? 3D models in After Effects tend to behave sluggishly (a high-end professional graphics card certainly helps) and have the following fundamental limitations:

▶ Textures, lighting, even anti-aliasing can be adjusted only in Photoshop.

▶ To adjust such Photoshop-only features, use Edit Original (**Ctrl+E/Cmd+E**), make the changes in Photoshop, then save and they appear in After Effects. It's not what you'd call "interactive."

▶ After Effects lighting, material options, and motion blur have no effect on Photoshop 3D layers, and there's no easy way to articulate or otherwise work with the individual components of a complex model. Forget about spinning the propeller of that aircraft for some natural motion blur.

Figure 9.13 shows the basic Photoshop 3D setup in After Effects. The source Photoshop file has a single layer, but the comp generated upon import into After Effects contains three: a camera, a Controller layer, and the 3D image itself. You can replace or even eliminate the camera layer, but the other two must remain together or the layer becomes ordinary again, like Cinderella after midnight.

Figure 9.13 The Photoshop Import dialog accommodates Photoshop 3D layers; just check the Live Photoshop 3D box. The resulting comp (right) contains a camera, the image, and a controller layer; the image has a Live Photoshop 3D effect applied to it, which links it to the Controller via a set of expressions (in red).

To transform the 3D object, you work with the controller layer, a null. You can apply any standard image effects to the layer that contains the image itself. More fundamental changes to the appearance of the model are no more available than they would be in third-party software such as Maya, which can also render a much nice-looking image using modern lighting and shading techniques available in Mental Ray or Pixar Renderman.

If the lack of motion blur is the main thing standing in your way of using Photoshop 3D elements in After Effects, you can try adding an adjustment layer at the top of the comp containing your 3D animation. Next:

▶ Apply the Timewarp effect to that layer. Change speed to 100 and toggle Enable Motion Blur, then set the other Motion Blur settings to get the look you want.

▶ Apply CC TimeBlend for a less render-intensive approach that won't work with heavy motion (and is frankly a bit eccentric to preview—if it looks strange, try hitting the Clear button at the top of the effect and regenerating the preview).

These are the same workarounds you would use if for some reason your 3D render had no motion blur; it's a less accurate and, especially in the case of Timewarp, more render-intensive approach. More about using Timewarp to generate motion blur can be found in Chapter 2.

Stereo Output

With Nuke, the Foundry has led stereo compositing with dedicated tools such as Ocula to smooth the process. After Effects leaves you largely on your own to figure out how to work on two image channels simultaneously in order to change them. Not that much has changed in After Effects regarding 3D comping since the days when we comped movies such as *Spy Kids 3D* at the Orphanage, back when stereo display was considered kind of retro.

The big problem comping in stereo is twofold. First, you can only preview the resulting 3D image when you put on your 3D glasses and look at a final image, which is to say, when you stop working. The more difficult problem is that

CLOSE-UP

DigiEffects FreeForm AE for 3D Displacement and Warps

After Effects CS5 adds a plug-in which at long last can bend any layer into true 3D space instead of limiting image data to the "postcards in space" model. Many plug-ins including Particular and 3D Stroke operate in true 3D and interact with the After Effects camera. Only DE_FreeFormAE, however, can take an existing image and either warp it, via a mesh, or displace it, using a bitmap, into 3D space (so that as the camera moves around it, the shape is revealed to be three-dimensional).

You can use this plug-in to match objects in a scene—for example, replacing the label on a can that the camera moves around by bending it with a mesh—or to displace your own custom geometry (a staircase uses a row of gray bars, while more natural mountain or water topography can be re-created with a fractal noise map). To re-create the motion of a flag in 3D, you might both ripple it with a displacement map and create the broader flapping motion by keyframing a mesh animation. Tutorials showing how to use it are available at www.digieffects.com.

A simple 3D comp setup is found in 09_3D_setup_basic on the book's disc.

Duplink, Jeff Almasol's script introduced earlier, which is exclusive to this book and can be found on the disc (rd_Duplink.jsx), creates an instance layer whose properties are all linked to the original, allowing you to freely work in one channel and see updates in the other. You still have to set it up for each layer and effect you add, but it can certainly save tedious manual labor.

tiny incremental refinements that have any spatial component whatsoever have to be implemented the same, yet differently, on both channels. Roto is hard enough, but when the same element has to be rotoscoped identically on two channels that don't match, you have a dilemma. And quite possibly, a headache.

You can keep two comp viewers side by side—or perhaps more conveniently for the rest of the UI, top and bottom. Generally you make all of your edits to one or the other channel (usually based on which one is destined to be the "hero" channel that will be displayed in 2D-only playback of the movie). In an ideal world you could get one channel perfect, then duplicate that comp, swap in the other channel, and make the necessary adjustments in one pass.

Unfortunately I never seem to spot any job listings from this "ideal world." No matter how hard you try to get one layer to final before starting on the other one, there will be changes, and these must of course be consistent on both layers, with spatial offsets. And unless you set it up carefully and pay close attention, that turns into a game of whack-a-mole—only less fun.

The only procedural solution is to link as many elements together between left and right as possible. The biggest recent feature addition that would have helped me comp 3D features in After Effects a few years ago is the ability to link masks together with expressions; you simply apply an expression to a mask shape and then pick whip to the mask whose shape you want it to inherit. True, there's no easy way to offset it automatically, but you can turn any expression into keyframes using Animation > Keyframe Assistant > Convert Expression to Keyframes and then offset the whole set or individual vertices using the Key Tweak script introduced in Chapter 7.

Convergence and 3D Previews

Previewing 3D in After Effects is most possible in anaglyph view (typically with red and blue glasses). Anaglyph does horrendous things to color and contrast, as each primary becomes effectively invisible in the corresponding eye. But prepping the channels for this type of display is simple with the Shift Channels effect. First create a render comp containing only the left and right channel composites. Now just turn off one channel in one eye, turn off the other two channels in the other eye, and set whichever layer is higher in the stack to Add mode to combine the two.

The other item necessary in this render comp is an *interocular* control, a fancy name for the distance between the two views. The proper way to set this is to match the average distance between human eyes, which is approximately 2.5 inches. Move the left and right channels further or closer horizontally and the apparent depth (and *convergence point*, if any) changes, more or less respectively. You can rig a simple expression to a Slider Control to offset the secondary channel (as in **Figure 9.14**).

If you happen to be doing a lot of 3D compositing, you will no doubt want to do better than a simple offset in the render comp, however. Offsetting 2D images fails to re-create true parallax, in which it's possible to widen the interocular for more depth without changing the convergence point. There's also the question of whether the cameras are aimed straight ahead for *parallel* orientation (as in most stereo movies) or *toe in*, where the cameras are angled toward the center of the plane of convergence (as was favored by Jim Cameron for *Avatar*).

NOTES

The 8-bit 3D Glasses effect offers a few other options for display which you can re-create via channel effects, without clipping output to 8 bpc. It's there for convenience, not necessity.

Figure 9.14 After Effects doesn't include a UI setup for stereo viewing, but it does give you the means to customize your own. By using the View > New Viewer (**Alt+Shift+N/Opt+Shift+N**) command you can create more than one Composition viewer for a two up stereo view (left) or an anaglyph output (right). The key is to lock each view so they don't switch as you change the active timeline.

Beyond Anaglyph

Figure 9.14 shows a preview in anaglyph view, where the right channel has only red active, and that is added to the left channel with red disabled (making it cyan). This is the simplest 3D image to preview, since it just requires cheap glasses and ordinary display technology. But only when Hollywood figured out how to deliver stereo movies inexpensively and effectively by distributing passive (polarized) or active (scanning) glasses to the audience did the headaches go away and the resurgence of 3D occur. It was also only at this point that it became possible to put a pure red or cyan object in frame (which would otherwise disappear from one channel entirely). The question, then, is what alternatives do you have to anaglyph to preview a 3D image directly from After Effects?

You're not stuck. When working with a single still image, as is the case during the compositing process, the basic alternative to anaglyph for previewing purposes is a dedicated display system for 3D previews. Fortunately, these exist without replacing your monitor or even adding hardware, but this functionality is not built into After Effects.

Always keep in mind where the audience's attention is focused in order to best make use of the magician's technique—misdirection. If you're worried about a detail that is so obscure that the only way the audience would notice it is if they're bored with the story, your project has problems you'll never solve single-handedly!

In such a case, you'll want to create some expressions-based 3D camera rigs. You can set controls in the master composition to angle and offset your cameras, then link all left/right camera rigs to those controls. That way, as the need arises to change the interocular, you have one master control where you preview the result. The following chapter gives more clues as to how you might set something like this up.

It's typical to render two separate full-color images for 3D output unless the shortest possible route to anaglyph view is required. Therefore any repositioning in a master composition is passed through—again via expressions—to separate comps, one for each channel, with any offset retained.

Camera and Story

Locked-off shots are essential to signature shots by Welles, Hitchcock, Kubrick, and Lucas, among others, but these days they are the exception rather than the norm. Beginning in the 1970s, the neutral view of the static shot and the God-like perspective of the sweeping crane shot were no longer the only options, as the human documentary point of view of the handheld shot along with its smoother cousin, the steadicam, came to the fore.

In the bad old days of optical compositing, it was scarcely possible to composite anything but a static camera point of view. Nowadays, most directors aren't satisfied being limited to locked-off shots, yet the decision to move the camera might not happen on set, or it might have to be altered in postproduction.

It's helpful to create a rough assemble with camera animation as early in the process of creating your shot as possible, because it will tell you a lot about what you can get away with and what needs dedicated attention. The "Sky Replacement" section in Chapter 13 contains an example in which a flat card stands in for a fully dimensional skyline (**Figure 9.15**). The audience is focused on watching the lead character walk through the lobby, wondering what he has in his briefcase.

Figure 9.15 Prominent though it may appear in this still image, the audience isn't focused on that San Francisco skyline outside the window. There's no multiplaning as the camera moves because the background skyline is a still image; no one notices because viewer attention is on the foreground character. (Image courtesy of the Orphanage.)

Camera Animation

The most common confusion about the After Effects camera stems from the fact that, by default, it includes a *point of interest*, a point in 3D space at which the camera always points, for auto-orientation. The point of interest is *fully optional*, and thankfully with CS5 the toggle is no longer concealed in an obscure dialog but instead resides right in the Camera Settings (Figure 9.5).

A single-node camera is just like the ones we use in the real world, and thus is the one I find most useful and intuitive. For cases where you truly want the camera to orient around a point, the two-node camera's Point of Interest property can even be linked to that point with an expression (and the pick whip for a moving target).

The main problem with the two-node camera, besides that it has no direct equivalent in the physical world, is that it becomes cumbersome to animate a camera move that involves both the camera and its point of interest. To transform the camera and its point of interest together, don't attempt to match keyframes for the two properties—this is sheer madness! Parent the camera to a null and translate that instead. This can help with the other surprise about the auto-oriented two-node camera, that it always maintains an upright position; cross over the X/Y plane above the center and the camera flips unless you do so via a parented null (or just use a one-node camera).

TIP

The Unified Camera tool (**C**) lets you use a three-button mouse to orbit, track, and zoom the camera without having to cycle through the tools. The better your graphics card, the snappier this tool will be.

NOTES

The Y axis is upside-down in After Effects 3D, just as in 2D; an increased Y value moves a layer downward.

You can even orient the camera along its motion path, so that it maintains tangency (rotating in the direction it travels). For that, Layer > Transform > Auto Orient contains a toggle shown in Figure 9.15. You are still free to rotate a camera that is auto-oriented, but it usually gets a little hairy, since any change to a position keyframe changes the rotation too.

The preceding points come into play only with more elaborate camera animations; more modest use of the 3D camera, such as a simple camera push, raises other more aesthetic questions.

Push and Zoom

A camera *push* moves the camera closer to the subject; a *zoom* lengthens the lens, reframing the shot to be closer up while the camera remains stationary. **Figure 9.16** demonstrates the difference in perspective, which is just as noticeable with multiple 3D elements in After Effects as with objects in the real world. The zoom has a more extreme effect on the foreground/background composition of the shot and calls more attention to the camera itself. Zooming is most appropriate to reality or documentary shooting as it makes the viewer aware of the camera operator reframing the shot; in a push, the point of view moves naturally through the space like a human (or other nonmechanical) view would.

Figure 9.16 Frame a similar shot with a long (left) and wide (right) lens and you see the difference between a zoom and a push. A zoomed image has a flattened perspective.

Dramatic zooms for the most part had their heyday in 1960s-era Sergio Leone movies and have since declined dramatically in popularity, although they also re-create the live documentary feel of a camera operator reaching quickly for a shot. And that's really the point; because your eye does not zoom, this move calls attention to the camera apparatus itself, and to the camera operator. Its use is therefore limited.

The push, on the other hand, is a dramatic staple. The question when creating one in After Effects is, does it require a 3D camera when you can simply scale 2D layers?

Scaling a 2D layer (or several, parented to a null) works for a small move; however, to re-create progression through z space, scaling is linear when it should be logarithmic—halve the distance from the camera to an object and it does not merely appear at twice its former size. A 3D camera move creates the proper scale difference naturally, making it simple to add eases, stops, and starts, a little bit of desta-bilization—whatever works, as if with an actual camera.

Natural camera motion contains keyframe eases (Chapter 2) for the human aspect. A little bit of irregularity lends the feeling of a camera operator's individual personality (**Figure 9.17**), or even dramatic interest (hesitation, caution, intrigue, a leap forward—the possibilities are many).

Animation > Keyframe Assistant > Exponential Scale is the old-school, pre-3D way to fake the illusion of a camera move on a 2D layer. There is no good reason to employ this feature when you can instead animate a 3D camera.

Figure 9.17 The Graph Editor shows where you've created organic motion in ease curves, although the smoothness of this camera push as it eases to a stop may itself lack that extra human imperfection, which would also show up in the curves.

Do you have a bunch of coplanar layers you're making 3D just so you can push in on them? Precomp them together first to avoid little rounding errors that can easily occur where they overlap in 3D.

For this example, check out 09_camera_projection_basic on the disc, or try 09_camera_projection_advanced for the more complicated setup from previous editions.

Lack of perspective can easily cause a move in or out of a completely 2D shot to look wrong. Likewise, all but the subtlest tracking and panning shots, crane-ups, and other more elaborate camera moves blow the 2.5D gag. Certain types of elements—soft, translucent organic shapes, such as clouds, fog, smoke, and the like—can be layered together and staggered in 3D space, fooling the eye into seeing 3D volume. Chapter 13 gives details.

Camera Projection

Camera projection (or *camera mapping*) begins with a still photo or locked-off (stabilized) moving image. Imagine this image to be a slide, projected onto three-dimensional blank surfaces that match the position of planes in the image. As you move around, the projection holds its place on the surfaces, providing the illusion of depth and perspective (right up until the illusion breaks by going too far and revealing missing or stretched textures).

Previous editions of this book featured an ambitious animation of a still photo assembled by Stu Maschwitz that includes a couple of Hummers parked in the foreground. That project can still be found on the disc, but to simplify and clarify the process, here's a simpler setup involving a locked-off shot across McCovey Cove (**Figure 9.18**).

Suppose you desire a shot of the camera crossing the open water. A helicopter could do it, or possibly a very large crane, to some extent. Or you could plant a tripod on the shore, take a locked-off plate like the one provided, and project the scene to animate it yourself (**Figure 9.19**).

Figure 9.18 The difference between a simple reframe of the shot (left), which is a lot like a zoom (center), and a camera projection move, which is more like a dolly shot across the water (right), is not entirely subtle. The water surface appears soft in the projection because it is effectively scaled dramatically by the camera move.

Figure 9.19 It's easier to see what's really happening here, in Perspective view: The water, the waterfront wall, and stadium each have their own individual layer.

How is it that the one "texture" (the photo) sticks to the 3D objects? The steps to projecting any still image into 3D space are as follows:

1. Begin with an image that can be modeled as a series of planes. In this case, the water and stadium are at least two planes, but there is the option of separating the front wall from the rest of the stadium, and even the sky and background skyscraper from that for a total of four or five planes. The more easily definable planes you can add, the more perspective you can derive.

2. Create a white solid for the first dimensional plane in the image, the background. Enable 3D, and under Material Options, change Accepts Lights to Off.

3. Add a camera named Projection Cam; if you know the Angle of View of your source image, add that value, but if not, it's not necessarily a big deal.

4. Add a Point light called Projector Light. Set its position to that of Projection Cam, then parent it to Projection Cam. Set Casts Shadows to On.

5. Duplicate the source image, naming this layer Slide. Enable 3D, and in Material Options, change Casts Shadows to Only and Light Transmission to 100%.

6. Slide not located properly? Add a null object called Slide Repo; set its position to that of Projection Cam, and parent it to Projection Cam. Now parent Slide to it, and adjust its scale downward until the image is cast onto the white planes, as if projected.

TIP

If a projected image looks softer than it should, go into the Advanced tab of Composition Settings, click Options, and change Shadow Map Resolution to at least double the frame size.

This much can be done for you by the CameraProjectionSetup script, other than specifying any unusual Angle of View (from step 3).

7. Now it's time to do a little—very little—3D modeling.

   The backing plane is already set, although it will be further edited, but the first layer to add is the ground plane. You can simply duplicate and rename the solid Plane then enable multiple views to make it easy to rotate it 90 degrees and move it down and outward until it lines up with the edge of the water against the dock.

   Having done that, I recommend at least one further breakdown. Duplicate the backing plane and name it Wall. Create a masked shape around the low wall above the water on the backing plane. Move the other layer (in the original position with no masks) back in z space, say 1000 pixels. Your setup should now begin to look something like that in Figure 9.19.

8. With a more complicated setup, if planes that you know to be at perpendicular 90 degree angles don't line up, adjust the Zoom value of the Projection Cam, scaling the model and slide as needed.

9. Once everything is lined up, duplicate and disable Projection Cam, and rename the duplicate Anim Cam. Freely move this camera around the scene.

SCRIPT

Included on the disc is CameraProjectionSetup, a script that Jeff Almasol and I designed to accomplish the basic camera projection setup automatically.

A simple move forward across the water reveals a flaw: The top of the wall was doubled as the camera moved closer to it. A simple move downward, closer to the surface of the water, not only solves this problem, it makes the effect of crossing the water more compelling.

There's no need to stop here. The bland, blue sky is just begging to be replaced, and that skyscraper to the right of frame could also use a plane of its own. Each of these presents a challenge: You need to mask or paint out the flag covering the building (I would just remove it) so it doesn't travel with the building. The sky can be keyed out, but you should do that in a precomp since you can't easily apply the matte to a projection.

You can freely add elements to the 3D environment of a camera-projected scene. If you wanted a logo to hover over the water or a giant dinosaur to lumber along the walkway beside the right field fence, these elements with alpha channel can be composited with the scene at the appropriate position (and scale) in x, y, and, most importantly, z space.

Depth of Focus

Elements out of focus have optical characteristics completely unique from those of ordinary blurred elements. Shallow depth of field creates a cinematic point of view by guiding the viewer's attention, often while creating a lovely aesthetic. It's worth re-creating in post even though doing so is a bit more trouble than simply blurring the image.

The standard consumer video camera has fairly limitless depth of field under normal shooting conditions, which can be seen as an advantage or a limitation. Shallow focal depth not only produces a beautiful image one would almost automatically call "cinematic," it focuses the viewer's attention and thus provides the director with a powerful storytelling tool. Not everyone subscribes to this aesthetic, of course: Orson Welles and his cinematographer Gregg Toland invented their own camera to increase the focal depth of shots in *Citizen Kane* to the maximum possible amount. But look at contemporary cinema and dramatic television and you will notice a lot of beautiful shots with very shallow depth of field.

It can be a lot of work to re-create depth effects in After Effects; it's better to get them in camera if possible. Nonetheless, you can create specific cinematic blur effects such as a *rack focus* shot, in which the plane of focus shifts from a subject at one distance to another. This is a device to create anticipation and change the object of attention while creating a beautiful aesthetic.

Limited focal range is a natural part of human vision. Camera lenses contribute their own unique blur characteristics that in the contemporary era are considered aesthetically pleasing the world over—particularly in Japan, where the term *boke* (literally meaning "fuzzy") was coined to describe the quality of out-of-focus light as viewed through a lens.

NOTES

Camera Mapper is a standalone plug-in for camera projection from Digieffects that reduces the steps required for setup.

A solid description of boke with links lives on the Web at http://en.wikipedia.org/wiki/Bokeh.

This example can be found in 09_rack_focus on the book's disc.

Figure 9.20 Check Enable Depth of Field in Camera Settings to activate Focus Distance (the distance in pixels of the focal point, which can be toggled to Lock to the Zoom). A low F-Stop (or high Aperture) with a Blur Level of 100% creates a shallow focal effect.

Figure 9.21 With Enable Depth of Field on, the Focus Distance is denoted by a red boundary line, easily viewed and animated in isometric views.

Boke and depth-of-field effects can be re-created in After Effects, using a combination of tools built in to the software, third-party tools to support the process, and a careful observation of optics and nature.

Image Planes and Rack Focus

Any shot with distinct planes of depth can include a rack focus animation, in which the camera's focus is pulled from one subject to another with a different depth. All you need is a focal point to animate and a depth of field narrow enough to create blur everywhere but the immediate plane of focus.

Narrow depth of field is created on a real camera by lowering the f-stop value, which lowers exposure as well. Not so with the After Effects 3D camera. Its Aperture and F-Stop settings (**Figure 9.20**) affect only focal depth, not exposure or motion blur. The two settings have an inverse relationship. F-Stop is the setting more commonly referenced by camera operators, and yet only Aperture appears as a property in the Timeline.

After Effects' depth of field settings can be matched to those found in a camera report, provided that it includes the f-stop setting used when the footage was shot. If so, open up the Camera Settings dialog (**Ctrl+Shift+Y/Cmd+Shift+Y**, or double-click the Camera in the Timeline panel), check the box labeled Enable Depth of Field, and enter the value.

Offset at least one layer in z space so that it falls out of focal range. Now, in the Top view, set the Focus Distance (under Options) to match the layer that will be in focus at the beginning of the shot, add a keyframe, then change the Focus Distance at another frame to match a second layer later in the shot (**Figure 9.21**).

A static focus pull doesn't look quite right; changing focus on a real camera will change the framing of the shot slightly. To sell the example shot, which starts on a view of the city and racks focus to reveal a sign in the foreground, I animate the camera pulling back slightly, augmented by a nice shift that then occurs in the offset planes of focus (**Figure 9.22**).

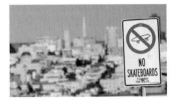

Figure 9.22 The final shot combines a rack focus with a gentle pullback, using ease keyframes to animate Position and Focus Distance.

Boke Blur

Racking focus in this manner generates camera blur that is accurate relative to the plane of focus, but it does not truly create the look of a defocused lens, because it is the lens itself that generates that look.

Boke features the phenomenon whereby points of light become discs of light (also called *circles of confusion*) that take on the character of the lens itself as they pass through the camera lens and aperture. Like lens flares (covered in Chapter 12) these are purely a phenomenon of the camera lens, not human vision; many shooters prize the beauty and suspense they can add to a shot. Illuminated out-of-focus elements in a shot are, after all, mysterious; visual intrigue is created as the shot resolves in or out of a wash of color and light (**Figure 9.23**).

Figure 9.23 With shallow depth of field, highlights in the foreground retain blur even in a focused shot.

A perfectly formed lens passes a defocused point of light to the back of the camera as a soft, spherical blur. A bright point remains bright but is enlarged and softened in the process. Ordinary blur of a low-dynamic-range image in 8 or 16 bit per channel color mode instead merely dims the highlights (**Figure 9.24**).

Figure 9.24 Begin with a source image that includes bright highlights (top left); blur it via conventional means, and the result is gray and desaturated (top right), unless the source image is HDR and the comp is 32 bpc (bottom left), which approaches the look of real camera motion blur (bottom right).

Most camera lenses are not perfect, so instead of perfect blurred spheres, boke spheres may be brighter toward the edges than in the middle. An anamorphic lens will show squashed spheres, and as with lens flares, the shape of the aperture itself may be visible in the circles, making them hexagonal (or pentagonal, and so on, depending on the number of blades in the opening). Believe it or not, if you skip this level of detail, the result is far less likely to succeed even with the casual viewer.

Go for Boke

To accurately create the bloom of highlights as they are blurred requires 32 bit per channel color and source highlights that are brighter than what would be called full white in 8 or 16 bpc. The process of creating such an image is explored and explained in Chapter 11.

Check out boke blur creation with After Effects in the 09_lens_blur_ boke folder on the disc.

The Lens Blur effect does not operate in 32 bpc—it instead mimics the behavior of bright highlights through a lens. It's more or less a direct port from Photoshop; as such, it can be slow and cumbersome in After Effects. It won't blur beyond 100 pixels, and the effect does not understand nonsquare pixels (it creates a perfect circle every time).

Instead of 3D camera or layer data, Lens Blur can use a Depth Map Layer, using pixel values (brightness) from a specified Depth Map Channel. You can rack focus by adjusting Blur Focal Distance. Iris Shape defines polygons around the highlights, corresponding to the number of blades in the iris; you can also specify Iris Blade Curvature and Iris Rotation (this rotates the polygon).

The actual amount of blur is determined by Iris Radius, the bloom by Specular Threshold (all pixels above this value are highlights) and Specular Brightness, which creates the simulation of highlight bloom. These are the controls you'll tweak most (**Figure 9.25**).

NOTES

The most respected third-party tool for lens blurs is Frischluft's Lenscare. The default settings are not reliable, but with adjustments and depth maps (for 3D footage), you can derive some lovely results (you'll find Lenscare at www.frischluft. com and on the book's disc).

Figure 9.25 The result of a Lens Blur effect (left) doesn't look so hot compared to the real thing (center), while the Lenscare plug-in from Frischluft (right) is remarkably close. Sometimes the tools matter.

The Noise controls are designed to restore noise that would be removed by the blur operation; they don't relate to the blur itself and can be ignored in favor of grain techniques described in the following section.

By no means do the settings in Lens Blur (or for that matter, third-party alternatives such as Lenscare from Frischluft) exhaust the possibilities for how defocused areas of an image might appear, especially when illuminated. Keep looking at the reference and thinking of ways to re-create what you see in it (**Figure 9.26**).

Figure 9.26 Does an image with shallow depth of field look more cinematic? What do you see happening in the defocused background?

Grain

Once the image passes through the camera lens and is recorded, it takes on another characteristic of motion pictures: grain. Grain is essentially high-frequency noise readily apparent in each channel of most recorded footage, although progress in image gathering technology has led to a gradual reduction of grain. Digitally produced animations such as Pixar movies have no native grain at all, save when the story calls for a deliberate re-creation of archival footage, as in the opening scenes of *The Incredibles*.

Grain can, however, be your friend, subtly adding life to a static background or camouflaging foreground edge detail. It is not simply switched on or off, but requires careful per-channel adjustment. There are two basic factors to consider:

▶ size of the grain, per channel

▶ amount of grain, or amount of contrast in the grain, per channel

The emphasis here is that these factors typically vary from channel to channel. Blue is almost universally the channel likeliest to have the most noise; happily, the human eye is less sensitive to blue than red or green.

NOTES

Excessive grain is often triggered by a low amount of scene light combined with a higher effective ASA, particularly with lower-quality image sensors.

How much grain is enough? As with color in Chapter 5, the goal is typically to match what's there already. If your shot has a background plate with the proper amount of grain in it, match foreground elements to that. A computer-generated still or scene might have to be grain-matched to surrounding shots.

Grain Management Strategies

After Effects includes a suite of three tools for automated grain sampling, grain reduction, and grain generation: Add Grain, Match Grain, and Remove Grain. Add Grain relies on your settings only, but Match Grain and Remove Grain can generate initial settings by sampling a source layer for grain patterns.

I don't always recommend the automated solution, but in this case, Match Grain usually comes up with a good first pass at settings; it can get you 70% to 80% there and is just as adjustable thereafter. To refine grain settings:

1. Look for a section of your source footage with a solid color area that stays in place for 10 to 20 frames. Most clips satisfy these criteria (and those that don't tend to allow less precision).

2. Zoom 200% to 400% on the solid color area, and create a Region of Interest around it. Set Work Area to the 10 or 20 frames with little or no motion.

3. Add a solid small enough to occupy part of the region of interest. Apply a Ramp effect to the solid, and use the eyedropper tools to select the darkest and lightest pixels in the solid color area of the clip. The lack of grain detail in the foreground gradient should be clearly apparent (**Figure 9.27**).

4. Apply the Match Grain effect to the foreground solid. Choose the source footage layer in the Noise Source Layer menu. As soon as the effect finishes rendering a sample frame, you have a basis from which to begin fine-tuning. You can RAM preview at this point to see how close a match you have. In most cases, you're not done yet.

NOTES

Try grain matching for yourself with the material in the 09_grain_match folder.

Figure 9.27 A gradient is placed right over the talent's head as a reference for grain matching the window above it. Even without slamming the image it's clear that the added window looks too flat in this grainy scene, but slamming with the addition of a gradient gives you a clear target.

5. Twirl down the Tweaking controls for Match Grain, and then twirl down Channel Intensities and Channel Size. You can save yourself a lot of time by doing most of your work here, channel by channel.

6. Activate the green channel only in the Composition panel (**Alt+1/Opt+1**) and adjust the Green Intensity and Green Size values to match the foreground and background. Repeat this process for the green and blue channels (**Alt+2/Opt+2** and **Alt+3/Opt+3**). If you don't see much variation channel to channel, you can instead adjust overall Intensity and Size (**Figure 9.28**). RAM preview the result.

7. Adjust Intensity, Size, or Softness controls under Tweaking according to what you see in the RAM preview. You may also find it necessary to reduce Saturation under Color, particularly if your source is film rather than video.

Figure 9.28 In this unusual case, there is little variation of grain channel to channel, and the automatic match is pretty good; a slight boost to the overall Intensity setting under the Tweaking controls does the trick.

In most cases, these steps yield a workable result (**Figure 9.29**). The effect can then be copied and pasted to any foreground layers that need grain. If the foreground layer already contains noise or grain, you may need to adjust the Compensate for Existing Noise percentage for that layer.

Figure 9.29 Even in this printed figure, the matching grain is somewhat evident. Grain matching is often best reviewed in motion with a boosted exposure.

Use Noise as Grain

Prior to the addition of Add Grain and Match Grain to After Effects version 6.5 Professional, the typical way to generate grain was to use the Noise effect. The main advantage of the Noise effect over Match Grain is that it renders about 20 times faster. However, After Effects doesn't make it easy for you to separate the effect channel by channel, and scaling requires a separate effect (or precomping).

You can use three solid layers, with three effects applied to each layer: Shift Channels, Noise, and Transform. Use Shift Channels to set each solid to red, green, or blue, respectively, set Blending Modes to Add, and set their Opacity very low (well below 10%, adjusting as needed). Next, set the amount of noise and scale it via the Transform effect.

If the grain is meant to affect a set of foreground layers only, hold them out from the background plate either via precomping or track mattes. If this sounds complicated, it is, which is why Match Grain is preferable unless the rendering time is really killer.

Obviously, whole categories of controls within Match Grain remain untouched with this approach; the Application category, for example, contains controls for how the grain is blended and how it affects shadows, midtones, and highlights individually. These are typically overkill, as are the Sampling and Animation controls, but how far you go in matching grain before your eye is satisfied is, of course, up to you.

Grain Removal

Removing grain, or sharpening an image in general, is an entirely different process from adding grain. On a well-shot production, you'll rarely have a reason to reach for the Remove Grain tool.

If you do, the reason for doing so may be unique to your particular footage. In such cases, you may very well find that leaving Remove Grain at the default settings gives you a satisfactory result. If not, check into the Fine Tuning and Unsharp Mask settings to adjust the grain.

Remove Grain is often best employed stealthily—not necessarily across the entire frame (**Figure 9.30**), or as part of a series of effects. It is a reasonably sophisticated solution (compared with the current alternatives) that can really help in seemingly hopeless situations.

Grain removal can also help with grain matching by allowing you to start with a clean slate instead of applying grain over more grain. When matching grainy footage to other footage with a different grain structure or pattern, it's a necessary step.

Figure 9.30 The left side of frame is clearly less grainy than the right as a result of applying Remove Grain and letting it automatically sample the footage.

When to Manage Grain

The most obvious candidates for grain addition are computer-generated or still image layers that lack the moving grain found in film or video footage. As soon as your shot has to match anything that came from a camera, and particularly in a large format such as HD or film, you must work with grain.

Blurred elements may also need grain addition, even if they originate as source footage. Blurry source shots contain as much grain as focused ones because the grain is an artifact of the medium recording the image, not the subject itself. Elements that have been scaled down in After Effects contain scaled-down grain, which may require restoration. Color keying can also suppress grain in the channel that has been keyed out.

Other compositing operations will instead enhance grain. Sharpening, unless performed via Remove Grain, can strongly emphasize grain contrast in an element, typically in a not-so-desirable manner. Sharpening also brings out any nasty compression artifacts that come with footage that uses JPEG-type compression, such as miniDV video.

Lack of grain, however, is one of the big dead giveaways of a poorly composited shot. It is worth the effort to match the correct amount of grain into your shot even if the result isn't apparent as you preview it on your monitor.

TIP

If you're using Remove Grain to improve a bluescreen or greenscreen key, consider applying the result as an alpha track matte. This offers the best of both worlds: a clean matte channel and preservation of realistic grain on the source color layer.

Lens Optics & Looks

The real fun comes when you start to add your own recipe of looks to an image, whether to make it look as though it were shot on some different medium, or to make it look as cinematic as possible. In either case, you will find yourself effectively degrading your footage: adding effects related to lens limitations, cropping the image to be shorter (and thus appear wider), pushing the color into a much more limited, controlled range.

The question of how to create a cinematic image without a professional film crew (or budget) is greatly expanded upon in *The DV Rebel's Guide: An All-Digital Approach to Making Killer Action Movies on the Cheap* (Peachpit Press, 2006),

CLOSE-UP

Garbage In, Garbage Out

You don't need me to tell you how difficult it is to bring a poorly shot image back from the dead, but check *The DV Rebel's Guide* for a thorough rundown of factors that go into a well-shot image. If possible go on set to help eliminate flaws that will be difficult to fix in post. Among the less obvious points from the book:

▶ When shooting digitally, keep the contrast low and overall light levels well below maximum; you are shooting the negative, not the final (**Figure 9.31**).

▶ If using a small, light camera, mount it to something heavy to move it; that weight reads to the viewer as more expensive and more natural motion.

Figure 9.31 Shooting low-contrast (top) with a camera that has a healthy contrast range allows you to bring out hidden detail and color, even tone-mapping to do so only in specific areas of frame (bottom).

by Stu Maschwitz. The first chapter lists the major factors that influence production value. Many of these, including image and sound quality, location, and lighting, cannot be "fixed in post," which must be why Stu's book includes a bunch of information on how to actually shoot.

Achieving a particular look is well within the realm of tricks you can pull off consistently in After Effects. You can take control of the following to develop a look and maximize production value:

▶ **Lens artifacts.** We love defects! In addition to the aforementioned boke and other defocus imperfections, along with chromatic aberration, are such filmic visual staples as the vignette and the lens flare.

▶ **Frame rate.** Change this to alter the very character of footage. For the most part, frame rate needs to be determined when shooting in order for things to go smoothly.

▶ **Aspect ratio.** The format of the composition makes a huge perceptual difference as well. Wide connotes big-budget Hollywood epic and thus is not always appropriate.

▶ **Color look.** Nothing affects the mood of a given shot like color and contrast. It's a complex subject revisited in Chapter 12.

Lens Artifacts and Other Happy "Accidents"

Reality as glimpsed by the camera includes lens artifacts (visual phenomena that occur only through a camera, not the lens of your eye) such as lens distortion and lens blur (or boke), but that's not all. Also on your palette are "flaws" that good cinematographers avoided right up until *Easy Rider* showed that a lens flare goes with a road movie the way mustard goes with a hot dog.

Vignettes, the darkening around the corners of the frame that results from a mismatch between a round lens and a rectangular frame (when the frame is too large for the image) are almost completely avoidable these days, yet they've never been more popular among designers and photo graders.

Chromatic aberration is exactly the combination it sounds to be: an aberration (which sounds bad) of color (we all like that). It, too, is always the result of a mismatch between a lens and a camera and rarely shows up unless the shooter is doing something crazy or using a very cheap camera.

All of these effects provide texture, variety, and spontaneity to an image; in other words, they can bring a shot to life.

The Lens Flare

When a bright light source such as the sun appears in shot it causes secondary reflections to bounce around among the lens elements; there's so much light, it reflects back on the surface of the many individual lenses that make up what we call a lens. Your eye can resolve an image using one very flexible lens, but camera lenses beyond the simplest Brownie (one lens) or pinhole (none) camera require a series of inflexible glass lens elements. A complex zoom lens might consist of 20 elements. Each is coated to prevent the reflections that create flares, but there's a limit.

Because they occur within the lens, lens flares appear superimposed over the image. If the light source is partially occluded by a foreground object or figure, the flare may diminish or disappear, but you'll never see a full-strength lens flare partially blocked by a foreground subject. Each flare appears as a complete disc, ring, star, or other shape.

Artists love lens flares and can develop the bad habit of playing a bit fast and loose with them. As with anything, the game is to keep it real first, and then bend the rules around to the look you want, if necessary. Fundamentally, only if the shot was clearly taken with a long lens do you have any business with the types of crazy multi-element flares you get, for example, by the default setting of the paltry Lens Flare effect that ships with After Effects.

In addition to the glass elements, aperture blades contribute to the appearance of flares. Their highly reflective corners result in streaks, the number corresponding to the number of blades. As with boke, the shape of the flares might correspond to the shape of the aperture (a pentagon for a five-sided aperture, a hexagon for six). Dust and scratches on the lens even reflect light.

The Lens Flare effect that ships with After Effects is limited to three inflexible 8 bit per channel presets and had become old a decade ago. Knoll Light Factory is highly customizable and is derived from careful study of lens behaviors; it's being updated as of press time. The major newcomer on the scene is Optical Flares from Video Copilot.

Chapter 12 shows that flares can also be caused by bright specular pings and other reflected highlights in a scene and offer a further opportunity to enhance the reality of a shot. These can be re-created with those same plug-in effects, or by creating your own and using a blending mode (typically Add) to apply it.

The Vignette

When the edges of the frame go dark, our attention becomes more focused on what's at the center. Lens manufacturers have gone to significant trouble to eliminate this effect when shooting, but pay attention to the corners of the images you see and you'll notice an awful lot of vignettes added in post these days.

Vignette controls are included with "film look" software such as Magic Bullet Looks, but this is also an easy effect to create:

1. Create a black solid the size of your frame as the top layer and name it Vignette.

2. Double-click the Ellipse tool in the toolbar; an elliptical mask fills the frame.

3. Highlight the layer in the Timeline and press **F** to reveal Mask Feather.

4. Increase the Mask Feather value a lot—somewhere in the low triple digits is probably about right.

5. Lower the Opacity value (**T**) until the effect looks right; you might prefer a light vignette (10% to 15%) or something heavier (40% to 50%).

SCRIPT

Designing your own array of lens elements isn't out of the question, and in order to array them in a classic mult-element zoom lens arrangement, you can use Trajectory (http://aescripts.com/trajectory/), a script from Michael Cardeiro, that aligns layers between two null objects.

A vignette would be elliptical or round depending on whether it was shot with an anamorphic lens (**Figure 9.32**). There would be no reason for a lens vignette to be offset, but you're not limited to such realistic limitations if it suits your scene to offset and rotate a soft ellipse. Generally, vignettes look best just below the threshold where we would clearly notice that the corners and edges have gone a little dark.

Chromatic Aberration

Chromatic Aberration is an even rarer visual phenomenon. This fringing or smearing of light that occurs when a lens cannot focus various colors on the spectrum to a single point, because of the differing wavelengths, yields a rainbow of colors something like that of light passing through a prism. The effect is more pronounced closer to the edge of frame. It can occur during projection as well; alas, I have seen it in low-budget cinemas.

Like lens flares and boke, a little bit of aberration can bring a scene life and spontaneity. Some simple steps to re-create this effect at its most basic level:

1. Duplicate the layer twice and precompose all three.

2. Use the Shift Channels effect to leave only red, green, or blue on for each layer (so you end up with one of each).

3. Set the top two layers to Add mode.

4. Scale the green channel to roughly 101% and the blue channel to roughly 102%.

5. Add a small amount of Radial Blur (set to Zoom, not the default Spin).

A before and after comparison using this setup appears in **Figure 9.33**. Better yet, pick up Satya Meka's Separate RGB effect (http://aescripts.com/separate-rgb/) where you can name your own price. This Pixel Bender plug-in lets you transform individual channels of color directly.

Figure 9.32 A vignette is created with a feathered mask applied to a solid (top). If the image is reframed for display in another format, such as anamorphic, you may have to use that framing instead of the source (bottom).

SCRIPT

ft-Cubic Lens Distortion by François Tarlier (http://aescripts.com/ft-cubic-lens-distortion/) is in fact a pixel bender plug-in but has in common with scripts that it is donation-ware and freely available to try. It uses the Syntheyes cubic lens distortion algorithm and can not only add or remove lens distortion but apply chromatic aberration to a shot.

Figure 9.33 A simulation of chromatic aberration (right), the color ringing that is caused when different wavelengths of light have different focal lengths; most lenses correct for it with an added diffractive element (left).

Frame Rate and Realism

It's no accident that film images are still displayed at 24 frames per second nearly a century after this seeming limitation was imposed, and that even the newest electronic formats that can be optimized for 30 or 60 also tend to gain legitimacy when they add a 24p, or full frame 24 fps mode, but it makes no sense. Why not gather more data if you can?

The answer does not seem entirely logical. The truth seems to be that your eye has an effective "refresh rate" somewhere slightly upward of 60 times per second, and so the 60 interlaced fields of 29.97 American television feel a lot like direct reality. 24 fps, on the other hand, is barely above the threshold where the eye loses persistence of vision, the phenomenon that allows it to see continuity from still images shown in series.

Cinema may have gone for 24 fps due to limitations of equipment and money. Fewer frames per second meant a sizable reduction in film stock costs. If so they accidentally also got with this compromise the more ephemeral and dream-like quality that goes with it. As with shallow depth of field (earlier in this chapter) and color reduction (ahead), less can be more. Once again, re-creating cinematic reality requires that you reduce data.

After Effects is quite forgiving about letting you change frame rates midstream compared with most video applications; details on how the conversion actually works

29.97 fps Is for Soap Operas and Reality Television

The debate about raising the frame rate above the 24 fps you see in the cinema has been raging since long before the digital era. The invention of videotape in the 1950s made it cheap and fast to record imagery more directly in the format of television.

One particular experiment from this era stands out. For six episodes, the producers of *The Twilight Zone* tried tape before they evidently realized it was ruining the show's mystique. Video's higher frame rate transformed this masterpiece of irony and suspense into something resembling a soap opera. Judge for yourself—check out Season 2's videotaped episodes: "Static," "Night of the Meek," "The Lateness of the Hour," "The Whole Truth," "Twenty-Two," or "Long Distance Call." The experiment was quickly ended and in five total seasons the show never appeared on videotape again.

appeared back in Chapter 2. However, it is very difficult to convert 29.97 fps footage to 24 fps without introducing a lurching cadence to smooth motion as every sixth frame is dropped. When working at 29.97 fps, it can still make sense to animate and render whole frames instead of interlacing to 60 fields per second to give a little more of that cinematic quality to the result.

Format and Panoramas

As the world transitions from standard-definition to high-definition broadcast television, formats are undergoing the same transition that they made in film half a century ago. The nearly square 4:3 aspect is being replaced as standard by the wider 16:9 format, but 1.85 Academy aperture and 2.35 Cinemascope also appear as common "widescreen" formats.

In response to the growing popularity of television in the 1950s, Hollywood conjured up a number of different widescreen formats through experiments with anamorphic lenses and film stocks as wide as 70 mm. These systems—CinemaScope, VistaVision, Panavision, and so on—themselves faded away but not without changing the way films are displayed.

Standard 35 mm film has an aspect ratio of 4:3, which is not coincidentally the same as a television. Movies tend to be filmed in this format as if originally intended for the small screen. When shown in a theater using a widescreen aspect of 1.85:1 (also known as 16:9, the HDTV standard) or 2.39:1 (Cinemascope), the full 4:3 negative is cropped (**Figure 9.34**). The wider formats also tend to have been shot anamorphically, squeezing the wider image into the narrower frame.

16:9 widescreen high-definition televisions and projectors have taken over, so clearly the wider aspect ratio won. Is 2.4:1 even better? This format seems to go best with sweeping vistas: the majestic desert of *Lawrence of Arabia* and the Millennium Falcon's jump to light speed. If you choose this format, you are saying to your audience that they should expect to see some pretty spectacular views, and if you don't deliver, the format choice may disappoint.

The numbers "1.85" and "2.35" or "2.4" give the width, relative to a height of 1, so it's like saying 1.85:1 or 2.39:1 (the actual widescreen ratio). The 16:9 format, which has become popular with digital video and HD, is equivalent to a 1.77:1 ratio, slightly narrower than Academy, but wide compared to the standard television format of 4:3 (1.33: 1), which is also that of old movies such as *Casablanca*.

Figure 9.34 "Wide" film formats would more accurately be called "shorter" because they typically involve cropping the original 4:3 image.

Also, and ironically, when shown in HD the widescreen image is the lowest resolution—only 800 pixels tall, making small detail less discernable, especially once compression has been applied.

Less Color Is More

This entire section has been about how corrupting, degrading and reducing data in an image can bring it to cinematic life. Color grading can transform an ordinary image into one that resonates emotionally, and it does so, paradoxically, by reducing the accuracy and range of the hues in the source image.

In her book *If It's Purple, Someone's Gonna Die*, author Patti Bellantoni explores many scenes from cinema whose color palette is dominated by one color, and why this choice resonates with us, including analogues with other visual art forms such as paintings. It's surprisingly rare for a shot in a movie to be dominated by more than three shades, and there is no doubt that the dominant color influences the emotional impact of the scene.

Figures 9.35 through **9.38** offer a simple demonstration of how color choices can influence the look of a scene, along with showing the primary corrections that were made in Colorista to achieve them.

Figure 9.35 The source image does not by itself convey any particular emotion through its color palette, although the natural vignette-like effect caused by the backlight does focus one's attention. (Source clip courtesy of Eric Escobar.)

Figure 9.36 A miracle is about to occur.

Figure 9.37 Does this city care about people, or just money and efficiency?

Figure 9.38 The day the world almost came to an end.

Primary color correction—creating the look in post—typically is done via a three-way color corrector such as is found in Color Finesse or Colorista. You might start by pushing shadows in one direction—typically the cooler blue/green range to offset the next step, pushing highlights in the yellow/red (but truly, orange) direction. The midtone might then set the mood.

This process may reduce the range of hues in the shot but emotionally, done right, it will make the frame sing. However, this is merely one of many methods one could use to establish a look. For more ideas, watch others as they work in videos on color correction, as are freely available at places like Red Giant Software. This topic is probably worthy of a book of its own.

Overall, if you're new to the idea of developing a color look for a film or sequence, look at references. Study other people's work for the effect of color on the mood and story in a shot, sequence, or entire film, and give yourself the exercise of re-creating it. Don't be hard on yourself, just notice what works and what's missing. Once you have that down, you're ready to create your own rules and even break those set by others.

Conclusion

And really, this chapter just scratched the surface of what's possible. You can and should always look for new methods to replicate the way that the camera sees the world, going beyond realism to present what we really want to see—realism as it looks through the lens.

10

Expressions

Music is math.

—Michael Sandison and Marcus Eoin
(Boards of Canada)

Expressions

Expressions are cool. You can use them to create amazing procedural effects that would otherwise be impossible (or at least impractical). You can also use them to create complex relationships between various parameters. Unfortunately, many After Effects users are afraid of expressions. Don't be.

The fact that you're reading this chapter indicates that you are at least curious about expressions. That's a good start. By the end of the chapter, you'll see how expressions can open new doors for you, and, hopefully, you'll have the confidence to give them a try.

The best way to learn about expressions is to examine working examples to figure out what makes them tick. The examples in this chapter focus on how you can use expressions to create or control effects.

As you work through the examples (don't be discouraged if you need a couple passes or more to understand it all), please keep in mind that I'm mainly a code guy—not a special effects or motion graphics artist. My examples may not be very visually impressive, but using these same techniques, you'll be able to create your own dazzling effects.

What Expressions Are

The After Effects expression language is a powerful set of tools with which you can control the behavior of a layer's properties. Expressions can range in complexity from ridiculously simple to mind-numbingly complicated. At the simple end of the spectrum, you can use expressions to link one property to another or to set a property to a static value. At the other extreme, you can create complex linkages, manipulate time, perform calculations in 3D space, set up tricky procedural animations, and more.

Sometimes you'll use expressions instead of keyframes (most properties that can be keyframed can be controlled by expressions). In other cases you'll use expressions to augment the keyframed behavior. For example, you could use keyframes to move a layer along a specific path and then add an expression to add some randomness to the motion.

Expressions Have Limitations

Although the After Effects expression language presents you with an impressive arsenal of powerful tools, it's important to understand the limitations of expressions so that you can avoid making assumptions that lead you astray.

▶ An expression may generally be applied only to a property that can be keyframed, and it can affect only the value of that property. That is, an expression can affect one and only one thing: the value of the property to which it is applied. This means there are no global variables. This also means that although an expression has access to many composition and layer attributes (layer width and height, for example) as well as the values of other properties, it can only read, not change, them.

▶ Expressions can't create objects. For example, an expression cannot spawn a new layer, add an effect, create a paint stroke, change a blend mode—the list goes on and on. Remember, if you can't keyframe it, you can't create an expression for it.

▶ Expressions can't access information about individual mask vertices.

▶ Expressions can't access text layer formatting attributes, such as font face, font size, leading, or even the height and width of the text itself.

▶ Expressions cannot access values they created on previous frames, which means expressions have no memory. If you've had a little Flash programming experience, you might expect to be able to increment a value at each frame. Nope. Even though you can access previous values of the property using `valueAt-Time()`, what you get is the pre-expression value (the static value of the property plus the effect of any keyframes). It's as if the expression didn't exist. There is no way for an expression to communicate with itself from one frame to the next. Note, however, just to make things more confusing, the postexpression value of a property *is* available to any other expression, just not the one applied to that property. In fact, the postexpression value is the *only* value available to expressions applied to other properties. To summarize: An expression has access only to the pre-expression value of the property to which it is applied, and it only has access to the postexpression values for other properties with expressions. It's confusing at first, but it sinks in eventually.

Creating Expressions

The easiest way to create an expression is to simply **Alt**-click (**Opt**-click) the stopwatch of the property where you want the expression to go. After Effects then creates a default expression, adds four new tool icons, changes the color of the property value to red (indicating that the value is determined by an expression), and leaves the expression text highlighted for editing (**Figure 10.1**).

Figure 10.1 When you create an expression, After Effects creates a default expression with the text highlighted for editing, changes the color of the property value to red, and adds four new tool icons: an enable/disable toggle, a Graph Editor toggle, a pick whip, and an Expression Language menu fly-out.

At this point you have a number of options. You can simply start typing, and your text will replace the default expression. Note that while you're in edit mode, the **Enter** (**Return**) key moves you to a new line in the expression (this is how you can create multiline expressions) and leaves you in edit mode.

Another option while the text is highlighted is to paste in the text of an expression that you have copied from a text editor. This is the method I generally use if I'm working on a multiline expression.

Instead of replacing all the default text by typing or pasting, you can click somewhere in the highlighted text to create an edit point for inserting additional text.

Alternatively, you can drag the expression's pick whip to another property or object (the target can even be in another composition), and After Effects will insert the appropriate text when you let go. Note that if an object or property can be referenced using the pick whip, a rounded rectangle appears around the name as you drag the pick whip over it. If this doesn't happen, you won't be able to pick whip it.

Finally, you can also use the Expression Language menu to insert various language elements.

After creating your expression, exit edit mode by clicking somewhere else in the timeline or pressing **Enter** on the numeric keypad. If your expression text contains an error, After Effects displays an error message, disables the expression, and displays a little yellow warning icon (**Figure 10.2**). You can temporarily disable an expression by clicking on the enable/disable toggle.

Figure 10.2 If your expression contains an error, After Effects disables the expression, changes the enable/disable toggle to the disabled state, returns the Property value to its normal color, displays an error icon, and displays an error message dialog box.

Working with existing expressions is as easy as creating them. Some common operations include

▶ **editing.** Click in the expression text area to select the entire expression; you now have the same options as when creating a new expression. If your expression consists of multiple lines, you may need to expand the expression editing area to be able to see all (or at least more) of it by positioning the cursor over the line below the expression text until you see a double-ended arrow and then clicking and dragging.

▶ **deleting.** Simply **Alt**-click (**Opt**-click) the property's stopwatch, or you can delete all the text for the expression and press **Enter** on the numeric keypad.

▶ **exposing.** Select a layer in the Timeline and press **EE** to expose any expressions applied to that layer.

▶ **copying.** In the Timeline panel, select a layer property containing an expression and choose Edit > Copy Expression Only to copy just the property's expression. You now can select as many other layers as you'd like and Edit > Paste to paste the expression into the appropriate property of the other layers.

The Language of Expressions

The After Effects expression language is based on a subset of JavaScript. JavaScript is a scripting language used largely for Web page design and includes many features specifically aimed at that task. The JavaScript implementation for expressions includes the core features only. That means there's a lot about JavaScript that you won't need to know, but it also means that any JavaScript reference you pick up (and you're going to need one if you really want to master expressions) is going to have a lot of content that will be of little or no use to you.

The rest of the expression language consists of extensions that Adobe has added specifically for After Effects. This means that in addition to a good JavaScript reference, you'll also be frequenting Adobe's *After Effects Expression Element Reference*. The most up-to-date version of this reference can be found at Adobe's Help on the Web. The After Effects Help menu will take you there: Help > After Effects Help, or you can go to www.adobe.com/support/aftereffects.

This chapter focuses on working examples rather than the details of JavaScript. The book's disc, however, contains an abbreviated JavaScript guide, and I recommend that you glance through it before you really dive into the sample expressions discussed here. In addition, I'll point you to the appropriate sections of that guide as you encounter new JavaScript elements for the first time.

Linking an Effect Parameter to a Property

Here's the scenario: You want to link an effect to an audio track. Specifically, you want to link the Field of View (FOV) parameter of the Optics Compensation effect to the amplitude of an audio layer. Expressions can't access audio levels directly, so first you have to use a keyframe assistant (Animation > Keyframe Assistant > Convert Audio to Keyframes) to create a null layer named Audio Amplitude with Slider Controls keyframed for the audio levels of the Left, Right, and Both channels (for a stereo source). Next, you just **Alt**-click (**Opt**-click) the stopwatch for the FOV parameter of the Optics Compensation effect and drag the pick whip to the Both Channels Slider property of the Audio Amplitude layer (**Figure 10.3**). Doing so generates this expression:

```
thisComp.layer("Audio Amplitude").effect("Both
Channels")("Slider")
```

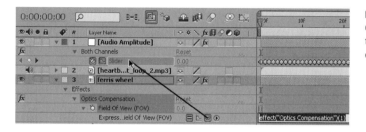

Figure 10.3 Select the Both Channels slider with the pick whip to replace the highlighted default expression text.

Take a closer look at its syntax: From JavaScript, the After Effects expression language inherits a left-to-right "dot" notation used to separate objects and attributes in a hierarchy. If your expression references a property in a different layer, you first have to identify the composition. You can use `thisComp` if the other layer happens to be in the same composition (as in this example). Otherwise, you would use `comp("other comp name")`, with the other composition name in quotes. Next you identify the layer using `layer("layer name")` and finally, the property, such as `effect("effect name")("property name")` or possibly `transform.rotation`.

In addition to objects and properties, the dot notation hierarchy can include references to an object's attributes and methods. An attribute is just what you would guess: a property of an object, such as a layer's height or a composition's duration. In fact, in JavaScript documentation, attributes are actually referred to as properties, but in order to avoid confusion with the layer properties such as Position and Rotation (which existed long before expressions came along), in After Effects documentation (and here) they're referred to as attributes. For example, each layer has a height attribute that can be referenced this way:

```
comp("Comp 1").layer("Layer 1").height
```

Methods are a little harder to grasp. Just think of them as actions or functions associated with an object. You can tell the difference between attributes and methods by the parentheses that follow a method. The parentheses may enclose some comma-separated parameters.

It's important to note that you don't have to specify the full path in the dot notation hierarchy if you're referencing attributes or properties of the layer where the expression resides. If you leave out the comp and layer references, After Effects assumes you mean the layer with the expression. So, for example, if you specify only width, After Effects assumes you mean the width of the layer, not the width of the composition.

NOTES

If you're not familiar with JavaScript arithmetic operators (such as the * for multiplication used in this example), you might want to take a look at the "Operators" section of the JavaScript guide on the book's disc.

Let's forge ahead. You linked the amplitude of your audio layer to your effect parameter, but suppose you want to increase the effect that the audio level has on the parameter. You can use a little JavaScript math to multiply the value by some amount, like this

```
thisComp.layer("Audio Amplitude").effect("Both
Channels")("Slider") * 3
```

Toward the end of the chapter you'll see a much more complicated and powerful way of linking an effect to audio.

Using a Layer's Index

A layer's index attribute can be used as a simple but powerful tool that allows you to create expressions that behave differently depending on where the layer is situated in the layer stack. The index attribute corresponds exactly to the number assigned to the layer in the Timeline window. So, the index for the layer at the top of the stack is 1, and so on.

Time Delay Based on Layer Index

Suppose you keyframed an animation for one layer. Now you want to create a bunch of identical layers, but you want their animations to be delayed by an amount that increases as you move down the layer stack. You also want to rotate each copy by an amount proportional to its position in the layer stack. To do so, you first apply an expression like this to the top layer's animated properties:

```
delay = 0.15;
valueAtTime(time - (index-1)*delay)
```

Then you apply an expression like this to the Rotation property:

```
offsetAngle = 3;
value +(index-1)*offsetAngle
```

Finally, duplicate the layer a bunch of times. The animation of each layer will lag behind the layer above it by 0.15 seconds and the rotation of each layer will be 3 degrees more than the layer above (**Figure 10.4**).

What's going on here? In the first expression, the first line defines a JavaScript variable named delay and sets its value to 0.15 seconds. The second line is where all the action is, and it's packed with new things. For example, notice the use of time. It represents the current composition time, in seconds. In other words, time represents the time at which the expression is currently being evaluated.

You use valueAtTime() to access a property's pre-expression value at some time other than the current comp time (to access the pre-expression value at the current comp time, use value() instead, as in the Rotation expression). The parameter passed to valueAtTime() determines that time:

```
time - (index-1)*delay
```

Subtracting 1 from the layer's index and multiplying that result by the value of the delay variable (0.15) gives the total delay (in seconds) for this layer. Subtracting 1 from index means that the delay will be 0 for the first layer. So, for Layer 1, the total delay is 0, for Layer 2 it is 0.15, for Layer 3 it is 0.30, and so on. You then subtract the total delay from the current comp time. The result of this is that Layer 1's animation runs as normal (not delayed). Layer 2's animation lags behind Layer 1 by 0.15 seconds, and so on.

Figure 10.4 Notice how the blaster shot created by each layer lags that of the previous layer and is at a slightly different angle.

NOTES

If you're not familiar with JavaScript variables, see the "Variables" section of the JavaScript guide on the accompanying disc.

TIP

Remember, if you don't specify a comp and layer when referencing a property or attribute, After Effects assumes you mean the layer with the expression. When you reference an attribute of the property housing the expression, After Effects makes a similar assumption, allowing you to specify only the attribute name (without the entire comp/layer/property path). One side benefit of not having to specify the entire path is that you can apply the same expression to any property, without having to modify it at all.

The Rotation expression is very similar except that it doesn't reference time. The reason for this is that the first expression is used to offset a keyframed animation in time, while the second expression simply creates a static (not animated) offset for the Rotation property. The first line of the expression defines a variable named offsetAngle. This variable defines the rotation amount (in degrees) by which each layer will be offset from the layer above it. The second line tells After Effects to calculate the layer's offset and add it to the pre-expression value of the property.

You'll see other ways to use index in later examples.

Looping Keyframes

The expression language provides two convenient ways to loop a sequence of keyframes: loopOut() and loopIn().

TIP

A small glitch in the cycle version of loopOut() drops the first keyframe from each of the loops. If you want the frame with the first keyframe to be included, add a duplicate of the first keyframe one frame beyond the last keyframe.

Suppose you keyframed a short animation and you want that sequence to repeat continuously. Simply add this expression to the keyframed property

```
loopOut("cycle")
```

and your animation will loop for the duration of the comp (**Figure 10.5**).

There are three other variations of loopOut(), as well:

▶ loopOut("pingpong") Runs your animation alternately forward, then backward.

▶ loopOut("continue") Extrapolates the animation beyond the last keyframe, so the value of the property keeps moving at the same rate (and in the same direction, if you're animating a spatial property such as

Figure 10.5 The solid line in the graph represents the keyframed bounce action. The dotted line represents the subsequent bounces created by loopOut("cycle").

Position) as the last keyframe. This can be useful, for example, if you're tracking an object that has moved offscreen and you want After Effects to extrapolate where it would be if it kept moving at the same speed and in the same direction.

▶ loopOut("offset") Works similarly to "cycle" except that instead of returning to the value of the first keyframe, each loop of the animation is offset by an amount equal to the value at the end of the previous loop. This produces a cumulative or stair-step effect.

loopIn() operates the same way as loopOut(), except that the looping occurs before the first keyframe instead of after the last keyframe. Both loopIn() and loopOut() will accept a second, optional parameter that specifies how many keyframes to loop. Actually, it's easier to think of it as how many keyframed segments to loop. For loopOut() the segments are counted from the last keyframe toward the layer's In point. For loopIn() the segments are counted from the first keyframe toward the layer's Out point. If you leave this parameter out (or specify it as 0), all keyframes are looped. For example, this variation loops the segment bounded by the last and next-to-last keyframes:

loopOut("cycle",1)

Two variations on the expressions—loopOutDuration() and loopInDuration()—enable you to specify the time (in seconds) as the second parameter instead of the number of keyframed segments to be looped. For loopOutDuration(), the time is measured from the last keyframe toward the layer's In point. For loopInDuration(), the time is measured from the first keyframe toward the layer's Out point. For example, this expression loops the two-second interval prior to the last keyframe:

loopOutDuration("cycle",2)

If you leave out the second parameter (or specify it as 0), the entire interval between the layer's In point and the last keyframe will be looped for loopOutDuration(). For loopInDuration(), the interval from the first keyframe to the Out point will be looped.

Using Markers

The expression language gives you access to the attributes of layer (and composition) markers. This can be extremely useful for synchronizing or easily establishing timing relationships between animated events.

The marker attributes that appear most frequently in expressions are time and index. As you might guess, the time attribute represents the time (in seconds) where the marker is located on the timeline. The index attribute represents the marker's order on the timeline, where 1 represents the left-most marker. You can also retrieve the marker nearest to a time that you specify by using nearestKey(). For example, to access the layer marker nearest to the current comp time use

```
marker.nearestKey(time)
```

This can be handy, but more often you'll want to know the most recent previous marker. The code necessary to retrieve it looks like this:

```
n = 0;
if (marker.numKeys > 0){
  n = marker.nearestKey(time).index;
  if (marker.key(n).time > time){
    n--;
  }
}
```

Note that this piece of code by itself is not very useful. When you do use it, you'll always combine it with additional code that makes it suitable for the particular property to which the expression will be applied. Because it's so versatile and can show up in expressions for virtually any property, it's worth looking at in detail.

The first line creates a variable, n, and sets its value to 0. If the value is still 0 when the routine finishes, it means that at the current time no marker was reached or that there are no markers on this layer.

The next line, a JavaScript if statement, checks if the layer has at least one marker. If there are no layer markers,

After Effects skips to the end of the routine with the variable n still set to 0. You need to make this test because the next line attempts to access the nearest marker with the statement

```
n = marker.nearestKey(time).index;
```

If After Effects attempted to execute this statement and there were no layer markers, it would generate an error and the expression would be disabled. It's best to defend against these kinds of errors so that you can apply the expression first and add the markers later if you want to.

If there is at least one layer marker, the third line of the expression sets n to the index of the nearest marker. Now all you have to do is determine if the nearest marker occurs before or after the current comp time with the statement

```
if (marker.key(n).time > time){
    n--;
}
```

This tells After Effects to decrement n by 1 if the nearest marker occurs later than the current time.

The result of all this is that the variable n contains the index of the most recent previous marker or 0 if no marker has yet been reached.

So how can you use this little routine? Consider a simple example.

Trigger Animation at Markers

Say you have a keyframed animation that you want to trigger at various times. All you need to do is drop a layer marker (just press * on the numeric keypad) wherever you want the action to be triggered. Then, apply this expression to the animated property:

```
n = 0;
if (marker.numKeys > 0){
  n = marker.nearestKey(time).index;
  if (marker.key(n).time > time){
    n--;
```

TIP

For more explanation of if statements, check out the "Conditionals" and "Comparison Operators" sections of the JavaScript guide.

TIP

If you're wondering about the JavaScript decrement operator (--), it's described in the "Operators" section of the JavaScript guide.

```
  }
}if (n == 0){
  valueAtTime(0);
}else{
  t = time - marker.key(n).time;
  valueAtTime(t)
}
```

As you can see, it's the previous marker routine with six new lines at the end. These lines tell After Effects to use the property's value from time 0 if there are no previous markers. Otherwise, variable t is defined to be the time since the most recent previous marker, and the value for that time is used.

The result of this is that the animation will run, beginning at frame 0, wherever there is a layer marker.

Play Only Frames with Markers

Suppose you want to achieve a stop-motion animation effect by displaying only specific frames of your footage, say playing only the frames when your actor reaches the apex of a jump so he appears to fly or hover.

First enable time remapping for the layer, then scrub through the Timeline and drop a layer marker at each frame that you want to include. Finally, apply this expression to the Time Remap property:

```
n = marker.numKeys;
if (n > 0){
  f = timeToFrames(time);
  idx = Math.min(f + 1, n);
  marker.key(idx).time
}else{
  value
}
```

In this expression, the variable n stores the total number of markers for the layer. The if statement next checks whether there is at least one marker. If not, the else clause executes, instructing After Effects to run the clip at normal speed. If there are markers, the expression first calculates the current frame using `timeToFrames()`, which converts whatever time you pass to it into the appropriate frame number. Here, it receives the current comp time and returns the current frame number, which is stored in variable `f`.

Next you need to convert the current frame number to a corresponding marker index for the frame you actually want to display. It turns out that all you need to do is add 1. That means when the current frame is 0, you actually want to show the frame that is at marker 1. When frame is 1, you want to show the frame at marker 2, and so on. The line

```
idx = Math.min(f + 1, n);
```

calculates the marker index and stores it in the variable `idx`. Using `Math.min()` ensures the expression never tries to access more markers than there are (which would generate an error and disable the expression). Instead, playback freezes on the last frame that has a marker.

Finally, you use the `idx` variable to retrieve the time of the corresponding marker. This value becomes the result of the expression, which causes After Effects to display the frame corresponding to the marker (**Figure 10.6**).

NOTES

See "The Math Object" in the Java-Script guide for more information on `Math.min()`.

Figure 10.6 The bottom line in the graph represents how the Time Remap property would behave without the expression. As you would expect, it is a linear, gradual increase. The upper, stair-stepped line is the result of the expression. Because the expression plays only frames with markers (represented in the graph by small triangles), time advances much more quickly.

Time Remapping Expressions

There are many ways to create interesting effects with time remapping expressions. You've already seen one (the last expression in the previous section). Here are a few more illustrative examples.

Jittery Slow Motion

Here's an interesting slow-motion effect where frames 0, 1, 2, and 3 play, followed by frames 1, 2, 3, and 4, then 2, 3, 4, and 5, and so on. First, enable time remapping for the layer and then apply this expression to the Time Remap property:

```
cycle = 4;
f = timeToFrames();
framesToTime(Math.floor(f/cycle) + f%cycle);
```

The first line sets the value of the variable cycle to the number of frames After Effects will display in succession (4 in this case). The second line sets variable f to the frame number corresponding to the current comp time. Next comes a tricky bit of math using JavaScript's Math.floor() method and its % modulo operator. The result is a repeating sequence (whose length is determined by the variable cycle) where the starting frame number increases by 1 for each cycle.

Wiggle Time

This effect uses multiple copies of the same footage to achieve a somewhat creepy echo effect. This effect actually involves three short expressions: one for Time Remap, one for Opacity, and one for Audio Levels. First, you enable time remapping for the layer. Then apply the three expressions and duplicate the layer as many times as necessary to create the look you want (**Figure 10.7**).

Figure 10.7 The time-wiggling effect with multiple layers.

Note that this time-wiggling effect is interesting, even with a single layer. The Opacity and Audio Levels expressions are necessary only if you want to duplicate the layer.

The expression for the Time Remap property is

```
Math.abs(wiggle(1,1))
```

`wiggle()` is an extremely useful tool that can introduce a smooth or fairly frenetic randomness into any animation, depending on your preference. `wiggle()` accepts five parameters, but only `frequency` and `amplitude` are required. Check the After Effects documentation for an explanation of what the remaining three optional parameters do.

The first parameter, `frequency`, represents the frequency of the wiggle in seconds; `wiggle(1,1)` varies the playback speed at the rate of once per second. The second parameter is the amplitude of the wiggle, given in the units of the parameter to which `wiggle()` is applied, which in this case is also seconds. So, `wiggle(1,1)` lets the playback time deviate from the actual comp time by as much as one second in either direction.

You use `Math.abs()` to make sure that the wiggled time value never becomes less than 0, which would cause the layer to sit at frame 0.

The Opacity expression gives equal visibility to each layer. Here's what it looks like:

```
(index/thisComp.numLayers)*100
```

This is simply the ratio of the layer's index divided by the total number of layers in the comp, times 100%. That means if you duplicate the layer four times (for a total of five layers), the top layer will have an Opacity of 20%, the second layer will have an Opacity of 40%, and so on, until the bottom (fifth) layer, which will have an Opacity of 100%. This allows each layer to contribute equally to the final result.

If the footage has audio, you have a couple of choices. You can turn the audio off for all but one of the layers, or you can use an expression for Audio Levels that normalizes

NOTES

For more detail on `Math.abs()`, see "The Math Object" section of the online JavaScript guide.

them so that the combined total audio level is roughly the same as it would be for a single layer. I think the second option enhances the creepiness of the effect; here's the Audio Levels expression for a stereo audio source (for a mono source you could just leave out the second line of the expression):

```
db = -10*Math.log(thisComp.numLayers)/Math.log(10);
[db,db]
```

This is just a little decibel math that reduces the level of each layer based on how many total layers there are (using the comp attribute `numLayers`). You'll also notice a couple of JavaScript elements you haven't encountered before: `Math.Log()` and an array (the second line of the expression). In expressions, you specify and reference the value of a multidimensional property, such as both channels of the stereo audio level, using array square bracket syntax.

NOTES

For more information on `Math. log()` see the "Math Object" section of the JavaScript guide on the accompanying disc; for more on arrays see the "Arrays" section.

Random Time

In this example, instead of having the time of each layer wander around, the expression offsets each layer's playback time by a random amount. The expression you need for the Time Remap property is

```
maxOffset = 0.7;
seedRandom(index, true);
time + random(maxOffset);
```

The first thing to notice about this expression is the use of `seedRandom()` and `random()` and the relationship between these functions. If you use `random()` by itself, you get a different random number at each frame, which is usually not what you want. The solution is `seedRandom()`, which takes two parameters. The first is the seed. It controls which random numbers get generated by `random()`. If you specify only this parameter, you will have different random numbers on each frame, but they are an entirely new sequence of numbers. It's the second parameter of `seedRandom()` that enables you to slow things down. Specifying this parameter as `true` tells After Effects to generate the same random numbers on each frame. The default value is `false`, so if you don't specify this parameter at all, you get different numbers on each frame. It's important to note that `seedRandom()` doesn't generate anything by itself. It just defines the subsequent behavior of `random()`.

Here's an example. This Position expression randomly moves a layer to a new location in the comp on each frame:

```
random([thisComp.width,thisComp.height])
```

This variation causes the layer to stay in one random location:

```
seedRandom(1,true);
random([thisComp.width,thisComp.height])
```

This version is the same as the previous one, except that it generates a different, single random location because the value of the seed is different:

```
seedRandom(2,true);
random([thisComp.width,thisComp.height])
```

Let's get back to the Time Remap expression. The first line creates the variable `maxOffset` and sets it to the maximum value, in seconds, that each layer's playback time can deviate from the actual comp time. The maximum for the example is 0.7 seconds.

The next line tells After Effects that you want the random number generator (`random()`) to generate the same random number on each frame.

The last line of the expression calculates the final Time Remap value, which is just the sum of the current comp time plus a random offset between 0 and 0.7 seconds.

Next, you would apply the Opacity and Audio Levels expressions from the `wiggle()` example so that each layer's video and audio will be weighted equally. Duplicate the layer as many times as necessary to get the effect you like.

Layer Space Transforms

In the world of expressions, layer space transforms are indispensible, but they present some of the most difficult concepts to grasp. There are three coordinate systems in After Effects, and layer space transforms provide you with the tools you need to translate locations from one coordinate system to another.

CLOSE-UP

More About random()

There are several ways to use `random()`. If you call it with no parameters, it will generate a random number between 0 and 1. If you provide a single parameter (as in the Random Time example), it will generate a random number between 0 and the value of the parameter. If you provide two parameters, separated by a comma, it will generate a random number between those two parameters. It's important to note that the parameters can be arrays instead of numbers. For example, this expression will give you a random 2D position somewhere within the comp:

```
random ([thisComp.width,
thisComp.height])
```

In addition to `random()`, After Effects provides `gaussRandom()`, which operates in much the same way as `random()` except that the results have more of a Gaussian distribution to them. That is, more values are clustered toward the center of the range, with fewer at the extremities. Another difference is that with `gaussRandom()`, sometimes the values may actually be slightly outside the specified range, which never happens with `random()`.

One coordinate system represents a *layer's own space*. This is the coordinate system relative (usually) to the layer's upper-left corner. In this coordinate system, [0, 0] represents a layer's upper-left corner, [width, height] represents the lower-right corner, and [width, height]/2 represents the center of the layer. Note that unless you move a layer's anchor point, it, too, will usually represent the center of the layer in the layer's coordinate system.

The second coordinate system represents *world space*. World coordinates are relative to [0, 0, 0] of the composition. This starts out at the upper-left corner of a newly created composition, but it can end up anywhere relative to the comp view if the comp has a camera and the camera has been moved, rotated, or zoomed.

The last coordinate system represents *comp space*. In this coordinate system, [0, 0] represents the upper-left corner of the camera view (or the default comp view if there is no camera), no matter where the camera is located or how it is oriented. In this coordinate system, the lower-right corner of the camera view is given by [thisComp.width, thisComp.height]. In comp space, the Z coordinate really doesn't have much meaning because you're only concerned with the flat representation of the camera view (**Figure 10.8**).

Figure 10.8 This illustration shows the three coordinate systems of After Effects. Positions in the yellow layer's coordinate system are measured relative to its upper-left corner. The 3D null is positioned at [0,0,0] in the comp so that it shows the reference point of the world coordinate system (here it's exactly the same as the null's layer coordinate system). The comp's coordinate system is always referenced to the upper-left corner of the Comp view, which in this case no longer matches the world coordinate system because the camera has been moved and rotated.

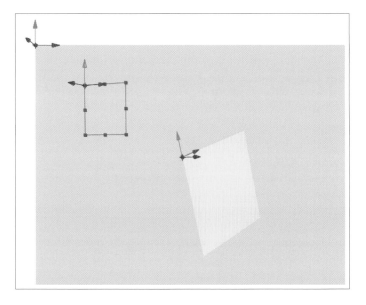

So when would you use layer space transforms? One of the most common uses is probably to provide the world coordinates of a layer that is the child of another layer. When you make a layer the child of another layer, the child layer's Position value changes from the world space coordinate system to layer space of the parent layer. That is, the child layer's Position becomes the distance of its anchor point from the parent layer's upper-left corner. So a child layer's Position is no longer a reliable indicator of where the layer is in world space. For example, if you want another layer to track a layer that happens to be a child, you need to translate the child layer's position to world coordinates. Another common application of layer space transforms allows you to apply an effect to a 2D layer at a point that corresponds to where a 3D layer appears in the comp view. Both of these applications will be demonstrated in the following examples.

Effect Tracks Parented Layer

To start, consider a relatively simple example: You have a layer named "star" that's the child of another layer, and you want to rotate the parent, causing the child to orbit the parent. You have applied CC Particle Systems II to a comp-sized layer and you want the Producer Position of the particle system to track the comp position of the child layer. The expression you need to do all this is

```
L = thisComp.layer("star");
L.toComp(L.transform.anchorPoint)
```

The first line is a little trick I like to use to make the following lines shorter and easier to manage. It creates a variable L and sets it equal to the layer whose position needs to be translated. It's important to note that you can use variables to represent more than just numbers. In this case the variable is representing a layer object. So now, when you want to reference a property or attribute of the target layer, instead of having to prefix it with `thisComp.layer("star")`, you can just use L.

In the second line the `toComp()` layer space transform translates the target layer's anchor point from the layer's own space to comp space. The transform uses the anchor point because it represents the layer's position in its own layer space. Another way to think of this second line is "From the target layer's own layer space, convert the target layer's anchor point into comp space coordinates."

This simple expression can be used in many ways. For example, if you want to simulate the look of 3D rays emanating from a 3D shape layer, you can create a 3D null and make it the child of the shape layer. You then position the null some distance behind the shape layer. Then apply the CC Light Burst 2.5 effect to a comp-sized 2D layer and apply this expression to the effect's Center parameter:

```
L = thisComp.layer("source point");
L.toComp(L.anchorPoint)
```

(Notice that this is the same expression as in the previous example, except for the name of the target layer: source point, in this case). If you rotate the shape layer, or move a camera around, the rays seem to be coming from the position of the null.

Apply 2D Layer as Decal onto 3D Layer

Sometimes you may need to use more than one layer space transform in a single expression. For example, you might want to apply a 2D layer like a decal to a 3D layer using the Corner Pin effect. To pull this off you need a way to mark on the 3D layer where you want the corners of the 2D layer to be pinned. Apply four point controls to the 3D layer, and you can then position each of the 2D layer's corners individually on the surface of the 3D layer. To keep things simple, rename each of the point controls to indicate the corner it represents, making the upper-left one UL, the upper-right UR, and so on. Once the point controls are in place, you can apply an expression like this one for the upper-left parameter to each parameter of the 2D layer's Corner Pin effect:

```
L = thisComp.layer("target");
fromComp(L.toComp(L.effect("UL")("Point")))
```

The first line is just the little shorthand trick so that you can reference the target layer (the 3D layer in this case) more succinctly. The second line translates the position of point controls from the 3D layer's space to the layer space of the 2D layer with the Corner Pin effect. There are no layer-to-layer space transforms, however, so the best you can do is transform twice: first from the 3D layer to comp space and then from comp space to the 2D layer. (Remember to edit the expression slightly for each of the other corner parameters so that it references the corresponding point control on the 3D layer.)

So, inside the parentheses you convert the point control from the 3D layer's space into comp space. Then you convert that result to the 2D layer's space. Nothing to it, right?

Reduce Saturation Away from Camera

Let's change gears a little. You want to create an expression that reduces a layer's saturation as it moves away from the camera in a 3D scene. In addition, you want this expression to work even if the target layer and the camera happen to be children of other layers. You can accomplish this by applying the Color Balance (HLS) effect to the target layer and applying this expression to the Saturation parameter:

```
minDist = 900;
maxDist = 2000;

C = thisComp.activeCamera.toWorld([0,0,0]);
dist = length(toWorld(transform.anchorPoint), C);
ease(dist, minDist, maxDist, 0, -100)
```

The first two lines define variables that will be used to set the boundaries of this effect. If the target layer's distance from the camera is less than `minDist`, you'll leave the Saturation setting unchanged at 0. If the distance is greater than `maxDist` you want to completely desaturate the layer with a setting of −100.

The third line of the expression creates variable C, which represents the position of the comp's currently active camera in world space. It's important to note that cameras and lights don't have anchor points, so you have to convert a specific location in the camera's layer space. It turns out that, in its own layer space, a camera's location is represented by the array [0,0,0] (that is, the X, Y, and Z coordinates are all 0).

The next line creates another variable, dist, which represents the distance between the camera and the anchor point of the target layer. You do this with the help of length(), which takes two parameters and calculates the distance between them. The first parameter is the world location of the target layer and the second parameter is the world location of the camera, calculated previously.

All that's left to do is calculate the actual Saturation value based on the layer's current distance from the camera. You do this with the help of ease(), one of the expression language's amazingly useful interpolation methods. What this line basically says is "as the value of dist varies from minDist to maxDist, vary the output of ease() from 0 to –100."

Interpolation Methods

After Effects provides some very handy global interpolation methods for converting one set of values to another. Say you wanted an Opacity expression that would fade in over half a second, starting at the layer's In point. This is very easily accomplished using the linear() interpolation method:

```
linear(time, inPoint, inPoint + 0.5, 0, 100)
```

As you can see, linear() accepts five parameters (there is also a seldom-used version that accepts only three parameters), which are, in order:

▶ input value that is driving the change

▶ minimum input value

▶ maximum input value

▶ output value corresponding to the minimum input value

▶ output value corresponding to the maximum input value

In the example, time is the input value (first parameter), and as it varies from the layer's In point (second parameter) to 0.5 seconds beyond the In point (third parameter), the output of linear() varies from 0 (fourth parameter) to 100 (fifth parameter). For values of the input parameter

Expression Controls

Expression controls are actually layer effects whose main purpose is to allow you to attach user interface controls to an expression. These controls come in six versions:

▶ Slider Control

▶ Point Control

▶ Angle Control

▶ Checkbox Control

▶ Color Control

▶ Layer Control

All types of controls (except Layer Control) can be keyframed and can themselves accept expressions. The most common use, however, is to enable you to set or change a value used in an expression calculation without having to edit the code. For example, you might want to be able to easily adjust the `frequency` and `ampli-tude` parameters of a `wiggle()` expression. You could accomplish this by applying two slider controls to the layer with the expression (Effects > Expression Controls). It's usually a good idea to give your controls descriptive names; say you change the name of the first slider to frequency and the second one to amplitude. You would then set up your expression like this (using the pick whip to create the references the sliders would be smart):

```
freq = effect("frequency")("Slider");
amp = effect("amplitude")("Slider");
wiggle(freq, amp)
```

Now, you can control the frequency and amplitude of the wiggle via the sliders. With each of the control types (again, with the exception of Layer Control) you can edit the numeric value directly, or you set the value using the control's gadget.

One unfortunate side note about expression controls is that because you can't apply effects to cameras or lights, neither can you apply expression controls to them.

that are less than the minimum input value, the output of `linear()` will be clamped at the value of the fourth parameter. Similarly, if the value of the input parameter is greater than the maximum input value, the output of `linear()` will be clamped to the value of the fifth parameter. Back to the example, at times before the layer's In point the Opacity value will be held at 0. From the layer's In point until 0.5 seconds beyond the In point, the Opacity value ramps smoothly from 0 to 100. For times beyond the In point + 0.5 seconds, the Opacity value will be held at 100.

Sometimes it helps to read it from left to right like this: "As the value of time varies from the In point to 0.5 seconds past the In point, vary the output from 0 to 100."

The second parameter should always be less than the third parameter. Failure to set it up this way can result in some bizarre behavior.

Note that the output values need not be numbers. Arrays work as well. If you want to slowly move a layer from the composition's upper-left corner to the lower-right corner over the time between the layer's In point and Out point, you could set it up like this:

```
linear(time, inPoint, outPoint, [0,0], [thisComp.
width, thisComp.height])
```

There are other equally useful interpolation methods in addition to linear(), each taking exactly the same set of parameters. easeIn() provides ease at the minimum value side of the interpolation, easeOut() provides it at the maximum value side, and ease() provides it at both. So if you wanted the previous example to ease in and out of the motion, you could do it like this:

```
ease(time, inPoint, outPoint, [0,0], [thisComp.width,
thisComp.height])
```

Fade While Moving Away from Camera

Just as you can reduce a layer's saturation as it moves away from the camera, you can reduce Opacity. The expression is, in fact, quite similar:

```
minDist = 900;
maxDist = 2000;

C = thisComp.activeCamera.toWorld([0,0,0]);
dist = length(toWorld(transform.anchorPoint), C);
ease(dist, minDist, maxDist, 100, 0)
```

The only differences between this expression and the previous one are the fourth and fifth parameters of the ease() statement. In this case, as the distance increases from 900 to 2000, the opacity fades from 100% to 0%.

From Comp Space to Layer Surface

There's a somewhat obscure layer space transform that you haven't looked at yet, namely `fromCompToSurface()`. This translates a location from the current comp view to the location on a 3D layer's surface that lines up with that point (from the camera's perspective). When would that be useful?

Imagine you have a 2D comp-sized layer named Beam, to which you have applied the Beam Effect. You want a Lens Flare effect on a 3D layer to line up with the ending point of the Beam effect on the 2D layer. You can do it by applying this expression to the Flare Center parameter of the Lens Flare effect on the 3D layer:

```
beamPos = thisComp.layer("beam").effect("Beam")
("Ending Point");
fromCompToSurface(beamPos)
```

First, store the location of the ending point of the Beam effect into the variable `beamPos`. Now you can take a couple of shortcuts because of the way things are set up. First, the Ending Point parameter is already represented as a location in the Beam layer's space. Second, because the Beam layer is a comp-sized layer that hasn't been moved or scaled, its layer space will correspond exactly to the Camera view (which is the same as comp space). Therefore, you can assume that the ending point is already represented in comp space. If the Beam layer were a different size than the comp, located somewhere other than the comp's center, or scaled, you couldn't get away with this. You would have to convert the ending point from Beam's layer space to comp space.

Now all you have to do is translate the `beamPos` variable from comp space to the corresponding point of the surface of the layer with Lens Flare, which is accomplished easily with `fromCompToSurface()`.

You'll look at one more example of layer space transforms in the big finale "Extra Credit" section at the end of the chapter.

CLOSE-UP

More About sampleImage()

You can sample the color and alpha data of a rectangular area of a layer using the layer method `sampleImage()`. You supply up to four parameters to `sampleImage()` and it returns color and alpha data as a four-element array (red, green, blue, alpha), where the values have been normalized so that they fall between 0.0 and 1.0. The four parameters are

- ▶ sample point
- ▶ sample radius
- ▶ post-effect flag
- ▶ sample time

The sample point is given in layer space coordinates, where [0, 0] represents the center of the layer's top left pixel. The sample radius is a two-element array (x radius, y radius) that specifies the horizontal and vertical distance from the sample point to the edges of the rectangular area being sampled. To sample a single pixel, you would set this value to [0.5, 0.5], half a pixel in each direction from the center of the pixel at the sample point. The post-effect flag is optional (its default value is true if you omit it) and specifies whether you want the sample to be taken after masks and effects are applied to the layer (true) or before (false). The sample time parameter specifies the time at which the sample is to be taken. This parameter is also optional (the default value is the current composition time), but if you include it, you must also include the post-effect flag parameter. As an example, here's how you could sample the red value of the pixel at a layer's center, after any effects and masks have been applied, at a time one second prior to the current composition time:

```
mySample = sampleImage([width/
height]/2, [0.5,0.5], true, time
- 1);
myRedSample = mySample[0];
```

Color Sampling and Conversion

Here's an example that demonstrates how you work with colors in an expression. The idea here is that you want to vary the opacity of an animated small layer based on the lightness (or luminosity) of the pixels of a background layer that currently happen to be under the moving layer. The smaller layer will become more transparent as it passes over dark areas of the background and more opaque as it passes over lighter areas. Fortunately, the expression language supplies a couple of useful tools to help out.

Before examining the expression, we need to talk about the way color data is represented in expressions. An individual color channel (red, blue, green, hue, saturation, lightness, or alpha) is represented as a number between 0.0 (fully off) and 1.0 (fully on). A complete color space representation consists of an array of four such channels. Most of the time you'll be working in red, blue, green, and alpha (RGBA) color space, but you can convert to and from hue, saturation, lightness, and alpha (HSLA) color space. This example uses sampleImage() to extract RGBA data from a target layer called background. Then rgbToHsl() converts the RGBA data to HSLA color space so that you can extract the lightness channel, which will then be used to drive the Opacity parameter of the small animated layer. Here's the expression:

```
sampleSize = [width, height]/2;
target = thisComp.layer("background");
rgba = target.sampleImage(transform.position,
sampleSize, true, time);
hsla = rgbToHsl(rgba);
hsla[2]*100
```

First you create the variable sampleSize and set its value as an array consisting of half the width and height of the layer whose opacity will be controlled with the expression. Essentially this means that you'll be sampling all of the pixels of the background layer that are under smaller layers at any given time.

The second line just creates the variable target, which will be a shorthand way to refer to the background layer. Then sampleImage() retrieves the RGBA data for the area of the background under the smaller layer and stores the result-ing array in the variable rgba. See the sidebar "More About sampleImage()" earlier in the chapter for details on all the parameters of sampleImage().

Next rgbToHsl() converts the RGBA data to HSLA color space and stores the result in variable hsla. Finally, because the lightness channel is the third value in the HSLA array, you use the array index of [2] to extract it (see the "Arrays" section of the JavaScript guide if this doesn't make sense to you). Because it will be a value between 0.0 and 1.0, you just need to multiply it by 100 to get it into a range suitable to control the Opacity parameter (**Figure 10.9**).

Figure 10.9 The small blue layer becomes more transparent as it passes over darker areas of the background image.

Extra Credit

Congratulations on making it this far. The remaining exam-ples build on concepts covered earlier, but I have saved them for this section because they are particularly tricky or involve some complex math. I'm presenting them mainly to entice you to take some time to figure out how they work.

Fade as Turn Away from Camera

Let's briefly return to the world of layer space transforms and examine a simple idea that requires only a short expression, but one with a lot of complicated vector math going on under the hood. The idea is that you want a 3D layer to fade out as it turns away from the camera. This needs to work not only when the layer rotates away from the camera, but also if the camera orbits the layer. And of course, it should still work if either the layer or the camera happens to be the child of another layer. Take a look at an expression for Opacity that will accomplish this:

```
minAngle = 20;
maxAngle = 70;

C = thisComp.activeCamera.toWorld([0,0,0]);
v1 = normalize(toWorld(transform.anchorPoint) - C);
v2 = toWorldVec([0,0,1]);
angle = radiansToDegrees(Math.acos(dot(v1, v2)));
ease(angle, minAngle, maxAngle, 100, 0)
```

The first two lines just create two variables (`minAngle` and `maxAngle`) that establish the range of the effect. Here you set their values so that when the layer is within 20 degrees of facing the camera, it will be at 100% Opacity and Opacity will fade from 100% to 0% as the angle increases to 70 degrees. Beyond 70 degrees, Opacity will be 0%.

Next you create a variable `C` that represents the position of the comp's active camera in world space. You've seen this before, in the expression where the layer fades as it moves away from the camera.

Now starts the vector math. Things get a little bumpy from here. Briefly, a *vector* is an entity that has a length and a direction, but has no definite position in space. I like to think of vectors as arrows that you can move around, but they always keep the same heading. Fortunately the expression language provides a pretty good arsenal of tools to deal with vectors.

To figure out the angle between the camera and the layer with the expression, you're going to need two vectors. One will be the vector that points from the center of the layer toward the camera. The other will be a vector that points outward from the center of the layer along the z-axis.

To calculate the first vector (variable `v1`), convert the layer's anchor point to world space coordinates and subtract from that value the location of the camera in world space. What you're doing is subtracting two points in space. Remember, in After Effects, each 3D position in space is represented by an array: [x,y,z]. The result of subtracting two points like this gives you a vector. This vector has a magnitude representing the distance between the two points and a direction (in this case, the direction from the layer to the camera). You can use `normalize()` to convert the vector to what is known as a unit vector, which maintains the direction of the original vector but sets its length to 1. This simplifies the upcoming determination of the angle between two vectors.

Next you create the second vector (variable `v2`). You can create the necessary unit vector in one step this time by using `toWorldVec([0,0,1])` to create a vector of length 1 pointed along the layer's z-axis.

Now you have your two vectors. To calculate the angle between two vectors, you use what is known as the vector dot product. I won't go into great detail about how it works (there's a lot of information on the Internet if you're curious), but it turns out that if you use unit vectors, the vector dot product will directly give you the arc cosine of the angle between the two vectors. Luckily, the expression language gives us a built-in function, dot(), to calculate the dot product.

So now you can calculate the angle you need (and store it in variable angle) in three steps. First you take the dot product of the two vectors, producing the arc cosine of the angle. Then you use Math.acos() to convert that to an angle (see the "Math Object" section of the JavaScript guide for more information). Because the result of Math. acos() will be in radians, you need to convert it to degrees so that it will be in the same units as the limits minAngle and maxAngle. Fortunately, the expression language provides radiansToDegrees() to make the conversion.

The final step is to use the interpolation method ease() to smoothly execute the fade as the angle increases.

Audio Triggers Effect

Earlier, you learned about linking an effect to an audio level. You can take that idea one step further and use audio to trigger an animated effect. The difference is subtle but significant. In the earlier examples, the effect tracked the audio level precisely, leaving the result at the mercy of the shape of the audio level's envelope. Here, you're going to use the transitioning of the audio level above some threshold to trigger an animation. The animation will run until there is another trigger event, which will cause the animation to start again from the beginning.

This is a powerful concept and there are many ways to use it. This example triggers a decaying oscillation that is actually contained within the expression, but you could easily adapt this to run a keyframed animation using valueAt-Time() or to run a time-remapped sequence.

The heart of this expression is what I would call a "beat detector." The expression basically walks backward in time, frame by frame, looking for the most recent event where the audio level transitioned from below the threshold to above the threshold. It then uses the difference in time between the triggering event and the current comp time to determine how far along it should be in the animation. At each new beat, this time resets to 0 and runs until the next beat. Take a look at this monster:

```
threshold = 20.0;

A = thisComp.layer("Audio Amplitude").effect("Both
Channels")("Slider");

// beat detector starts here

above = false;
frame = timeToFrames();
while (true){
  t = framesToTime(frame);
  if (above){
    if (A.valueAtTime(t) < threshold){
      frame++;
      break;
    }
  }else if (A.valueAtTime(t) >= threshold){
    above = true;
  }
  if (frame == 0){
    break;
  }
  frame--;
}
if (! above){
  t = 0;
}else{
  t = time - framesToTime(frame);
}

// animation starts here

amp = 75;
freq = 5;
decay = 2.0;

angle = freq * 2 * Math.PI * t;
amp * (-Math.cos(angle)+1)/ Math.exp(decay * t);
```

This expression has three sections. The first section defines the audio level that you want to trigger the animation and stores it into the variable `threshold`. It then defines variable `A` to use as shorthand notation for the slider control containing the keyframed data for the audio level.

The next section is the actual beat detector. In general, the expression starts at the current comp time and determines if the level is currently above the threshold. If it is, the expression moves backward in time, frame by frame, until it finds the most recent frame where the audio level was below the threshold. It then determines that the triggering event occurred on the frame after that (the most recent frame where the level transitioned from below the threshold to above it). That transition frame is converted to time using `framesToTime()`, that value is subtracted from the current comp time, and the result (the time, in seconds, since the triggering event) is stored in variable `t`.

However, if instead the audio level at the current comp time is *below* the threshold, the expression has more work to do. It first moves backward from the current comp time, frame by frame, until it finds a frame where the audio level is above the threshold. Then it continues on, looking for the transition from below the threshold to above it. The elapsed time since the triggering event is then calculated and stored in variable `t`.

There are some other things going on in this routine, but they mostly have to do with special cases, such as a time when there hasn't yet been a triggering event (in which case the animation is held at the first frame), or when the level is above the threshold but it has been there since the first frame.

There are some JavaScript elements in this section that you haven't seen before. Two forward slashes, `//` , denotes the start of a comment. The routine consists mainly of a giant `while()` loop. This loop is unusual in that its terminating condition is set to `true`, so it will never end on its own. It will continue to loop until one of the `break` statements is executed.

When After Effects arrives at the last section of the expression, variable `t` contains the necessary information: how

NOTES

See the "Comments" section of the JavaScript guide for more details on comments and the "Loops" section for more information about `while()`, `break`, and loops in general.

long it has been since the last triggering event. The final section uses it to drive a decaying oscillation routine with Math.cos() and Math.exp(). First you define the amplitude of the oscillation with the variable amp. Then you define the frequency of the oscillation (oscillations per second) with the variable freq. Variable decay determines how fast the oscillation decays (a higher number means a faster decay).

Math.cos() creates an oscillating sine wave with amplitude amp and frequency freq, then Math.exp() reduces the amplitude of the oscillating wave at a rate determined by variable decay (**Figure 10.10**).

You might want to visit "The Math Object" section of the JavaScript guide for more information on Math.cos() and Math.exp().

Figure 10.10 The graph shows the decaying oscillation triggered whenever the audio threshold level is crossed.

Conclusion

This chapter covered a lot of ground, but still it really only provided a hint of what's possible with expressions. Here are a few resources where you can find additional information:

▶ **www.aenhancers.com:** A forum-based site where you can get your questions answered and take a look at expressions contributed by others

▶ **http://forums.creativecow.net/forum/adobe_after_effects_expressions:** A forum dedicated to expressions

▶ **http://forums.adobe.com/community/aftereffects_general_discussion/aftereffects_expressions:** Adobe's own After Effects forum, which has a subforum on expressions

▶ **www.adobe.com/support/aftereffects:** The online version of After Effects Help

▶ **www.motionscript.com:** The site of the author of this chapter, which has a lot of examples and analysis

11

Advanced Color Options and HDR

Don't you wish there was a knob on the TV to turn up the intelligence? There's one marked "Brightness," but it doesn't work.

—Gallagher

Advanced Color Options and HDR

Perhaps you are somewhere near your computer monitor, and there is a window near that monitor. Perhaps there is daylight outside that window, and although like most computer graphics artists you probably work with the shades closed, perhaps some of that light is entering the room. If you were to take a photo out that window from inside that room from where that monitor sits, and then display it on that monitor, would there be any difference between how the room appeared on screen and in reality?

The truth is obvious. No matter how good your camera or recording medium, and no matter how advanced the display, no way will that scene of daylight illuminating a room from the window look the same on a display and in actuality. Yet how exactly does the image fail to capture the full fidelity, range, and response of that scene, and what can you do about it? That is the subject of this chapter.

The point being made here is that you may be aware that the images you work with and the ways you work with them have limitations, but you may not be aware what those are or how to work with them. Specifically, digital images tend to fall short in the following ways:

▶ Color accuracy is not maintained, so hues and intensities slip and slide as an image makes its way through the pipeline.

▶ Dynamic range of the source image is limited, so that shadows and highlights lack detail that exists in the real world.

▶ The very model used internally by your computer's graphics system is, by default, inaccurate in how it adjusts and blends colors and highly limited in the colors that it can store or represent on the monitor.

The challenge set forth here, to take an image all the way through the pipeline so that the result matches the source, is of course impossible. As we've seen, your work is to create camera reality, not reality itself, and as soon as you capture an image you create an optical point of view that doesn't otherwise exist.

But it's too easy to just throw in the towel. As soon as you learn to work with light more like it actually exists in the world, you may realize how often you compromise and work around standard limitations of digital color. The computer's model of color is not the basis for your work—it's a limitation to overcome on the path from the rich outer world of visual data to the images in your final output.

In this chapter, we'll take a look at how higher bit depths, the built-in color management system of After Effects and 3D LUTs, and compositing in linear (1.0 gamma) color can enhance your work.

Dynamic Range: Bit Depth and Film

It may still be the case that the majority of After Effects artists spend the majority of time working in 8 bits per channel, also known as monitor color. This section details the many ways in which you can do better. The simplest and least costly of these is to move from 8-bpc to 16-bpc mode.

16-Bit-Per-Channel Composites

After Effects 5.0 added support for 16-bpc color for one basic reason: to eliminate color *quantization*, most commonly seen as banding, where subtle gradients and other threshold regions appear in an image. 16-bpc mode adds 128 extra gradations between each R, G, B, and A value of the familiar 8-bpc mode.

Those increments are typically too fine for your eye to distinguish (or your monitor to display), but the eye easily

NOTES

All but the oldest and most outdated effects and plug-ins support 16-bpc color. To discern which ones do, with the project set to 16 bpc, choose Show 16 bpc-Capable Effects Only from the Effects & Presets panel menu. Effects that are only 8 bpc aren't off-limits, but it may be helpful to place them at the beginning (or end) of the image pipeline, where they are least likely to cause quantization by mixing with higher-bit-depth effects.

notices banding, and multiple adjustments to 8-bpc images will cause banding to appear in areas of subtle shading, such as edge thresholds and shadows, making the image look bad. To raise project color depth, either **Alt**-click (**Opt**-click) the color depth setting at the bottom of the Project panel or use the Depth menu in File > Project Settings.

There are really only a couple of downsides to working in 16 bpc instead of 8. There is a performance hit from the increased memory and processing bandwidth, but on contemporary systems it is typically negligible.

The real resistance tends to come from the unfamiliarity of 16-bit color values, but switching to 16-bpc mode doesn't mean you're stuck with incomprehensible pixel values such as 32768, 0, 0 for pure red or 16384, 16384, 16384 for middle gray. The panel menu of the Info panel allows you to choose whichever numerical color representation works for you, including familiar 8-bpc values when working in 16 bpc (**Figure 11.1**). The following sections use the 8-bpc values of your monitor despite referring to 16-bpc projects.

The Info panel menu color value settings determine color values everywhere in the application, including the Adobe Color Picker.

Figure 11.1 Love working in 16 bpc but hate analyzing 16-bit values that go up to 32768? Choose 8 bpc in the Info panel menu to display familiar 0 to 255 values. Or better yet, use Decimal values in all bit depths.

Even if your output is 8 bpc, the higher precision of 16 bpc will eliminate quantization and banding. However, there is more to color flexibility than toggling 16 bpc in order to avoid banding. You may even have source images with values beyond standard 8-bit color.

Film and Cineon Files

Although film as a recording medium is on the wane, the standards and formats of film remain common in the pipelines of studios working on digital "films" for the big screen. 10-bit Cineon .dpx files remain a common format for storing feature film images. The process of working with film can teach plenty about how to handle higher dynamic ranges in general, and even newer formats can output film-style .dpx sequences, so here's a brief description of the process.

After 35mm or 16mm film has been shot, the negative is developed, and shots destined for digital effects work are scanned frame by frame. During this *Telecine* process, some initial color decisions are made before the frames are output as a numbered sequence of Cineon files, named after Kodak's now-defunct film compositing system. Both Cineon files and the related format, DPX, store pixels uncompressed at 10 bits per channel. Scanners are usually capable of scanning 4K plates, and these have become more popular for visual effects usage, although many still elect to scan at half resolution, creating 2K frames around 2048 by 1536 pixels and weighing in at almost 13 MB.

The world's most famous Cineon file is Kodak's original test image, affectionately referred to as Marcie (**Figure 11.2**) and available from Kodak's web site (www.kodak.com/US/en/motion/-support/dlad/) or the book's disc. To get a feel for working with film, drop the file called dlad_2048X1556.cin from the 11_output_simulation folder into After Effects, which imports Cineon files just fine.

The first thing you'll notice about Marcie is that she looks funny, and not just because this photo dates back to the '80s. Cineon files are encoded using a logarithmic (log) tone response curve. To make Marcie look more natural, open the Interpret Footage dialog, select the Color Management tab, click Cineon Settings, and choose the Over Range preset (instead of the default Full Range). Aah, that looks better; the log image is now converted to the monitor's color space.

Figure 11.2 This universal sample image has been converted from film of a bygone era to Cineon format found on the book's disc.

Also included on the book's disc is a Cineon sequence from the RED Camera (courtesy of fxphd.com), showing off that digital camera's dynamic range and overall image quality. This is one example of Cineon format that is remaining viable with digital source.

Figure 11.3 When you convert an image from log space (left) to linear (center) and then back to log (right), the brightest details are lost.

It would seem natural to convert Cineon files to the monitor's color space, work normally, and then convert the end result back to log, but to do so would be to throw away valuable data. Try this: Apply the Cineon Converter effect and switch the Conversion Type from Linear to Log. This is a preview of how the file would be written on output back to a Cineon log file. Upon further examination of this conversion, you see a problem: In an 8-bpc (or even 16-bpc) project, the bright details in Marcie's hair don't survive the trip (**Figure 11.3**).

What's going on with this mystical Cineon file and its log color space that makes it so hard to deal with? And more importantly, why? Well, it turns out that the engineers at Kodak know a thing or two about film and have made no decisions lightly. But to properly answer the question, it's necessary to discuss some basic principles of photography and light.

NOTES

As becomes evident later in the chapter, the choice of the term "linear" as an alternative to "log" space for Cineon Converter is unfortunate, because "linear" specifically means neutral (1.0) gamma; what Cineon Converter calls "linear" is in fact gamma-encoded.

Dynamic Range

The pictures shown in **Figure 11.4** were taken in sequence from a roof on a winter morning. Anyone who has ever tried to photograph a sunrise or sunset with a digital camera should immediately recognize the problem at hand, even in an era in which a phone camera can deliver HDR images. With a standard exposure, the sky comes in beautifully, but foreground houses are nearly black. Using longer exposures you can bring the houses up, but by the time they are looking good the sky is completely blown out.

Figure 11.4 Different exposures when recording the same scene clearly produce widely varying results.

The limiting factor here is the digital camera's small dynamic range, which is the difference between the brightest and darkest things that can be captured in the same image. An outdoor scene has a wide array of brightnesses, but any digital device can read only a slice of them. You can change exposure to capture different ranges, but the size of the slice is fixed.

Our eyes have a much larger dynamic range and our brains have a wide array of perceptual tricks, so in real life the houses and sky are both seen easily. But even eyes have limits, such as when you try to see someone behind a bright spotlight or use a laptop computer in the sun. The spotlight has not made the person behind any darker, but when eyes adjust to bright lights (as they must to avoid injury), dark things fall out of range and simply appear black.

White on a monitor just isn't very bright, which is one reason professionals work in dim rooms with the blinds pulled down. When you try to represent the bright sky on a dim monitor, everything else in the image has to scale down in proportion. Even when a digital camera can capture extra dynamic range, your monitor must compress it in order to display it.

A standard 8-bpc computer image uses values 0 to 255 to represent RGB values. If you record a value above 255—say 285 or 310—that represents a pixel beyond the monitor's dynamic range, brighter than white or overbright. Because 8-bpc pixels can't actually go above 255, overbright information is stored as floating-point decimals where 0.0 is black and 1.0 is white. Because floating-point numbers are

NOTES

Floating point decimal numbers (which are effective for storing a wide range of precise values efficiently) and high dynamic range numbers (which extend beyond monitor range) have tended to be lumped together, but each is a separate, unique concept. If your 8-bit color range is limited to 0 to 255, then as soon as you have a value of 256, or –1, you are in high dynamic range territory. Floating-point values are merely a method used to store those out-of-range values without hitting an absolute low or high cutoff.

virtually unbounded, 0.75, 7.5, or 750.0 are all acceptable values, even though everything above 1.0 will clip to white on the monitor (**Figure 11.5**).

In recent years, it has become simpler to create still HDR images from a series of exposures—files that contain all light information from a scene (**Figure 11.6**). The best-known paper on the subject was published by Malik and Debevec at SIGGRAPH '97 (www.debevec.org has details). In successive exposures, values that remain within range can be compared to describe how the camera is respond-ing to different levels of light. That information allows a computer to connect bright areas in the scene to the darker ones and calculate accurate HDR pixel values that combine detail from each exposure.

But with all the excitement surrounding HDR imaging and improvements in the dynamic range of video cam-eras, many forget that for decades there has been another medium available for capturing dynamic range far beyond what a computer monitor can display or a digital camera can capture.

That medium is film.

Figure 11.5 Monitor white represents the upper limit for 8-bpc and 16-bpc pixels, while 32-bpc values can go arbitrarily higher (depending on for-mat) or lower; the range also extends below absolute black, 0.0—values that are theoretical and not part of the world you see (unless you're in outer space, staring into a black hole).

Figure 11.6 Consider the floating-point pixel values for this HDR image; they relate to one another proportionally, and continue to do so whether the image is brightened or darkened, because the values do not need to clip at 1.0.

Cineon Log Space

A film negative gets its name because areas exposed to light ultimately become dark and opaque, and areas unexposed are made transparent during developing. Light makes dark. Hence, negative.

Dark is a relative term here. A white piece of paper makes a nice dark splotch on the negative, but a lightbulb darkens the film even more, and a photograph of the sun causes the negative to turn out darker still. By not completely exposing to even bright lights, the negative is able to capture the differences between bright highlights and really bright highlights. Film, the original image capture medium, has always been high dynamic range.

If you were to graph the increase in film "density" as increasing amounts of light expose it, you'd get something like **Figure 11.7**. In math, this is referred to as a logarithmic curve. I'll get back to this in a moment.

Even the modern DSLR camera lacks the dynamic range to capture an outdoor scene with heavy contrast such as Figure 11.13 on a single pass, so most of these cameras include an option to shoot a series of stills with bracketed exposures above and below the target. The stills can then be combined into a single high dynamic range image using Photoshop's Merge to HDR Pro feature.

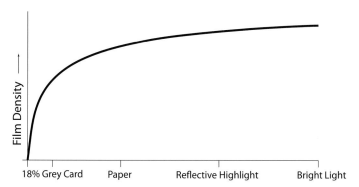

Figure 11.7 Graph the darkening (density) of film as increasing amounts of light expose it and you get a logarithmic curve.

Digital Film

If a monitor's maximum brightness is considered to be 1.0, the brightest value film can represent is officially considered by Kodak to be 13.53 (although using the more efficient ICC color conversion, outlined later in the chapter, reveals brightness values above 70). Note this only applies to a film negative that is exposed by light in the world as opposed to a film positive, which is limited by the brightness of a projector bulb, and is therefore not really considered high dynamic range. A Telecine captures the entire range of each frame and stores the frames as a sequence of 10-bit Cineon files. Those extra two bits mean that Cineon pixel values can range from 0 to 1023 instead of the 0 to 255 in 8-bit files.

Having four times as many values to work with in a Cineon file helps, but considering you have 13.53 times the range to record, care must be taken in encoding those values. The most obvious way to store all that light would simply be to evenly squeeze 0.0 to 13.53 into the 0 to 1023 range. The problem with this solution is that it would only leave 75 code values for the all-important 0.0 to 1.0 range, the same as allocated to the range 10.0 to 11.0, which you are far less interested in representing with much accuracy. Your eye can barely tell the difference between two highlights that bright—it certainly doesn't need 75 brightness variations between them.

A proper way to encode light on film would quickly fill up the usable values with the most important 0.0 to 1.0 light and then leave space for the rest of the negative's range. Fortunately, the film negative itself with its logarithmic response behaves just this way.

Cineon files are often said to be stored in a log color space. Actually, it is the negative that uses a log response curve and the file is simply storing the negative's density at each pixel. In any case, the graph in **Figure 11.8** describes how light exposes a negative and is encoded into Cineon color values according to Kodak, creator of the format.

Figure 11.8 Kodak's Cineon log encoding is also expressed as a logarithmic curve, with labels for the visible black and white points that correspond to 0 and 255 in normal 8-bit pixel values.

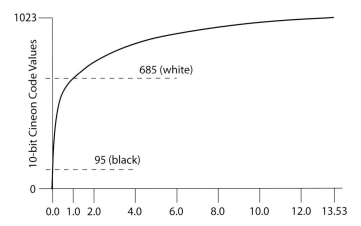

One strange feature in this graph is that black is mapped to code value 95 instead of 0. Not only does the Cineon file store whiter-than-white (overbright) values, it also has some blacker-than-black information. This is mirrored in the film lab when a negative is printed brighter than usual and the blacker-than-black information can reveal itself. Likewise, negatives can be printed darker and take advantage of overbright detail. The standard value mapped to monitor white is 685, and everything above is considered overbright.

Although the Kodak formulas are commonly used to transform log images for compositing, other methods have emerged. The idea of having light values below 0.0 is dubious at best, and many take issue with the idea that a single curve can describe all film stocks, cameras, and shooting environments. As a different approach, some visual effects facilities take care to photograph well-defined photographic charts and use the resultant film to build custom curves that differ subtly from the Kodak standard.

As much as Cineon log is a great way to encode light captured by film, it should not be used for compositing or other image transformations. This point is so important that it just has to be emphasized again:

Encoding color spaces are not compositing color spaces.

To illustrate this point, imagine you had a black pixel with Cineon value 95 next to an extremely bright pixel with Cineon's highest code value, 1023. If these two pixels were blended together (say, if the image was being blurred), the result would be 559, which is somewhere around middle gray (0.37 to be precise). But when you consider that the extremely bright pixel has a relative brightness of 13.5, that black pixel should only have been able to bring it down to 6.75, which is still overbright white! Log space's extra emphasis on darker values causes standard image processing operations to give those values extra weight, leading to an overall unpleasant and inaccurate darkening of the image. So, final warning: If you're working with a log source, don't do image processing in log space!

All About Log

You may first have heard of logarithmic curves in high school physics class, if you ever learned about the decay of radioactive isotopes.

If a radioactive material has a half-life of one year, half of it will have decayed after that time. The next year, half of what remains will decay, leaving a quarter, and so on. To calculate how much time has elapsed based on how much material remains, a logarithmic function is used.

Light, another type of radiation, has a similar effect on film. At the molecular level, light causes silver halide crystals to react. If film exposed for some short period of time causes half the crystals to react, repeating the exposure will cause half of the remaining to react, and so on. This is how film gets its response curve and the ability to capture even very bright light sources. No amount of exposure can be expected to affect every single crystal.

The description of gamma in video is oversimplified here somewhat because the subject is complex enough for a book of its own. An excellent one is Charles Poynton's *Digital Video and HDTV Algorithms and Interfaces* (Morgan Kaufmann).

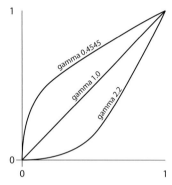

Figure 11.9 Graph of monitor gamma (2.2) with file gamma (0.4545) and linear (1.0). These are the color curves in question, with 0.4545 and 2.2 each acting as the direct inverse of the other.

Video Gamma Space

Because log spaces certainly don't look natural, it probably comes as no surprise that they are bad color spaces to work in. But there is another encoding color space with which you definitely have a working familiarity: the video space of your monitor.

You may have always assumed that 8-bit monitor code value 128, halfway between black and white, makes a gray that is half as bright as white. If so, you may be shocked to hear that this is not the case. In fact, 128 is much darker—not even a quarter of white's brightness on most monitors.

A system where half the input gives you half the output is described as linear, but monitors (like many things in the real world) are nonlinear. When a system is nonlinear, you can sometimes describe its behavior using the gamma function, shown in **Figure 11.9** and in the equation

```
Output = inputgamma 0 <= input <= 1
```

In this function, the darkest and brightest values (0.0 and 1.0) are always fixed, and the gamma value determines how the transition between them behaves. Successive applications of gamma can be concatenated by multiplying them together. Applying gamma and then 1/gamma has the net result of doing nothing. A curve with a gamma of 1.0 is linear.

Mac OS previously used a gamma of 1.8, while Windows used a gamma value of 2.2. Because the electronics in your screen are slow to react from lower levels of input voltage, a 1.0 gamma is simply too dark in either case; boosting this value compensates correctly.

The reason digital images do not appear dark, however, is that they have all been created with the inverse gamma function baked in to prebrighten pixels before they are displayed (**Figure 11.10**). Yes, all of them.

Because encoding spaces are not compositing spaces, working directly with images that appear on your monitor can pose problems. Similar to log encoding, video gamma encoding allocates more values to dark pixels, so they weigh more than they should. Video color space is not much more valid than Cineon color space for re-creating the way light behaves in the world at large.

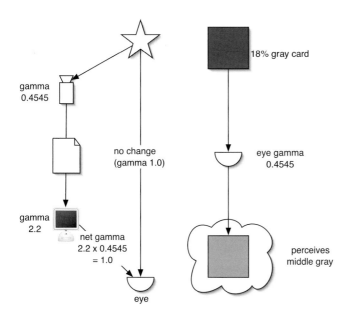

Figure 11.10 The gamma settings in the file and monitor complement one another to result in faithful image reproduction.

Linearized Working Space

In the real world, light intensity is linear. Double the wattage and the entire scene is twice as bright. Unless you work linear, with these *scene-referred* values, this is not how color intensity behaves on your computer's *monitor-referred* values, which also clip at an intensity well below the whitest white your eye can see. If only your computer had the same color and light model as the real world, you could use light values the same way they are used in nature.

Let's take a trip now to a magical land where computer and real-world light values are one; to reach our destination, we need go no further than the Project Settings dialog.

Open Project Settings in any project and take a look at Color Settings. By default the dialog might look like that in **Figure 11.11** (left). There are a couple of pull-down menus, a few checkboxes (one or two of which might be grayed out) and some complicated looking fine print below.

CLOSE-UP

Gamma-rama

In case all this gamma talk hasn't already blown your mind, allow me to clarify how monitor gamma and human vision work together. The question often comes up—why is middle gray 18% and not 50%? And why does 50% gray look like middle gray on my monitor, but not on a linear color chart?

It turns out that your eyes also have a nonlinear response to color—your vision brightens low light, which helps you to see where it's dim, a survival advantage. The human eye is very sensitive to small amounts of light, and it gets less sensitive as brightness increases. Your eye effectively brightens the levels, and objects in the world are, in fact, darker than they appear—or, they become darker when we represent their true linear nature. The subjective observation that 18% gray, give or take a percentage point, appears to be the midpoint between black and white indicates that your eye (or more accurately, the human vision system) applies a gamma correction of 2.5, which can be calculated as follows: $0.5 = 0.18^{(1/2.5)}$.

NOTES

To follow this discussion, choose Decimal in the Info panel menu (this is the default for 32 bpc). 0.0 to 1.0 values are those falling in low dynamic range, or LDR—those values typically described in 8 bit as 0 to 255. Any values outside this range are HDR, 32 bpc only.

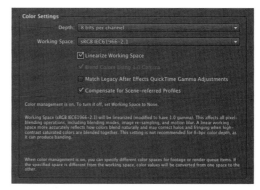

Figure 11.11 This is how default Color Settings might look in the Project Settings dialog.

If there's one thing I know about visual artists, it's that we're generally impatient with fine print and are enamored of visual examples, so try the following:

1. Set a working space to enable color management. It doesn't really matter for this exercise which you choose—more on the specific choice later—but if you want the most common and flexible one, choose sRGB (or, use its more complete and impossible-to-remember name, sRGB IEC61966-2.1), which is designed to correspond to your monitor itself.

2. Note that the checkboxes are now all live (none are grayed out), including Linearize Working Space. Enable that one, and leave Compensate for Scene-referred Profiles enabled, then click OK (**Figure 11.11**, right).

3. For simplicity's sake, make sure in Preferences > General that Use System Color Picker is disabled so that you're working with the Adobe Color Picker.

NOTES

What's up with the name? sRGB's cumbersome full name tells us that it comes from the IEC, a standards management board founded a century ago by Lord Kelvin in the famously neutral country of Switzerland. Like so many engineering specs, its numerical name connects it to a version number of a long and detailed document—51 pages long, in this case, or roughly 10% longer than this chapter

4. Create a new solid layer. Click on the Color swatch to open the Adobe Color Picker. Notice that it looks different—strange and unfamiliar, even (**Figure 11.12**). Set Brightness to 50% and notice a tone much brighter than what would be considered middle gray.

Figure 11.12 When you set the working space to be linearized, the Adobe color picker responds in kind by presenting linear color values. Notice how far below center middle gray appears to be.

5. Now try switching that Brightness value to 18%.

   Aha. In a linearized working space, After Effects accommodates the 18% middle gray of real-world color.

Now the question becomes, how does that help? This type of change should generally not be introduced to a project already in progress, since all of the solids and other color selections will shift and need to be reset, and any blends will also be linear, so even composites without color selections will shift. Plus, it's confusing not to have middle gray at 50%, isn't it?

What's the point?

Color Realism: Linear HDRI

The examples in **Table 11.1** show the difference between making adjustments to digital camera photos in their native video space and performing those same operations in linear space. In all cases, an unaltered photograph featuring the equivalent in-camera effect is shown for comparison.

The table's first column contains the images brightened by one stop, an increment on a camera's aperture, which controls how much light is allowed through the lens. Widening the aperture by one stop allows twice as much light to enter. An increase of three stops brightens the image by a factor of eight (2 x 2 x 2, or 2^3).

To double pixel values in video space is to quickly blow out bright areas in the image. Video pixels are already encoded with extra brightness and can't take much more.

TABLE **11.1** Comparison of Adjustments in Native Video Space and in Linear Space

	BRIGHTEN ONE STOP	LENS DEFOCUS	MOTION BLUR
Original Image			
Filtered in Video Space			
Filtered in Linear Space			
Real-World Photo			

The curtain and computer screen lose detail in video space that is retained in linear space. The linear image is nearly indistinguishable from the actual photo for which camera exposure time was doubled (another practical way to brighten by one stop).

The second column simulates an out-of-focus scene using Fast Blur. You may be surprised to see an overall darkening with bright highlights fading into the background—at least in video space. In linear, the highlights pop much better. See how the little man in the Walk sign stays bright in linear but almost fades away in video because of the extra emphasis given to dark pixels in video space. Squint your eyes and you notice that only the video image darkens overall. Because a defocused lens doesn't cause any less light to enter it, regular 8-bpc blur does not behave like a true defocus.

The table's third column uses After Effects' built-in motion blur to simulate the streaking caused by quick panning as the photo was taken. Pay particular attention to the highlight on the lamp; notice how it leaves a long, bright streak in the linear and in-camera examples. Artificial dulling of highlights is the most obvious giveaway of nonlinear image processing.

Artists have dealt with the problems of working directly in video space for years without even knowing we're compensating all the time. A perfect example is the Screen transfer mode; while it's additive in nature, its calculations are clearly convoluted when compared with the pure Add transfer mode. Screen uses a multiply-toward-white function with the advantage of avoiding the clipping associated with Add. But Add's reputation comes from its application in bright video-space images. Screen was invented only to help people be productive when working in video space, without overbrights; Screen darkens overbrights (**Figure 11.13**). Real light doesn't screen, it adds. Add is the new Screen, Multiply is the new Hard Light, and many other blending modes fall away completely in linear floating point.

Figure 11.13 Watch those highlights. Double up the explosion (top left) in video space with Add blows out (top right), but Screen in video looks better if washed out (bottom left). Adding in linear is best (bottom right).

NOTES

Examples with over-range source on the disc can be found in 11_experiments_hdr_source and 11_hdr_overrange_RED_source. 11_hdr_from_ldr_afternoon and 11_hdr_from_ldr_sunrise are examples from previous editions making use of 32-bpc compositing of low dynamic-range source.

TIP

Linear blending is available without 32-bpc HDR; in Project Settings, choose Blend Colors using 1.0 Gamma. This feature is described in detail near the end of the chapter.

HDR Source and Linearized Working Space

Should you be fortunate enough to have high-bit-depth source images with over-range values, or even if you have reason to push images into HDR by adding overexposure, glows, and so on, working in 32-bpc linear has indisputable benefits—even if your final output uses a plain old video format that cannot accommodate these values.

In **Figure 11.14**, the lights are severely clipped by video space, which is not a problem so long as the image is only displayed; all of the images look fine printed on this page or displayed on your monitor. Add motion blur, however, and you see the problem at its most exaggerated; the

Figure 11.14 An HDR image (left) is blurred without floating point (center) and with floating point (right).

points of light should not lose their intensity simply by being put into motion.

The benefits of floating point aren't restricted to blurs, however; those just happen to be an easy place to see the difference. Every operation in a compositing pipeline gains extra realism from the presence of floating-point pixels and linear blending.

Figure 11.15 features an HDR image on which a simple composite is performed, once in video space and once using linear floating point. In the HDR version, the dark translucent layer behaves like sunglass lenses on the bright window, revealing extra detail exactly as a filter on a camera lens would. The soft edges of a motion-blurred object also behave realistically as bright highlights push through. Without over-range values there is no extra information to reveal, so the window looks clipped and dull and motion blur doesn't interact with the scene properly.

Terminology

Linear floating-point HDR compositing uses *radiometrically linear*, or *scene-referred*, color data. For the purposes of this discussion, this is perhaps best called "linear light compositing" or "linear." The alternative mode to which you are accustomed is "gamma-encoded," "monitor color space," or simply "video."

Figure 11.15 A source image with over-range values in the highlights (top) is composited in LDR (bottom left) and HDR (bottom right).

Included on the disc are two similar images, sanityCheck.exr and sanityCheck.tif. The 32-bpc EXR file is linearized, but the 8-bpc TIFF file is not. Two corresponding projects are also included, one using no color profile, the other employing a linear profile. These should help illustrate the different appearances of a linear and a gamma-encoded image.

Figure 11.16 Exposure is an HDR preview control that appears in the Composition panel in 32-bpc mode.

Keep in mind that for each 1.0 adjustment upward or downward of Exposure, you double (or halve) the light levels in the scene. Echoing the earlier discussion, a +3.0 Exposure setting sets the light levels 8× (or 2^3) brighter.

32 Bits per Channel

Although it is not necessary to use HDR source to take advantage of an HDR pipeline, it offers a clear glimpse of this brave new world. Open 11_treeHDR_lin.aep; it contains a comp made up of a single image in 32-bpc EXR format (used to create Figure 11.19). With the Info panel clearly visible, move your cursor around the frame.

As your cursor crosses highlights—the lights on the tree, specular highlights on the wall and chair, and especially in the window—the values are seen to be well above 1.0, the maximum value you will ever see doing the same in 8-bpc or 16-bpc mode. Remember that you can quickly toggle between color depths by **Alt**-clicking (**Opt**-clicking) the project color depth identifier at the bottom of the Project panel.

You might assume that there is no detail in that window—it appears blown out to solid white forevermore in LDR. However, you may have noticed an extra icon and accompanying numerical value that appears at the bottom of the composition panel in a 32-bpc project (**Figure 11.16**). This is the Exposure control; its icon looks like a camera aperture and it performs an analogous function—controlling the exposure (total amount of light) of a scene the way you would stop a camera up or down (by adjusting its aperture).

Drag to the left on the numerical text and something amazing happens. Not only does the lighting in the scene decrease naturally, as if the light itself were being brought down, but at somewhere around –10.0, a gentle blue gradient appears in the window (**Figure 11.17**, left).

Drag the other direction, into positive Exposure range, and the scene begins to look like an overexposed photo; the light proportions remain and the highlights bloom outward (**Figure 11.17**, right).

The Exposure control in the Composition panel is a preview-only control (there is an effect by the same name that renders); scan with your cursor, and Info panel values do not vary according to its setting. This control offers a quick

Figure 11.17 At −10 Exposure (left), the room is dark other than the tree lights and detail becomes visible out the window. At +3, the effect is exactly that of a camera that was open three stops brighter than the unadjusted image.

way to check what is happening in the out-of-range areas of a composition. With a linear light image, each integer increment represents the equivalent of one photographic stop, or a doubling (or halving) of linear light value.

Mixed Bit Depths and Compander

Many effects don't, alas, support 32 bpc, although there are dozens that do. Apply a 16-bpc or (shudder) 8-bpc effect, however, and the overbrights in your 32-bpc project disappear—all clipped to 1.0. Any effect will reduce the image being piped through it to its own color space limitations. A small warning sign appears next to the effect to remind you that it does not support the current bit depth. You may even see a warning explaining the dangers of applying this effect.

Of course, this doesn't mean you need to avoid these effects to work in 32 bpc. It may mean you have to cheat, and After Effects includes a preset allowing you to do just that: Compress-Expand Dynamic Range (contained in Effects & Presets > Animation Presets > Image – Utilities; make certain Show Animation Presets is checked in the panel menu).

This preset actually consists of two instances of the HDR Compander effect, which was specifically designed to bring HDR back into LDR range. The first instance

CLOSE-UP

Floating-Point Files

As you've already seen, there is one class of files that does not need to be converted to linear space: floating-point files. These files are already storing scene-referred values, complete with overbright information. Common formats supported by After Effects are Radiance (.hdr) and floating-point .tif, not to mention .psd, but the most universal and versatile is Industrial Light + Magic's OpenEXR format. OpenEXR uses efficient 16-bpc floating-point pixels, can store any number of image channels, supports lossless compression, and is already supported by most 3D programs thanks to being an open source format.

After Effects offers expanded support of the OpenEXR format by bundling plug-ins from fnord software, which provide access to multiple layers and channels within these files. EXtractoR can open any floating-point image channel in an EXR file, and Identifier can open the other, non-image channels such as Object and Material ID.

Figure 11.18 Effects & Presets > Animation Presets > Presets > Image–Utilities includes the Compress-Expand Dynamic Range preset, also known as the Compander (Compressor/Expander). Two instances of the HDR Compander effect are linked together with expressions to work in opposition, and the idea is to sandwich them around an 8- or 16-bpc effect (such as Match Grain).

TIP

8- and 16-bpc effects clip only the image that they process. Apply one to a layer, and you clip that layer *only*. Apply one to an adjustment layer and you clip everything below. Add an LDR comp or layer to an otherwise HDR comp in a 32-bpc project, and it remains otherwise HDR.

is automatically renamed Compress, and the second, Expand, which is how the corresponding modes are set. You set the Gain of Compress to whatever is the brightest overbright value you wish to preserve, up to 100. The values are then compressed into LDR range, allowing you to apply your LDR effect. Gain (as well as Gamma) of Expand is linked via an expression to Compress so that the values round-trip back to HDR (**Figure 11.18**).

This prevents clipping of over-range values. If banding appears as a result of Compress-Expand, Gamma can be adjusted to weight the compressed image more toward the region of the image (probably the shadows) where the banding occurs. Image fidelity is thus sacrificed in order to preserve a compressed version of the HDR pipeline.

Additionally, there are smart ways to set up a project to ensure that Compander plays the minimal possible role. As much as possible, group all of your LDR effects together, and keep them away from the layers that use blending modes where HDR values are most essential. For example, apply an LDR effect via a separate adjustment layer instead of directly on a layer with a blending mode. Also, if possible, apply the LDR effects first, then boost the result into HDR range to apply any additional 32-bpc effects and blending modes.

Blend Colors Using 1.0 Gamma

After Effects includes a fantastic option to linearize image data only when performing blending operations: the Blend Colors Using 1.0 Gamma toggle in Project Settings (**Figure 11.19**). This allows you to take advantage of linear blending, which makes Add and Multiply blending modes actually work properly, even in 8-bpc or 16-bpc modes.

Figure 11.19 This checkbox is all you need to get the benefits of linear light compositing without the extra overhead of 32-bpc floating-point color.

The difference is quite simple. A linearized working space does all image processing in gamma 1.0, as follows

```
footage --> to linear PWS ->
   Layer ->
      Mask -> Effects -> Transform ->
         Blend With Comp ->
   Comp -> from linear PWS to OM space ->
output
```

whereas linearized blending performs only the blending step, where the image is combined with the composition, in gamma 1.0

```
footage --> to PWS ->
   Layer ->
      Mask -> Effects -> Transform -> to linear PWS
->
         Blend With Comp -> to PWS ->
   Comp -> from PWS to OM space ->
output
```

(Special thanks to Dan Wilk at Adobe for detailing this.)

Because effects aren't added in linear color, blurs no longer interact correctly with overbrights (although they do composite more nicely), and you don't get the subtle benefits to Transform operations. After Effects' oft maligned scaling operations are greatly improved in linear 32bpc. Also, 3D lights behave more like actual lights in a fully linearized working space.

I prefer the linear blending option when in lower bit depths, and there is no need to manage over-range values; it gives me the huge benefit of more elegant composites and blending modes without forcing me to think about managing effects in linear color. Certain key effects, in particular Exposure, helpfully operate in linear, 1.0 gamma mode.

Chinese Menu

So to review, there are three fundamental ways to move beyond standard monitor color in After Effects. Simply by enabling 32-bpc color, you get out-of-range handling, without enabling linear blending. Or, you can enable linear blending and use it in all three color modes, not just 32 bpc. Finally, by setting a project working space you can linearize the color of the entire project, as shown at the end of the previous section.

One thing you cannot do is enable 32 bpc just for one comp—it's the whole project or nothing. But you can work in 16 bpc and enable 32 bpc only when it's time to render, if the performance at the higher bit depth is too great. Not only do per-frame render times lengthen in 32 bpc, RAM previews become shorter as each frame is required to hold exponentially more data. Remember, 32 bits is not double 16; it doubles each pixel value eight times.

Output

Finally, what good is it working in linear 32-bpc color if the output bears no resemblance to what you see in the Composition viewer? Just because you work in 32-bpc color does not mean you have to render your images that way.

Keeping in mind that each working space can be linear or not, if you work in a linearized color space and then render to a format that is typically gamma encoded (as most are), the gamma-encoded version of the working space will also be used. After Effects spells this out for you explicitly in the Description section of the Color Management tab (**Figure 11.20**).

Figure 11.20 Suppose you work in a color-managed 32-bpc linear project but want to dump out a simple reference QuickTime without thinking about it. After Effects does the right thing and even spells out in the fine print what it's doing: leaving the output gamma (because the format doesn't support 32 bpc) and baking in the profile (because the format can't embed it) so as best to preserve the appearance of the comp.

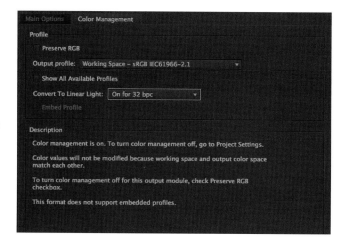

To this day, the standard method to pass around footage with over-range values, particularly if it is being sent for film-out, is to use 10-bit log-encoded Cineon/DPX. This is also converted for you from 32-bpc linear, but be sure to choose Working Space as the output profile and in Cineon Settings, use the Standard preset.

The great thing about Cineon/DPX with a standard 10-bit profile is that it is a universal standard. Facilities around the world know what to do with it even if they've never encountered a file with an embedded color profile. As was detailed earlier in the chapter, it is capable of taking full advantage of the dynamic range of film, which is to this day the most dynamic display medium widely available.

Color Fidelity: Management, Depth, LUTs

Color and light would seem to be arbitrary, and the idea that they could be measured and made consistent as a source image works its way from camera to output seems ludicrous and even undesirable. While it's true that your goal is rarely if ever the one set out at the beginning of the chapter—to make output match source exactly—there are stages along the way in which this is absolutely what you want. Once you've decided how the image should look, arbitrary changes are unwelcome surprises.

While color is a phenomenon of vision and does not apparently exist in the absence of an eye to see it and a mind to process it, color also corresponds to measurable wavelengths and intensities that can be regulated and profiled. This is a huge improvement over the way color is natively handled by your computer.

We're all familiar with the concept of a digital image as three color channels, each containing an 8-bit luminance value. Web designers may convert this value into more concise hex color values (white is FFFFFF, black 000000, pure blue 0000FF, and so on), but they're merely the same 8-bit combinations described in a different language.

The fantasy is that these 8-bit RGB values are reliable, since they seem to be so exact. The reality is they are tied directly to a highly imprecise and arbitrary device, your monitor, no two of which are completely identical in how they appear right out of the box. Those R, G, and B values are only monitoring how much current—electrical power—is given to each channel. How precise do RGB or Hex values sound now?

So although 8-bit RGB remains the lingua franca of digital imaging, there are tools available so that color isn't so arbitrary. We'll look at these first, before focusing on getting more out of the images themselves.

Adobe Color Management

Although not enabled by default, a color management system in After Effects allows you to work with profiles attached to otherwise arbitrary points in the image pipeline. It is most useful in the following cases:

▶ An After Effects project features a color-managed graphic with an embedded ICC profile, typically a still element created in other Adobe software such as Photoshop or Illustrator.

▶ All monitors in a given facility have been assigned profiles using a hardware colorimeter and profiling software, and you want what appears on each monitor to match.

▶ Output from an After Effects project will be a still format that supports color profiles. This is rare, since the typical moving image formats don't work with Adobe's color management system.

▶ A precise output format such as projected film or HDTV has been identified, and you need to accurately preview how an image will appear in that format right on the computer monitor (not via an external device).

Depending on your setup, at least one of those may be a reason to learn a bit about the color management system. The first essential step is that you work on a calibrated monitor.

Monitor Calibration

As was explained above, RGB values alone cannot describe exact colors; connect a still-working decade-old CRT monitor to your system and it will represent those values precisely in terms of how much voltage is sent to each pixel, while the monitor itself is likely to have a strong uncorrected bluish or yellow cast or to be too bright or too low in contrast.

Third-party color calibration hardware and software can be used to generate a profile that is then stored and set as a system preference. This monitor profile is used by the system so that it displays regular RGB color more accurately, but it also offers software such as After Effects a reliable platform on which to create an accurate colorimetric image pipeline, which is just a fancy way of saying what you see is what you get.

Actual monitor calibration technologies and methods are beyond the scope of this book; suffice it to say that for a small investment you can do much better than an adjustment by eye, and you can get a set of monitors to match how they display an image. This is best recalibrated once each quarter at the very least. It's the first step in eliminating variables that can wreak havoc once your images are handed off.

Color Management: Disabled by Default

Import a file edited in another Adobe application such as Photoshop or Lightroom and it likely contains an embedded ICC color profile. This profile can tell After Effects how the colors should be interpreted and appear, instead of remaining as raw electrical signals.

A file called sanityCheck.tif on the book's disc contains data and color gradients to help elucidate linear color later in the chapter. For now, import this file into After Effects and choose File > Interpret Footage > Main (**Ctrl+F/Cmd+F**, or context-click instead). Note that Interpret Footage includes a Color Management tab.

Figure 11.21 shows how this tab appears with the default settings. The image does indeed carry a profile. Assign Profile is grayed out (and the profile ignored) because, as the Description text explains, Color Management is off and color values are not converted. Color Management is enabled as soon as you assign a working space.

If monitor calibration via a colorimeter isn't available, at least go into Display settings in the system and follow the basic steps to calibrate your monitor by eye.

Is there an external broadcast monitor attached to your system (set as Output Device in Preferences > Video Preview)? Color Management settings do not apply to that device.

Figure 11.21 Until Color Management is enabled for the entire project, the embedded profile of a source image is not displayed in the Project panel, nor is it used.

Project Working Space

Project Working Space is designed to match the "output intent," a color space that corresponds to the target device. The Working Space menu containing all possible choices is located in File > Project Settings (**Ctrl+Alt+K/Cmd+Opt+K,** or just click where you see the "bpc" setting along the bottom of the Project panel).

There is no hard-and-fast rule for which one to use in a particular case. Profiles above the line are considered by Adobe to be the most likely candidates. Those below might include profiles used by such unlikely output devices as a color printer (**Figure 11.22**).

Figure 11.22 For better or worse, all of the color profiles active on the local system are listed as Working Space candidates, even such unlikely targets as the office color printer.

By default, Working Space is set to None (and thus Color Management is off). Make a selection on the Working Space menu and Color Management is enabled, triggering the following:

▶ Assigned profiles in imported files are activated and displayed atop the Project panel when it's selected.

▶ Imported files with no assigned profile are assumed to have a profile of sRGB IEC61966-2.1, hereafter referred to as simply *sRGB*.

▶ Actual RGB values *can and will change* to maintain consistent color values.

Choose wisely; it's a bad idea to change your working space midproject once you've begun adjusting color, because it will change the fundamental look of source footage and comps. But how do you choose?

There's a rather large document, included on the disc and also available at www.adobe.com/devnet/aftereffects/articles/color_management_workflow.html, that has a table itemizing each and every profile included in After Effects. We can forgo that for the time being and surmise that

▶ for HD display, HDTV (Rec. 709) is Adobe-sanctioned, but sRGB is similar and more of a reliable standard

▶ for monitor playback, sRGB is generally most suitable

▶ SDTV NTSC or SDTV PAL theoretically lets you forgo a preview broadcast monitor, although it's also possible to simulate these formats without working in them (see "Display Management and Output Simulation" below)

▶ film output is an exception (discussed later in this chapter)

To say that a profile is "reliable" is like saying that a particular brand of car is reliable or that scrambled eggs reliably taste better cooked with butter: experience, rather than science, informs the decision. A profile such as sRGB has been used and abused by artists around the world and shown not to mess up the colors. If you want to see messed-up colors, try a few of those profiles below the dividing line, such as the ones for paper print output.

Gamut describes the range of possible saturation; keep in mind that any pixel can be described by its hue, saturation, and brightness as accurately as its red, green, and blue. The range of hues accessible to human vision is fixed, but the amount of brightness and saturation possible is not—32-bpc HDR addresses both. The idea is to match, not outdo (and definitely not undershoot) the gamut of the target.

You might think that the widest possible gamut is best; the problem with that approach is that if it gives too much weight to colors that your display or output medium can't even properly represent, then the more useful colors become underrepresented. Suppose that of your 256 shades of red in 8-bpc color, the top 128 were all of a higher brightness and saturation than your monitor could display. That would cut down the usable number of reds if your output medium was a similar monitor. But if that medium was film, it might make sense to do it that way, especially using some of the other tools mentioned ahead

A small yellow plus sign appears in the middle of the Show Channel icon to indicate that Display Color Management is active (**Figure 11.23**).

Figure 11.23 When Use Display Color Management is active in the View menu (the default after you set a working space), this icon adds a yellow plus symbol at its center.

to translate those colors into something you can see on your monitor.

Working spaces, then, change RGB values. Open sanity-Check.tif in a viewer and move your cursor over the little bright red square; its values are 255, 0, 0. Now change the working space to ProPhoto RGB. Nothing looks different, but the values are now 179, 20, 26, meaning that with this wider gamut, color values do not need to be nearly as large in order to appear just as saturated, and there is headroom for far more saturation. You just need a medium capable of displaying the more saturated red in order to see it properly with this gamut. Many film stocks can do it, and your monitor cannot.

Input Profile and MediaCore

If an 8-bpc image file has no embedded profile, sRGB is assigned (as in Figure 11.21), which is close to monitor color space. Setting this target allows the file to be color managed, to preserve its appearance even in a different color space. Toggle Preserve RGB in the Color Management tab and the appearance of that image can change with the working space—not, generally, what you want, which is why After Effects goes ahead and assigns its best guess.

In many ways, MediaCore's automation is a good thing. After Effects 7.0 had a little check box at the bottom of Interpret Footage labeled "Expand ITU-R 601 Luma Levels" that obligated you to manage incoming luminance range. With MediaCore, however, you lose the ability to override the setting. Expanded values above 235 and below 16 are pushed out of range, recoverable only in 32-bpc mode.

Video formats (QuickTime being by far the most common) don't accept color profiles, but they do require color interpretation based on embedded data. After Effects uses an Adobe component called MediaCore to interpret these files automatically; it operates completely behind the scenes, invisible to you.

You know that MediaCore is handling a file when that file has Y'CbCr in the Embedded Profile info, including DV and YUV format files. In such a case the Color Management tab is completely grayed out, so there is no option to override the embedded settings.

Display Management and Output Simulation

Output Simulation simulates how your comp will look on a particular device and is fun to try out. The "device" in question can include film projection, and the process of

Check out 11_output_simulation for examples of this setup in action.

representing that environment on your monitor works better than you might expect.

Suppose you need to know how an image (**Figure 11.24**) would appear on NTSC and PAL standard definition television, and you don't have a standard def broadcast monitor to preview either of those formats.

Figure 11.24 The source image (courtesy of Michael Scott) is adjusted precisely in a color-managed project.

No problem. With the viewer selected choose View > Simulate Output > SDTV NTSC. Here's what happens:

▶ The appearance of the footage changes to match the output simulation. The viewer displays After Effects' simulation of an NTSC monitor.

▶ Unlike when the working space is changed, color values do not change due to output simulation.

▶ The image is actually assigned two separate color profiles in sequence: a scene-referred profile to simulate the output profile you would use for NTSC (SDTV NTSC) and a second profile that actually simulates the television monitor that would then display that rendered output (SMPTE-C). To see what these settings are, and to customize them, choose View > Simulate Output > Custom to open the Custom Output Simulation dialog (**Figure 11.25**).

This process becomes fun with simulations of projected film (**Figure 11.26**)—not only the print stock but the appearance of projection is simulated, allowing an artist to work directly on the projected look of a shot instead of waiting until it is filmed out and projected.

Figure 11.25 This Custom Output Simulation dialog now nicely shows the four stages from source RGB image to the monitor. The middle two stages are those set by Output Simulation; the first occurs on import, the final when the image is displayed.

Interpretation Rules

A file on your system named "interpretation rules. txt" defines how files are automatically interpreted as they are imported into After Effects. To change anything in this file, you should be something of a hacker, able to look at a line like

```
# *, *, *, "sDPX", * ~ *, *, *,
*, "ginp", *
```

and, by examining surrounding lines and comments, figure out that this line is commented out (with the # sign at the beginning), and that the next to last argument, "*ginp*" in quotes, assigns the Kodak 5218 film profile if the file type corresponds with the fourth argument, "*sDPX*". If this makes you squirm, don't touch it, call a nerd. In this case, removing the # sign at the beginning would enable this rule so that DPX files would be assigned a Kodak 5218 profile (without it, they are assigned to the working space).

If this isn't your cup of tea, as it won't be for most artists, leave it to someone willing to muck around with this stuff.

Figure 11.26 The result of Output Simulation shows bluer highlights, deeper blacks (which may not read on the printed page), and a less saturated red dress. If you wanted the image to appear different when projected, you would now further adjust it with this view active. It might then look "wrong" with Output Simulation off, but "right" when finally filmed out and projected.

Here's a summary of what is happening to the source image in the example project:

1. The source image is interpreted on import (on the Footage Settings > Color Management tab) according to its Working Space setting.

2. The image is transformed to the Project Working Space; its color values will change to preserve its appearance.

3. With View > Simulate Output and any profile selected

   a. color values are transformed to the specified output profile.

   b. color appearance (but not actual values) is transformed to a specified simulation profile.

4. With View > Display Color Management enabled (required for step 3) color appearance (but not actual values) is transformed to the monitor profile (the one that lives in system settings, which you created when you calibrated your monitor, remember?).

That leaves output, which relies only on steps 1 and 2. The others are only for previewing, although you may wish to render an output simulation (to show the filmed-out look on a video display in dailies, for example). To replicate the two-stage color conversion of output simulation:

TIP

Having trouble with View > Simulate Output appearing grayed-out? Make sure a viewer window is active when you set it; it operates on a per-viewer basis.

1. Apply the Color Profile Converter effect, and match the Output Profile setting to the one listed under View > Simulate Output > Custom. Change the Intent setting to Absolute Colorimetric.

2. Set a second Color Profile Converter effect, and match the Input Profile setting to the Simulation Profile under View > Simulate Output > Custom (leaving Intent as the default Relative Colorimetric).

The output profile in the render queue then should match the intended display device.

Simulation isn't likely something you'll use all the time; it's merely there if you need it. So let's leave it behind and examine what happens when you attempt to preserve actual colors in rendered output (which is, after all, the point of all of this effort, right?).

Output Profile

By default, After Effects uses the working space as the output profile, usually the right choice assuming the working space was chosen appropriately. Place the comp in the render queue and open the output module; on the Color Management tab you can select a different profile to apply on output. The pipeline from the last section now adds a third step to the first two:

1. The source image is interpreted on import (on the Footage Settings > Color Management tab).

2. The image is transformed to the working space; its color values will change to preserve its appearance.

3. The image is transformed to the output profile specified in Output Module Settings > Color Management.

If the profile in step 3 is different from that of step 2, color values will change to preserve color appearance. If the output format supports embedded ICC profiles (presumably a still image format such as TIFF or PSD), then a profile will be embedded so that any other application with color management (presumably an Adobe application such as Photoshop or Illustrator) will continue to preserve those colors.

In Photoshop, there is no Project Working Space option, only the document Working Space, because there are no projects (no need to accommodate multiple sources together in a single nondestructive project).

In the real world, of course, rendered output is probably destined to a device or format that doesn't support color management and embedded profiles. That's OK, except in the case of QuickTime, which may further change the appearance of the file, almost guaranteeing that the output won't match your composition without special handling.

QuickTime

QuickTime continues to have special issues of its own separate from but related to Adobe's color management. The QuickTime format is a moving target because it has its own internal and seemingly ad-hoc color management system (whose spec Apple does not even reveal, which sometimes changes from one version of QuickTime to the next, and which also can change depending on which system or software is displaying it). Even Apple's own software applications are not necessarily consistent about how they display QuickTime color, and if that's not a danger signal about the format, what is?

The gamma of QuickTime files is interpreted uniquely by each codec, so files with Photo-JPEG compression have a different gamma than files with H.264 compression. Even files with the default Animation setting, which are effectively uncompressed and assumedly neutral, display an altered (inconsistent) gamma.

The Match Legacy After Effects QuickTime Gamma Adjustments toggle in Project Settings is not only the longest-titled checkbox in the entire application, it is an option you should not need, in theory at least, unless you've opened up an old 7.0 (or earlier) project, or you need a Composition to match what you see in QuickTime Player.

However, many of us deliver client review files as QuickTime movies, so the best bet is to enable Color Management for any project intended to output QuickTime video. The option to disable the Match Legacy toggle is reserved for cases in which that approach doesn't work; these do unfortunately crop up and remain a moving target as new versions of QuickTime are released, further revising the standard.

If in doubt, at least compare QuickTime output by eye to what you see in your After Effects comp, particularly if using a format notorious for gamma shifts, such as the otherwise useful H.264. If such shifts are seen to occur—and they will generally be obvious if so—either adjust gamma on output to compensate (squirrely but reliable) or use the above variable settings to try to track down where the shift can be eliminated.

Bypass Color Management?

Headaches like these make many artists long for simpler days. If you prefer to avoid color management altogether, or to use it only selectively, you can disable the feature and return to After Effects 7.0 behavior:

1. In Project Settings, set Working Space to None (as it is by default, **Figure 11.27**).

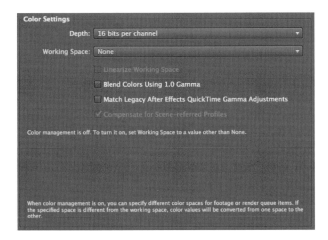

Figure 11.27 The Working Space setting (along with the fine print) indicates that color management is disabled.

2. Enable Match Legacy After Effects QuickTime Gamma Adjustments.

Being more selective about how color management is applied—to take advantage of some features while leaving others disabled for clarity—is tricky and tends to stump some pretty smart users. Here are a couple of final tips that may nonetheless help:

▶ To disable a profile for incoming footage, check Preserve RGB in Interpret Footage (Color Management tab). No attempt will be made to preserve the appearance of that clip.

▶ To change the behavior causing untagged footage to be tagged with an sRGB profile, in interpretation rules.txt find this line

```
# soft rule: tag all untagged footage with an sRGB
profile
*, *, *, *, * ~ *, *, *, *, "sRGB", *
```

and add a # at the beginning of the second line to assign no profile, or change "sRGB" to a different format (options listed in the comments at the top of the file).

▶ To prevent your display profile from being factored in, disable View > Use Display Color Management and the pixels are sent straight to the display.

▶ To prevent any file from being color managed, check Preserve RGB in Output Module Settings (Color Management tab).

Note that any of the preceding tips may lead to unintended consequences, and the hope is that such nerdery is never actually required.

LUT: Color Look-Up Table

LUTs are a worldwide standard for compositing, editing, and color software the world over, except for Adobe software—until CS5, which adds the ability to use and even create a LUT.

What is a LUT? A color look-up table essentially takes one set of color values and translates them to another set of values; it is an array of values that can be saved and reapplied and shared on any system that supports a LUT. The classic usage of a LUT is to preview how, for example, a 10-bpc log file will look as a film print using a particular film stock.

As you probably realize, After Effects has long had apparent alternatives to LUTs. For previewing, there is the feature set we just finished looking at, Color Management, and for actual transformations of images there are effects such as Cineon Converter as well as good old Levels and Curves, saved as effects presets.

There's a bit more to a LUT than there is to an effect preset. A 1D or one-dimensional LUT is a lot like Levels—taking a single value and changing it to a different value—but the new Apply Color LUT plug-in supports a couple of the common 3D LUT formats. A 3D LUT adjusts all three color channels interdependently and nonlinearly, so that saturation and brightness can be adjusted independent of one another. This allows color adjustments to mimic different gamuts, such as the wider gamut of film.

You can create your own 3D LUT using Color Finesse. Make adjustments, even using just the Simplified Interface, then enable the Full Interface in order to use File > Export and write one of the 10 or so listed 3D LUT formats. If you want this LUT to be readable by the Apply Color LUT effect, choose either one of the Autodesk formats to create a .3DL file, or use Truelight Cube to create a .cube file (**Figure 11.28**).

Figure 11.28 The way to create a LUT in After Effects: Use Color Finesse and export from Full Interface.

What's the point? For one, the color adjustment is ubiquitous and can be interchanged with many other types of computer graphics systems. More importantly, if someone working in Lustre, Smoke, Flame, or Scratch wants to send you a LUT, he can do so without apologies provided he chooses one of the compatible formats.

There are two basic usages of a LUT. A *Calibration LUT* is like color management—it is meant only to show how an image might look in a different setting. To use a LUT this way in After Effects requires that you apply it to an Adjustment layer and set that layer as a Guide layer so that it doesn't render—but this means you must apply it to all layers below.

More appropriate to the After Effects implementation of a LUT, perhaps, is the *Viewing LUT* that would be used to apply a color correction look to footage. This one is intended to alter and render the pixel values, not merely preview them.

Most After Effects artists won't have an immediate need for the color LUT, but with this explanation you know what to do if someone sends you one, and you have the option of creating and sending your own with Color Finesse.

Conclusion

This chapter concludes Section II, which focused on the most fundamental techniques of effects compositing. In the next and final section, you'll apply those techniques. You'll also learn about the importance of observation, as well as some specialized tips and tricks for specific effects compositing situations that re-create particular environments, settings, conditions, and natural phenomena.

SECTION III

Creative Explorations

12

Light

Light seeking light doth light of light beguile.
—William Shakespeare

Light

There's more to light than physics and optics, although those are certainly essential components. The work of a compositor is akin to that of a painter or cinematographer, in that a combination of technical knowledge, interpretation, and even intuition all contribute to getting a scene "right."

Other areas of digital production rely on elaborate models to simulate the way light works in the physical world. Like a painter, the compositor observes the play of light in the three-dimensional world in order to re-create it two-dimensionally. Like a cinematographer, you succeed with a feeling for how lighting and color decisions affect the beauty and drama of a scene and how the camera gathers them.

Several chapters in this book have already touched upon principles of the behavior of light. Chapter 5 is about the bread and butter work of the compositor—matching brightness and color of a foreground and background. Chapter 9 is all about how the world looks through a lens. Chapter 11 explores more advanced technical ways in which After Effects can re-create the way color and light values behave.

This chapter is dedicated to practical situations involving light that you as a compositor must re-create. It's important to distinguish lighting conditions you can easily emulate and those that are essentially out of bounds—although, for a compositor with a good eye and patience, the seemingly "impossible" becomes a welcome challenge and the source of a favorite war story.

Source and Direction

In many scenes, there is clearly more involved with light than matching brightness and contrast channel by channel. Light direction is fundamental, especially where the quality of the light is *hard* (direct) rather than *soft* (diffuse).

Such a huge variety of light situations are possible in a shot, and in an infinite array of combinations, that it becomes difficult to make any broad statements stand up about lighting. This section, however, attempts to pin down some general guidelines and workflows for manipulating the light situation of your scene.

Location and Quality

You may have specific information about the lighting conditions that existed when source footage was shot. On a set, you can easily identify the placement and type of each light, and away from set, this information may be found in a camera report or on-set photos. For a naturally lit shot, it's mostly a question of the position of the sun relative to the camera and the reflectivity of the surrounding environment.

Sometimes the location and direction of light is readily apparent, but not as often as you might think. Hard, direct light casts clear shadows and raises contrast, and soft, diffuse light lowers contrast and casts soft shadows (if any). That much seems clear.

These, however, are broad stereotypes, which do not always behave as expected in the real world. Hard light aimed directly at a subject from the same direction as the camera actually flattens out detail, effectively decreasing contrast. And artificial lighting is usually from multiple sources in a single scene, which work against one another to diffuse hard shadows (**Figure 12.1**).

TIP

One of the primary responsibilities of the on-set visual effects supervisor is to record light conditions on set to augment what shows up in the image and what appears in the camera report.

Figure 12.1 Interior sets, like interior environments, are typically lit by more than one source, creating multiple soft highlights and shadows.

Neutralize Direction and Hotspots

Mismatched direction or diffusion of light on a foreground element is clearly a fundamental problem for the compositor and can only be the result of poor planning or limited resources. The solution is generally to neutralize the mismatch by isolating and minimizing it. Relighting the element in 2D generally offers a result that might technically be called "cheesy."

Every shot in the world has unique light characteristics, but a couple of overall strategies apply. Once you've exhausted simple solutions such as flopping the shot (if the lighting is simply backward), you can

▶ isolate and remove directional clues around the element, such as cast shadows (typically by matting or rotoscoping them out)

▶ isolate and reduce contrast of highlights and shadows in the element itself, typically with a Levels or Curves adjustment (potentially aided by a luma matte, described later in this chapter)

▶ invert the highlights and shadows with a counter-gradient

The simple way to undo evidence of too strong a keylight in a scene is to create a counter-gradient as a track matte for an adjustment layer; a Levels or Curves effect on this layer affects the image proportionally to this gradient. The Ramp effect can be set and even animated to the position of a keylight hotspot (**Figure 12.2**).

Figure 12.2 Counter-gradients (this one created with the Ramp effect) can serve as an adjustment layer used to lower the brightness and contrast in the hotspot region.

A radial ramp is merely linear, which is not the correct model for light falloff. Light's intensity diminishes proportionally to its distance from the source squared, according to the *inverse square law*. An object positioned twice as far from a single light source is illuminated by one-quarter the amount of light. To mimic this with a gradient, precomp it, duplicate the radial gradient layer, and set the upper of the two layers to a Multiply blending mode (**Figure 12.3**).

Figure 12.3 A standard Ramp gradient (top left) is linear, as can be seen in the histogram, but light falls off in a logarithmic, inverse-square pattern, so the matte used in Figure 12.2 multiplies together two linear gradients (bottom left) with Linear blending enabled (bottom right) in Project Settings even though it's not a 32-bpc linear HDR project. Again, light works in linear.

Of course, you don't want to fight the fundamental source lighting in this way unless you absolutely must; hopefully you will rarely have to "fix" lighting and will most often want to work with what you've got to make it even stronger and more dramatic.

Color Looks

Have you ever seen unadjusted source clips or behind-the-scenes footage from a favorite movie? It's a striking reminder about the bold and deliberate use of color in modern films. Look at the work prints or on-set making of video—the magic more or less disappears.

In older films color looks had to be accomplished optically and photochemically. The well-known *bleach-bypass method* would be used to strip certain colors out in the film lab. Nowadays, a digital production pipeline has made the photo-chemical approach rarer, although optical filters still play a large role in shooting. Meanwhile, it's becoming more and more common for an entire feature-length production to be graded through a *digital intermediate*, or *D.I.*

After Effects has an advantage over D.I. software such as DaVinci Resolve in that it is a true compositing system with fine controls over image selection. After Effects was not created principally with the colorist in mind, so its primary color tools (as described in Chapter 5) are simpler and less interactive. Third-party solutions such as Colorista and Magic Bullet Looks, both from Red Giant, help bridge this gap.

Keeping in mind that your job as a compositor is to emulate the world as it looks when viewed with a camera, it can be effective to begin by emulating physical lens elements.

The Virtual Lens Filter

Suppose a shot (or some portion of it) should simply be "warmer" or "cooler." With only a camera and some film, you might accomplish this transformation by adding a lens filter. It could be a solid color (blue for cooler, amber to warm things up) or a gradient (amber to white to change only the color of a sky above the horizon).

Add a colored solid and set its blending mode to Color. Choose a color that is pleasing to your eye, with brightness and saturation well above 50%. Use blue or green for a cooler look, red or yellow for a warmer one (**Figure 12.4**).

Figure 12.4 Here, the four color filters are applied as a test with a Color blending mode, and with the Linear mode, so that they behave a lot like lens filters of an equivalent color.

At 100%, this is the equivalent of a full-color tint of the image, which is too much. Dial Opacity down between 10% and 50%, seeking the threshold where the source colors remain discernable, filtered by the added color to set the look.

To re-create a graded filter, typically used to affect only the sky, apply the Ramp effect to the solid color and change the Start Color to your tint color; an amber filter adds the look of a smoggy urban day. The Add mode (with Blend Colors using 1.0 Gamma enabled in Project Settings) re-creates the real-world optics of a color gradient filter over an image.

Black and White

Counterintuitively, Hue/Saturation is not effective to create a black-and-white image because it maintains luminance proportions, and as mentioned in a sidebar back in Chapter 6, that's not how the eye sees color. **Figure 12.5** illustrates the difference.

NOTES

The use of solids as if they were lens filters can be found in the 12_solid_color_filters folder on the disc. One project is linear color, the other standard video.

NOTES

The flag of Mars is a red, green, and blue tricolor selected by the Mars Society and flown into orbit by the Space Shuttle Discovery. It was not used by Marvin the Martian to claim Planet X.

Figures 12.5 This is the flag of Mars (left): it shows three fields of pure red, green, and blue. Tint (center) compensates for the perceptual differences in human color vision when desaturating, Hue/Saturation (right) does not.

Figure 12.6 A real color-to-grayscale conversion may involve carefully rebalancing color, contrast, or saturation. Here, the face and lamp are important and get individual adjustments in color prior to conversion. (Images courtesy of 4charros.)

NOTES

Check the 12_black_and_white_conversion folder on the disc to compare the methods described here.

If it's truly a black-and-white version of the color source that is required, several options will work better than lowering Saturation to 0.0:

▶ Tint effect at the default settings weights the color channels, as does a fully desaturated solid (black, white, or gray, it doesn't matter) with a Color blending mode.

▶ For more control of color weighting, you can make use of the Black & White effect added to After Effects CS5. Because this effect originated in Photoshop, it doesn't support 32 bits per channel, but if you're applying it directly to 8- or 16-bit source, even in a 32-bpc project, that limitation won't cost the image any accuracy.

Taking care with the conversion from color to black and white and in particular the weighting of the color channels can heavily influence the look of the shot (**Figure 12.6**).

Day for Night

Stronger optical effects are often possible, such as making a daytime scene appear as if it were shot on a moonlit night. Known in French as *la nuit américaine* (and immortalized in Francois Truffaut's ode to filmmaking of the same name), this involves a simple trick. Shoot an exterior scene under ordinary daylight with a dark blue lens filter to compensate for the difficulty of successful low-light night shoots. If there is direct sunlight, it's meant to read as moonlight.

Lighting techniques and film itself have improved since this was a common convention of films, particularly Westerns, but digital cameras tend to produce noisy and muddy footage under low light.

Figure 12.7 shows the difference between a source image that is blue and desaturated and an actual night look; if instead you're starting with a daylight image, look at the images on the book's disc, which take the image more in that direction. Overall, remember that the eye cannot see color without light, so only areas that are perceived to be well illuminated should have a hue outside the range between deep blue and black.

TIP

Many images benefit from a subtle reduction in overall Saturation using the Hue/Saturation tool. This moves red, green, and blue closer together and can reduce the "juicy" quality that makes bright-colored images hard to look at.

Figure 12.7 An ordinary twilight shot of a house at dusk (left) becomes a spooky Halloween mansion. Converting day for night avoids the problems associated with low-light shooting. (Images courtesy of Mars Productions.)

Color Timing Effects

Digital tools can of course go far beyond what is possible with lens filters. The industry standard tools rely on a *three-way color corrector*, which allows you to tint the image in three basic luminance ranges—highlights, midtones, and shadows—adjusting each separately via wheels that control hue and brightness.

Just such a color corrector is now found in Synthetic Aperture Color Finesse 3, included with After Effects. Twirl down the Simplified Interface and there you find the Hue Offset controls, known colloquially as "color pots," along with the three main color correction tools introduced in Chapter 5: Curves, HSL (equivalent to Hue/Saturation), and RGB (which contains the Levels controls, minus the histogram—for that, click Full Interface).

A contemporary color look will have you pushing (via clicking or dragging) the Shadows control in a blue-green direction and Highlights in the opposite pink-yellow direction. (In fact, the Mojo plug-in from Red Giant is predicated on the concept that color looks take shadow/highlight areas toward cyan/orange. This look endures in large part because of the orange character of human skin tones—the contrasting shadows can give them an even warmer and healthier glow to make talent look best.)

Having set that contrast, you're now free to set the overall mood with the Midtones control, or change the entire look by adjusting the Master color. If things get a little juicy you can pull back saturation for any or all of these color ranges, particularly if you've increased contrast using Curves or RGB controls.

TIP

Red Giant Software has several useful plug-ins for colorists: In addition to Mojo, Colorista applies Lift/Gamma/Gain via color pots, and the all-encompassing Looks creates an entire color pipeline that is actually fun to use, thanks to its engaging production metaphor.

Once a *hero* grade is established, it can then be saved and applied across several shots in what is traditionally called the *color timing* process—literally, making color consistent across time, which typically involves much more than simply applying the same adjustment to every shot. You can use the techniques described here and in Section II to first balance a shot, then add its color look, finally bringing out any key exceptional details. As as soon as you understand someone asking you to "silver it up" or "crush" it, voilà, you're a colorist—here's your Ferrari.

Source, Reflection, and Shadow

Sometimes you work with source footage that contains strong lighting and thus offers a clear target. Other times, it's up to you to add a strong look. Either way, reference is your friend. You will be surprised how much bolder and more fascinating nature's choices are than your own.

Unexpected surprises that simply "work" can be the *kiss of love* for a scene—that something extra that nobody requested but everyone who is paying attention appreciates. Details of light and shadow are one area where this extra effort can really pay off.

Big, bold, daring choices about light don't call attention to themselves if appropriate to a scene, adding to the dramatic quality of the shot instead of merely showing off what you as an artist can do.

Backlighting and Light Wrap

The conditions of a backlit scene are a classic example where a comped shot falls short of what actually happens in the real world.

This technique is designed for scenes that contain backlighting conditions and a foreground that, although it may be lit to match those conditions, lacks light wrapping around the edges (**Figure 12.8**).

The light wrap formula outlined below has been converted to a script created by Jeff Almasol. You can find it on the book's disc as rd_Lightwrap. Select the matted source layer and let this script do the work.

Figure 12.8 The silhouetted figure is color corrected to match but lacks any of the light wrap clearly visible around the figures seated on the beach.

A lot of people wish for an After Effects light wrap plug-in. Simply creating light around the edges of a figure just doesn't look right. The light needs to be motivated by what is behind the subject, and that presents a difficult procedural problem for a plug-in. The following method has you create your own color reference for light wrapping and use that.

Check out the 12_lightwrap folder on the disc to see this example in action.

Set up a light wrap effect as follows:

1. Create a new composition that contains the background and foreground layers, exactly as they are positioned and animated in the master composition. You can do this simply by duplicating the master comp and renaming it something intuitive, such as Light Wrap. If the foreground or background consists of several layers, it will probably be simpler to precompose them into two layers, one each for the foreground and background.

2. Set Silhouette Alpha blending mode for the foreground layer, punching a hole in the background.

3. Add an adjustment layer at the top, and apply Fast Blur.

4. In Fast Blur, toggle the Repeat Edge Pixels on and crank up the blurriness.

5. Duplicate the foreground layer, move the copy to the top, and set its blending mode to Stencil Alpha, leaving a halo of background color that matches the shape of the foreground (**Figure 12.9**, top). If the light source is not directly behind the subject, you can offset this layer to match, producing more light on the matching side.

6. Place the resulting comp in the master comp and adjust opacity (and optionally switch the blending mode to Add, Screen, or Lighten) until you have what you're after. You may need to go back to the Light Wrap comp to further adjust the blur (Figure 12.9, bottom).

When there is no fill light, the foreground subject might appear completely silhouetted. Because the foreground subjects are often the stars of the scene, you might have to compensate, allowing enough light and detail in the foreground that the viewer can see facial expressions and other important dramatic detail.

In other words, this might be a case where your reference conflicts with what is needed for the story. Try to strike a balance, but remember, when the story loses, nobody wins.

Figure 12.9 The background is blurred into the matte area (top) in a precomp and added back into the scene to better integrate the silhouette (bottom).

Flares

For our purposes a "flare" is any direct light source that appears in shot, not just a cheesy 17-element lens flare whenever the sun pokes around the moon in some science-fiction television show from the early 1990s (or even a few shots from *Hancock*). These don't come for free in After Effects; 3D lights don't even create a visible source if placed in shot until you add the Trapcode Lux effect (included on this book's disc).

Real lens flares aren't cheesy, but natural, even beautiful artifacts the eye accepts without necessarily understanding anything about what actually causes them (**Figure 12.10**). ILM in particular seems to excel at great-looking light optics (and cannot be held responsible for the over-the-top look on the bridge of *Star Trek*).

Figure 12.10 You might think of a lens flare as one of those element rings caused by a zoom lens pointing at the sun, but flares occur anytime a bright light source appears in or near frame. Here, the green traffic light causes a large flare without even appearing in frame, and numerous other lights bloom and flare. (Image from *Quality of Life*, courtesy of Benjamin Morgan.)

Therefore, to get lens flares or even simple glints right, good reference is often key. Only a tiny percentage of your viewers may know the difference between lens flares from a 50 mm prime and a 120 mm zoom lens, yet somehow, if you get it wrong, it reads as phony. Odd.

CLOSE-UP

What Causes a Lens Flare?

Unlike your eye, which has only one very flexible lens, camera lenses are typically made up of a series of inflexible lens elements. These elements are coated to prevent light from reflecting off of them under normal circumstances. Extreme amounts of light, however, are reflected somewhat by each element.

Zoom lenses contain many focusing elements and tend to generate a complex-looking flare with lots of individual reflections. Prime lenses generate fewer.

Many factors besides the lens elements contribute to the look of a flare. Aperture blades within the lens cause reflective corners that often result in streaks; the number of streaks corresponds to the number of blades. The shape of the flares sometimes corresponds to the shape of the aperture (a pentagon for a five-sided aperture, a hexagon for six). Dust and scratches on the lens also reflect light. And few light elements look as badass as the anamorphic lens flare you might get shooting into a light source for 2.39:1 widescreen scope display.

Lens flares also appear very different depending on whether they were shot on film or video; excess light bleeds out in different directions and patterns.

NOTES

Prior to the 1970s-era of *Easy Rider* and moon shots, flares were regarded as errors on the part of the cinematographer, and shots containing them were carefully noted on the camera report and retaken.

Here are some things you should know about lens flares:

▶ They are consistent for a given lens. Their angles vary according to the position of the light, but not the shape or arrangement of the component flares.

▶ The big complex flares with lots of components are created by long zoom lenses with many internal lens elements. Wider prime lenses create simpler flares.

▶ Because they are caused within the lens, flares beyond the source appear superimposed over the image, even over objects in the foreground that partially block the source flare.

Moreover, not every bright light source that appears in frame will cause a lens flare—not even the sun.

The Lens Flare effect included with After Effects is rather useless as it contains only three basic presets. Knoll Light Factory, available from Red Giant Software, is much more helpful both because the presets correspond to real lenses and because the components can be fully customized in a modular fashion. The new challenger on the lens flare scene is Optical Flares from videocopilot.net. Either of these will improve dramatically upon what you can achieve with the built-in effect, so investment in one or the other is recommended for this purpose (assuming you're not the type of nerd to create your own lens flares as a 3D precomp, which would be much more time consuming).

Figure 12.11 This sequence shows the glint that plays off the chrome areas of the taxi as it passes a spot in the frame where the sun is reflected directly into the camera lens.

Reflected Light

Reflected light is another "kiss of love" opportunity for a scene. You might not notice that it's missing, but a glimmer, glint, or full reflection can add not only realism but pizzazz to a shot.

Glints are specular flares that occur when light is reflected toward the camera from shiny parts of an element in scene, such as the chrome of the taxi in **Figure 12.11**, taken from the Chapter 5 color matching example.

The same plug-ins used for flares (Trapcode Lux, Knoll Light Factory, Tinderbox, and Optical Flare) can be used to create glints, with more modest settings that don't create all the lens reflections. **Figure 12.12** shows that there's

Figure 12.12 There's not a whole lot
to a glint when you look at it closely,
but it helps sell the plane.

not necessarily a whole lot to a single glint. An Add mode makes these work even in 32-bpc HDR (in which case they create over-range values, just as they would on film).

Light Scattering and Volume

Light scatters as it encounters particles in the air, most dramatically causing the phenomena of volumetric light or "God rays." Our atmosphere does not permit light to travel directly to the camera, uninterrupted, as it does in outer space. Instead, the light ricochets off tiny particles in the air, revealing its path.

The effect can be subtle. Lights that appear in the scene, casting their beams at the camera, tend to have a glowing halo around them. If the light traveled directly to the camera, the outline of the source light would be clear. Instead, light rays hit particles on their way to the camera and head off in slightly new directions, causing a halo (**Figure 12.13**).

Add more particles in the air (in the form of smoke, fog, or mist), and a halo may appear, along with the conditions under which volumetric light occurs. God rays are the result of the fact that light from an omnidirectional source, such as the sun, travels outward in a continuous arc (**Figure 12.14**).

CLOSE-UP

Three Ways to Blur

After Effects offers quite a few blur effects, but three are most common for general usage: Gaussian Blur, Fast Blur (which at best quality is no different), and Box Blur, which can match the other two but offers more flexibility.

At the default Iterations setting (1), a Box Blur can seem crude and, well, boxy, but it can approximate the look of a defocused lens without all the more complex polygons of Lens Blur. You can also hold it out to the horizontal or vertical axis to create a nice motion blur approximation (where Directional Blur is actually too smooth and Gaussian).

Raising the Box Blur Iterations setting above 3 not only amplifies the blur but refines the blur kernel beyond anything the other two effects are capable of producing. What actually occurs is that the blur goes from a square appearance (suiting the name box blur) to a softer, rounder look. You're more likely to notice the difference working with over-range bright values in 32-bit HDR.

Fast Blur and Box Blur also each include a Repeat Edge Pixels check box; enable this to avoid dark borders when blurring a full-frame image. The same setting with these two effects will not, alas, produce the same amount of blur even if Box Blur is set to 3 iterations (to match Fast Blur).

Figure 12.13 You're so used to light halation (left) that it looks wrong to lower the exposure so that it disappears.

Figure 12.14 God rays, with which nature evokes the vast and eternal from an ordinary sunset.

NOTES

To see the setup used to create volumetric light with built-in After Effects tools, check out 12_godrays_built_in_effects on the disc.

The CC Light Rays effect is probably most helpful among those included with After Effects to re-create volumetric light effects and even God rays. The honest truth is that Trapcode Shine outperforms it, but where possible, this book provides methods that don't involve buying a plug-in.

Light Rays not only boosts and causes halation around the source light, but it also adds rays coming straight at camera. These rays can be made more prominent by boosting radius and intensity, but in order to create a God rays effect and not overwhelm an entire image with rays, it's usually best to make a target source and apply the effect to that. For example:

1. Add a solid of your preferred color.

2. Apply Fractal Noise (default settings are acceptable to begin).

3. Mask the solid around the target God rays source area. Feather it heavily.

4. Apply CC Light Rays. Place Center at the God rays target. Boost Intensity and Radius settings until the rays are prominent.

5. For rays only (no fractal noise) set Transfer Mode to None.

6. Set a Subtract mask or Alpha Inverted track matte to create occluded areas for the rays to wrap around, as in **Figure 12.15**.

You can further hold out and mask out the rays as needed, even precomping and moving the source outside of frame if necessary. To make the rays animate, keyframe the Evolution property in Fractal Noise or add an expression such as time*60 to make them undulate over time. Different Fractal Type and Noise Type settings will also yield unique rays.

Shadows

As there is light, so must there be shadows. Unfortunately, they can be difficult to re-create in 2D because they interact with 3D space and volume, none of which 2D layers have. The behavior of shadows can be unpredictable, but luckily, your audience typically doesn't know how they should look in your scene either (until there is some reference right there in the shot).

You can certainly cast a shadow from a matted layer onto a plane by positioning each of them in 3D space and properly positioning a light. Be sure that you first change Casts Shadows for the matted layer from its default Off setting to On or Only (the latter option making it possible to create a precomp containing only the shadow).

Figure 12.15 The included CC Light Rays effect is essential to creating your own volumetric light effects in After Effects. Masks or mattes can be used to occlude rays.

A more straightforward plug-in for volumetric light is Trapcode Lux, which can derive volume and a flare from any After Effects 3D light simply by applying it to an adjustment layer.

Figure 12.16 Compare the fake 3D shadow (left) with the real thing and you instantly grasp the problem with this approach. You can cast a good shadow head-on, but not at this steep an angle.

You can instead corner pin the matte to the angle at which the shadow should fall and avoid the 3D setup altogether. In either case, the problem is that the illusion breaks if the light source is more than 10 degrees off-axis from the camera. The more you light a 2D element from the side, the more it just breaks (**Figure 12.16**).

There's also the possibility of cheating: If it's easy to add ground surface that would obscure a shadow (for example, grass instead of dirt), do so, and no one will even expect to see a shadow because it no longer belongs there.

Contact Shadows and Indirect Light

For the most part, successful shading in a 2D scene relies on achieving what you can practically, and getting creative when practical shadows aren't present. There are plenty of cases where a full cast shadow would be correct and no shadow at all would clearly look wrong, but a simple contact shadow can at least remove glaring contrast so that no one really notices.

A contact shadow is a lot like a drop shadow—basically just an offset, soft, dark copy directly behind the foreground. A drop shadow, however, is good only for casting a shadow onto an imaginary wall behind a floating logo, whereas a contact shadow is held out to only the areas of the foreground that have contact with the ground plane.

Figure 12.17 shows the foreground layer duplicated and placed behind the source. A mask is drawn around the base, and it is then offset downward. A blur is applied to soften the transparency channel. That gives you the matte. Red Giant Warp includes a Shadow effect that not only facilitates the process of creating this type of shadow, but adds the ability to project across a floor and a back wall, with an angle and position that are determined parametrically.

NOTES

Some simple shadow-casting setups can be found in the 12_shadow_casting_basic folder on the disc.

Figure 12.17 A simple contact shadow (middle) can make the difference between an object that appears to sit on a surface and an object that appears to float in space.

A real shadow is often not just black; it's an area of reduced light and therefore color. Instead of darkening down the matte itself to create the shadow, create an adjustment layer just below the contact shadow layer and set an alpha track matte. Add a Levels (or if you prefer, Curves) effect and adjust brightness and gamma downward to create your shadow. Treat it like a color correction, working on separate channels if necessary; the result is more interesting and accurate than a pool of blackness (**Figure 12.18**).

Reflected light is another type of contact lighting that plays a role in how things look in the real world, and thus can play a role in your composited scenes. Most objects in the world have diffuse surfaces that reflect light; when the object is prominent or colorful enough, your eye simply

Figure 12.18 By applying the shadow layer as a track matte to an adjustment layer, you can treat it as a color correction and match the color and contrast of the scene's existing shadows (top). Add a color correction pass and a day-lit American street takes on a more exotic vibe (bottom).

Figure 12.19 The color influence of indirect light is not always so evident as with a bright saturated object, but it is always in play in a natural setting.

expects it to affect other more neutral neighboring surfaces, whether or not your brain is aware of the phenomenon (**Figure 12.19**).

In 3D computer graphics this situation is re-created via global illumination, which includes light and surface interactions in a render. If you're working with a computer-generated scene, aim for a pass that includes these types of light interactions. If you have to create the effect from scratch, the method is similar to that of shadows or color matching: Create a selection of the area reflecting light, including any needed falloff (that may be the hard part), and use color correction tools to color match the adjacent object reflecting color.

Multipass 3D Compositing

Lighting in computer-generated scenes has advanced to an astonishing extent, with stunning scenes from *Avatar* or *Toy Story 3* displaying all of the loveliness of natural light with no compositing needed. Nonetheless, when attempting to match a computer-generated element to a live-action backplate, it's more effective to divide the render of a single element into multiple passes.

This is different from simply rendering in layers, which while also useful for compositing is really only about separating foreground elements from the background.

Multipass rendering is the technique of isolating individual surface qualities and creating a separate render for each. "Surface qualities" are things like specularity, shadows, and wear and tear (or grunge). In his excellent book *Digital Lighting & Rendering, Second Edition* (Peachpit Press, 2006), Jeremy Birn calls out multiple benefits yielded by rendering a model on multiple passes:

▶ **Changes** can be made with little or no re-rendering. If a shadow is too dark or a glow is the wrong color, the adjustment can be made right in After Effects.

▶ **Integration** often requires multiple passes where the model interacts with the scene, casting a shadow on the ground or being reflected in water. If the cast shadow is simply part of a single render, you lose all control over its appearance and cannot apply it as recommended in the previous section.

▶ **Reflections**, which often consume massive amounts of time to process, can be rendered at lower quality and blurred in After Effects.

▶ **Bump Maps** can be applied more selectively (held out by another pass such as a highlight or reflection pass).

▶ **Glows** can be created easily in 2D by simply blurring and boosting exposure of a specular pass.

▶ **Depth of Field** can be controlled entirely in 2D by using a Z pass as a matte for a blur adjustment layer.

▶ **Less render power and time** is required to render any one pass than the entire shaded model, so a lower powered computer can do more, and redoing any one element takes far less time than redoing the entire finished model.

Putting multiple passes to use is also surprisingly simple; the artistry is in all of the minute decisions about which combination of adjustments will bring the element to life. **Table 12.1** (on the next page) describes some common render passes and how they are typically used.

Other passes for specific objects might include a *Fresnel* (or *Incidence*) pass showing the sheen of indirect light and applied to an adjustment layer with a luma matte (raise Output Black in Levels to re-create sheen); a *Grunge* or

RPF and EXR

RPF files are an Autodesk update to RLA. After Effects offers limited native support for these files (via the effects in the 3D Channel menu), but more robust support for some of the finer features of RPF such as Normal maps is only available via third-party plug-ins. Commercially available plug-ins that can translate normal maps for use in After Effects include ZBornToy (which also does amazing things with depth maps) from Frischluft and WalkerFX Channel Lighting, part of the Walker Effects collection. There is a free option for Windows called Normality (www.minning.de/software/normality).

As mentioned in Chapter 8, After Effects can also extract camera data from RPF files (typically generated in 3DS Max or Flame); place the sequence containing the 3D camera data in a comp and choose Animation > Keyframe Assistant > RPF Camera Import.

The most popular way to get a multipass render into After Effects these days is via the EXR format, which can store all of the various passes and related data in a single file. EXR is now supported directly in After Effects via EXtractoR and IDentifier, two plug-ins from fnordware.

Got UV Maps? After Effects has the means to use them with the RE:Map plug-in from RE:Vision Effects. This allows you to map a texture to an object, using the UV map for coordinates, without returning to the 3D app that generated it or waiting for Live Photoshop 3D to support mapping in After Effects.

TABLE **12.1** Ten Typical Multipass Render Layer Types

TYPE	COLOR/ GRAYSCALE	TYPICAL BLENDING MODE	DESCRIPTION	USE
Diffuse	Color	Normal	Full color render; includes diffuse illumination, color correction, and texture; excludes reflections, highlights, and shadows	Color basis for the element; main target for primary color
Specular	Color	Add or Screen	Isolated specular highlights	Control how highlights are rendered; can be reused to create a glow pass by simply blurring and raising exposure
Reflection	Color	Add or Screen	Self-reflections, other objects, environment	Control the prominence and color of reflections
Shadow	Grayscale	Luma Inverted Matte	Isolated translucent shadows in scene	Control appearance, color, and softness of shadows; applied as a track matte to an adjustment layer with a Levels or Curves effect
Ambient	Color	Color	Color and texture maps without diffuse shading, specular highlights, shadows, or reflections	Color reference, can be used to make the color/texture of an object more pure and visible
Occlusion	Grayscale	Luma Inverted Matte	Shadows that result from soft illumination, simulating light from an overcast sky or well-lit room	Adds natural soft shadows to an object; these can be tinted to reflect the color of reflected light
Beauty	Color	Normal	A render of all passes	Reference: this is how the object or scene would appear if rendered in a single pass
Global Illumination	Color	Add or Screen	Indirect light added to the scene by global illumination, potentially including ray-traced reflections and refractions	Control intensity of indirect lighting in scene
Matte/ Mask/ Alpha	Grayscale	Luma Matte	Can be used to contain multiple transparency masks for portions of the object or scene, one each on the red, green, blue, and alpha channels	Straight alpha for any channel
Depth/Z-depth/ Depth Map	Grayscale or non-image floating point	Luma Matte	Describes the distance of surface areas from the camera	Can be used to control depth effects such as fog and lens blur, as well as light falloff

Dirt map, applied as a luma inverted matte, allowing you to dial in areas of wear and tear with Levels on an adjustment layer; a *Light* pass for any self-illuminated details; and a *Normal* pass showing the direction of surface normals for relighting purposes. Many, many more are possible—really anything that you can isolate in a 3D animation program. **Figure 12.20** shows a model set up for multipass rendering and a few of its component render layers.

A

B   C   D   E

F   G   H   I

Figure 12.20 A basic multipass setup (**A**) with the beauty pass (**B**) as reference, made up of the following color passes: diffuse (**C**), specular (**D**), and reflection (**E**) as well as grayscale passes applied as luma mattes to adjustment layers, each containing a Levels effect: grunge (**F**), incidence (**G**), and occlusion (**H**). A depth matte (**I**) can be applied in various ways; here it is used as reference for a lens blur on an adjustment layer (to give the appearance of shallow depth of field).

It's more typical to simply apply grayscale layers via blending modes such as add or multiply (**Figure 12.21**)

None of these passes necessarily requires a transparency (alpha) channel, and in old-school effects it is customary not to render them, since multiple passes of edge transparency can lead to image multiplication headaches.

The general rules for multipass compositing are simple:

▶ Use the Diffuse layer as the base.

▶ Apply color layers meant to illuminate the base layer, such as specular and reflection, via Add or Screen blending modes.

▶ Apply color layers meant to darken the base layer, if any, via Multiply or Darken blending modes.

▶ Apply grayscale maps as luma mattes for adjustment layers. Apply Levels, Curves, and Hue/Saturation to allow these mattes to influence the shading of the object or scene.

▶ Control the strength of any layer using Opacity.

Check out the 12_multipass folder on the disc for a couple of setups, and try your own versions!

Multipass renders provide an excellent opportunity to enable Blend Colors Using 1.0 Gamma in Project Settings, whether or not you assign a working space (and whether or not that working space is linearized). With this setting enabled, specular and reflection passes naturally light the model via Add mode and shadow, grunge, or ambient occlusion passes naturally darken it via Multiply.

Multipass rendering is only partially scientific and accurate; successful use of multiple passes is a highly individualized and creative sport. I personally like to cheat heavily instead of going by the book if I'm happy with the result. With the correct basic lighting setup you can use multipass renders to place a given 3D element in a variety of environments without the need for a complete re-render.

Varied environments are themselves the subject of the following chapter.

A

B

C

D

E

F

G

H

I

J

Figure 12.21 Just to show there's no hard-and-fast rule for multipass rendering, here's a setup (and set of source layers) completely unique from the previous. The color pass (**A**) is minimal. Precomping the canopy (**B**) and glass (**C**) separately with Collapse Transformations on gives individual control of that translucent element.. The decals (**D**) are held out by a hi-con pass (**E**) to give the color pass most of its surface attributes. A specular (**F**) and three individual reflection passes (**G-I**) give full control over the plane's salient shininess. The ambient occlusion pass (**J**) is multiplied in to give weight to the shadows, and an adjustment layer applies HDR Highlight Compression to this 32-bpc assembly so that it can be rendered and used as an 8- or 16-bit element if necessary.

13

Climate and the Environment

*Conversation about the weather is the last refuge
of the unimaginative.*

—Oscar Wilde

Yes, yes, let's talk about the weather.
—W. S. Gilbert, *The Pirates of Penzance,*
or the *Slave of Duty*

Climate and the Environment

Even if you're not called upon to re-create extreme climate conditions, even a casual glance out the window demonstrates that meteorological phenomena are always in play: A breeze is blowing in the trees, or water and particulates in the air are changing the appearance of buildings and the land closest to the horizon.

This chapter offers methods to create natural elements such as particulates and wind effects, as well as to replace a sky, or add mist, fog, smoke, or other various forms of precipitation. All of these generally are more easily captured with a camera than re-created in After Effects, but sometimes the required conditions don't materialize on the day of a shoot. Mother Nature is, after all, notoriously fickle, and shooting just to get a particular environment can be extraordinarily expensive and random.

It's rare indeed that weather conditions cooperate on location, and even rarer that a shoot can wait for perfect weather or can be set against the perfect backdrop. Transforming the appearance of a scene using natural elements is among the more satisfying things you can do as a compositor.

Particulate Matter

Particulate matter in the air influences how objects appear at different depths. What is this matter? Fundamentally, it is water and other gas, dust, or visible particulates usually known as pollution. In an ideal, pristine, pollution-free environment there is moisture in the air—even in the driest desert, where there also might be heavier forms of particulates like dust and sand. The amount of haze in the air offers clues as to

▶ the distance to the horizon and of objects in relation to it

▶ the basic type of climate; the aridness or heaviness of the weather

▶ the time of year and the day's conditions

▶ the air's stagnancy (think *Blade Runner*)

▶ the sun's location (when it's not visible in shot)

The color of the particulate matter offers clues to how much pollution is present and what it is, even how it feels: dust, smog, dark smoke from a fire, and so on (**Figure 13.1**).

Particulate matter in the air lowers the apparent contrast of visible objects; secondarily, objects take on the color of the atmosphere around them and become slightly diffuse. This is a subtle yet omnipresent depth cue: With any particulate matter in the air, objects lose contrast further from the camera; the apparent color can change quite a bit, and detail is softened. As a compositor, you use this to your advantage, not only to re-create reality but to provide dramatic information.

NOTES

It will not come as news that atmospheric haze occurs only in the presence of an atmosphere. Examine photos of the moon landscape, and you'll see that the blacks in the distance look just as dark as those in the foreground.

Figure 13.1 Same location, different conditions. Watch for subtleties: Backlighting emphasizes even low levels of haze and reduces overall saturation (left); more diffuse conditions desaturate and obscure the horizon while emphasizing foreground color (right).

Depth Cues

Figure 13.2 shows how the same object at the same size indicates its depth by its color. The background has great foreground and background reference for black and white levels; although the rear plane looks icy blue against gray, it matches the look of gray objects in the distance of the image.

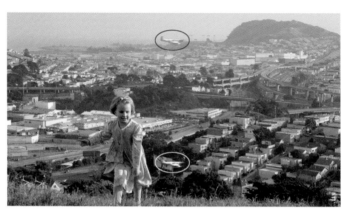

Figure 13.2 One plane (circled in white) is composited as if it is a toy model in the foreground, the other (circled in black) as if it is crossing the sky further in the distance (far right). A look at just the planes (near right) shows them to be identical but for their color. The difference between a toy model airplane flying close, a real airplane flying nearby, and the same plane in the distant sky is conveyed with the use of Scale, but just as importantly, with Levels that show the influence of atmospheric haze.

The plane as a foreground element seems to make life easier by containing a full range of monochrome colors. When matching a more colorful or monochrome element, you can always create a small solid and add the default Ramp effect. With such a reference element, it is simple to add the proper depth cueing with Levels and then apply the setting to the final element (**Figure 13.3**).

Figure 13.3 If your foreground layer lacks the full range of values, match a grayscale gradient, then swap in the element. These gradient squares have the same settings as the planes in 13.2.

Depth Maps

To re-create depth cues in a shot from scratch, you must somehow separate the shot into planes of distance. If the source imagery is computer-generated, the 3D program that created it can also generate a depth map for you to use. If not, you can slice the image into planes of distance, or you can make your own depth map to weight the distance of the objects in frame (**Figure 13.4**).

There are several ways in which a depth map can be used, but the simplest approach is probably to apply it to an adjustment layer as a luma (or luma inverted) matte, and then add Levels or other color correction adjustment to the adjustment layer. Depth cueing applies to the most distant elements, so setting a luma inverted matte and then *flashing* the blacks (raising the Output Black level in Levels) adds the effect of atmosphere on the scene.

Figure 13.4 This grayscale depth map is made up of individual roto shapes, each shaded for relative distance (further elucidated in the excellent *Advanced Rotoscoping Techniques for Adobe After Effects* by Pete O'Connell, Creative Cow).

Depth data may also be rendered and stored in an RPF file, as in **Figure 13.5**. RPF files are in some ways crude, lacking even thresholding in the edges (let alone higher bit depths), but they can contain several types of 3D data, as listed in the 3D Channel menu. This data can be used directly by a few effects to simulate 3D, including Particle Playground, which accepts RPF data as an influence map.

TIP

Roto Brush is a perfect tool to quickly create a decent depth map in 20% or less of the time it would take to do the roto by hand.

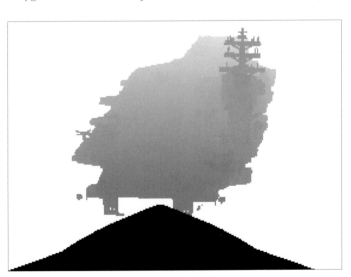

Figure 13.5 Note the jaggies in an RPF image. A depth map does not have to be perfectly pristine. (Created by Fred Lewis; used with permission from Inhance Digital, Boeing, and the Navy UCAV program.)

One good reason to use a basic 3D render of a scene as the basis for a matte painting is that the perspective and lens angle can be used not only for reference but to generate a depth map, even if the entire scene is painted over.

Examples of keying and replacing a sky are found in the 13_sky_ replacement folder on the disc.

More extreme conditions may demand actual 3D particles, which are saved for later in the chapter.

Sky Replacement

Sky replacement is among the most inexpensive and fundamental enhancements that can be made to a shot. Not only can a bland sky be upgraded to a dramatic, lovely one, you can change the very location of the shot by changing its sky backdrop. This is much easier and in many cases less expensive than scouting the perfect location.

Skies are always part of the story—sometimes only subliminally, but often as a starring element. An interior with a window could be anywhere, but show a recognizable skyline outside the window and locals will automatically gauge the exact neighborhood and city block of that location, along with the time of day, time of year, weather, outside temperature, and so on, possibly without ever really paying conscious attention to it.

You could spend tens (or even hundreds) of thousands of dollars for that apartment with a view on Central Park East to film a scene at golden hour (the beautiful "hour" of sunset that typically lasts more like 20 minutes and is missing on an overcast day). The guerrilla method is to use a friend's apartment, shoot all day, and add the sunset view in post. In many cases, the real story is elsewhere, and the sky is a subliminal (even if beautiful) backdrop that must serve that story (**Figure 13.6**).

The Sky Is Not (Quite) a Blue Screen

Study the actual sky (perhaps there's one nearby) or even better, study reference images, and you may notice that the blue color desaturates near the horizon, cloudless skies are not always easy to come by, and even clear blue skies are not as saturated as they might sometimes seem.

Some combination of a color keyer, such as Keylight, and a hi-con luminance matte pass or a garbage matte, as needed, can remove the existing sky in your shot, leaving nice edges around the foreground. Chapter 6 focuses on

Figure 13.6 For an independent film with no budget set in San Francisco, the director had the clever idea of shooting it in a building lobby across the bay in lower-rent Oakland (top left), pulling a matte from the blue sky (top center), and match moving a still shot of the San Francisco skyline (from street level, top right) for a result that anyone familiar with that infamous pyramid-shaped building would assume was taken in downtown San Francisco (bottom). (Images courtesy of the Orphanage.)

strategies that put these to use, and Chapter 7 describes supporting approaches when keys and garbage mattes fail.

The first step of sky replacement is to remove the existing "sky" (which may include other items at infinite distance, such as buildings and clouds) by developing a matte for it. As you do this, place the replacement sky in the background; a sky matte typically does not have to be as exacting as a blue-screen key if the replacement sky is also fundamentally blue, or if the whole image is radically color corrected as in **Figure 13.7**.

Figure 13.7 A very challenging matte for several reasons, not the least of which is the uneven desaturated quality of the sky. Placing the subject in a radically different environment requires color and grain matching to compensate for a less than stellar source.

Infinite Depth

A locked-off shot can be completed with the creation of the matte and a color match to the new sky. But if there is camera movement in the shot, you might assume that a 3D track is needed to properly add a new sky element.

Typically, that's overkill. Instead, consider the following:

▶ When matching motion from the original shot, look for anything in the source sky that can be tracked. Also, spot opportunities to cheat and hand-animate when the ground plane leaves the shot.

▶ If only your foreground can be tracked, you might want to try the suggestions in Chapter 8 for applying a track to a 3D camera: Move the replacement sky to the distant background (via a Z Position value well into four or five digits, depending on camera settings). Scale up to compensate for the distance.

▶ A push or zoom shot (Chapter 9 describes the difference) may be more easily re-created using a tracked 3D camera (but look at Chapter 8 for tips on getting away with a 2D track).

The basic phenomenon to re-create is the scenery at infinite distance that moves less than objects in the foreground. This is the parallax effect, which is less pronounced with a long, telephoto lens, and much more obvious with a wide angle. For the match in Figure 13.6, a 2D matte painting of a skyline (no perspective) was skewed to match the correct angle and tracked in; the lens angle was long enough and the shot brief enough to get away with it. A simpler example is included on the disc.

NOTES

Want smoke? A few modest examples are in the 13_smoke folder on the disc.

Fog, Smoke, and Mist

An animated layer of translucent clouds is easy to re-create in After Effects. The basic element can be fabricated by applying the Turbulent Noise effect to a solid. An Add or Screen blending mode gives the reflective light quality, and a separate Multiply pass can add weight and thickness.

NOTES

Turbulent Noise is a faster and more natural looking alternative to Fractal Noise.

Turbulent Noise at its default settings already looks smoky (**Figure 13.8**); switching the Noise Type setting from the default, Soft Linear, to Spline improves it. The main extra

Figure 13.8 The new Turbulent Noise effect (shown at the default setting, left) is a decent stand-in for organic-looking ambient smoke and fog. Animate the Evolution effect if you want any billowing of the element. The same alternate Fractal Types as found in the older Fractal Noise effect are available, as seen in the pop-up menu.

ingredient is motion, which I like to do with a simple expression applied to the Evolution property: `time*60` (I find 60 an appropriate rate in many situations; follow your own taste). The Transform properties within Fractal Noise can be animated, causing the overall layer to move as if being blown by wind.

Brightness, Contrast, and Scale settings influence the apparent scale and density of the noise layer. Complexity and Sub settings also affect apparent scale and density, but with all kinds of undesirable side effects that make the smoke look artificial. The look is greatly improved by layering at least two separate passes via a blending mode (as in the example project).

Masking and Adjusting

When covering the entire foreground evenly with smoke or mist, a more realistic look is achieved using two or three separate overlapping layers with offset positions (**Figure 13.9**). The unexpected byproduct of layering 2D particle layers in this manner is that they take on the illusion of depth and volume.

CLOSE-UP

Add vs. Multiply: Light and Occlusion

Multiply mode is appropriate for elements such as smoke, mist, and fog—these are dark and occlude what is behind them, and Multiply enhances dark tones and omits light ones. Add mode is best for light elements (especially those shot against dark backgrounds such as pyrotechnics); it has the characteristic of brightening what is behind it. For an element with light and dark tones such as a thick plume of smoke, you may want to use a combination of both, at varying levels of opacity.

Figure 13.9 Overlay layers of fabricated smoke to add dimensionality and depth.

Fractal Noise texture maps maintain the advantage over Turbulent Noise in that they can loop seamlessly (allowing reuse on shots of varying length). In Evolution Options, enable Cycle Evolution, and animate Evolution in whole revolutions (say, from 0° 2 × 0.0°). Set the Cycle (in Revolutions) parameter to the number of total revolutions (2). The first and last keyframes now match, and a loopOut("cycle") expression continues this loop infinitely.

The eye perceives changes in parallax between the foreground and background and automatically assumes these to be a byproduct of full three-dimensionality, yet you save the time and trouble of a 3D volumetric particle render. Of course, you're limited to instances in which particles don't interact substantially with movement from objects in the scene, although that's not off-limits for one who is patient; techniques to shape the motion of liquid elements follow later in this chapter.

Particle layers can be combined with the background via blending modes, or they can be applied as a luma matte to a colored solid. As always, choose whichever gives the most control via the fewest steps.

To add smoke to a generalized area of the frame, a big elliptical mask with a high feather setting (in the triple digits even for video resolution) does the trick; if the borders of the smoke area are apparent, increase the mask feather even further (**Figure 13.10**).

Figure 13.10 This mask of a single smoke element from the shot in Figure 13.8 has a feather value in the hundreds. The softness of the mask helps to sell the element as smoke and works well overlaid with other, similarly feathered masked elements.

Moving Through the Mist

The same effect you get when you layer several instances of Turbulent or Fractal Noise can aid the illusion of moving forward through a misty cloud. That's done simply enough (for an example of flying through a synthetic cloud, see the Smoky Layers project on the disc), but how often does your shot consist of just moving through a misty cloud? Most of the time, clouds of smoke or mist are combined with an existing shot.

The secret is that these organic "liquid" 2D layers take on the illusion of volume as they are overlaid and arrayed in 3D. By "liquid" we mean any element with flowing organic motion and no hard-surface shape, so gases and fire are even included. To make this work, keep a few points in mind:

▶ Each instance of Fractal Noise uses a soft elliptical mask.

▶ The mask should be large enough to overlap with another masked instance but small enough to hold its position as the angle of the camera changes.

▶ A small amount of Evolution animation goes a long way, and too much will blow the gag. Let the movement of the camera create the interest of motion.

▶ Depending on the length and distance covered in the shot, be willing to create at least a half-dozen individual masked layers of Fractal Noise.

The Smoky Flyover features just such an effect of moving forward through clouds. It combines the tracking of each shot carefully into place with the phenomenon of parallax, whereby overlapping layers swirl across one another in a believable manner. Mist and smoke seem to be a volume, but they actually often behave more like overlapping, translucent planes—individual clouds of mist and smoke.

Billowing Smoke

Fractal Noise works fine to create and animate thin wispy smoke and mist, but is of little help to fabricate thick, billowing plumes or clouds. Instead of a plug-in effect, all that's required is a good still cloud element and you can animate it in After Effects. And all you need to create the

CLOSE-UP

Selling the Effect with Diffraction

There is more to adding a cloud to a realistic shot than a simple A over B comp; liquid particles in the air, whether in spray, mist, or clouds, not only occlude light but diffract it. This diffraction effect can be simulated by applying Compound Blur to an adjustment layer between the fog and the background and using a precomposed (or prerendered) version of the fog element as its Blur layer.

This usage of Compound Blur is detailed further in the next chapter, where it is used to enhance the effect of smoky haze.

element is a high-resolution reference photo—or even a bag of cotton puffs, as was used to create the images in **Figure 13.11**.

Figure 13.11 A good static image, even cotton puffs arranged on black posterboard, photographed in daylight, can be used as the foundation of billowing smoke.

To give clouds shape and contour, open the image in Photoshop, and use the Clone Stamp tool to create a cloud with the shape you want. You can do it directly in After Effects, but this is the kind of job for which Photoshop was designed. Clone in contour layers of highlights (using Linear Dodge, Screen, or Lighten blending modes) and shadows (with Blending set to Multiply or Darken) until the cloud has the look you're after (**Figure 13.12**).

Figure 13.12 The elements from Figure 13.11 are incorporated into this matte painting, and the final shot contains a mixture of real and composited smoke.

So now you have a good-looking cloud, but it's a still. How do you put it in motion? This is where After Effects' excellent distortion tools come into play, in particular Mesh Warp and Liquify. The Smoke Cloud project containing just such a cloud animation is found on the disc.

Mesh Warp

Mesh Warp displays a grid of Bezier handles over the frame; to animate distortion, set a keyframe for the Distortion Mesh property at frame 0, then move the points of the grid and realign the Bezier handles associated with each point to bend to the vertices between points. The image to which this effect is applied follows the shape of the grid.

By default, Mesh Warp begins with a seven-by-seven grid. Before you do anything else, make sure that the size of the grid makes sense for your image; you might want to increase its size for a high-resolution project, and reduce the number of rows to fit the aspect ratio of your shot, for a grid of squares (**Figure 13.13**).

You can't typically get away with dragging a point more than about halfway toward any other point; watch carefully for artifacts of stretching and tearing as you work, and preview often. If you see stretching, realign adjacent points and handles to compensate. There is no better way to learn about this than to experiment.

I have found that the best results with Mesh Warp use minimal animation of the mesh, animating instead the element that moves underneath it. This works well with any organic, flowing liquid.

Liquify

Mesh Warp is appropriate for gross distortions of an entire frame. The Liquify effect is a brush-based system for fine distortions. The Smoke Cloud project includes a composition that employs Liquify to swirl a cloud. Following is a brief orientation to this toolset, but as with most brush-based painterly tools, there is no substitute for hands-on experience.

TIP

Mesh Warp, like many distortion tools, renders rather slowly. As you rough in the motion, feel free to work at quarter resolution. When you've finalized your animation, you can save a lot of time by pre-rendering it (see Chapter 4).

Figure 13.13 The Mesh Warp controls are simple, just a grid of points and vectors. You can preset the number and quality; more is not necessarily better. Points can be multiselected and dragged, and each point contains Bezier handles for warping the adjacent vectors.

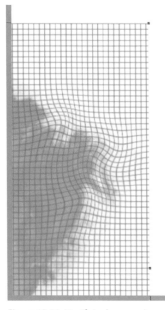

Figure 13.14 Liquify is also a mesh distortion tool, only the mesh is much finer than Mesh Warp's and it is controlled via brushes, allowing more specific distortions.

The principle behind Liquify is actually similar to that of Mesh Warp; enable View Mesh under View Options and you'll see that you're still just manipulating a grid, albeit a finer one that would be cumbersome to adjust point by point—hence the brush interface.

Of the brushes included with Liquify, the first two along the top row, Warp and Turbulence, are most often used (**Figure 13.14**). Warp has a similar effect to moving a point in Mesh Warp; it simply pushes pixels in the direction you drag the brush. Turbulence scrambles pixels in the path of the brush.

The Reconstruction brush (rightmost on the bottom row) is like a selective undo, reversing distortions at the default setting; other options for this brush are contained in the Reconstruction Mode menu (which appears only when the brush is selected).

Liquify has the advantage of allowing holdout areas. Draw a mask around the area you want to leave untouched by Liquify brushes, but set the Mask mode to None, disabling it. Under Warp Tool Options, select the mask name in the Freeze Area Masked menu.

Liquify was a key addition to the "super cell" element (that huge swirling mass of weather) for the freezing of the New York City sequence in *The Day After Tomorrow*. Artists at the Orphanage were able to animate matte paintings of the cloud bank, broken down into more than a dozen component parts to give the effect the appropriate organic complexity and dimension.

Wind and Ambience

What is wind doing in this chapter? While not itself visible, its effects are omnipresent in most any exterior shot. Therefore, suggesting the influence of wind can help bring a matte painting or other static background to life.

Most still scenes in the real world contain ambient motion of some kind. Objects directly in the scene as well as reflected light and shadow might be changing all the time in a scene we perceive to be motionless. The next time you are at a good outdoor vantage point, notice what subtle motion you see in the environment and think about what you could easily re-create.

As a compositor, you often look for opportunities to contribute to the realism of a scene without stealing focus. Obviously, the kinds of dynamics involved with making the leaves and branches of a tree sway are mostly beyond the realm of 2D compositing, but there are often other elements that are easily articulated and animated ever so slightly. Successful examples of ambient animation should not be noticeable, and they often will not have been explicitly requested, so this can be an exercise in subtlety.

CLOSE-UP

Primary and Secondary

Primary animation is the gross movement of the object, its movement as a whole. *Secondary animation* is the movement of individual parts of the object as a result of inertia. So, for example, a helicopter crashes to the ground: That's the primary animation. Its rotors and tail bend and shudder at impact: That's the secondary animation.

Adding Elements and Animation

Using the Puppet tools is one method to organically add a little motion to a solid-body element. You also have the option of acquiring and adding elements that indicate or add to the effect of wind motion. **Figure 13.15** is an element of blowing autumn leaves shot against a black background for easy removal and matting. Granted, you could add an element this turbulent only to a scene that either already had signs of gusts in it or that contained only elements that would show no secondary motion from wind whatsoever.

Figure 13.15 Sometimes you can find elements that will enliven your scene when comped in, such as this clip of blowing leaves shot over black. (Footage courtesy of Artbeats.)

Remember, too, how easily you can grab an effects element if the sky is your background. **Figure 13.16** shows a wind-blown element that was shot on the fly and then stabilized for effects usage. Re-creating a dynamic animation of an element even as, ahem, simple as a single palm tree is really not worth the trouble if it's just an ambient element.

Figure 13.16 VFX elements can be shot sideways to maximize image fidelity, and the fact that I was missing a tripod the day I took this doesn't invalidate it as an element, thanks to motion stabilization.

Smoke Trails, Plumes, and More

Many effects, including smoke trails, don't require particle generation in order to be re-created faithfully. This example shows how, with a little creativity, you can combine techniques in After Effects to create effects that you might think require extra tools.

Initial setup of such an effect is simply a matter of starting with a clean plate, painting the smoke trails in a separate still layer, and revealing them over time (presumably behind the aircraft that is creating them). The quickest and easiest way to reveal such an element over time is often by animating a mask, as in **Figure 13.17**. Or, you could use techniques described in Chapter 8 to apply a motion tracker to a brush.

The second stage of this effect is dissipation of the trail; depending on how much wind is present, the trail might drift, spread, and thin out over time. That might mean that in a wide shot, the back of the trail would be more dissipated than the front, or it might mean the whole smoke trail was blown around.

Figure 13.17 No procedural effect is needed; animating out masks is quick, simple, and gives full control over the result.

One method is to displace with a black-to-white gradient (created with Ramp) and Compound Blur. The gradient is white at the dissipated end of the trail and black at the source (**Figure 13.18**); each point can be animated or tracked in. Compound Blur uses this gradient as its Blur Layer, creating more blur as the ramp becomes more white. Another method, also shown in Figure 13.18, uses a different displacement effect, Turbulent displace, to create the same type of organic noise as in the preceding cloud layers.

Figures 13.18 To dissipate a smoke trail the way the wind would, you can use a gradient and Compound Blur, so that the smoke dissipates more over time, or use the Turbulent Displace effect (right) that, like Turbulent Noise, adds fractal noise to displace the straight trails from Figure 13.17.

Precipitation

You might want to create a "dry for wet" effect, taking footage that was shot under clear, dry conditions and adding the effects of inclement weather. Not only is it impractical to time a shoot so that you're filming in a storm (in most parts of the world, anyway), but wet, stormy conditions limit shooting possibilities and cut down on available light. Re-creating a storm by having actual water fall in a scene is expensive, complicated, and not necessarily convincing.

I like Trapcode Particular (see the demo on the book's disc) for particles of accumulating rain or snow. This effect outdoes After Effects' own Particle Playground for features, flexibility, and fast renders. As the following example shows, Particular is good for more than just falling particles, as well.

The Wet Look

Study reference photographs of stormy conditions and you'll notice some things that they all have in common, as well as others that depend on variables. Here are the steps taken to make a sunny day gloomy (**Figure 13.19**):

1. Replace the sky: placid for stormy (**Figure 13.20, part A**).

2. Adjust Hue/Saturation—LA for Dublin—to bring out the green mossiness of those dry hills, I've knocked out the blues and pulled the reds down and around toward green (**Figure 13.20, B**).

Want to see this project already set up? Look at 13_dry_for_wet on the book's disc.

Figure 13.19 An ordinary exterior where "it never rains" (left) becomes a deluge.

3. Exchange Tint—balmy for frigid—a bluish cast is common to rainy scenes **(Figure 13.20, C).**

4. Fine-tune Curves—low light for daylight—aggressively dropping the gamma while holding the highlights makes things even moodier (**Figure 13.20, D**).

That's dark, but it looks as dry as a lunar surface. How do you make the background look soaked? It seems like an impossible problem, until you study reference. Then it becomes apparent that all of that moisture in the air causes distant highlights to bloom. This is a win-win adjustment (did I really just type that?) because it also makes the scene lovelier to behold.

You can simply add a Glow effect, but it doesn't offer as much control as the approach I recommend.

Follow these steps:

1. Bring in the background layer again (you can duplicate it and delete the applied effects—**Ctrl+Shift+E/ Cmd+Shift+E**).

2. Add an Adjustment Layer below it and set the duplicated background as Luma Matte.

3. Use Levels to make the matte layer a hi-con matte that isolates the highlights to be bloomed.

4. Fast Blur the result to soften the bloom area.

5. On the Adjustment Layer, add Exposure and Fast Blur to bloom the background within the matte selection.

Create Precipitation

Trapcode Particular contains all the controls needed to generate custom precipitation (it contains a lot of controls, period). A primer is helpful, to get past the default animation of little white squares emanating out in all directions (click under Preview in Effect Controls to see it). To get started making rain, create a comp-sized 2D solid layer and apply Particular. Next:

1. Twirl down Emitter and set an Emitter Type. For rain I like Box so that I can easily set its width and depth, but anything besides the default Point and Grid will work.

A

B

C

D

E

Figure 13.20 The progression to a heavy, wet day (top to bottom). Image **E** shows the result—it now looks like a wet, cold day, but where's the rain?

NOTES

The 13_snowfall folder on the disc contains a setup very much like this one. Customize it or use it to start on the path to creating your own.

2. Set Emitter Size to at least the comp width in X, to fill the frame.

3. Set Direction to Directional.

4. Set X Rotation to –90 so that the particles fall downward.

5. Boost velocity to go from gently falling snow speed to pelting rain.

You might think it more correct to boost gravity than velocity, but gravity increases velocity over time (as Galileo discovered) and rain begins falling thousands of feet above. Don't think too hard, in any case; what you're after here is realistic-looking weather, not a physics prize.

You do, however, need to do the following:

1. Move the Emitter Y Position to 0 or less so that it sits above frame.

2. Increase the Emitter Size Y to get more depth among those falling particles.

3. Crank up the Particles/sec and Physics Time (under Physics) to get enough particles, full blast from the first frame.

4. If the particles are coming up short at the bottom of frame, increase the Life setting under Particle.

5. Enable Motion Blur for the layer and comp to get some nice streaky rain (**Figure 13.21**).

From here, you can add Wind and Air Resistance under Physics. If you're creating snow instead of rain, you might want to customize Particle Type, even referring to your own Custom layer if necessary for snowflakes.

Composite Precipitation

What is the color of falling rain? The correct answer to this Zen Koan–like question is that raindrops and snowflakes are translucent. Their appearance is heavily influenced by the background environment, because they behave like tiny falling lenses. They diffract light, defocusing and

Figure 13.21 In the "good enough" category, two passes of rain, one very near, one far, act together to create a watery deluge. Particular could generate this level of depth with a single field, and the midground rain is missing, but planes are much faster to set up for a fast-moving shot like this. The rain falls mainly on two planes.

lowering the contrast of whatever is behind them, but they themselves also pick up the ambient light.

Therefore, on *The Day After Tomorrow* our crew found success with using the rain or snow element as a track matte for an adjustment layer containing a Fast Blur and a Levels (or Exposure) effect, like a reflective, defocused lens. This type of precipitation changes brightness according to its backlighting, as it should. You may see fit to hold out specific areas and brighten them more, if you spot an area where a volumetric light effect might occur.

The final result in Figure 13.19 benefits from a couple of extra touches. The rain is divided into multiple layers, near and far, and motion-tracked to match the motion of the car from which we're watching this scene. Particular has the ability to generate parallax without using multiple layers, but I sometimes find this approach gives me more control over the perspective. Although you rarely want one without the other, it's one more example of choosing artistry over scientific accuracy.

Because we're looking out a car window, if we want to call attention to the point of view—because the next shot reverses to an actor looking out this window—it's only appropriate that the rain bead up. This is also done with Particular, with Velocity turned off and Custom particles for the droplets.

And because your audience can always tell when you have the details wrong, even if they don't know exactly what's wrong, check out **Figure 13.22** for how the droplet is designed.

Once again, it is attention to detail and creative license that allow you to simulate the complexities of nature. It can be fun and satisfying to transform a scene using the techniques from this chapter, and it can be even more fun and satisfying to design your own based on the same principles: Study how it really works, and notice details others would miss. Your audience will appreciate the difference every time.

The next chapter heats things up with fire, explosions, and other combustibles.

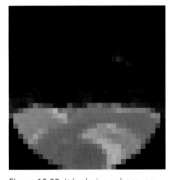

Figure 13.22 It looks jaggy because you don't want particles to be any higher resolution than they need to be, or they take up massive amounts of render time. There are two keys to creating this particle: It uses the adjusted background, inverted, with the CC Lens effect to create the look. Look at raindrops on a window sometime and notice that, as little lenses, they invert their fish-eye view of the scene behind them.

14

Pyrotechnics:
Heat, Fire, Explosions

My nature is to be on set, blowing things up.
— Ken Ralston (winner of five
Academy Awards for visual effects)

Pyrotechnics:
Heat, Fire, Explosions

It may not be the true majority, but plenty of people—guys mostly—first become interested in a visual effects career as borderline pyromaniacs or even gun nuts. You have to follow your passion in life, I suppose. Creating a conflagration on the computer isn't quite as much fun as simply blowing shit up, but maybe it keeps these people off of our streets.

The truth is that many types of explosions are still best done through a combination of practical and virtual simulations. There are, however, many cases in which compositing can save a lot of time, expense, and hazard. Blowing up models and props is fun, but it involves extensive setup and a not insubstantial amount of danger to the cast and crew. Second chances don't come cheap.

On the other hand, there's often no substitute for the physics of live-action mayhem. I hope it doesn't come as a disappointment to learn that not everything pyrotechnical can be accomplished start to finish in After Effects. Some effects require actual footage of physical or fabricated elements being shot at or blown up, and good reference of such events is immensely beneficial. Practical elements might rely on After Effects to work, but pyrotechnical shots are equally reliant, if not more so, on practical elements.

Firearms

Blanks are dangerous, and real guns deadly. To safely create a shot with realistic gunfire requires

▶ a realistic-looking gun prop in the scene

▶ some method to mime or generate firing action on set

- ▶ the addition of a muzzle flash, smoke, cartridge, or shell discharge (where appropriate)
- ▶ the matching shot showing the result of gunfire: debris, bullet hits, even blood

After Effects can help with all of these to some extent, and handles some of them completely, relieving you of the need for more expensive or dangerous alternatives.

The Shoot

For the purposes of this discussion let's assume that you begin with a plate shot of an actor re-creating the action of firing a gun, and that the gun that was used on set produces nothing: no muzzle flash, no smoke, no shell. All that's required is some miming by the actor of the recoil, or kick, which is relatively minor with small handguns, and a much bigger deal with a shotgun or fully automatic weapon.

Happily, there's no shortage of reference, as nowhere outside of the NRA is the Second Amendment more cherished than in Hollywood movies and television. Granted, most such scenes are themselves staged or manipulated, not documentary realism, but remember, we're going for cinematic reality here, so if it looks good to you (and the director), by all means use it as reference.

Figure 14.1 shows something like the minimal composite to create a realistic shot of a gun being fired (albeit artfully executed in this case). Depending on the gun, smoke or a spent cartridge might also discharge. As important as the look of the frame is the timing; check your favorite reference carefully and you'll find that not much, and certainly not the flash, lingers longer than a single frame.

NOTES

Stu Maschwitz's book, *The DV Rebel's Guide* (Peachpit Press), is definitive on the subject of creating an action movie, perhaps on a low budget, with the help of After Effects. Included with the cover price, you get a couple of nifty After Effects tools for muzzle flashes and spent shells, and some serious expertise on the subject of making explosive action exciting and real.

Figure 14.1 Much of the good reference for movie gunfire is other movies; you typically want the most dramatic and cinematic look, which is a single frame of muzzle flash and contact lighting on surrounding elements (right). (Image courtesy of Mars Productions.)

The actual travel of the bullet out of the barrel is not generally anything to worry about; at roughly one kilometer per second, it moves too fast to be seen amid all the other effects, particularly the blinding muzzle flash.

Muzzle Flash and Smoke

The clearest indication that a gun has gone off is the flash of light around the muzzle, at the end of the barrel. This small, bright explosion of gunpowder actually lasts about $\frac{1}{50}$ second, short enough that when shot live it can fall between frames of film (in which case you might need to restore it in order for the action of the scene to be clear). Real guns don't discharge a muzzle flash as a rule, but movie guns certainly do.

A flash can be painted by hand, cloned in from a practical image, or composited from stock reference. The means you use to generate it is not too significant, although muzzle flashes have in common with lens flares that they are specific to the device that created them. Someone in your audience is bound to know something about how the muzzle flash of your gun might look, so get reference: Certain guns emit a characteristic shape such as a teardrop, cross, or star (**Figure 14.2**).

Figure 14.2 The angle of the shot and the type of gun affect the muzzle flash effect. The image at left is from an M16 rifle; the one on the right is from a handgun. (Images courtesy of Artbeats.)

Any such explosion travels in two directions from the end of the barrel: arrayed outward from the firing point and in a straight line out from the barrel. If you don't have source that makes this shape at the correct angle, it's probably simplest to paint it.

The key is to make it look right on one frame; this is a rare case where that's virtually all the audience should see, and where that one frame can be almost completely different from those surrounding it. If it looks blah or only part of the way there, it's too well matched to the surrounding frames. Focus on the one frame until you believe it for explosiveness and dramatic flourish.

Technically speaking, some guns—for example, rifles—may cause quite a bit of smoke, but most emit little or none at all. If you do make a smoke puff with Turbulent Noise held out by a soft mask, which you certainly could, my advice is to make it evaporate relatively quickly so you don't blow the gag.

Shells and Interactive Light

If the gun in your scene calls for it, that extra little bit of realism can be added with a secondary animation of a shell popping off the top of a semi-automatic. **Figure 14.3** shows how such an element looks being emitted from a real gun and shot with a high-speed shutter.

It's definitely cool to have a detailed-looking shell pop off of the gun, although the truth is that with a lower camera shutter speed, the element will become an unrecognizable two-frame blur anyway, in which case all you need may be a four-point mask of a white (or brass-colored) solid.

The bright flash of the muzzle may also cause a brief reflected flash on objects near the gun as well as the subject firing it. Chapter 12 offers the basic methodology: Softly mask a highlight area, or matte the element with its own highlights, then flash it using an adjustment layer containing a Levels effect or a colored solid with a suitable blending mode.

As a general rule, the lower the ambient light and the larger the weapon, the greater the likelihood of interactive lighting, whereby light (and shadows) contact surrounding surfaces with the flash of gunfire. A literal "shot in the dark" would fully illuminate the face of whomever (or whatever) fired it, just for a single frame. It's a great dramatic effect, but one that is very difficult to re-create in post. Firing blanks on set or any other means of getting contact lighting of a flash on set would be invaluable here.

By contrast, or rather by reduced contrast, a day-lit scene will heavily dampen the level of interactivity of the light.

Figure 14.3 A shell pops off of the fired gun, but it could just as well be a shape layer with motion blur (or check *The DV Rebel's Guide* for a Particle Playground–based setup to create it automatically). (Images courtesy of Artbeats.)

Figure 14.4 This sequence of frames shows a second bullet hitting the cab of the truck, using two elements: the painted bullet hit (top) and the spark element, whose source was shot on black and added via Screen mode. (Images courtesy of markandmatty.com.)

Instead of a white hot flash, you might more accurately have saturation of orange and yellow in the full muzzle flash element, and the interactive lighting might be minimal. This is where understanding your camera and recording medium can help you gauge the effect of a small aperture hit by a lot of light.

Hits and Squibs

Bullets that ricochet on set are known as *squib hits* because they typically are created with *squibs*, small explosives with the approximate power of a firecracker that go off during the take. Squibs can even be actual firecrackers. It is possible to add bullet hits without using explosives on set, but frenetic gunplay will typically demand a mixture of on-set action and postproduction enhancement.

Figure 14.4 shows a before-and-after addition of a bullet hit purely in After Effects. Here the bullet does not ricochet but is embedded directly into the solid metal of the truck. In such a case, all you need to do is add the results of the damage on a separate layer at the frame where the bullet hits; you can paint this (it's a few sparks). The element can then be motion-tracked to marry it solidly to the background.

At the frame of impact, and for a frame or two thereafter, a shooting spark and possibly a bit of smoke (if the target is combustible—but not in the case of a steel vehicle) will convey the full violence of the bullets. As with the muzzle flash, this can vary from a single frame to a more fireworks-like shower of sparks tracked in over a few frames (**Figure 14.5**).

A bullet-hit explosion can be created via a little miniature effects shoot, using a fire-retardant black background (a flat, black card might do it) and some firecrackers (assuming you can get them). The resulting flash, sparks, and smoke stand out against the black, allowing the element to be composited via a blending mode (such as Add or Screen) or a hi-con matte (Chapter 6). Better yet, try a pixel bender effect designed for the purpose of both keying out and unmultiplying the black areas of the image. If dangerous explosives aren't your thing, even in a

Figure 14.5 A source spark element shot against black can be composited using Add or Screen blending mode—no matte needed. (Images courtesy of markandmatty.com.)

controlled situation, stock footage is available. If debris is also part of the shot, however, the more that can be done practically on set, the better (**Figure 14.6**).

So to recap, a good bullet hit should include

- ▶ smoke or sparks at the frame of impact, typically lasting between one and five frames
- ▶ the physical result of the bullet damage (if any) painted and tracked into the scene
- ▶ debris in cases where the target is shatterable or scatterable

Later in this chapter, you'll see how larger explosions have much in common with bullet hits, which are essentially just miniature explosions. In both cases, a bit of practical debris can be crucial to sell the shot.

Energy Effects

There is a whole realm of pyrotechnical effects that are made up of pure energy. At one end of the very bright spectrum is lightning, which occurs in the atmosphere of our own planet daily; on the other end are science fiction weapons that exist only in the mind (not that the U.S. military under Ronald Reagan didn't try to make them a reality).

A lightning simulation and a light saber composite have quite a bit in common, in that they rely on fooling the

Figure 14.6 Animating debris is tedious and unrewarding when compared with shooting a BB gun at breakaway objects and hurling debris at the talent. (Images courtesy of the Orphanage.)

Figure 14.7 Spectacular dueling action from *Ryan versus Dorkman*. (Sequence courtesy of Michael Scott.)

NOTES

The 14_lightsaber_ryan_vs_dorkman folder on the disc contains this effect as well as the sequence containing these clips.

eye into seeing an element that appears white hot. The funny thing about human vision is that it actually looks for the decay—the not-quite-white-hot areas around the hot core—for indications that an element is brighter than white and hotter than hot.

The Hot Look: Core and Decay

In previous editions of this book I half-joked that the recipe for creating a filmic light saber blur was top secret. This time around I'm motivated to spill the beans instead of going the quick and easy route, thanks to the Internet superstars of the low-budget light saber, Ryan and Dorkman, who have provided an entire light saber battle on the disc (**Figure 14.7**).

You may find the light saber to be somewhat played out after three decades, but the techniques you need to make a good light saber battle apply to any other energy-driven effect. There is also still plenty of interest these days in a funny *Star Wars* parody or take-off such as *Ryan vs. Dorkman*, from which the example used in this section is taken (**Figure 14.7**).

The Beam effect (Effect > Generate > Beam) automatically gives you the bare minimum, a core and surrounding glow. It is 32 bpc and can be built up, but like so many automated solutions it's a compromise. The real thing is created by hand, and it's not all that much more trouble considering how much better the result can be. Greater control over the motion and threshold areas equals a much better look.

Figure 14.8 shows the basics for a single light saber effect:

1. In the first comp, make the background plate (**Figure 14.8**, top left) a guide layer, because this is not the final comp, and create a masked white solid. In this case, the position and arcs of the light sabers are all rotoscoped by hand (top right), as detailed in Chapter 7.

2. Drop (or precomp) this comp into a new comp, apply Fast Blur to the resulting layer (turn on Repeat Edge Pixels), and set the blending mode to Add (or Screen).

Figure 14.8 The initial roto comp is set up with generous padding (top left) so that masks can move out of frame without being cut off. The roto itself is shaped to frame the full area of motion blur, where applicable, from the source (top right). The glow effect (middle left) comes from layering together several copies of the roto, each with different amounts of Feather on the mask. This is then tinted as a single element (middle right) and tweaked in Levels (bottom) for the proper glow intensity.

3. Duplicate this layer several times, and adjust Fast Blur so that each layer has approximately double the blur of the one above it. With six or seven layers you might have a Blur Radius ranging from 5 on the top level (the core) down to 400 or so.

To automate setup you could even apply this expression text to the duplicate layer's Blurriness setting:

```
thisComp.layer(index-1).effect("Fast Blur")
("Blurriness")*2
```

This takes the Blurriness value from the layer above and doubles it so that as you duplicate the layer, each one below the top is twice as soft (Figure 14.8, middle left).

4. Drop this comp into your main composition to combine it with footage and give it color (Figure 14.8, middle right). The Ryan versus Dorkman approach uses Color Balance and is composited in 16 bpc; one 32-bpc alternative (because Color Balance doesn't work in HDR) is simply to use Levels, adjusting Input White and Gamma on individual red, green, and blue channels. You could also apply Tint and Map White To values brighter than white (Figure 14.8, bottom).

That's the fundamental setup; here are some other ways to really sell a scene like this. You can use

▶ motion blur; notice how by rotoscoping the arc of movement and adding the edge threshold you get this for free in the preceding figures

▶ contact/interactive lighting/glow (**Figure 14.9**)

Figure 14.9 You get a few things for free: Contact lighting occurs on the face from the blue glow; it could and should be boosted in low light. Layer order of the sabers doesn't matter when they cross; either way their values are added together.

Figure 14.10 Flashes occur dozens of times throughout the battle; each one appears to have a unique shape, but they all use the same four-frame flare, and its unique shape comes from being composited with the rest of the scene.

▶ physical damage/interaction with the environment; the same types of interactions described for bullet hits apply, so add sparks, flares, and other damage to the surrounding environment

▶ flashes/over-range values (**Figure 14.10**)

I don't even need to tell you that these techniques are good for more than light sabers; suppose you intend to generate a more natural effect such as lightning. Reference shows this to possess similar qualities (**Figure 14.11**) and the same techniques will sell the effect.

There are a couple of built-in effects that will create lightning in After Effects. With either Lightning or Advanced Lightning, you're not stuck with the rather mediocre look of the effect itself; you can adapt the light saber methodology here and elsewhere. Turn off the glow and use the effect to generate a hard white core, and follow the same steps as just described. It's worth the trouble to get beyond the canned look, and it opens all of the possibilities shown here and more.

In some cases you might go beyond these examples and create an element that throws off so much heat and energy that it distorts the environment around it.

Figure 14.11 Actual reference images contain energy effects with realistic thresholding and interaction with the surrounding environment. (Image courtesy of Kevin Miller via Creative Commons license.)

Heat Distortion

Heat distortion, that strange rippling in the air that occurs when hot air meets cooler air, is another one of those effects compositors love. Like a lens flare, it's a highly visible effect that, if properly motivated and adjusted, adds

Figures 14.12 Heat haze by itself can look a little odd (top) but adds significantly to the realism of a scene containing a prominent heat source (bottom).

NOTES

Check out 14_heat_displacement on the disc for this setup.

instant realism even if your viewers don't know that hot gas bends light.

Figures 14.12 shows the fabricated results of heat distortion in a close-up of a scene that will also incorporate fire. When your eye sees heat distortion, it understands that something intense is happening, just like with the decay/ threshold of bright lights, as described earlier. The mind is drawn to contrast.

What Is Actually Happening

Stare into a swimming pool, and you can see displacement caused by the bending of light as it travels through the water. Rippled waves in the water cause rippled bending of light. There are cases in which our atmosphere behaves like this as well, with ripples caused by the collision of warmer and cooler air, a medium that is not quite as transparent as it seems.

As you might know from basic physics, hot air rises and hot particles move faster than cool ones. Air is not a perfectly clear medium but a translucent gas that can act as a lens, bending light. This "lens" is typically static and appears flat, but the application of heat causes an abrupt mixture of fast-moving hot air particles rising into cooler ambient air. This creates ripples that have the effect of displacing and distorting what is behind the moving air, just like ripples in the pool or ripples in the double-hung windows of a 100-year-old house.

Because this behavior resembles a lens effect, and because the role of air isn't typically taken into account in a 3D render, it can be adequately modeled as a distortion overlaid on whatever sits behind the area of hot air.

How to Re-create It

The basic steps for re-creating heat distortion from an invisible source in After Effects are as follows:

1. Create a basic particle animation that simulates the movement and dissipation of hot air particles in the scene.

2. Make two similar but unique passes of this particle animation—one to displace the background vertically, the other to displace it horizontally—and precomp them.

3. Add an adjustment layer containing the Displacement Map effect, which should be set to use the particle animation comp to create the distortion effect. Apply it to the background.

   Particle Playground is practically ideal for this purpose because its default settings come close to generating exactly what you need, with the following minor adjustments:

   a. Under Cannon, move Position to the source in the frame where the heat haze originates (in this case, the bottom center, as the entire layer will be repositioned and reused).

   b. Open up Barrel Radius from the default of 0.0 to the width, in pixels, of the source. Higher numbers lead to slower renders.

   c. Boost Particles Per Second to something like 200. The larger the Barrel Radius, the more particles are needed.

   d. Under Gravity, set Force to 0.0 to prevent the default fountain effect.

   The default color and scale of the particles is fine for this video resolution example, but you might have to adjust them as well according to your shot. A larger format (in pixels) or a bigger heat source might require bigger, softer particles.

4. Now duplicate the particles layer and set the color of the duplicated layer to pure green. As you'll see below, the Displacement Map effect by default uses the red and green channels for horizontal and vertical displacement. The idea is to vary it so that the particles don't overlap by changing Direction Random Spread and Velocity Random Spread from their defaults.

It can be useful to generate the particles for the displacement map itself in 3D animation software, when the distortion needs to be attached to a 3D animated object, such as a jet engine or rocket exhaust. The distortion is still best created in After Effects using that map.

The 14_fire folder on the disc contains the still comps used for these figures, as well as a moving image shot that can be used to create your own dynamic shot with the same fire elements.

Figure 14.13 This displacement layer, matted against gray merely for clarity, was created with the included steps and used with the Displacement Map effect to produce the effect shown in Figure 14.12.

5. The heat animation is almost complete; it only needs some softening. Add a moderate Fast Blur setting (**Figure 14.13**).

Now put the animation to use: Drag it into the main comp, and turn off its visibility. The actual Displacement Map effect is applied either directly to the background plate or preferably to an adjustment layer sitting above all the layers that should be affected by the heat haze. Displacement Map is set by default to use the red channel for horizontal displacement and the green channel for vertical displacement; all you need to do is select the layer containing the red and green particles under the Displacement Map Layer menu.

Heat displacement often dissipates before it reaches the top of the frame. Making particles behave so that their life span ends before they reach the top of the frame is accurate, but painstaking. A simpler solution is to add a solid with a black-to-white gradient (created with the Ramp effect) as a luma matte to hold out the adjustment layer containing the displacement effect. You can also use a big, soft mask.

Fire

Within After Effects, fire synthesis (from scratch) is way too hot to handle; there's no tool, built-in or plug-in, to make convincing-looking flames. If fire is at all prominent in a shot, it will require elements that come from somewhere else—most likely shot with a camera, although 3D animators have become increasingly talented at fabricating alternatives here and there.

Creating and Using Fire Elements

Figure 14.14 shows effects plates of fire elements. The big challenge when compositing fire is that it doesn't scale very realistically—a fireplace fire will look like it belongs in the hearth, no matter how you may attempt to scale or retime it.

Fire elements are ideally shot in negative space—against a black background, or at least, at night—so that they can be

Figure 14.14 Fire elements are typically shot in negative (black) space or occasionally in a natural setting requiring more careful matting. By adjusting Input Black in Levels, you can control the amount of glow coming off the fire as it is blended via Add mode, lending the scene interactive lighting for free. (Images courtesy of Artbeats.)

composited with blending modes and a minimum of roto-scoping. Fire illuminates its surroundings—just something to keep in mind when shooting.

This, then, is a case where it can be worth investing in proper elements shot by trained pyrotechnicians (unless that sounds like no fun, but there's more involved with a good fire shoot than a camera rental and a blowtorch). In many cases, stock footage companies, such as Artbeats (examples on the book's disc), anticipate your needs. The scale and intensity may be more correct than what you can easily shoot on your own; like anything, pyro is a skill whose masters have devoted much trial and error to its practice.

All Fired Up

Blending modes and linear blending, not mattes, are the key to good-looking fire composites. Given a fire element shot against black (for example, the Artbeats_RF001H_fireExcerpt.mov included on the disc and used for the depicted example), the common newbie mistake is to try to key out the black with an Extract effect, which will lead to a fight between black edges and thin fire.

A first step is to simply lay the fire layer over the background and apply Add mode. To firm up a fire, flare, or other bright element you can

▶ ascertain that Blend Colors Using 1.0 Gamma is enabled in Project Settings

▶ apply Alpha from Max Color (this free pixel bender plug-in mentioned earlier in the chapter makes all black areas of the image transparent)

▶ fine-tune the result with a Levels effect, pushing in on Input White and Black (as well as color matching overall)

▶ add an Exposure effect (with a boosted Exposure setting) to create a raging inferno

▶ add interactive lighting for low-lit scenes (next section)

▶ create displacement above the open flames (as detailed in the previous section)

▶ add an adjustment layer over the background with a Compound Blur effect, using transparency of the fire and smoke as a blur layer (**Figure 14.15**)

Where there's fire there is, of course, smoke, which can at a modest level be created with a Fractal Noise effect as described in the previous chapter, bringing this shot home (**Figure 14.16**).

Figure 14.15 The effect of steam or fog can be re-created with a subtle Compound Blur effect.

Figure 14.16 All of the techniques described here build to a result that gives the furniture motivation to jump out the windows.

NOTES

Compound Blur simply varies the amount of blur according to the brightness of a given pixel in the Blur layer, up to a given maximum. It's the right thing to use not only for fire and smoke but for fog and mist; heavy particulates in the air act like little tiny defocused lenses, causing this effect in nature.

Light Interacts

Provided that your camera does not rotate too much, a 2D fire layer, or a set of them, offset in 3D space, can read as sufficiently three-dimensional. The key to making it interact dimensionally with a scene, particularly a relatively dark one, is often interactive light. As stated earlier, fire tends to illuminate everything around it with a warm, flickering glow.

Figure 14.17 Input White and Black on the RGB and Red channels of the Levels effect offer control of the natural glow around the element. The better the dynamic range of the source image, the harder you can push this—another case for higher bit depth source.

As shown in **Figure 14.17**, a fire element may include a certain amount of usable glow. Input White and Input Black in Levels control the extent to which glow is enhanced or suppressed (right), respectively.

Note, however, that this glow isn't anything unique or special; you can re-create it by using a heavily blurred duplicate of the source fire or a masked and heavily feathered orange solid, with perhaps a slight wiggle added to the glow layer's opacity to flicker the intensity.

Dimensionality

You can pull off the illusion of fully three-dimensional fire, especially if the camera is moving around in 3D space, directly in After Effects. I was frankly surprised at how well this worked when I created the shot featured in **Figure 14.18**, back in the early days of After Effects 3D.

As shown, the background plate is an aerial flyby of a forest. Because of the change in altitude and perspective, this shot clearly required 3D tracking (touched upon at the end of Chapter 8). The keys to making this shot look fully dimensional were to break up the source fire elements into discrete chunks and to stagger those in 3D space so that as the plane rose above them, their relationship and parallax changed (**Figure 14.19**).

TIP

For a shot featuring a character or object that reflects firelight, there's no need to go crazy projecting fire onto the subject. In many cases, it is enough to create some flickering in the character's own luminance values, for example, by wiggling the Input White value at a low frequency in Levels (Individual Controls).

Figure 14.18 Before-and-after sequential stills of a flyover shot. Because of the angle of the aerial camera, the shot required 3D motion tracking, in this case done with 2D3's Boujou. (Images courtesy of ABC-TV.)

Figure 14.19 A top view of the 3D motion-tracked camera from Figure 14.18 panning past one set of fires (of which the final composition had half a dozen). The pink layers contain fire elements, the gray layers smoke.

It is easy to get away with any individual fire element being 2D in this case. Because fire changes its shape constantly, there is nothing to give away its two-dimensionality. Borders of individual fire elements can freely overlap without being distracting, so it doesn't look cut out. The eye sees evidence of parallax between a couple dozen fire elements and does not think to question that any individual one of them looks too flat. The smoke elements were handled in a similar way, organized along overlapping planes. As mentioned in the previous chapter, smoke's translucency aids the illusion that overlapping smoke layers have dimensional depth.

Explosions

The example forest fire shot also contains a large explosion in a clearing. There is not a huge fundamental difference between the methods to composite an explosion and mere fire, except that a convincing explosion might be built up out of more individual elements. It is largely a question of what is exploding.

All explosions are caused by rapidly expanding combustible gases; implosions are caused by rapid contraction. Just by looking at an explosion, viewers can gauge its size and get an idea of what blew up, so you need to design the right explosion for your situation or your result will be too cheesy even for 1980s television sci-fi. How do you do it?

Light and Chunky

Each explosion you will see is unique, but to narrow the discussion, I'll organize all explosions into two basic categories. The easier one to deal with is the gaseous explosion— one made up only of gas and heat. These explosions behave just like fire; in fact, in the shot in **Figure 14.20** (left) the explosion is fire, a huge ball of it, where something very combustible evidently went up very quickly.

Some shots end up looking fake because they use a gaseous explosion when some chunks of debris are needed. This is a prime reason that exploding miniatures are still in use, shot at high speed (or even, when possible, full-scale explosions, which can be shot at standard speed). The slower-moving and bigger the amount of debris, the bigger the apparent explosion.

If your shot calls for a chunky explosion, full of physical debris, and the source lacks them, you need an alternate source. Many 3D programs these days include effective dynamics simulations; if you go that route, be sure to

Figure 14.20 Pyrotechnics footage is just the thing when you need a big explosion filled with debris. (Images courtesy of Artbeats.)

generate a depth map as well because each chunk will be revealed only as it emerges from the fireball. Many other concerns associated with this are beyond the scope of this discussion because they must be solved in other software.

One effect that seems to come close in After Effects is Shatter, but it's hard to recommend this unless you're simulating a pane of glass or some other pane breaking. Shatter isn't bad for a decade-old dynamics simulator, but its primary limitation is a huge one: It can employ only extruded flat polygons to model the chunks. A pane of glass is one of the few physical objects that would shatter into irregular but flat polygons, and Shatter contains built-in controls for specifying the size of the shards in the point of impact. Shatter was also developed prior to the introduction of 3D in After Effects; you can place your imaginary window in perspective space, but not with the help of a camera or 3D controls.

A wide selection of pyrotechnic explosions is available as stock footage from companies such as Artbeats. In many cases, there is no substitute for footage of a real, physical object being blown to bits (Figure 14.20, right).

In a Blaze of Glory

With good reference and a willingness to take the extra step to marry your shot and effect, you can create believable footage that would require danger or destruction if taken with a camera. Even when your project has the budget to actually re-create some of the mayhem described in this chapter, you can almost always use After Effects to enhance and build upon what the camera captures. Boom. Sometimes you get to go out with a bang.

Index

What's on the DVD?

Although this book is designed not to rely on tutorials, many of the techniques described in the text can be further explored via the dozens of projects and accompanying footage and stills included on the disc. These range from simple demonstrations of single concepts to completed shots, and make use of live action effects footage custom shot for the book or borrowed from a professional shoot. Wherever possible, HD (1920×1080) clips are incorporated; other examples use NTSC footage or stills if that is all that's required to get the point across.

Additionally, the DVD includes demos of more than a dozen plug-ins and applications. These demos are similar to the real software for everything but output, allowing you to experiment with your own footage. In the Scripts folder on the disc, you'll also find a PDF with a list of scripts mentioned in the book and links to download them from aescripts.com, a donation-ware site.

▶ **Custom scripts from redefinery**. A number of custom scripts created by Jeff Almasol are included with this edition in the Scripts folder on the disc, including **Lightwrap** and **CameraProjectionSetup**, which duplicate the exact steps described to set those up (Chapters 12 and 9, respectively); three scripts described in the appendix on the accompanying disc; and two scripts included with previous editions: **Duplink**, which creates "instance" objects, and **Merge Projects**, which integrates the structure of an imported project into the master project. More information on these is included as comments in the scripts themselves (which can be opened with any text editor).

▶ **SynthEyes** (Andersson Technologies) provides fully automatic, as well as user-controlled, matchmoving for single or batchprocessed shots; it's a stand-alone program that exports to After Effects.

▶ **Camera Tracker** (The Foundry) also provides fully automatic (and user-controlled) 3D matchmoving but does so directly in After Effects.

▶ **Kronos** (The Foundry) is an alternative to After Effects' built-in Timewarp effect for optical-flow-based retiming of footage.

▶ **Lenscare** (Frischluft) creates a more natural and beautiful lens blur than the Photoshop filter included with After Effects.

▶ **Knoll Light Factory Pro** (Red Giant Software) includes such pre-built lighting effects as lens flares, sparkles, glows, and more. It also provides individual lens components so you can create your own custom effects and has been newly revamped for After Effects CS5.

- **Magic Bullet Colorista 2** (Red Giant Software) is 3-way Lift/Gamma/Gain color control to After Effects that now also includes powerful secondary color selection tools.

- **Magic Bullet Looks** (Red Giant Software) is an intuitive, real-world based application that lets you dramatically change the color look of your footage via an intuitive user interface metaphor that mirrors film production itself.

- **Magic Bullet Mojo** (Red Giant Software) provides a quick way to get color balance typical of cinematic projects.

- **Primatte Keyer** (Red Giant Software) is a great alternative to Keylight, particularly for cases where the matte is uneven or of a nonstandard color.

- **Trapcode Form** (Red Giant Software) is a cousin to Trapcode Particular and allows you to array particles across a mesh, so that they can hold a three dimensional shape.

- **Trapcode Horizon** (Red Giant Software) creates 3D-aware gradients and spherical maps, which is useful to create skies and multi-color gradients for use with a 3D camera.

- **Trapcode Lux** (Red Giant Software) allows After Effects' built-in lights to create visible light flares and volume.

- **Trapcode Particular 2** (Red Giant Software) designs 3D particle systems that simulate air resistance, gravity, and turbulence. It provides a real-time preview, as well as controls that allow you to freeze time and manipulate a camera in the scene.

- **Warp** (Red Giant Software) is a natural companion to mocha for After Effects and allows you to corner pin both from and to an angled plane, as well as including a nice shadow creation tool.

- **Silhouette v4** (SilhouetteFX) is available as both a stand-alone application and a shape import/export plug-in for AE. It's designed to rotoscope and generate mattes.

- **ReelSmart Motion Blur** (RE: Vision Effects) allows you to procedurally generate motion blur for moving elements in a shot which lack it (or lack enough of it). After Effects' built-in motion blur is available only on animated elements.

- **PV Feather** (RE: Vision Effects) adds features long missing from After Effects and available in comparable packages such as Shake: the ability to control per-vertex (or per-spline) mask feather.

- **Twixtor** (RE: Vision Effects) is an alternative to After Effects' built-in Timewarp effect for optical-flow-based retiming of footage.

WATCH
READ
CREATE

Meet Creative Edge.

A new resource of unlimited books, videos and tutorials for creatives from the world's leading experts.

Creative Edge is your one stop for inspiration, answers to technical questions and ways to stay at the top of your game so you can focus on what you do best—being creative.

All for only $24.99 per month for access—any day any time you need it.

creative edge

peachpit.com/creativeedge